Japan Business and Economics Series

This series provides a forum for empirical and theoretical work on Japanese business enterprises, Japanese management practices, and the Japanese economy. Japan continues to grow as a major economic world power, and Japanese companies create products and deliver services that compete successfully with those of the best firms around the world. Much can be learned from an understanding of how this has been accomplished and how it is being sustained.

The series aims to balance empirical and theoretical work, always in search of a deeper understanding of the Japanese phenomenon. It also implicitly takes for granted that there are significant differences between Japan and other countries and that these differences are worth knowing about. The series editors expect books published in the series to present a broad range of work on social, cultural, economics, and political institutions. If, as some have predicted, the twenty-first century sees the rise of Asia as the most powerful economic region in the world, the rest of the world needs to understand the country that is, and will continue to be, one of the major players in this region.

Japan Business and Economics Series

Remade in America

Transplanting and Transforming Japanese Management Systems

Edited by
Jeffrey K. Liker
W. Mark Fruin
Paul S. Adler

New York   Oxford

Oxford University Press

1999

Oxford University Press

Oxford   New York
Athens   Auckland   Bangkok   Bogotá   Buenos Aires   Calcutta
Cape Town   Chennai   Dar es Salaam   Delhi   Florence   Hong Kong   Istanbul
Karachi   Kuala Lumpur   Madrid   Melbourne   Mexico City   Mumbai
Nairobi   Paris   São Paulo   Singapore   Taipei   Tokyo   Toronto   Warsaw

and associated companies in
Berlin   Ibadan

Library of Congress Cataloging-in-Publication Data
Remade in America : transplanting and transforming Japanese
management systems / edited by Jeffrey K. Liker, W. Mark Fruin,
Paul S. Adler.
p.   cm. — (Japan business and economics series)
Includes bibliographical references and index.
ISBN 0-19-511815-4
1. Industrial management—Japan—Case studies.   2. Industrial
management—United States—Case studies.   3. Technology
transfer—Japan—Case studies.   4. Technology transfer—United
States—Case studies.   5. Comparative management.   I. Liker, Jeffrey K.
II. Fruin, W. Mark, 1943–   III. Adler, Paul S.   IV. Series.
HD70.J3 R46   1999
658.4'00952—dc21   98-24205

9 8 7 6 5 4 3 2 1

Printed in the United States of America
on acid-free paper

Preface

In 1991, at the instigation of Senator Jeff Bingaman of New Mexico, the U.S. Congress provided $10 million to the Department of Defense to establish a program for U.S.-Japanese industry and technology management training. The goal of the program was to improve American industrial competitiveness by helping to develop engineers and managers who can speak Japanese and thus learn about Japanese technology management practices directly from experience in Japan during the course of their academic and professional careers. Another chief component of the program was to research and analyze the technology management practices that give top Japanese companies a competitive edge in their industries. The University of Michigan's Japan Technology Management Program (JTMP) was one of the first recipients of a grant from this program, administered by the Air Force Office of Scientific Research (AFOSR) (over time, twelve such programs were funded by AFOSR). The JTMP focused much of its early efforts on research covering a broad spectrum of the technology life cycle, from basic research to manufacturing. One product of that early effort was *Engineered in Japan: Japanese Technology Management Practices* (Oxford University Press, 1995), which went on to win a 1996 Shingo Prize for Excellence in Manufacturing Research. Now we are happy to share this second book focusing on Japanese manufacturing management systems as they have been brought over to the United States in what some call "transplant operations."

At the time the idea for this book evolved in 1996, the JTMP had been in operation for five years. It seemed time to begin another major book-writing effort. Mark Fruin, on the faculty at the University of British Columbia, was visiting the University of Michigan for several years, and Paul Adler at the University of Southern California agreed to join our team. We all had direct experience with Japanese manufacturing operations in the United States and agreed on three things: first, there were some truly high-performing Japanese manufacturing plants in the United States; second, some top U.S. firms were emulating successful manufacturing practices from Japanese plants located in both Japan and the United States; third, the management systems in these Japanese transplants and in their U.S.-owned emulators were neither exactly like what we had seen in Japan nor like traditional American plants— they were hybrids. In addition, there were still legions of traditional American plants that clearly had not learned the lessons available to them from world-class Japanese operations. We concluded that it was urgent to identify the ways in which the approaches that had proven themselves in Japanese manufacturing could be effectively brought to the United States.

We therefore decided to create an edited volume that would bring together the most knowledgable scholars in the field to summarize the available evidence and present the most compelling theories. Early in 1996, we identified these scholars and invited them to draft papers for the projected volume. That September, we invited the authors and a number of other experts to a conference in Ann Arbor. At the conference, each paper was critiqued by the other attendees; we conducted a broad-ranging discussion of the key issues underlying the projected volume, and authors were encouraged to rework their papers to incorporate the results of this discussion. The resulting papers constitute the chapters in this book (some will also appear in different versions in journals). As editors, we drafted an introductory chapter that provided a conceptual framework for the collection.

What emerges is a complex, multifaceted, but coherent picture of the transfer of Japanese manufacturing management principles to the United States. Taken as a whole, the chapters make clear that this transfer is not linear and mechanical but, rather, a complex and evolutionary process. As we plunge into an increasingly global economy, we need to learn how better to manage that process. We hope the present volume offers some conceptual handles on that huge challenge.

This book was written for scholars interested in Japanese business, engineering, and manufacturing management and for managers and engineers with interests in manufacturing. The chapters provided a mix of in-depth case studies, conceptual frameworks, and statistical studies. We have avoided specialized academic jargon, though we assume some familiarity with basic concepts of Japanese manufacturing methods (e.g., JIT, pull systems, and SPC) and with general management concepts.

Many people and organizations made this book possible. We must first thank our contributors, who joined this venture without realizing how demanding the editors would be. We also thank colleagues who are not represented in this volume but who participated in the September 1996 conference as discussants and reviewers and who significantly shaped the book: Steve Babson, Bruce Kogut, Will Mitchell, and Mayer Zald. We thank the Air Force Office of Scientific Research for its financial support and, in particular, Koto White, who ran the program at AFOSR, for her enthusiastic and effective leadership. We greatly appreciate the hard work and dedication beyond the call of duty of Heidi Tietjen, associate director of the Japan Technology Management Program. One of our inspirational leaders for this book was John Shook, director of JTMP, who provided sage advice at our conference and influenced our thinking in countless ways through sharing his experiences in bringing the Toyota Production System to the United States. John Campbell and Brian Talbott, codirectors of JTMP, also contributed wit, wisdom, and generous support. Finally, we thank Herb Addison at Oxford University Press for his invaluable support and encouragement.

Ann Arbor, Michigan   J. K. L.
San Jose, California   W. M. F.
Los Angeles, California   P. S. A.
February 1998

Acknowledgments

Chapter 2: This article is an extended version of an article in the *Journal of World Business* (Pil and MacDuffie 1999). It is based in part on research at NUMMI conducted jointly with David Levine and Barbara Goldoftas. Partial funding was provided by MIT's International Motor Vehicle Program. This version has benefited from comments by Ed Lawler, Terje Gronning, Charles Heckscher, Seok-Woo Kwon, Katherine Xin, and other contributors to this volume.

Chapter 4: We are grateful to NSK Corporation for opening the door to us, providing generously of staff time, and openly sharing information with us. Specific individuals at NSK who gave generously of their time and support include S. Fuchigami, H. Otsuka, D. Rathmann, D. Reinhart, H. Tazaki, and T. Yano. Professors Paul Adler, Susan Helper, Bruce Kogut, and Eleanor Westney offered valuable comments on earlier drafts. This project was supported by a faculty fellowship from Joel Tauber Manufacturing Institute and support from the Japan Technology Management Program at the University of Michigan (under Air Force Office of Scientific Research grant DOD-G-F49620-93-1-0612).

Chapter 5: An abridged version of this chapter appeared in *California Management Review,* vol. 39, no. 4 (summer 1997). We are grateful to Honda of America Manufacturing and the Honda suppliers who generously provided time and access to their operations for this project. Thanks also to Paul Adler, Robert Cole, Mark Fruin, Martin Kenney, Ann Marie Knott, David Levine, Jeffrey Liker, Charles Sabel, and participants in Wharton's Organizational

Learning Seminar for comments on an earlier draft. Funding for this research was provided by the International Motor Vehicle Program of MIT; the Jones Center for Management Policy, Strategy, and Organization at Wharton; and the Center for Regional Economic Issues at Case Western Reserve University.

Chapter 6: The material presented here draws from selected portions of my book *Managing Quality Fads: How American Business Learned to Play the Quality Game*, published by Oxford University Press. Preparation of the book was supported by National Science Foundation Grant no. SES-9022192 and the Air Force Office of Scientific Research under AFOSR Grant no. F49620-95-1-0042.

Chapter 8: I thank Shoko Tanaka for assisting in the interviews used in this paper and Paul Adler, W. Mark Fruin, and Jeffrey Liker for their helpful comments. I also thank Shuichi Hashimoto, Michio Nitta, and Keisuke Nakamura for their assistance in finding previous Japanese research. I thank the Alfred P. Sloan Foundation for funding research on the television industry.

Chapter 10: Research funding was provided by a grant from the Alfred P. Sloan Foundation. Paul Osterman supplied the data from his 1992 survey of U.S. manufacturing establishments. Michael Massagli oversaw the collection of the transplant survey data. Mitsumasa Motoya provided research assistance.

Chapter 11: M. Nakamura's research is in part supported by the Social Sciences and Humanities Research Council of Canada.

Contents

Contributors

Paul S. Adler
University of Southern California

Mary Yoko Brannen
San Jose State University

Robert E. Cole
University of California, Berkeley

Richard Florida
Center for Economic Development
Carnegie Mellon University

W. Mark Fruin
School of Business
University of Michigan

Susan Helper
Case Western Reserve University

Davis Jenkins
Great Cities Institute
University of Illinois

Martin Kenney
Department of Human and
    Community Development
University of California, Davis

Jeffrey K. Liker
Industrial and Operations
    Engineering
University of Michigan

John Paul MacDuffie
Wharton Business School
University of Pennsylvania

Masao Nakamura
Faculty of Commerce, Institute of
    Asian Research, & Faculty of
    Applied Science
University of British Columbia

T. K. Peng
Chinese Navy Academy

Mark F. Peterson
Texas Tech University &
Florida Atlantic University

Frits K. Pil
University of Pittsburgh

Sadao Sakakibara
Keio University

Roger G. Schroeder
Curtis L. Carlson School of
    Management
University of Minnesota

Peter B. Smith
University of Sussex & Roffey Park
    Management College

D. Eleanor Westney
M.I.T. Sloan School of Management

Remade in America

1

Bringing Japanese Management Systems to the United States

Transplantation or Transformation?

Jeffrey K. Liker

W. Mark Fruin

Paul S. Adler

The Goals of This Volume

Over the past two decades, Japanese firms have challenged U.S. dominance in many manufacturing industries. At first the challenge appeared in the form of imports, and early analyses often attributed Japanese success to an under-valued yen, low labor costs, and unfair trade practices. However, Japanese firms have increasingly brought their competitive challenge to the United States in the form of transplant operations, and recognition has spread that their success owes much to superior manufacturing management. Despite the ups and downs of the business cycle in Japan, there remains a core of world-class companies in Japan that have evolved manufacturing management systems that companies throughout the world have been striving to emulate.

This book aims to clarify the challenges that face firms—both Japanese- and U.S.-owned—when they attempt to implement these management tech-niques in a U.S. context. While the most successful of the Japanese manufac-turing transplants rely, in varying degrees and in varying ways, on home-country management techniques, the transplants have had to adapt them to fit U.S. conditions. Similarly, the growing number of U.S. firms that are adopting these techniques to strengthen their own positions face a con-siderable challenge in transforming them to fit local conditions. This book, therefore, addresses the following questions: which aspects of their manage-

3

ment systems explain Japanese manufacturing firms' export successes? Which aspects can be transferred relatively intact to the United States? Which parts need to be modified, and in what ways? What U.S. management practices need to change to support the adoption of these management approaches from Japan?

The Machine That Changed the World (Womack, Jones, and Roos, 1990), a publication of MIT's International Motor Vehicle Program, traced the superior performance of Japanese auto companies and their U.S. transplants to a set of practices called "lean production." The exemplar of the lean production paradigm is the Toyota Production System. However, Japanese firms have systematically outperformed their U.S. counterparts in several industries besides the auto industry, most notably in office equipment (copiers, faxes, laptops), tires, and consumer and industrial electronics (Kenney and Florida, 1993). Although successful Japanese firms in these industries do not always follow every tenet of the Toyota Production System, there is a strong family resemblance among their production systems.

The success of Japan's leading industrial firms has also been attributed to features of their broader management systems, those that govern the factory and the corporation rather than the shop floor alone. Many observers highlight the importance of Japanese approaches to human resource management, organizational design, management decision making, and industrial and supplier relations in buttressing the shop floor production systems. Here, too, notwithstanding differences among firms and industries, there are notable family resemblances.

We use the term "Japanese management systems" (JMSs) to refer to the family of production, factory, and corporate management practices found in world-class Japanese firms. This volume explores the sources of competitive advantage that JMSs provide and the ways in which they are being transplanted and transformed in the United States. Of course, there is variation in the performance of firms in Japan just as there is any place in the world. Our focus, however, is on those industrial firms that have proven capable of sustained success at home and in international competition.

We focus on two industries, auto and electronics, and analyze the different patterns of transplantation and transformation found in each. Our focus on two industries and on the United States distinguishes this volume from other scholarly efforts, as it allows us to analyze in greater depth the dynamics of transfer, transplantation, and transformation.

Our choice of the auto and the electronics industries is motivated by their large share of the flow of foreign direct investment. To take a recent and unexceptional year, 1995, Japan's total foreign direct investment overseas was some $50 billion. Of this, $22 billion, or nearly one half, went to the United States, and, of that $22 billion, $7 billion was in manufacturing. This represented accumulated investment in opening and expanding about 1,700 manufacturing plants across the United States. Of the direct investment in manufacturing, 18 percent was in the electrical machinery sector and 15 percent in the transport machinery sector (according to the Japanese Ministry of Finance).

This introduction outlines a common conceptual backdrop that ties together the following chapters. We begin by defining in detail what we mean by Japanese management systems. The next section identifies a number of partially competing but mostly complementary theories of the sources of effectiveness of JMSs. We then sketch the range of forces that shape the transfer of JMSs and the degree of transformation. Finally, we summarize the key ideas of the chapters.

Defining Japanese Management Systems

There are numerous possible interpretations of the success evidenced by world-class Japanese firms. On the one hand, some have argued that this success is due to the broader institutional context within which these firms operate in Japan, including close government-business and labor-management relations, and to the Confucian cultural patterns that predispose Japanese citizens to work hard and sacrifice for the community. On the other hand, some have argued that their success is due to their mastery of the fundamentals of good manufacturing, such as inventory control, quality, maintenance, and training.

As long as the success of Japanese firms was in the form of exports, the debate was difficult to resolve, since all the possible determinants of performance were confounded. But during the 1980s, a growing number of Japanese firms established transplant operations in North America. Many transplants proved to be highly effective, and a consensus emerged that, although broad contextual factors are important, much of the competitive strength of Japanese firms is attributable to the policies and practices that shape day-to-day operations on the shop floor, or what the Japanese call the "production system." World-class Japanese firms demonstrate the immense pay-offs that accrue to a disciplined implementation of a coherent set of policies that govern production. Many U.S. firms, by contrast, even some highly profitable ones, manage production under a disjointed set of policies and ad hoc decisions.

Since the publication of *The Machine That Changed the World*, the Toyota Production System (TPS) has become the standard reference point for many American firms (Womack and Jones 1996). Its core features, such as just-in-time (JIT) inventory, production leveling, mixed-model production, continuous improvement, visual control, errorproofing, production teams, and standardized work, have become well known and widely admired. However, in our view, JMSs cannot be reduced to TPS. First, not every high-performing Japanese firm in the auto industry practices TPS. Honda, for example, practices neither leveled production schedules nor pure JIT to the same extent as Toyota.

Second, and more significant, Japanese firms have shown exceptional performance in a number of industries where TPS does not seem to provide a universal template, such as memory chips, cameras, tires, information technology, and consumer and industrial electronics (Odagiri and Goto, 1997). At least some elements of TPS may not be well suited to industries where product life cycles are short—a matter of months rather than years, as in the auto industry—and where even a small plant's product variety is several orders of magnitude greater than that found in the auto industry.

If JMSs encompass a rather heterogeneous set of practices and philosophies that differ depending on production technology, product variety, and the duration of product life cycles, we nevertheless observe some strong family resemblances across the production systems of world-class Japanese firms. For example, successful factories that do not have energetic, small-group activities contributing to the continuous improvement of production are clearly outliers. Similarly, good factories without strong commitments to building-in quality and to highly disciplined work and quality assurance procedures are hard to imagine.

The list of such generic features is long but worth repeating. In every world-class Japanese plant, we would expect to find spotlessly clean shop floors with a place for everything and everything in its place. Excellent product and process engineering with a shop floor focus (*genbashugi* in Japanese) is the norm (Imai, 1997). By *genbashugi* we mean that many of the highly trained and educated employees (especially engineers) are deployed in their daily work activities to support shop floor activities. In addition, there are many tools aimed at simplifying and making transparent manufacturing operations so that all shop floor employees can be involved in improvement. For example, across a range of industries we see simple, visual ways of tracking progress, and preventive maintenance programs where operators armed with detailed checklists do most of the routine maintenance and troubleshooting. While not all high-performing Japanese factories use Toyota's elaborate *kanban* system for pulling products through plants and the supply chain, they all pay a great deal of attention to keeping inventory levels at a minimum in order to accelerate problem detection. They are also likely to emphasize the importance of reducing changeover times and keeping lot sizes down. Finally, it is now well established that Japanese factories are not especially "high tech" but are, rather, characterized by the creative use of low-cost automation, often custommade in house to assure quality, efficiency, and flexibility (Whitney, 1995; Fruin, 1997).

An Embedded Layer Model of JMSs

If, as argued in the previous subsection, the source of Japanese firms' successes is not reducible to the Toyota Production System, neither is it reducible to a generic set of production system characteristics. The effectiveness of Japanese production systems is greatly conditioned by the structure of the broader factory organization and by the corporate management system within which individual factories operate. We therefore identify three layers in the structure we call Japanese management systems:

Layer 1: Shop floor production systems
Layer 2: Factory organization and management
Layer 3: Corporate structure and systems

To these three layers of the management system, we could add a fourth, representing the social and institutional context within which firms operate (see Figure 1.1).

The successes of the best transplants have shown that JMSs—or variants of them adapted to the local context—can function effectively in foreign institutional and social contexts. Much less clear are the fate and the role of each of the three layers of JMSs in the transplantation process. Knowledgeable observers agree that all of these layers are closely interwoven and interdependent in Japan (Aoki, 1994; Aoki and Patrick, 1994; Fruin, 1992; Odagiri, 1992), but previous research leaves unresolved two key issues that are the foci of this volume. First, what changes to the production system, the inner core of JMSs, are made in the process of transfer? Second, what outer-layer policies and practices are found in firms that attempt to transplant the core, and how do they differ from those found in Japan?

Since the four-layer model plays a key role in our conceptualization of these issues, we briefly describe each layer here.

Layer 1: Shop floor production system. To recapitulate the previous section, this layer encompasses hard technologies (equipment, tooling, and so forth), as well as organizational technologies directed toward shop floor operations in the form of rules, procedures, and work practices, including quality standards, quality procedures, standardized

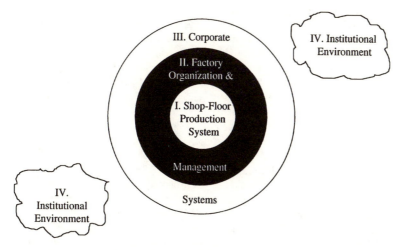

Figure 1.1 A layered model of Japanese management systems.

work sheets, preventive maintenance practices, quick die changes, and *kanban*. Organizational practices that directly affect operations, such as teams, job classification schemes, and continuous improvement activities, are also included in this layer. We also include manufacturing philosophies that are enacted on the shop floor, like the pull system under TPS, built-in quality, and standardized work.

Layer 2: Factory organization and management. This layer includes a broader set of factory-level systems and structures that buttress the production system, most notably human resources practices, industrial and supplier relations policies, organizational culture, formal and informal structure, communication, and learning processes. We should note that some features of Japan's factory management system find their counterparts in U.S. firms only at the corporate layer. Indeed, there is a growing literature that highlights the distinctiveness of Japanese factories' abundant technical resources and considerable autonomy with respect to deploying those resources (Cusumano, 1991; Fruin, 1992; Imai, 1997). Moreover, in certain industries, Japan's factories are distinguished by multifunctional, multiproduct, and multifocal capabilities that are only rarely found in Western factories (Fruin, 1997). The managerial and technical intensity of factories (Layer 2)—as compared to corporate offices (Layer 3)—seems high relative to that in prototypical Western firms.

Layer 3: The corporate layer. This layer includes the business and management systems, support staff, and union structures outside the factory. It encompasses corporate R & D, strategy, human resources policies, and the relation of the firm to capital markets and to its supply chain. Horizontal and vertical *keiretsu* are also features of this layer (Miyashita and Russell, 1994; Nishiguchi, 1994; Lincoln, Gerlach, and Ahmadjian, 1996; Lincoln, Gerlach, and Takahashi, 1992; Odagiri, 1992), although others have argued that vertical *keiretsu* are really part of the factory management system (Fruin, 1997). Because of Japan's distinctive interorganizational practices, in particular its bank-and technology-centered business groupings, *kigyo shudan* and *keiretsu*, we classify this closely knit network within the corporate level, rather than as part of the institutional environment.

There may be more written about the corporate layer of Japanese firms than about either of the other two layers of JMSs. Beginning with James Abegglen's *The Japanese Factory*, published in 1958, a large corpus of work has grown that covers the distinctive behavioral, organizational, managerial, and employment practices of Japan's industrial firms. There has also been some work on patterns of growth and diversification among Japan's industrial firms that points to their distinctive differences (Fruin, 1992; Gerlach, 1992; Morikawa, 1992; Shiba and Shimotani, 1997). Likewise, the ways in which factories are integrated into larger divisional and corporate structures may be distinctive relative to the M-form model that describes multidivisional practices in many Western industrial firms (Chandler, 1990; Fruin, 1992). Masahiko Aoki's description of the Japanese firm as a system of attributes encompasses much of what we have said about layers 1, 2, and 3 (Aoki, 1994).

Layer 4: Institutional environment. For our purposes, the institutional environment is everything outside the corporate system. This includes consumer preferences, the legal and regulatory environment, the educational system broadly defined, and the more diffuse elements of national culture and values orientation.

It is noteworthy that much of what falls into Layer 3 in Japan, such as company unions, close and enduring relations with main banks and financial intermediaries, high levels of in-company education, and low levels of labor market mobility, depends on the distinctive nature of the broader Japanese institutional environment. Thus, one of the biggest challenges in the transfer of JMSs is the need for identifying adequate substitutes for the many organizational arrangements that are institutionally embedded in Japan or making the system work despite the lack of substitutes.

The Sources of JMSs' Effectiveness

If we postulate that management systems underlie the success of world-class Japanese firms, to what do we attribute the effectiveness of these systems? This requires more than a definition of JMSs: it requires a theory of JMSs. Research to date has not led to consensus on this question, and this volume does not attempt to create one. Instead, the various contributors call on several different, somewhat competing but largely complementary theories. In this section, we identify the four main theories invoked or implied in the following chapters and identify some of the challenges to transfer that each theory implies.

JMSs as Well-designed Management Tools and Techniques

The most straightforward theory of the source of JMSs' effectiveness emphasizes the production system and the specificity, rational design, and coherence of policies that guide production (Juran, 1988; Monden, 1983; Schonberger, 1982; Shingo, 1989). Notwithstanding our argument that the outer layers are critical components of JMSs, there is good reason to believe that the innermost layer—the production system's tools and techniques, such as preventive maintenance, visual control, quality standards, zero defects, and the 5Ss—are themselves immensely powerful.

Many U.S. firms now take for granted that these tools and techniques are worthy of emulation. All of the U.S. Big Three auto makers, for example, have committed publicly to implementing versions of TPS in their worldwide manufacturing operations (Liker, 1997). However, ten or twenty years ago, the strengths of JMSs' tools and techniques were not so obvious to American managers. Big Three auto makers, for example, knew about TPS for at least fifteen years before they made serious efforts at its implementation. And the process of implementing these methods is far from straightforward in these companies (Liker, 1997). Robert Cole's chapter in this volume provides a vivid account of the initial resistance of Hewlett-Packard managers to TQM as it was presented to them in the course of learning from Yokogawa-Hewlett-Packard, their Japanese joint venture; moreover, this resistance occurred despite what was in many ways an ideal set of circumstances for borrowing.

One reason for this slow acceptance by U.S. firms was that some of the core technical features of JMSs contradict taken-for-granted tenets of American mass production (Womack et al., 1990; Koenigsaeker, 1997). For example, just-in-time production is diametrically opposed to the economic order quantity principles of American manufacturing and to reliance on technologies such as MRP II for shop floor scheduling. In JIT, material is pulled through plants to replenish downstream processes, and advance scheduling of raw and intermediate inputs is eliminated to the extent possible.

A second reason for U.S. firms' difficulty in adopting these tools and techniques lies in their relation to some of the basic principles that underlie the broader management system that constitute Layer 2 of our model. According to one interpretation, these tools and techniques function far more effectively when implemented in an organization that is significantly less autocratic and more participative than has been the norm in the Big Three plants and in many other sectors of U.S. manufacturing. Allowing shop floor workers to do their own methods engineering, for example, flies in the face of the traditional form of Taylorism, which was based on the assumption that only engineering experts can develop scientifically accurate work methods (Adler, 1993).

A second interpretation of JMSs as tools and techniques argues that the source of their performance benefits lies in the resulting intensification of work. Some observers (Babson, 1995; Fucini and Fucini, 1990; Graham, 1995; Rinehart, Huxley, and Robertson, 1997) argue that continuous improvement leads to a continuous elimination of the "pores" in the working day that represent rest times for labor but lost time for capital. In part, the accuracy of this alternative interpretation depends on how the production system is implemented (whether work is in fact intensified or unproductive work is replaced by productive work) and how the resulting gains are distributed. Under either interpretation, however, it is clear that much of the challenge of implementing JMSs tools and techniques lies in their dependence on the broader organizational context to "involve" workers: such involvement requires considerable change to traditional U.S. management, worker, and union orientations.

This technical theory of JMSs' effectiveness also highlights a third difficulty in transfer to the United States: their industry-specificity. Efforts on the part of U.S. firms to emulate successful Japanese practices were sometimes handicapped by lack of information concerning these more subtle differences across industries. Several chapters in this volume, most notably the chapters by Kenney, Jenkins and Florida, and Nakamura, Sakakibara, and Schroeder, analyze these issues, comparing configurations of technical production systems found in different industries.

JMSs as Knowledge-Creating Small-Group Activity

Some authors have argued that the success of JMSs is due not to the efficiency properties of the production system's tools and techniques but, rather, to JMSs' superior ability to create practical knowledge (Fruin, 1997; Adler, 1993; Kenney and Florida, 1993). In very broad strokes, we might say that the basis of wealth and power over the past few centuries has progressed from land, to labor, to capital, and, finally, at the end of the twentieth century, to knowledge. From this perspective, JMSs have succeeded because they reintegrate the old manual/mental labor divide and allow for more effective factory-based knowledge creation in the form of both continuous improvement and more radical product-process innovation. JMSs' effectiveness—and, indeed, the effectiveness of the tools and techniques embodied in the production system—derive in great part from the way they encourage organizations to continually augment their knowledge stocks.

A key feature of JMSs highlighted in this view is the commitment to small-group activities as processes that integrate individual and organizational learning (Cole, 1979; Fruin, 1998a; Lillrank and Kano, 1989). It is standard practice to involve many different kinds of employees in across-the-board efforts to identify new and better routines and to diffuse them throughout the organization. On-line teams encourage team-level sharing of best practices, and off-line teams—quality circles, new model changeover teams, *kaizen* teams, and so on—strengthen factory knowledge-creation capabilities. Thus, in this perspective, JMSs are distinctive in their ability to integrate knowledge from workers, technical specialists, researchers, and suppliers, since everybody involved with designing, making, and marketing products is linked together in small-group activities.

Small-group activities promote learning in three ways. First, they are a powerful vehicle for generating new knowledge that is likely to lead to operational improvements. Second, such activities help diffuse this knowledge across the organization. Within teams, knowledge can be shared by apprenticeship-like practices ("socialization" in Nonaka and Takeuchi's [1995] terminology): when employees are mobilized in teams, they bring with them their augmented knowledge base and impart it to new team members. Third, small-group activities are important for creating a sense of belonging, involvement, and participation. These values are essential for maintaining a workplace environment that is open to knowledge creation and diffusion.

We should note that small-group activity has sometimes been interpreted more negatively. Graham (1995), for example, describes one auto transplant's team-based structure as a means of encouraging compliance by both the internalization of management values and peer pressure. Graham interprets the "human relations" aspects of small-group activity as its only rationale—arguing that the teams she studied generated little *kaizen*—and that this human relations strategy is essentially manipulative rather than collaborative.

Whether interpreted positively or negatively, there are numerous problems in attempting to transfer Japan's small-group activities to the United States. Here we mention one difficulty that is discussed in several of the following chapters. Small-group activity in Japan often involves a significant amount of top-down direction on the part of management to focus the goals toward management's business priorities (Fruin and Nakamura, 1997). Cole thus notes (1979) that in Japan small-group activities rely on strong first-line supervisors. In the United States, by contrast, efforts to strengthen employee involvement often deliberately bypass shop floor supervisors to "empower" production workers in ways foreign to Japanese organizations. In the chapter on NSK, we learn that Japanese managers attributed the failure of quality circles at their U.S. operations to giving too much power to workers to choose their own projects—projects that generally focused on "creature comforts" rather than on productivity and quality. Several other chapters discuss the challenges to traditional forms of authority from attempts to use small-group activities for knowledge creation.

JMSs as Enabling Bureaucracies

If, on the one hand, Japanese firms seem to rely on small-group processes to stimulate learning, many also evidence a rather high degree of vertical hierarchy formalization and standardization, at least in their production cores. (Other parts of their management systems may be far less bureaucratic.) Standardized work sheets, for example, lay out in great detail exactly how each job is to be done, and these standardized methods are taken far more seriously than in comparable U.S. firms. Japanese firms can mobilize production workers to perform preventive maintenance because these tasks have been extensively documented and standardized. Unlike the American enthusiasm for "flat" organizational structures, Japanese organizations typically have finely graduated and thickly populated vertical hierarchies.

However, the form of bureaucracy found in JMSs is strikingly different from that found in traditional U.S. firms and echoed in traditional organization theory. The traditional form of bureaucracy is designed for the purposes of control and compliance. The imposition of formal procedures, standards, and hierarchy is a way of ensuring that potentially recalcitrant and irresponsible employees do the right thing. When bureaucracy is designed and implemented with this coercive rationale, its efficiency comes at great cost to lost worker commitment, operational flexibility, and improvement momentum. But the bureaucratic features of at least some Japanese firms appear to have a different rationale and different effects: formal procedures and standards are designed with the participation of line personnel, rather than imposed by staff specialists. These procedures and standards serve to identify best practices and opportunities for improvement, rather than merely setting performance standards for the purpose of deterring shirkers. The hierarchy is based primarily on expertise rather than on positional authority, and hierarchically differentiated layers collaborate rather than battle it out. When bureaucracy takes this "enabling" form (Adler and Borys, 1996), it does not undercut commitment, flexibility, and innovation. It can simultaneously assist in the collaborative control of routine tasks and in collaborative creativity on nonroutine tasks.

Here, too, we should note that JMSs' bureaucratic features have been interpreted more negatively, as a more refined, pervasive, and invasive form of coercion (Babson, 1995; Fucini and Fucini, 1990). Some critics dispute the positive assessment of commitment and performance outcomes presented earlier, and argue that Japanese firms' successes are obtained despite, not because of, their bureaucratic form. Other critics accept that at least some Japanese bureaucracy takes this more benign form but argue that this happens only because workers' compliance is ensured by other, more structural means. When the cost of losing one's job is very high—as is the case in systems of lifetime employment (Sullivan and Peterson, 1991)—then it is not surprising, critics argue, that the details of procedures, standards, and reporting relationships do not have to take a strongly coercive form. Workers will naturally acquiesce to the discipline of an apparently enabling bureaucracy and may indeed evidence a range of commitment behaviors that mask an underlying indifference or hostility.

Under either of these interpretations of the enabling bureaucracy view, new hurdles to the transfer of JMSs are identified. Japanese firms' success with this approach appear to be very dependent on the internalization by workers and managers at all levels of certain values of discipline and group affiliation. Their re-creation in a foreign society with fundamentally different concepts of individual rights and democracy is unlikely without some fundamental rethinking.

JMSs as a Multistakeholder Model of Governance

The three views we have summarized up to this point have focused our attention inside the factory. But the effectiveness of JMSs, it could be argued, depends even more strongly on broader governance structures. Corporations in Japan link stakeholders like communities, unions, banks, suppliers, and shareholders in distinctive ways (Aoki and Patrick, 1994; Dore, 1988; Fruin, 1983; Miyashita and Russell, 1994; Morikawa, 1992; Odagiri, 1992). Many of the agency, property rights, and transaction cost models of governance that are based on the experience of Western firms do not apply very well in Japan:

- Management and unions are not determined adversaries. The asymmetries between managers and regular employees in terms of wages, authority, voice, rights, and benefits are significantly muted.
- Close and long-standing relations with creditors and debtors encourage a long-term view of the nature of competition and cooperation.

Board members and top executives are generally promoted from within firms. Hostile takeovers are rare and corporate control is not contested (Gerlach, 1992; Kester, 1989).

• Suppliers cooperate closely and without great concern for the appropriation of intellectual property, the risk of losing key employees to competitors, or partners' opportunism (Nishiguchi, 1994). Top executives of supplier firms are often dispatched from or recently retired from large manufacturing firms. Suppliers are an integral part of the Japanese system of production; they are part of a core firm's operations in spite of their legal independence. Production systems are integrated across the supply chain, organizational learning spans company boundaries, and network position often defines the evolution of technical capabilities (Fruin and Nishiguchi, 1993; Stuart and Podolny, 1996).

It should be noted that this stakeholder model, too, permits a more negative interpretation. In the eyes of some observers, the influence of multiple stakeholders limits the flexibility of individual firms (Sakai, 1990). This model may have served Japanese firms well in the past, argue these critics, but only because Japanese industry was enjoying the advantages of late development. Now that Japanese firms must begin to innovate rather than imitate, they will no longer be able to afford this handicap.

Whatever the merits of this critique, many of the following chapters show that the more successful Japanese transplants are indeed attempting to re-create something akin to the Japanese model in the United States, at least with respect to unions and suppliers (less so with banks). This represents a huge challenge, since it requires reshaping the expectations and norms of local actors—expectations and norms that have been formed by a long and very different industrial, legal, and social history. The empirical research reported in this volume casts light on the opportunities and constraints in the process.

Transfer: Transplanting and Transforming

One empirical goal of the present volume is to identify the parts of JMSs that can be transferred to the U.S. relatively intact, the parts that undergo significant transformation in transfer, and those that must be created anew. Once we frame this question in terms of our layer model, a pattern emerges from the chapters of this volume and other research on this question: it is easiest to transfer shop floor production systems, somewhat more difficult to transfer the wider factory organization, and far more difficult to transfer the institutional linkages that underpin a corporate system.

A key theoretical goal of this book is to understand why such a pattern should prevail. Here, we outline three broad perspectives that help situate the contributions of the various chapters to our understanding of this pattern. Like the various theories of JMSs' effectiveness, these perspectives are largely complementary.

However, before turning to these explanatory perspectives, it is useful to recall that transferring practices across societies and nations is an age-old process that did not start with Japan. While we do not pretend to be able to synthesize the rich history of technical and institutional transfer in this chapter, we can at least give a few general examples to help situate the transfer of JMS.

The international diffusion of Japanese management systems has parallels in earlier diffusions of other management innovations. Ideas and institutions have been borrowed from and imposed by one regime or another since the beginnings of civilization. Indeed, by the time of the great Mediterranean and Chinese conquest dynasties, and hence well before the time of Christ, patterning a region's political and economic affairs on another's was commonplace in the more densely settled and well-developed regions of the world.

Physical modeling—imitating structures such as causeways, aqueducts, and temples—was the least complex sort of modeling. Political and economic modeling were far more complex, but they were attempted nevertheless, and with some success. In most of these cases, the effort was directed toward securing the compliance of local elites, who, in turn, were responsible for erecting the facade, if not the substance, of the new model.

The nineteenth century saw a dramatic rise in worldwide commerce, industry, and diplomacy which greatly accelerated international intercourse, and the twentieth century's global conflicts offered ample opportunities for victors to impose their ways on the conquered. The United States, as the twentieth century's preeminent world power, both promoted and benefited from the acceleration of international learning. Through postwar treaties, lend-lease programs, the Marshall Plan, economic aid and advisement, and the promotion of its free market and democratic ideals, the United States sought to influence the political economies of its allies and its rivals. Internationally, through the United Nations, NATO, the International Monetary Fund, the World Bank, and other international bodies, the power and influence of the United States was globally evident.

In the management domain, the United States was the starting point for the international diffusion of Taylorism and Fordism in the early years of the twentieth century, the multidivisional corporation somewhat later, and the corporate culture movement still later, during the 1970s. Research on these models' diffusion shows that the characteristics of receiving countries affected the willingness to adopt them, the specific aspects adopted, and the modification and reinvention of the innovations (Kogut and Parkinson, 1993; Westney, 1987; Wilkins, 1970, 1974).

The Innovation Diffusion Perspective

In this dependence on receiving countries, the diffusion of new management approaches is similar to the diffusion of social and technical innovations in general. A large literature on innovations has shown that the speed and extent of their diffusion depends on sender and receiver characteristics, on the communication process between senders and receivers, and on what is being sent (Damanpour, 1991; Rogers, 1983; Tornatzky and Fleischer, 1990; Wolfe, 1994).

The application of this body of theory to JMSs is subject to two caveats. First, JMSs are more complex than the innovations typically studied in this literature. They embody more components, more layers, and subtler linkages. Second, JMSs are not obviously an innovation waiting to be transferred. JMSs become an innovation only through a complex process of interpretation, learning, and social construction, both within Japan and afar, in the United States. As we have already pointed out, when observers first began to think that Japanese approaches to management were not only different but perhaps superior, it was not clear that these approaches were in any meaningful way separable, conceptually or practically, from the broader pattern of Japanese culture. However, both these caveats are a matter of degree rather than kind, since some innovations are very complex and, some theorists would argue, all are to a degree socially "constructed." Several aspects of the transfer of JMSs to the United States can be usefully intepreted using the diffusion of innovations lens.

Receiver (Transplant) Characteristics

Looking first at receivers/adopters, research shows that the diffusion of innovations depends on the characteristics of individual firms and the broader aggregates of potential adopter firms (Tornatzky and Fleischer, 1990). Several characteristics are strong predictors of receptivity to innovations and of the ability to use innovations effectively: size, resources, and dependence on the innovation for survival and success.

Size of adopter.   Size plays a critical but complex role. On the one hand, larger firms have the human and financial resources to keep abreast of the latest technological and management innovations, as well as the resources to adopt and implement them. On the other hand, smaller companies are often more flexible, and they implement innovations more rapidly than larger, bureaucratic firms. A recent collection of case studies of U.S. firms that implemented versions of the Toyota Production System found that implementation was more rapid in smaller companies because larger companies, took more time up-front to communicate, train, and get competing political factions on board (Liker, 1997).

Evidence also suggests that larger firms are more likely to adopt new technologies, but smaller firms go broader and deeper when they adopt (Rees, Briggs, and Hicks, 1984; Wiarda, 1987). This is consistent with U.S. evidence that the implementation of just-in-time manufacturing practices is more effective in smaller than in larger firms (Inman and Mehra, 1990). We note, however, that these broad patterns leave considerable room for variation. The majority of the firms studied in this book are medium- to large-size and it is clear that they have devoted considerable resources (e.g., travel, legal, consulting) to transfer activities.

Slack resources of adopter.   Research has demonstrated a clear link between the availability of slack resources among potential adopters and the likelihood of adopting and of effectively implementing innovations. Smaller firms are slower to adopt innovations because they lack resources. In contrast, the leading Japanese firms discussed in this book commit considerable resources to support investment in their overseas operations and adopt innovations as a long-term investment. To take one example: Toyota's financial performance during the 1980s left it with considerable free cash flow, and the company could afford to send hundreds of engineers to NUMMI and TMMK to make sure those start-ups were successful.

Dependence of the adopter on the innovation.   It is hardly surprising that when firms are dependent on effective implementation of a given innovation for prosperity or survival, they are more serious about adopting it. The converse also holds. Cole's chapter describes how even the stunning success of TQM at the Yokogawa-HP joint venture was not enough to motivate other HP divisions to adopt TQM—until they concluded that TQM was critical to their own survival and success.

The diffusion of innovations depends not only on the charactertistics of individual potential adopters but also on the characteristics of aggregates of potential adopter plants and companies. Two factors are relevant:

Adopter population demographics. Other things being equal, diffusion is easier in populations composed of a few large potential adopters than in populations composed of many small, independent potential adopters. The chapter by MacDuffie and Helper shows how much effort is needed for Honda to diffuse its practices to a small number of suppliers and one can imagine how much more difficult it would be if the supplier base were composed of a larger number of firms.

Communication between adopters. Other things being equal once again, diffusion is easier when there are multiple communication links among potential adopters, enabling them to learn from one another. Cole's chapter shows that the diffusion of TQM across divisions within Hewlett-Packard was greatly facilitated by the ability of each division to observe results in peer divisions.

Sender (Home Company) Characteristics

Diffusion, however, depends not only on the receiver but also on the sender. Some industries and some firms in Japan may be more committed to, and better at, transferring management techniques to U.S. subsidiaries and suppliers (Kenney and Florida, 1993). The chapter by Martin Kenney suggests that Japanese TV manufacturers were not nearly as focused as their counterparts in auto at transferring JMSs to the United States. Fruin likewise shows that Toshiba's efforts to transfer its photocopier technology to the United States were similarly handicapped. Tornatzky and Fleischer's (1990) review shows two key sender characteristics that influence innovation diffusion—the resources senders devote to deployment and their commitment.

Sender resources.   The resources that senders can make available to support diffusion are closely linked to the sender's size, but also to its business situation at a given time. Some of the case studies in this volume portray senders who are very aware of these constraints. The chapter by Brannen, Liker, and Fruin shows that NSK intentionally delayed major investments in their Ann Arbor plant in order to concentrate resources on plants in Iowa and in England.

Sender commitment.   The diffusion of innovations—especially ones as complex as JMSs—takes time and resources. Given competition for scarce resources, diffusion depends critically on the commitment of the sender to a sustained effort. As the chapters on Toyota, Toshiba, and NSK show, the decision to set up an overseas plant represents not only an up-front commitment of financial and technical resources but also a commitment to a broad-range and long-lasting effort to create the dedicated human and organizational capabilities required for world-class performance. It seems that, in the case of television plants in the United States described by Kenney, Japanese companies were not highly committed to the United States, given that, ultimately, North American television production was to be concentrated in Mexico, where labor rates were cheaper.

Communication Mechanisms

Diffusion dynamics depend not only on the characteristics of receivers and senders but also on the communication processes linking them. The success of diffusion depends critically on communications. Face-to-face communication supports the diffusion of innovations that rely on more ambiguous information, while arms'-length communication mechanisms are more cost-effective for dealing with relatively unambiguous problems (Daft and Lengel, 1986).

Considering the nature of the boundaries and the communication mechanisms available to surmount them, it is hardly surprising that the transfer of JMSs is easier from Japanese parents to U.S. transplants than from U.S. transplants to U.S.-owned suppliers or arms'-length emulation by U.S. rivals. As several of the chapters make clear, Japanese companies that set up transplant operations in the United States do not rely exclusively on formal, written communications. Americans are brought to Japan to experience JMSs firsthand, and Japanese advisers are sent to American plants for extended stays. Showing and direct tutelage are often more effective than verbal explanations, particularly when communicating across cultures.

A common practice described in this book is the pairing of what are variously called "mother" or "sister" plants in Japan with transplant operations. The term "sister plant" is clearly euphemistic, because the Japanese "siblings" are far more experienced and generally act as a template for the U.S. plants. The "mother plant" designation is far more accurate (albeit still quaintly sexist). Manufacturing equipment is set up and debugged in mother plants prior to being sent to the United States, and American managers, engineers, and workers are brought to mother plants to train on new equipment under the guidance of Japanese peers. Expatriates are deployed from mother plants to help launch new transplants and to set up new generations of equipment in them, and they often stay on to help in training and technical improvements. While some analysts have interpreted this tutelage as a centralization of power, in this volume such hands-on guidance appears more often as an apprenticeship that serves as an effective way of building autonomous local capabilities. The Honda BP process analyzed by MacDuffie and Helper represents a kind of apprenticeship model.

Innovation Characteristics (The JMSs)

Research on innovation diffusion has shown that the dynamics of diffusion depend crucially on the characteristics of the innovation itself. Summarizing a large literature on the diffusion of innovations, Rogers (1983) argues that innovations are more easily diffused if they have the following features: high relative advantage, high compatibility with existing practices, low intrinsic complexity, high trialability, and high observability. Table 1.1 summarizes our assessment of JMSs under these five headings.

Three features of JMSs drive these five dimensions in a direction that makes diffusion more difficult. First, JMSs represent a radical departure from many of the basic precepts of American manufacturing management. Arguably, this radicalness is central to JMSs' relative advantage, but it also reduces compatibility with existing practices. Second, JMSs' systemic quality (Downs and Mohr, 1976; Bird and Beechler, 1995)—the complementarities between subsystems in each of the three layers and between the three layers themselves—reduces compatibility with existing practices, adds greatly to complexity, and reduces trialability. Finally, the tacitness of the knowledge embedded in and underlying JMSs (Nonaka and Takeuchi, 1995) and the tacitness of the skill required to manage multiple interdependencies between these practices reduce trialability and observability. These relationships between the three JMS attributes and Rogers's innovation characteristics are shown in Figure 1.2.

These characteristics of JMSs interact with other diffusion factors to render the diffusion of JMSs to the United States particularly difficult. Potential adopters have found it difficult to know if JMSs were indeed critical to Japanese firms' success. The complexity of JMSs meant that Japanese headquarters and mother plants needed not only substantial resources but also broad-

Table 1.1 Attributes of JMSs That Influence Ease of Diffusion

Dimension[a]	Attributes of JMSs
Relative advantage	Initially: difficult to decide if JMSs provide advantage to Japanese firms Later: difficult to decide what features of JMSs provide advantage
Compatibility	Key components of JMSs are incompatible with prevailing American practices
Complexity	Individual tools and techniques are relatively simple But complementarity of JMSs' components creates considerable complexity
Trialability	Individual production system components can be tested easily But outer layer subsystems much harder to test
Observability	Efficiency and quality outcomes are easy to observe But JMSs subsystem complementarity within and across layers is difficult to observe

a. Dimensions taken from Rogers (1983).

based commitment to support diffusion to their U.S. transplants and to their suppliers. This complexity and uncertainty also meant that communication between senders and receivers needed to be particularly rich and intense.

A Structuralist Perspective

The literature on the diffusion of innovations leaves in the background another, more amorphous set of factors that explain the diffusion process—the role of "context." In this literature, context is left in the background for a good reason: unless we can theoretically define the structure of this context, there seems little point in highlighting it; better to let its theoretical effects surface in our characterization of senders and receivers.

The broader literature on global systems and international management, however, suggests a way of giving some structure and explanatory power to context (Mueller, 1994; Smith and Meiskins, 1995). Adapting this research, we see four kinds of forces—operating at successively more concrete levels of analysis—that shape the international diffusion of JMSs. While the four layers of JMSs represent four empirically distinct domains, these four forces are differentiated theoretically rather than empirically, and they jointly determine the international transfer of management models such as JMSs.

1. At the most general level, the *capitalist firm* everywhere must compete and is thus under pressure to adopt productive ways of organizing. JMSs

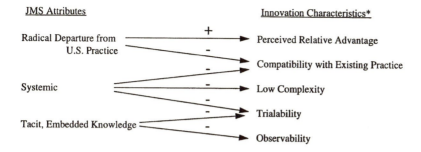

JMS Attributes   Innovation Characteristics*

* Innovation Characteristics from Rogers (1983) associated with ease of diffusion.

Figure 1.2 Relationships of JMS attributes to innovation characteristics that influence ease of diffusion.

have proven their potential at this level, even if, as we have seen, the source of their effectiveness remains in debate. At this level of analysis, we need to be sensitive to differences in the specifics of JMSs in more and less capital-intensive industries, in activities with more or less well-defined technological challenges, in industries with more or less product variety, and so forth.

2. At a more concrete level of analysis, we need to distinguish organizations on the basis of their location in the *international division of labor*. On the one hand, the transplants are mainly branch plants, subordinate to parent plants in Japan, and therefore they may not need the full range of capabilities afforded by JMSs. Many transplants do not have product design capabilities and thus don't get to wrestle with the problem of how to develop new designs that are manufacturable. Many of these problems have been solved in Japan by Japanese engineers working with their mother plants. On the other hand, however, the United States is a sophisticated market, an "advanced" society, a relatively high-cost operating environment, and a powerful trading partner and competitor; branch plants in such a location must add significant value to products. They must be more than "screw-driver" plants, if only because local labor costs are too high. It is thus not surprising that Japanese and U.S.-owned plants located the United States seek to implement far more advanced versions of JMSs than are found in less developed regions. And *a contrario* most Japanese TV assembly plants in the United States are moving to Mexico. Such is the spatial logic of "commodity chains" (Kenney and Florida, 1994).

3. At the level of *specific societies*, the key issues are how transplants and local firms adapt JMSs to local institutional and economic environments (law, industry associations, capital markets, national cultures, work and management values) and whether those environments are conducive to the adoption of the most effective ways of doing things. Alternatively, if the local environment is not conducive, will the practices adopted by firms operating in the

United States really handicap them in global competition? This is the theoretical equivalent of layer 4 of our JMS model, and where the "societal effects" analyzed by Maurice, Sorge, and Warner (1980) are located.

4. At the level of *specific companies and plants*, the history of each organization, with its idiosyncratic strengths, weaknesses, and developmental trajectories, comes into play. The strategies of specific firms represent more or less self-conscious attempts both to come to grips with the constraints imposed by the forces operative on levels 1 through 3 and also to reshape those constraints. Different firms compete on different dimensions; they define the charter of specific plants differently, and they position themselves differently with respect to societal constraints in various countries. Plants, too, have a site-specific history. Plants are embedded in specific regions, they started up at different times, they inherited different legacies, and they developed their own strategies for accommodating and modifying their local operating environments.

These four levels are in reality superimposed. The associated forces can reinforce or counteract each other. Adler's chapter on two Toyota transplants affords an example: two Toyota transplants, one in California (NUMMI) and the other in Kentucky (TMMK), share a common company heritage (level 4) and have attempted to implement rigorously the Toyota production system, which they see as the best way of competing (level 1), but they have had to adapt to the U.S. context (level 2 and 3), and they have done so in different ways (level 4).

The interaction of forces at these four levels creates an immensely complex dynamic whose outcomes over time are intrinsically difficult to interpret, let alone to predict. The complexity becomes even more opaque when the parameters that characterize each level change, such as when economies become more open to international competition (strengthening the salience of level 1 relative to level 3), regions change roles in the international commodity chain (level 2), countries' legal or political systems evolve (level 3), or rival organizations attain or lose dominance (level 4).

One idea that allows us to get beyond total agnosticism concerning the evolution path created by this four-level interaction is simple enough: the lower levels of this hierarchy (plant, company) are in some meaningful sense generally subordinate to the higher levels (successively, country specificities, international division of labor, and competition). If a plant does not perform, sooner or later the company is likely to shut it down. If a company does not perform, sooner or later it will not be able to compete nationally and internationally. If the society cannot sustain its place in the international division of labor, it will sooner or later be forced to slip down the hierarchy of national economies. All this reflects the priority of competitive pressures to perform over other considerations in the modern global economy.

However, countervailing forces are not negligible, if only because competition rarely comes in a pure and perfect form. In particular, regions are somewhat isolated from global competition, and local stakeholders have some influence over the norms that govern performance assessment. Many observers have argued that competitive pressures (i.e., level 1 forces) are growing in pervasiveness and salience as trade barriers come down and capitalist competition penetrates all regions of the globe. Such an argument suggests that the whole hierarchical system of forces leans in favor of the diffusion of more productive management systems such as JMSs.

An Emergent Process Perspective

The perspectives on transfer discussed so far have been essentially structural in orientation, seeking to identify structural features of the transfer content or context that can explain the observed outcomes. But, as our comments in the previous subsection suggest, the complexity and the multiplicity of these structural determinants make causal attributions risky.

This indeterminacy may not be a purely epistemological problem; it may also reflect the real nature of the evolution of JMSs and their transfer. Indeed, the very structure of the layer model of JMSs that we have proposed suggests that such systems cannot be "designed" but are rather "emergent" in the sense of the evolutionary view of the firm advanced by Penrose (1959), Nelson and Winter (1982), Kogut and Zander (1993), and Noda and Bower (1996), among others. The tacitness of much of the knowledge that underpins the production system and of the values and assumptions that underpins the broader management system imparts a marked path-dependent and firm-specific quality to the development of these systems. The internal development of each firm's management system is only partly the result of deliberate planning and is more often the result of opportunistic and experimental forms of "ex post" learning (Fujimoto, 1995).

If such systems cannot be deliberately designed, it is even more difficult to imagine how they could be deliberately transferred. The tacitness of the key components of these systems ensures that local conditions will greatly—rather than marginally—affect the outcomes of transfer efforts. The differences between a Honda and a Toyota—not to speak of those between a Toyota and a Toshiba—are so subtle and so interconnected that it is difficult to imagine what a "transfer of best practices" across such firms could be if not a "reinvention." And if transfer within Japan is difficult, cross-border, cross-cultural transfer is doubly so. JMSs at leading Japanese firms may serve as a reference point, but, in the international transfer process, each facility will experience its own developmental sequence, and numerous unplanned adaptations or mutations will occur. That is why the transfer of JMSs is much more than transplantation; system attributes must be modified to fit a new environment. So, when we speak of transplantation and transformation, the emphasis must be on the latter term.

The necessity of transformation is clearly visible when JMSs are seen as institutionalized cognitive patterns (Tsoukas, 1996). First, sending firms in Japan develop models of what makes their systems work, but given the complexity, interconnectedness, and tacitness of many components, these models are necessarily imperfect. Second, receiving organizations have their own beliefs and values that filter and reshape understandings. Third, to the extent that two parties interact in the transfer process, the interaction generates new interpretations of what is being transferred, what is not being transferred, and how effectively transfer is progressing. Ultimately, transplants represent the emergent results in a process of negotiating new, partly shared cognitive and normative models—models that are likely to be different in important ways from those of the parent in Japan (Westney, 1987; see also Fruin's and Brannen et al.'s chapters).

If, on the one hand, transfer requires transformation, such transformation risks undermining the effectiveness of the JMSs. The complementarity among JMSs' attributes is strong even if poorly understood (Hennart and Ready, 1994). As a result, there is likely to be a greater performance payoff when the system is implemented as a whole, even if such a holistic approach seems more difficult. When JMSs are transformed, chances are great that some of this complementarity will be lost.

The emergent, processual view of transfer helps us understand the way this tension unfolds because it highlights the importance of the mode of transfer for transfer effectiveness. JMSs can be transferred abroad in three different ways—greenfield operations, brownfield operations, and joint ventures—each creating rather different transfer process dynamics and different site-specific development scenarios.

Of the three transfer modes, greenfield sites afford the best chances for successful transfer of a whole set of home-country attributes because the impact of the local environment is not confounded by a local partner's preexisting routines and practices. Under such conditions, it may be easier to transfer the whole system because the plant managers are in a better position to adjust the processes of local selection, learning, and self-reproduction that inevitably occur.

Transfer to brownfield sites is more problematic because preexisting routines and practices and new ones may be in conflict. Instead of a single point of reference, on-site managers are constantly debating not only how to transfer a given model but also which of the two alternative approaches is more appropriate for various parts of the management system (Brannen and Salk, 1997; Salk and Brannen, 1998). Given an imperfect understanding of the functioning of the Japanese model even in Japan, such debates are undecidable and their outcomes unpredictable.

These problems can be compounded in international joint ventures, where choices made by on-site managers are subject to review by the two parents. Issues of differential power and influence are even more likely to affect the developmental sequence and the ultimate configuration of the new site's characteristics. Where both parents share in shaping the new organization, the resulting attribute configurations are difficult to predict in advance. When one partner is left in full control of the internal structure however, as in the NUMMI case, the development of local capabilities follows a path that is less subject to abrupt changes of policy at higher levels. We also learn in Cole's chapter that the Yokogawa-Hewlett-Packard plant was a brownfield site, yet the venture was very successful in adopting Yokogawa's excellent quality philosophy and systems. In this case, HP was undergoing incredible change, including the shift from batch production to high-volume, high-quality production in consumer products, and top management recognized a strong need to change to meet the Japanese challenge. The joint venture was given a good deal of autonomy and was highly successful in transforming a brownfield plant.

In JMS transfer, differences and similarities in sending and receiving sites depend on the management systems of both parents, and how much they strive to preserve the traits and features that each considers important (or dominant). But transformation rather than transplantation is the rule, because environmental effects have to be considered. Environmental change forces selection and selection drives evolution. In other words, transplanting JMSs necessarily compels their transformation.

It is remarkable that, with all these hurdles facing transfer, the empirical evidence presented here and elsewhere strongly indicates that key aspects of JMSs are indeed transferable and that they work well in the U.S. environment. The success of the Toyota Production System in the United States is noteworthy (Liker, 1997, 1990; Womack et al.). However, the empirical record also tells us that JMSs are not transferred easily or in their entirety. The following chapters cast light on the transfer dynamics that explain these patterns.

An Overview of This Book

The body of this book is divided into four parts: the auto industry, the electronics industry, cross-industry comparisons, and theoretical perspectives.

Automotive and Automotive Parts

The first chapter of Part I lays a foundation for the other studies of the auto industry. Frits Pil and John Paul MacDuffie compare Japanese and local influences in a large sample of auto assembly plants. They use data from Round Two of the International Assembly Plant Study (sponsored by MIT's International Motor Vehicle Program; see Womack et al., *The Machine That Changed the World*, 1990) to compare eight Japanese transplants in North America with 25 plants from the U.S. "Big Three" companies, as well as with 12 plants in Japan. They look at a wide range of organizational practices that have been associated with superior performance of Japanese automobile producers, including work and human resources practices, automation, product choices, and supplier relations. This allows them to show that the extent of transfer overseas varies by type of practice. They find that the transplants, on average, follow work practices (e.g., on-line work teams, job rotation, suggestion programs, off-line problem-solving groups) that are similar to plants in Japan, although at different levels of intensity and coverage and often with some adaptation to the local context. For example, shop floor teams are typical in Japan and in the transplants, but quality circles is a very common practice with broad participation in Japan but relatively little participation in the transplants. In compensation practices, the transplants tend to follow U.S. Big Three norms and have only low levels of contingent pay. The data also show the high level of effort that the transplants put into training and other socialization activity for new hires in North America.

The gap between the performance of the transplants and their sister plants in Japan has narrowed even more than the gap between Big Three plants and Japanese plants. This suggests that the transfer process in the transplants has been largely effective in terms of economic performance. However, the success of this transfer also suggests that there is little to prevent local competitors from adopting the same practices. Pil and MacDuffie close their chapter with a discussion of the factors that will facilitate or constrain this imitative behavior by local competitors.

The subsequent chapters in Part I focus on more specific parts of the patterns identified by Pil and MacDuffie. Paul Adler discusses the human resource management policies at two Toyota transplants in the United States, one unionized (NUMMI, located in California) and the other not (TMMK, located in Kentucky). Both plants were quite thorough in their implementation of the Toyota production system. In analyzing their human resources management systems, Adler reaches four conclusions. First, these subsidiaries' HRM policies, viewed as a whole, were neither purely Japanese nor purely American, but rather hybrids. Second, Japanese approaches were adopted in policies addressing work organization, learning, and administration, whereas hybridization was the norm in the employment relations domain. Third, this hybridization drew not on one homogeneous host-country model but rather on two—a "progressive union" model and a "union substitution" model. Fourth, under rather different HRM systems, these two subsidiaries both achieved world-class levels of productivity and quality. Not only were different elements of the subsidiaries' HRM systems subject to different pressures, but the pressures coming from the local environment were neither entirely homogeneous nor entirely deterministic. In contrast to some theories of institutionalization and culture, these cases suggest that foreign subsidiaries operate within a complex cultural, social, and institutional context that affords—and, indeed, demands—interpretation, choice, and learning.

The chapter by Mary Yoko Brannen, Jeff Liker, and Mark Fruin analyzes NSK's attempt to transfer a highly effective production system from a mother plant in Ishibe to a subsidiary in Ann Arbor, Michigan. NSK was the largest Japanese manufacturer of wheel bearings. It was a very forward-looking firm, with a sophisticated global strategy. New equipment was designed and tested in Ishibe, and training for Ann Arbor operators was done there prior to shipping the equipment to the Unites States. There was a continual stream of expatriates from Ishibe to Ann Arbor and visitors from Ann Arbor to Ishibe. NSK made a conscious decision to encourage the autonomous development of its overseas plants and left the design of their human resources management policies in the hands of local management. NSK's transfer efforts focused on technical production system know-how and the associated practices.

Brannen and her coauthors show how, as the transfer process unfolded at the Ann Arbor plant, these practices were "recontextualized" and their meanings transformed by local actors. However, not all aspects of NSK's model underwent equally important transformations. The authors draw from the NSK a more general model that explains the likelihood of transformation of a given component as a function of the component's degree of system embeddedness and the degree of tacitness of its knowledge base.

In the last chapter of Part I, John Paul MacDuffie and Sue Helper analyze Honda's efforts to help improve their U.S.-based suppliers. Honda of America developed an approach to teaching its version of lean production to its suppliers—a version that differs in significant ways from the Toyota Production System. The centerpiece of these efforts was a program called BP (standing simultaneously for "Best Process," "Best Performance," and "Best Practice"), in which a cross-functional team of personnel from Honda and the supplier worked intensively for weeks or months on narrowly targeted improvement projects in the supplier's plant. BP has been very successful in enhancing supplier performance. Suppliers participating in the program in 1994 averaged productivity gains of 50 percent on lines reengineered by BP. However, Honda found there was high variation in the extent to which suppliers were able to transfer the lessons taught beyond the line or plant where the BP intervention occurred.

In exploring the reasons for this variation, MacDuffie and Helper examine how the BP process interacts with the broader relationship between customer and supplier, organizational learning, technology transfer, and the transplantation of Japanese management practices to the United States. Their chapter presents case studies of six of Honda's U.S. suppliers to illustrate the dynamics of the learning process and the complex relationship that emerged between "teacher" and "student." Comparing the more and less successful cases, MacDuffie and Helper find that achieving self-sufficiency with the lean production techniques taught by BP was more likely when the supplier had a moderate degree of identification with and dependency on the customer. If identification and dependency were too high, the supplier was tempted to continue to rely on the customer for assistance; if they were too low, the learning relationship was prone to breakdown. Honda achieved the greatest degree of supplier self-reliance with larger U.S.-owned companies, companies that had identities as strong, competent actors and that thus tried to reduce dependence on Honda by mastering the new knowledge quickly. Yet these larger suppliers were sometimes less responsive to Honda's needs than were small-to-medium suppliers whose capabilities could be boosted through Honda's supplier development activities.

The overall picture that emerges from these studies of the transfer of JMSs in the auto sector is one of considerable success. However, most of what has been transferred has been at or near the production system core in our four-layer model. As we move out beyond that core, transformation in the form of hybridization and adoption of U.S. practices become the norm. In the domain of work organization—a domain that is at the intersection of production and human resource management—the auto transplants display a commitment to teamwork and to broad, flexible work roles, but this is often embodied in practices that resemble Western concepts of self-managing work teams rather than Japanese teamwork. In the domain of compensation and benefits, the adoption of U.S. approaches is even more obvious. These chapters also show that, when Japanese companies are responsible for the transfer of their systems, they make impressive investments of time and resources in employee development and training, and their transplants have achieved performance levels rivaling those at factories in Japan. By contrast, the American companies that adopt Japanese practices do not go quite as far and do not get quite the performance. For example, the Big Three auto plants sampled by MacDuffie and Pil do not put the same level of effort into training and socialization and do not reach the performance levels of their Japanese competitors in Japan or in North America. And it is clear from the MacDuffie and Helper chapter that, although Honda's BP program had considerable success, this did not come without a struggle, and the success varied considerably across U.S. suppliers.

Electronics and Related Products

Part II focuses on the electronics industry. The first chapter in Part II, by Robert Cole, examines the process by which Hewlett-Packard adopted and adapted Japanese ideas about quality improvement. Cole argues that, to survive, these ideas had to be transformed to mesh with HP culture and practices. His case study identifies the specific route that led to successful outcomes. At a different level, Cole shows how actors bridged the gap between learning and doing. All too often, he reminds us, learning is equated with doing. His analysis of Hewlett-Packard's experience shows how that organization bridged the gap working with its joint venture partner in Japan, Yokogawa-Hewlett-Packard (YHP). In particular, he documents the most effective conjunction of learning and doing that occurred as a result of joint problem-solving activity on the part of HP and YHP managers in the course of normal business activity. Top management at Hewlett-Packard skillfully used some of these outcomes as models for the rest of the company. In the course of his analysis, Cole disentangles the many ways in which one company or plant can serve as a model for another. The model can provide trustworthy information, information about what is possible and different from what employees in the receiving organization are already thinking or doing, concrete outcome benchmarks, a transparent template for concrete processes and practices, and a broad conceptual template of how an organization should approach major organizational uncertainties. The absence of one or more of these is likely to limit the modeling that does occur. Finally, Cole concludes that the many serendipitous and unique factors that influence the transfer process should remind us that there are limits to the strategic design of organizations.

Mark Fruin's chapter uses three cases of Toshiba's transfer of photocopier and peripherals technology to investigate the importance of what he calls "site-specific organizational learning" (SSOL) in international technology transfer. Given that business environments differ greatly and that transplant organizations have to develop fitness levels well matched to local resources and constraints, successful transfer is really the creation of self-sustaining learning systems based on local practice. Of the three efforts at transplanting photocopier technology that Fruin analyzes, two were successful and one was not. Successful transfer was characterized by clear, unambiguous models of what was being transferred and by local learning that transformed the models to fit environmental demands. Unsuccessful transfer was handicapped by ambiguous models of what was being transferred and by a lack of focus and resources at the recipient site. SSOL is the selective, active learning that is crucial to establishing an evolving repertoire of skills and procedures that work well and make sense.

Also in Part II, Martin Kenney discusses Japanese television assembly operations in Japan and the United States. He finds that the production system used by the Japanese leaders in their home-country plants belongs to the family of JMSs we have described in this introduction. However, when these companies set up transplants in the United States, only some components of the production system core and virtually nothing of the personnel management practices or the broader management structure were transferred. Traditional U.S. approaches to the management system were used instead. The business results of these transplants were modest: they achieved relatively high levels of effectiveness in producing standardized products but evidenced only slow growth in their capabilities and performance over time.

The contrast with the auto transplants is striking. Kenney attributes this contrast in part to the different technical challenges faced in the two industries. Compared to auto assembly, TV assembly offers far fewer opportunities for worker input, particularly in the standardized production segment in which the TV transplants were concentrated. However, this technical factor does not explain why Japanese firms did not give their transplants more ambitious charters, charters that would have required more extensive adoption of JMSs. Kenney suggests that the more fundamental explanation lies in the fact that these TV transplants were built before Japanese managers were confident of their ability to transfer JMSs and that, once low levels of worker involvement are established, they became a self-reinforcing structure that is difficult to change. Furthermore, the economics of TV assembly—in particular, its relatively low level of automation and facilities specialization—are such that these plants can be moved quickly and cheaply to areas with lower labor costs. So, when competitive pressure intensified, rather than investing the effort to build site-specific innovation capabilities, transplants in the United States were shut down and production shifted to Mexico.

In the final chapter of this section, Mark Peterson examines the role of expatriate supervisors. Some Japanese firms—more in the electronics industry than in the auto industry—have chosen to include lower-level expatriate supervisors as part of their approach to transferring managerial practices and maintaining ongoing control of their U.S. transplants. This chapter describes one such transplant and presents the results of survey data on the way the Japanese supervisors were perceived by employees in comparison to the way U.S. supervisors in the same facility were viewed. The Japanese supervisors were described as being especially instrumental in providing the kind of work-oriented "planning" leadership that was especially important in initial technology transfer. In the broader pattern of results, Peterson finds that a supervisor's nationality shapes the meanings subordinates give to his or her actions and the ways employees respond. For example, in the organization Peterson studied, subordinates responded to considerateness and friendliness on the part of a Japanese supervisor by doing good work, but the same considerateness on the part of an American supervisor was seen as shirking responsibility. Peterson has also conducted similar research in other plants and has found that these results are not consistent across organizations and over time. He concludes that national stereotypes can substantially affect relationships between supervisors and subordinates and that the precise nature of this effect is difficult to predict in specific cases.

Compared to the chapters on the auto industry, these chapters on electronics portray an industry that is more heterogenous, both in terms of its technologies and in the success of JMSs transfer. The appearance of greater technological heterogeneity is due in part to the broader range of end products in electronics and in part to the narrow focus in our auto chapters on final assembly and its immediately upstream suppliers. The more problematic nature of the transfer is striking, in contrast with the relatively successful transfer found in all the auto tranplants. Perhaps this reflects a less well-defined model in Japanese electronics home-country operations: there is nothing in the electronics industry comparable to the Toyota Production System to serve as a common reference point for all the major players. It may also reflect a less focused and committed transfer effort. Finally, it may reflect the ease with with management weaknesses can be mitigated by moving production to lower cost regions.

Surveys across Industries

Part III consists of surveys across a somewhat broader range of industries. These surveys help put in perspective the findings in the chapter on the auto and electronics industries. The chapter by Davis Jenkins and Richard Florida examines the extent to which Japanese manufacturing plants in the United States have adopted approaches to managing production work that are commonly associated with manufacturing practice in Japan. Their analysis is based on the first survey of the production work practices of the population of Japanese-affiliated manufacturing plants in the United States.

The survey reveals considerable variation among the U.S.-based Japanese transplants in their methods of managing production work. At one end of the spectrum, many transplants have adopted a rather coherent set of innovative and highly effective practices. The practices that constitute this "innovative" work system model reflect a blending of Japanese and American influences. At the other end of the spectrum, a sizable proportion of the transplants manage production work using more traditional "Taylorist" methods characteristic of heavy industry in the United States. Jenkins and Florida find that the adoption of innovative work systems is significantly more prevalent among transplants that supply automobile industry customers than among transplants that supply other industries. However, these transplant suppliers to the auto industry were no more likely to be innovative in their work systems than were U.S.-owned suppliers to the auto industry. They conclude that the upstream effect of the auto industry's performance improvement efforts (i.e., in the Big Three) have driven changes in a broad range of first-tier suppliers.

In the second chapter in Part III, Masao Nakamura, Sadao Sakakibara, and Roger Schroeder analyze the effects of just-in-time production system policies on the performance of a large sample of U.S.-and Japanese-owned plants from a broad range of industries. They distinguish three levels of JIT practices: first, "core" JIT practices, such as lot size and setup time reduction and JIT scheduling; second, "infrastructure" JIT practices, such as quality and work force management; and third, economy-wide business practices and market patterns, such as long-term employment and capital *keiretsu*. These three levels correspond roughly to our embedded layer model of JMSs (though their level 3 combines elements of our levels 3 and 4). Their results show that implementation of core JIT practices is associated with a significant improvement in U.S. plants' manufacturing performance—even without change to infrastructure and corporate level practices.

These two broader survey results confirm and deepen the observations made in the two specific industries: much has been transferred effectively, though transformations have clearly occurred. The "innovative" work systems identified by Jenkins and Florida are a hybrid of Japanese and American practices. Nakamura et al. find evidence that JIT approaches are having sizable performance benefits in the United States despite the fact that much of the infrastructure that supports JIT in Japan was not transferred. The Jenkins and Florida survey also supports our observation from earlier sections that there is variation across industries in the management paradigms of Japanese transplants and that the auto sector has been the leader in adopting the innovative work systems.

Theoretical Perspectives

The concluding chapter by Eleanor Westney presents conceptual arguments that draw theoretical lessons from the preceding chapters and suggest directions for future research. Westney argues that in the organizational research literature over the past four decades, and reflected in the various contributions to this volume, we can identify three broad perspectives that are particularly useful for looking at organization-environment relations. One regards organizations as "strategic designs"—systems consciously constructed for the efficient accomplishment of certain tasks. A second regards them primarily as ideational constructs defined by shared interpretations, meaning, and value. And a third sees them as both arenas for and tools of power, politics, and competing interests. Westney goes on to argue that the three perspectives are in reality complementary, each providing the analogue of a flashlight in a dark and overcrowded attic, directing the observer to different and potentially equally important facets of reality. An organization is, in fact, simultaneously a strategic design, a social construct, and an arena for political conflict. Our understanding of the international diffusion of management innovations will be enhanced if we can analyze concurrently all three aspects.

This book focuses on what happens when Japanese companies and their U.S. emulators bring Japanese manufacturing approaches to the United States. Taken as a whole, the chapters make clear that this is a complex evolutionary process. As we plunge into an increasingly global economy, we need to learn how better to manage that process. We hope the present volume offers some conceptual handles on that huge challenge.

References

Abegglen, James C. 1958. *The Japanese Factory*. Glencoe, Ill.: Free Press.

Adler, P. S. 1993. "The Learning Bureaucracy: New United Motors Manufacturing, Inc." In Barry M. Staw and Larry L. Cummings, eds., *Research in Organizational Behavior*, vol. 15, pp. 111–194. Greenwich, Conn.: JAI Press.

Adler, Paul S., and B. Borys. 1996. "Two Types of Bureaucracy: Enabling and Coercive." *Administrative Science Quarterly* 41(1): 61–89.

Aoki, Masahiko. 1994. "The Japanese Firm as a System of Attributes." In M. Aoki and H. Patrick, eds., *The Japanese Firm*. Oxford: Oxford University Press.

Aoki, Masahiko, and Hugh Patrick. 1994. *The Japanese Main Bank System*. Oxford: Oxford University Press.

Babson, Steve. 1995. "Whose Team? Lean Production at Mazda, U.S.A." In Steve Babson, ed., *Lean Work: Empowerment and Exploitation in the Global Auto Industry*, pp. 3–24. Detroit: Wayne State University Press.

Bird, Allan, and Schon Beechler. 1995. "Links between Business Strategy and Human Resource Management Strategy." *Journal of International Business* 26(1): 23–46.

Brannen, M. Y., and J. E. Salk. 1999. "Partnering across Borders: Negotiating Organizational Culture in a German-Japanese Joint Venture," *Human Relations*.

Chandler, A. D. 1990. *Scale and Scope*. Boston: Harvard University Press.

Cole, Robert E. 1979. *Work, Mobility, and Participation: A Comparative Study of American and Japanese Industry*. Berkeley: University of California Press.

Cole, Robert E. 1987. *Strategies for Learning*. Berkeley: University of California Press.

Cusumano, Michael, 1991, *Japan's Software Factories*, New York: Oxford University Press.

Daft, R. L., and Lengel, R. H. 1986. "Organizational Information Requirements, Media Richness, and Structural Design." *Management Science* 32(5): 554–571.

Damanpour, F. 1991. "Organizational Innovation: A Meta-analysis of Effects of Determinants and Moderators." *Academy of Management Journal* 34(3): 555–590.

Dore, R. P. 1988. *Flexible Rigidities: Industrial Policy and Structural Adjustment in the Japanese Economy, 1970–1980*. Stanford, Calif.: Stanford University Press.

Fruin, W. Mark. 1983. *Kikkoman: Company, Clan, and Community*, Cambridge, Mass.: Harvard University Press.

Fruin, W. Mark. 1992. *The Japanese Enterprise System*. Oxford: Oxford University Press.

Fruin, W. Mark. 1997. *Knowledge Works—Managing Intellectual Capital at Toshiba*. New York: Oxford University Press.

Fruin, W. Mark. 1999a. "Double Time/Double Bind: The Time Value of Knowledge, Organizational Change, and Organizational Campaigning." In Joseph Porac and Raghu Garud, eds., *Cognition, Knowledge, and Organization*. Greenwich, Conn.: JAI Press.

Fruin, W. Mark. 1998b. "Governance, Managed Competition and Network Organization in a Toshiba Electronics Factory." In W. Mark Fruin, ed., *Networks, Markets, and the Pacific Rim*. New York: Oxford University Press.

Fruin, W. Mark, and M. Nakamura. 1997. "Top-down Production Management: A Recent Trend in the Japanese Productivity-Enhancement Movement." *Managerial and Decision Economics*, 18: 131–39.

Fruin, W. Mark, and Toshihiro Nishiguchi. 1993. "Supplying the Toyota Production System: Intercorporate Organizational Evolution and Supplier Subsystems." In Bruce Kogut, ed., *Country Competitiveness*, pp. 225–248. New York: Oxford University Press.

Fucini, Joseph J., and Fucini, Suzy. 1990. *Working for the Japanese: Inside Mazda's American Auto Plant*. New York: Free Press.

Fujimoto, Takahiro. 1995. "An Evolutionary Process of Toyota's Final Assembly Operations: The Role of Ex Post Capabilities." Paper presented at the Third International Workshop on Assembly Automation, University of Venice, Oct. 12–14.

Gerlach, Michael. 1992. *Alliance Capitalism*. Berkeley: University of California Press.

Graham, Laurie. 1995. *On the Line at Subaru-Isuzu*. Ithaca, N.Y.: ILR Press/Cornell University Press.

Imai, Masaaki. 1997. *Gemba Kaizen*. New York: McGraw-Hill.

Juran, J. M. 1988. *Juran on Planning for Quality*. New York: Free Press.

Kenney, Martin, and Richard Florida. 1993. *Beyond Mass Production*. New York: Oxford University Press.

Kenney, Martin, and Richard Florida. 1994. "Japanese Maquiladoras: Production Organization and Global Commodity Chains." *World Development* 22(1): 27–44.

Kester, Carl. 1989. *Japanese Takeover*. Boston: Harvard Business School Press.

Koenigsaecker, G. 1997. "Lean Production—The Challenge of Multidimensional Change." In J. K. Liker, ed., *Becoming Lean: Experiences of U.S. Manufacturers*, pp. 457–476. Portland, Ore.: Productivity Press.

Kogut, Bruce, and David Parkinson. 1993. "The Diffusion of American Organizing Principles to Europe." In Bruce Kogut, ed., *Country Competitiveness*, pp. 179–202. New York: Oxford University Press.

Kogut, B., and U. Zander. 1993. "Knowledge of the Firm and the Evolutionary Theory of the Multinational Corporation." *Journal of International Business* 24(4): 625–646.

Liker, Jeffrey K. 1997. *Becoming Lean: Inside Stories of U.S. Manufacturers.* Portland, Ore.: Productivity Press.

Lillrank, Paul, and Noriaki Kano. 1989. *Continuous Improvement: Quality Control Circles in Japanese Industry.* Ann Arbor: University of Michigan Press.

Lincoln, James R., Michael Gerlach, and Christina Ahmadjian. 1996. "Keiretsu Networks and Corporate Performance in Japan." *American Sociological Review* 61: 67–88.

Lincoln, James R., Michael Gerlach, and Peggy Takahashi. 1992. "Keiretsu Networks in the Japanese Economy." *American Sociological Review* 57: 561–585.

Martinez, J., and J. Jarillo. 1991. "Coordination Demands of International Strategies." *Journal of International Business* 22(3): 429–444.

Maurice, M. S. Sorge, and M. Warner. 1980. "Societal Differences in Organizing Manufacturing Units: A Comparison of France, West Germany and Great Britain." *Organization Studies* 1: 59–86.

Miyashita, K., and D. Russell. 1994. *Keiretsu: Inside the Hidden Japanese Conglomerates.* New York: McGraw-Hill.

Monden, Y. 1983. *Toyota Production System.* Atlanta: Institute of Industrial Engineers.

Morikawa, Hidemasa. 1992. *Zaibatsu.* Tokyo: University of Tokyo Press.

Mueller, Frank. 1994. "Societal Effect, Organizational Effect, and Globalization." *Organization Studies* 15(3): 407–428.

Nelson, Richard, and Sidney Winter. 1982. *An Evolutionary Theory of Economic Change.* Cambridge, Mass.: Belknap Press.

Nishiguchi, Toshihiro. 1994. *Strategic Industrial Sourcing.* New York: Oxford University Press.

Noda, Tomo, and Joseph Bower. 1996. "Strategy Making as Iterated Processes of Resource Allocation." *Strategic Management Journal* 17: 159–192.

Nonaka, I., and H. Takeuchi. 1995. *The Knowledge-Creating Firm.* New York: Oxford University Press.

Odagiri, H. 1992. *Growth through Competition, Competition through Growth.* Oxford: Oxford University Press.

Odagiri, H., and A. Goto. 1997. *Technology and Industrial Development in Japan.* Oxford: Oxford University Press.

Penrose, Edith. 1959. *The Theory of the Growth of the Firm.* New York: Wiley.

Rees, J., R. Briggs, and D. Hicks. 1984. *New Technology in the American Machinery Industry: Trends and implications.* Study prepared for the use of the Joint Economic Committee, Congress of the United States. Washington, D.C.: Government Printing Office.

Rinehart, James W., Christopher Huxley, and David Robertson. 1997. *Just Another Car Factory? Lean Production and Its Discontents.* Ithaca, N.Y.: IRL Press/Cornell University Press.

Rogers, E. M. 1983. *Diffusion of Innovation*, 3rd ed. New York: Free Press.

Sakai, K. 1990. "The Feudal World of Japanese Manufacturing." *Harvard Business Review* Nov.–Dec.: 38–49.

Salk, J. E., and M. Y. Brannen. 1999. "National Culture, Networks and Individual Influence in a Multinational Management Team," *Academy of Management Journal*.

Shiba, T., and M. Shimotani. 1997. *Beyond the Firm*. Oxford: Oxford University Press.

Schonberger, R. J. 1982. *Japanese Manufacturing Techniques: Nine Hidden Lessons in Simplicity*. New York: Free Press.

Shingo, S. 1989. *A Study of the Toyota Production System*. Portland, Ore.: Productivity Press.

Smith, Chris, and Peter Meiskins. 1995. "System, Society and Dominance Effects in Cross-National Organizational Analysis." *Work, Employment and Society* 9(2): 241–267.

Stuart, Toby, and Joel Podolny. 1996. "Local Search and the Evolution of Technological Capabilities." *Strategic Management Journal* 17: 21–38.

Sullivan, J., and R. Peterson. 1991. "A Test of Theories Underlying the Japanese Lifetime Employment System." *Journal of International Business Studies* 21(1): 79–97.

Tornatzky, L., and M. Fleischer. 1990. *The Processes of Technological Innovation*. Boston: Lexington Books.

Tsoukas, Haridimos. 1996. "The Firm as a Distributed Knowledge System: A Constructionist Approach." *Strategic Management Journal* 17: 11–25.

Westney, Eleanor. 1987. *Imitation and Innovation*. Cambridge, Mass.: Harvard University Press.

Whitney, Daniel E. 1985. "Nippondenso Co., Ltd.: A Case Study of Strategic Product Design." In J. K. Liker, J. E. Ettlie, and J. C. Campbell, eds., *Engineered in Japan: Japanese Technology Management Practices*, pp. 115–151. New York: Oxford University Press.

Wiarda, 1987. *Frostbelt Automation*. Ann Arbor, Mich.: Industrial Technology Institute.

Wilkins, Mira. 1970. *The Emergence of American Multinational Enterprise*. Cambridge, Mass.: Harvard University Press.

Wilkins, Mira. 1974. *The Maturation of Multinational Enterprise*. Cambridge, Mass.: Harvard University Press.

Wolfe, R. A. 1994, May. "Organizational Innovation: Review, Critique, and Suggested Research Methods." *Journal of Management Studies* 31(3): 405–431.

Womack, J. P., and D. T. Jones, and D. Ross. 1990. *The Machine That Changed the World*. New York: Rawson Associates, Macmillan.

Womack, J. P. and D. T. Jones, 1996. *Lean Thinking*. New York: Simon and Shuster.

Part I

Automotive and Automotive Parts

2

Transferring Competitive Advantage across Borders

A Study of Japanese Auto Transplants in North America

Frits K. Pil

John Paul MacDuffie

Countries differ in their underlying organizing principles of work. These principles develop within the confines of a local trajectory, and differences are eliminated more slowly across than within national or regional boundaries (Kogut, 1991). Furthermore, localized learning can lock countries into suboptimal trajectories (Stiglitz, 1987). As a result, companies in some countries may possess advantages over those in other countries—advantages that do not diffuse naturally across national or regional borders. One means by which such advantages can be transferred across national borders is foreign direct investment (FDI).

In this chapter, we explore whether organizing principles and practices can indeed be transferred from one cultural and institutional environment to another through FDI, utilizing a unique data set that enables us to compare Japanese-owned automobile plants in North America with Japanese-owned automobile plants in Japan and Big Three automobile plants in North America. We look at a range of practices and policies that have been associated with superior performance of Japanese automobile producers, including those affecting work organization, human resource management, production technology, product variety, and supplier relations. We find that the extent of transfer varies by type of practice. Furthermore, while environmental influences play a role, the plants can shape and alter that environment and can also buffer themselves from it. Despite modifications of their production systems, we find that the Japanese transplants in North America are able to achieve almost the same performance levels as plants in Japan.

The notion that companies in different countries may have different operating principles and practices concurs with what has long been predicted by organizational theory. Such principles and practices should be differentiated on the basis of the external environment the organizations face (Aldrich and Pfeffer, 1976; Lawrence and Lorsch, 1967). Companies that operate in different locations face different environments in the form of institutions, employment expectations, and educational systems and thereby develop different modes of behavior and operation. However, the same forces that drive differences across regions also induce similarity across companies within any given region (Pil, 1996, 1997). Organizations depend on interactions with the institutional environment for their success (Hannan and Freeman, 1989; Thompson, 1967). Companies that face the same institutional environment experience isomorphic pressures to adopt the same kinds of practices and policies (Dimaggio and Powell, 1983; Zucker, 1988).

As mentioned, one means by which advantages that develop in one country can be transferred across national borders is foreign direct investment (FDI). However, the same environmental influences that give rise to superior organizing principles and practices in a given region also make it difficult to exploit such practices in a multinational context. Westney (1987, 1989) observed that the transfer of practices overseas by a multinational organization is never 100 percent because of the cultural dependency of some social technologies. As noted throughout this volume, in the process of transfer, there are both conscious and unconscious departures from the original practices. However, this raises an interesting quandary: although multinationals can serve as conduits for best practice, the environmental factors that promoted the development of best practice in one country may not be present in another.

Japanese multinationals provide a unique opportunity to study whether organizing principles can be transferred across national, institutional, and cultural environments. As early as 1973, in-depth research appeared contrasting the "Japanese production system" with the manufacturing practices of the West (Dore, 1973). The recent literature is replete with anecdotal and other evidence proclaiming the wonders of Japanese manufacturing systems (see Young, 1992), and there is substantial evidence in several industries that these practices have been instrumental in allowing Japanese plants to outperform their competitors in both productivity and quality (Abegglen and Stalk, 1985; MacDuffie and Krafcik, 1992; MacDuffie and Pil, 1998). At the same time, there is significant evidence suggesting that the United States and Japan differ significantly on a host of dimensions, including culture, educational systems, religion, and history (Hofstede, 1980; Ralston et al., 1997; Ronen and Shenkar, 1985). These differences help explain the emergence of superior practices in Japan, but they are also suggestive of the difficulties that might accompany transfer of the practices to the United States.

As described in the introductory chapter, the Japanese production system has many distinctive characteristics, in terms of work systems, technology choices, product strategies, and purchasing philosophies. We argue here that the extent of transfer of these different elements is at least partially dependent on the degree of interdependence with the external environment. Work systems and HR practices are dependent on the cultural and institutional environment, but measures can be taken to reduce that dependence and to adapt practices to the local environments. Production practices, such as those related to inventory buffers, are less dependent on the environment, though they require certain capabilities in the supply base that may need to be developed. Technical equipment is even less dependent on the environment and is often transferred with few adaptations. Product variety is very dependent on the demands of the customer base, but we find that the capabilities needed to handle the more complex product configurations present in Japan are transferred. Finally, with respect to supplier relations, we see evidence of extensive efforts to mimic the pattern of relationships found in Japan.

Research Context and Data

The focus of this chapter is Japanese (OEMs) automobile plants in North America (hereafter "transplants"). Some authors (Kenney and Florida, 1993; Young, 1992) have argued that Japanese auto companies have maintained their manufacturing practices upon moving to the United States, rather than alter them to meet the needs of the U.S. environment. Others have argued that the Japanese production system is not well suited to the U.S. context and must be modified in order to function (Zipkin, 1991). Although much has been written about work practices in some of the individual Japanese automobile transplants (e.g., Adler, 1992; Brown and Reich, 1989; Fucini and Fucini, 1990), no one has provided a detailed comparison of a large set of Japanese transplants in North America with a similar set of plants in Japan, as well as with American-owned plants in North America. Furthermore, while much of the focus to date has been on work and HR practices at the transplants, little has been written about the broader production systems at the transplants, including their technology, use of buffers, relationships with suppliers, and so forth. In this chapter we explore these issues, and do so with the benefit of data on a large set of Japanese plants, transplants, as well as U.S.-owned automobile plants.

By focusing our analyses on the automobile industry, we can relate our findings to those of others who have undertaken case study work in this area. There are three other important reasons for concentrating on the automobile industry. The first is that it is quite clear that the Japanese automobile producers in Japan have been extremely successful from a productivity and quality standpoint, and much of that success has been attributed to their production systems, sourcing practices, and so forth (MacDuffie and Pil, 1998; Womack et al., 1990). Second, given that the Japanese automobile companies have a successful template to draw on when they establish subsidiaries overseas, the transferability of "Japanese" systems provides a good test of whether multinationals can exploit superior practices that have originated in the cultural and institutional environment of their home country outside that environment. Last, it provides a unique opportunity to explore what aspects of Japanese production systems can be transferred completely, which require adaptation, and which are not transferable. Furthermore, we are in the unique position to assess the performance implications of the transfer of practices.

The data reported on here are from an international survey of automobile assembly plants worldwide, sponsored by MIT's International Motor Vehicle Program (MacDuffie and Pil, 1995). Here we report plant-level survey data from eight of the eleven Japanese auto transplants in North America. Survey responses were collected from 1993 to 1994. In addition, we have collected the same survey data for twelve automobile plants in Japan.[1] We have done extensive visits at twelve Japan plants and interviewed the management personnel in ten plants, as well as corporate-level managers at three of the five major companies in Japan. For U.S.-owned plants in North America (the "Big Three" of Ford, General Motors, and Chrysler), we have collected survey data from twenty-five plants and have carried out interviews at many of them. The data we present are all based on the survey responses, but our commentary reflects insights we have developed during the course of visiting the plants and conducting our interviews.

Comparing Human Resources and Work Practices

The work practices and HR policies of Japanese plants in Japan are often considered key to the success of Japanese automobile producers (Abegglen and Stalk, 1985; MacDuffie and Pil, 1998; Pil 1996; Womack et al., 1990). The idea that work practices can help firms create competitive advantage is found not only in research on Japan but also in an extensive body of literature about the U.S. (e.g., Kochan, Katz, and McKersie, 1986; Lawler, 1992). However, Japanese work practices developed in a unique cultural and institutional environment, and, as such, the question of their transferability overseas is an interesting one.[2]

Previous work in the tradition of comparative industrial relations has argued that the so-called three pillars of the Japanese employment system—lifetime employment, enterprise unionism, and seniority wages—are critical to the success of large Japanese companies (Shimada, 1985). Others have argued for the importance of practices and policies directly related to work organization and skill development in the Japanese production system, including team-based production methods, worker participation in problem solving, job rotation, a small number of job classifications, few distinctions between management and employees, and high-training levels (Cole, 1979; Koike, 1989; MacDuffie and Krafcik, 1992; Smith and Misumi, 1989). Although these are less dependent on the institutional environment, an important prerequisite is believed to be a homogenous workforce. We first consider the "three pillars" of the Japanese employment system and subsequently examine in detail the work and human resource practices commonly associated with the Japanese production system.

Lifetime Employment

First, we consider lifetime employment. This is believed to be important for the successful implementation of a whole range of practices, including the provision of extensive training, successful teamwork, and employee commitment to continuous improvement. This permanent employment is offered to a set of core employees. Part-time, seasonal, and contract workers are used to handle demand fluctuations and do not receive employment guarantees (Dore, 1986). These temporary employees make up almost 10 percent of the workforce in the Japan-based plants we surveyed but less than 1 percent of the transplant workforce. With fewer temporary workers, we would expect that it is more difficult for the transplants to give employment security guarantees to their core employees. However, all have made an effort to offer some kind of long-term employment assurances. The two transplants in our sample that are unionized have included a commitment to employment security in their union contracts, with the condition that such a commitment not jeoparde the financial viability of the transplants. The nonunion transplants have no such formal agreements but have indicated a similarly strong commitment to maintaining long-term employment for their core workers. None of the transplants have had any layoffs of core employees to date. During downturns, workers not needed for efficient production typically receive additional training. However, like the Japan plants, the transplants make no employment commitment to their temporary workers. Mazda and Mitsubishi Diamond Star, for example, have already laid off some of these workers.

Enterprise Unionism

The second mainstay of Japanese employment system is purported to be enterprise unions. All the Japanese plants in Japan are unionized by enterprise unions. Only a third of the automobile transplants are unionized, and they belong to the United Auto Workers union. This is in contrast to the U.S.-owned plants which are all unionized. It appears that many of the transplants are making a conscious effort to avoid unions. Saltzman (1994) observed one transplant actively trying to remove pro-union applicants in their screening process.

While many of the transplants may be avoiding the UAW, there is some evidence that the transplants have tried to create dynamics similar to those existing with an enterprise union (see chapter 3, on Toyota, in this volume).[3] At the unionized transplants, the labor contract includes a union commitment to support the competitiveness of the plant (together with a management commitment to employment security) and establishes a variety of mechanisms for ongoing labor-management consultation. Five of the six nonunion transplants, in turn, have made efforts to implement some governance structure for employee representation by establishing committees of worker representatives (typically appointed by management) to provide worker representation. Thus, while the transplants do not have enterprise unions, they do try to create a similar venue for employee-management consultation and cooperation.

Seniority-Based Wages

Regarding the third "pillar" of the Japanese employment system, the use of seniority-based wages, what we find in Japan is that employees receive seniority-based promotions. A frequent claim regarding compensation in Japanese plants in Japan is that there is an emphasis on minimizing the pay differentials between categories of employees. This enhances the sense of community and equal status among employees at different levels (e.g., Womack et al., 1990). We find evidence that the pay differential between production workers and supervisors is indeed extremely low in Japan, with the highest paid production worker earning on average 10 percent more than the lowest paid supervisor (compared to up to 15 percent less at U.S.-owned plants and transplants). Much of this reflects seniority pay to the most senior production workers. It is interesting to note, however, that while between-category differentials may be low in Japan, the pay differentials between the lowest and the highest ranks within employee categories is much higher than in the Japanese transplants in the United States (see Table 2.1[4]). This differential is not due to differences in starting pay. Such differentials reflect the use of bonuses

Table 2.1 Pay Differentials

Pay Differential between Highest and Lowest Paid	Japan (%)	Transplants (%)	United States (%)	Test JP vs. T	Test T vs U. S.
Production worker	204	26	25	***	
Maintenance worker	205	12	11	***	**
First-line supervisor	117	31	52	***	**
Manufacturing engineer	446	130	89	**	*

Mann-Whitney t tests done using two-sided confidence interval levels: * = .1, ** = .05, *** = .01.

to reward individual-level differences in seniority, skill, and initiative in Japan-located plants, compared to the policy at the transplants of awarding bonuses equally to all employees in a given category.

The transplants seem to be following the compensation norms found in their local environment. Their pay differentials are almost equal to those of their Big Three counterparts for production workers and maintenance employees, despite the fact that they have fewer levels or job categories than either their Japan or their Big Three counterparts. While Japan plants on average have approximately five classifications for production workers and maintenance workers, the transplants in Round 2 have only one production worker classification and one or two maintenance worker classifications. This is very low for the North American context, in which U.S.-owned plants had an average of thirty-three levels for production workers and fifteen for maintenance in 1994. The U.S.-owned plants have been reducing their number of production worker classifications (average was about forty-five in 1989) and thus appear to be moving toward the Japan plants and the transplants in that respect.

As Table 2.2 shows, the Japan plants make extensive use of bonuses and merit increases in salary. These are provided on the basis of company performance, as well as individual performance. The contingent compensation offered at the transplants is minimal and is very similar to that offered by the U.S. companies. Many of the transplants, like the U.S.-owned plants, give bonuses for company performance. The "plant" bonuses at many of the transplants are synonymous with "company" when there is only one manufacturing plant associated with the U.S. subsidiary, although where a Japanese subsidiary has multiple plants, each plant does have a bonus plan tied to its own performance.

None of the transplants give bonuses or increases in salary to production workers on the basis of work group or individual performance. This is again very similar to the practices of their U.S.-owned counterparts. Furthermore, like the U.S.-owned plants, no transplant offers bonuses for seniority. This is very different from the Japan plants, where half do. Since the transplants have only one rank for production workers, promotion from rank to rank cannot be used as a means to reward seniority, as is the case in almost all the Japan plants. As a result, pay at the transplants bears little relationship to seniority.

As we have shown, the transplants make an effort to provide assurances of lifetime employment for core employees and create employee-management committees, which allow them to have some of the worker-management consultation found with enterprise unions. However, the transplants make no effort to create a seniority wage system. This shift away from seniority-based compensation may reflect the fact that Japanese companies are not happy with it. A full 72 percent of Japanese managers report that the seniority system adversely affects the morale of those who are the most able (Aoki 1990; Smith and Misumi, 1989).

Promotion at the transplants, most of which have grown rapidly and expanded repeatedly, has provided career advancement opportunities for high-

Table 2.2 Contingent Compensation

Percentage of Plants Reporting Compensation Type	Japan (%)	Transplants (%)	United States (%)	Chi-square Test JP vs. T	Chi-square Text T vs U.S.
Production workers					
Bonus for company performance	83	63	56		
Bonus for plant performance	0	38	4	**	**
Bonus for group performance	33	0	0	*	
Bonus for individual performance	50	0	0	**	
Bonus based on seniority	33	0	0	*	
Merit increase in salary for individual performance	92	0	0	***	
Supervisors					
Bonus for company performance	83	63	68		
Bonus for plant performance	0	25	4	*	*
Bonus for group performance	33	0	0	*	
Bonus for individual performance	50	13	4	*	
Bonus based on seniority	33	0	0	*	
Merit increase in salary for individual performance	92	88	92		

Pearson chi-square: * = .1, ** = .05, *** = .01. We also ran a chi-square for differences across the three categories of plants at once. In every case where we report a significant difference across two of the groups, we also found a significant difference across the three groups.

tenure employees. While seniority is not the basis for promotion, virtually all promotions are from the ranks of experienced employees. As such, promotion has undoubtedly served as a partial substitute for seniority wages, though only during times of growth.

In summary, two of the three so-called "pillars" of the Japanese employment system were transferred to the United States. We will see that critical elements of the work and HR system were transferred as well, including teamwork, suggestion programs, job rotation, and extensive training. However, many of these have been modified for the U.S. context.

Work Teams

The importance of on-line teams in Japanese plants has long been recognized by scholars (Aoki, 1990; Koiki, 1989). Like plants in Japan, the transplants make extensive use of such teams. They differ significantly from their American counterparts in this area (see Table 2.3). While only a third of the Big Three plants use teams, all the Japan plants and transplants do. Furthermore, on average, 70 percent of production workers in transplants and Japan plants are in work teams, compared to about half at Big Three plants with teams. There are also differences in what team leaders can influence. Table 2.3 compares Japanese plants, transplants, and U.S. plants on what the teams can influence based on five-point influence ratings. As shown, management generally appoints team leaders, although at the unionized transplants union officials are often involved in team leader selection. In contrast, at the Big Three plants with teams, management indicates that team members have more say in team leader selection. Teams in both Japan plants and transplants

Table 2.3 Team Influence

Team Influence on	Japan	Transplants	United States	Test JP vs. T	Test T vs. U.S.
Use of new technology on job	2.8	2.0	2.7		
Who should do what job	4.3	3.1	3.1	**	
The way work is done; revising methods	4.3	4.1	2.9		**
Performance evaluations	3.2	1.4	1.3	**	
Settling grievances/complaints	4.2	2.1	1.6	***	
Pace of work	2.7	2.0	2.2		
Work to be done in a day	2.4	1.6	2.0		
Selection of team leader	1.5	2.1	3.4		

U.S. category includes only plants with teams. Measured on 1–5 Likert-type scale, where 1 indicates no influence over decisions and 5 indicates extensive influence. Mann-Whitney t test done using two-sided confidence interval levels: * = .1, ** = .05, *** = .01.

are similar in the degree of influence they have in some areas, according to management respondents. Table 2.3 rank orders areas of influence from most influence to least influence of teams. Teams are reported to have the most influence over who should do what job and methods of work, and the least influence over the selection of team leaders and the amount of work to be done in a day and the pace of work. The key statistically significant differences between the two groups are in the area of employee voice, with teams in the Japan plants reported to have more influence than those in transplants or U.S. companies over performance evaluations and the settlement of grievances and complaints. Like their Big Three counterparts, teams at the transplants have little influence in these areas. On the other hand, teams at the transplants do resemble their Japanese counterparts in that team members have influence on issues related to revising work methods. The Big Three teams have less influence in this area.

Job Rotation

Like work teams, job rotation is a means to foster flexibility and involvement on the part of the workforce. Workers at the transplants rotate almost as much as workers in Japan plants, rotating not just within their teams but even across teams within a given department. In contrast, job rotation is still relatively uncommon in Big Three plants. The Big Three plants indicate that although workers are capable of doing other work tasks within their work group, they generally do not rotate jobs.

Problem-Solving Groups and Suggestion Systems

While we have discussed some similarities in high-involvement work practices used at the transplants and those used in Japan plants, there are also some important differences. For example, the transplants and Japan plants differ significantly in the extent to which their employees engage in continuous improvement of the production process (known as *kaizen*) through off-line problem solving. One such activity is quality circles. In the auto plants (Table 2.4) we find that only a quarter of production workers in transplants are involved in such circles, compared to an average of 80 percent in Japan plants (although there is quite a bit of variance among the transplants). The Japanese transplants resemble American-owned plants very closely in that respect. It is possible that like the workers at the Big Three plants, workers at transplants believe that *kaizen* can result in job loss (Young, 1992). However, the employment security assurances of the transplants are intended to address precisely those concerns. An alternative view comes from Kenney and Florida (1993), who suggest that the low level of quality circle and employee involvement activity in the transplants reflects their newness and that plants plan to increase their usage over time. However, three plants for which we have data in both 1989 and 1993–1994 showed only a minor increase in participation in quality circles. According to Cole (1979), participation in these "volun-

Table 2.4 Problem-Solving Activities

	Japan	Transplants	United States	Test JP vs. T	Test T vs. U.S.
% in quality circles	80	27	26	***	
No. suggestions/employee	23.2	3.9	0.26	***	***
% of suggestions implemented	84	70	41		*

Mann-Whitney t tests done using two-sided confidence interval levels: * = .1, ** = .05, *** = .01.

tary" small-group activities in Japan plants is more likely to be viewed as mandatory by employees, because of management and peer pressure, than in plants located in the United States. Like their Big Three counterparts, all but one of the transplants pays employees during the time their quality circle meets. In Japan, a third of the plants report having teams meet during non-paid time.

As with quality circles, the transplants make less use of suggestion programs than the Japan plants. Indeed, as shown in Table 2.4, the average worker in a transplant offers roughly four suggestions per year, compared to twenty-three a year for workers at Japanese plants in Japan. (Unlike with quality circles, the level of involvement with the suggestion system has risen steadily since the transplants opened.) In comparison, the U.S.-owned plants receive only one suggestion for every four employees. One of the differences between the Japan plants and the transplants is that many of the Japan plants actually use a quota system whereby production workers need to provide a minimum number of suggestions per month. The number of suggestions provided by production workers actually gets factored into their evaluations and individual bonuses.

While the number of suggestions received is an important indicator of the improvement efforts arising from bottom-up input, equally important is the percent of suggestions that are actually implemented. This gives some indication of the degree to which the suggestions provided by the production workers are useful and valued. In the U.S.-owned plants, not only are very few suggestions received, but only 41 percent of those suggestions are ever implemented compared to 84 percent in Japan plants and 70 percent in the transplants.

Status Barriers

Another indicator of the overall philosophy of management toward production workers is the extent of status barriers between production workers and management. We have data on four such barriers: whether or not production workers and managers eat in the same cafeteria and park in the same parking lot, whether there is a common uniform for everyone, and whether managers wear ties. The transplants closely resemble the Japan plants in that production workers and managers park in the same parking lot, eat in the same cafeterias, and wear a common uniform, and managers don't wear ties. This is the reverse of what is found at most U.S. plants. Indeed, the transplants go further in this direction than even the Japan plants, some of which do have separate parking lots or cafeterias. On the basis of discussions with management at two of the transplants, we believe the reason for this is that the transplants want to symbolically emphasize egalitarian norms as much as possible.

Recruitment and Selection

Before the transplants opened, one common expectation about the transferability of Japanese employment practices was that American workers were too individualistic, too diverse, and too poorly educated for the successful implementation of such practices. Yet the transplants have been able to introduce high-involvement work practices like team work, job rotation, and suggestion programs—practices uncharacteristic of the U.S. environment. One reason for this success may be that the transplants carefully select and socialize their employees. As such, although culture may differ from country to country, the cultural measures at the country level mask differences at the individual level. There is a range of attitudes and behaviors found in any population, and, with careful selection and socializing, one can develop a workforce whose characteristics differ from the norm.

Only three of the transplants have hired production workers recently. On average, they hired only 5 percent of those who applied. Those who are hired are very well educated, with almost 40 percent of production workers having some college education. The average for U.S.-owned plants is only 15 percent, and in Japan plants, less than 1 percent. We also surveyed the plants with regard to the importance they attach to various employee characteristics in the hiring process. We find that U.S.-owned plants place greater emphasis on employees possessing previous experience in a similar job or specific technical expertise, whereas the transplants stress willingness to learn new skills, and the ability to work with others. Selectivity at the transplants during the hiring process may mean that workers are homogeneous with respect to attitudes toward work and receptiveness to Japanese manufacturing philosophies and human resource practices.[5]

Training

While selection is one means by which to develop a workforce that is willing to operate in a Japanese-type work environment, further socialization can also occur within the plant through training. Although both Japan plants and transplants provide similar levels of training to new employees, the transplants provide significantly higher levels of training to experienced employees (Table 2.5). The transplants provide significantly more training than their American-owned counterparts for all experienced employees, as well as for newly hired production workers. The difference between the transplants and their Japanese and Big Three counterparts may reflect the fact that they are newer plants and their employees are less experienced. However, there is also some evidence that training at the transplants is viewed not just as a means to develop skills but as away to socialize employees. Indeed, a quarter of the experienced employee training provided at transplants deals with production methods and philosophies, compared to 10 percent at plants in Japan. Thus, while selectivity during the hiring process may mean that workers are relatively homogeneous with respect to attitudes toward work and receptiveness to Japanese manufacturing philosophies and human resource practices, the high amount of training in Japanese production methods also helps create a strong and consistent organizational culture.

Use of Expatriates

In addition to careful selection and training, another means to obtain individuals who are receptive to Japanese production methods is to make use of expatriates. However, the use of expatriates can have benefits that go beyond

Table 2.5 Training Levels

	Japan	Transplants	United States	Test JP vs. T	Test T vs. U.S.
Training during first year of employment					
Production worker	2.9	3.0	1.7		***
First-line supervisor	2.8	2.6	2.6		
Mechanical engineer	2.8	2.9	2.6		
Training of experienced employees					
Production workers	3.2	4.1	2.3	*	**
First-line supervisor	2.8	4.6	3.0	***	***
Mechanical engineer	2.0	4.5	3.0	***	**

For new employees, 1 = 0–40 hrs/year; 2 = 41–80 hrs/year; 3 = 81–160 hrs/year; 4 = 160+ hrs/year. For experienced employees, 1 = 1–20 hrs/year; 2 = 21–40 hrs/year; 3 = 41–60 hrs/year; 4 = 61–80 hrs/year; 5 = 80+ hrs/year. Mann-Whitney t tests done using two-sided confidence interval levels: * = .1; ** = .05; *** = .01.

having employees who are receptive to home country practices. Nelson and Winter (1982) observed that one method of replicating practices somewhere else is to move key personnel.[6] Almeida and Kogut (1999) observed empirically that the movement of personnel was a powerful explanatory variable for the movement of technology across regions.

The average transplant has almost sixty Japanese expatriates working in it. Since the average transplant employs about 3,400 people, roughly 2 percent of their workforce are expatriates. Almost half these expatriates are engineers who help with new equipment installation, new model introduction, and so forth. A large portion of the remainder are managers, with about six expatriates in top management positions and the remainder in middle management. However, there is large variance in the use of expatriates across transplants. This reflects differences in the life-cycle stage of different plants but also different company philosophies about the use of expatriates. Some plants use as few as twenty-five expatriate engineers, while others have more than 100 expatriates in a range of positions. While expatriates appear to play a role in the transfer of Japanese production practices in the transplants, several managers at the transplants have told us that much more significant in the transfer process is the assignment of U.S. managers, engineers, and even production workers to Japanese sister plants for periods ranging from a few weeks to a year.

Summary of HR and Work Practices

Overall, the transplants have implemented most of the work practices found at their sister plants in Japan. In some instances, they have not gone as far, as in the case of quality circles, and in others, they have had to make modifications (e.g., teams do not deal with certain issues in the United States), but they generally have implemented the same practices found in Japan. This is surprising, given the fundamentally different institutional and cultural environment found in the United States and in Japan (Ronen and Shenkar, 1985; Hofstede, 1980). However, despite the different cultural environment, the transplants have been careful to hire employees who do have the attitudes needed to work in a high-involvement workplace. In addition to having careful selection procedures, the transplants spend an extensive amount of time training, developing, and socializing new and experienced employees.[7] We also found that the transplants have been trying, at least in part, to recreate some of the institutional characteristics of their home country in the United States by implementing employment security guarantees, as well as some of the elements associated with enterprise unionism.

Inventory and Buffers

In addition to work and HR practices, low buffers are also believed to help the Japanese automobile producers achieve superior performance. Buffers are stocks of unused resources (sources of organizational slack) and can include things like in-process inventory and incoming inventory. High buffer levels indicate loosely coupled systems, which can be useful to isolate problems and reduce their impact on the rest of the system (Weick, 1976). However, they may also hide problems and reduce incentives for managers to resolve problems on a permanent basis.[8] In order for tightly coupled systems to be in place, contingencies need to be dealt with through other mechanisms. Continuous improvement activities are a means to handle such contingencies. These activities include the quality and suggestion programs discussed earlier. There is also greater reliance upon highly trained operators who can respond immediately to problems as they arise. According to Nishiguchi (1994) and MacDuffie (1995), the buffering at Japanese plants that was once handled on the equipment and inventory side has to be shifted to the skills and capabilities developed in the workforce.[9]

Table 2.6 shows how the Japanese, transplant, and U.S. plants compare in three types of buffers. The first is the average repair area at the end of assembly. This captures the amount of "breathing room" available to plants if problems arise on the line. If repair areas are small, problems cannot wait to the end of the line and have to be resolved in process. Japanese plants have traditionally had small repair areas. In part, these reflect the high cost of land in Japan, but operating effectively with such small repair areas would not be possible without the high levels of worker training, participation, and involvement discussed earlier. When building greenfield sites in the United States, the Japanese companies faced significantly cheaper land prices and significantly expanded the space available for repair. However, the repair areas at the transplants are still a third smaller than those found in typical U.S. plants.[10]

In terms of in-process buffers, the Japanese transplants closely resemble their Japanese counterparts. A good indicator of in-process inventory is the buffer between paint shops and final assembly. Here the Japanese plants and transplants have virtually identical levels of inventory—levels that are almost half those found at Big three plants. In part this reflects the philosophy of forcing problems to the surface. It also reflects the tendency of Japanese-owned plants to fix the production sequence early on in the body shop, thus reducing the need for resequencing vehicles after the paint process. However, this again increases the need for problems to be handled in-process and for efforts to eradicate recurring problems through quality circles, suggestion programs, and the like.

While Japanese plants generally have low buffers between processes, some experimentation is currently under way in the assembly area. Specifically, some Japanese plants and transplants are experimenting with small buffers built into the assembly line. These buffers separate groups of twenty to twenty-five employees, the goal being to foster group efforts.

The last measure of buffers is the incoming inventory found in the plant. This is the average for eight key high-cost parts.[11] While the Japanese plants in Japan and the transplants have similarly low inventory levels for these

Table 2.6 Buffer Levels

Buffer Type	Japan	Transplants	United States	Test JP vs. T	Test T vs. U.S.
Corrected repair area (% of assembly)	3.5	7.8	12.2	*	*
Paint ass'y buffer (% of 1 shift production)	16.5	18.2	35.4		*
Inventory level (in days, avg. of 8 parts)	0.6	0.8	1.4		

Mann-Whitney t tests done using two-sided confidence interval levels: * = .1; ** = .05; *** = .01.

parts, it is interesting to note that the U.S. plants have been working on reducing their inventory levels of these parts as well and, since 1989, have dropped the average level of these parts from 2.4 days to 1.4 days.

Automation and Technology

While workforce management and deployment is one important aspect of production, capital, and, more specifically, technology, is another. Caves (1982) argued that an organization's technical capabilities were a key driver of foreign direct investment. In this section, we explore whether the technical systems in place in Japan were transferred to the U.S. transplants and how those systems differ from what is found at U.S. plants. Compared to work and HR practices, technology is less dependent on an organization's institutional and cultural environment, and, as such, we should expect to see few modifications to technical equipment (see Brannen et al., this volume). Furthermore, because of the reduced dependence on the external environment and a tendency for companies to handle "make or buy" decisions about technical equipment centrally, we should expect to see greater variation across companies.

Automobile production at most assembly plants consists of three primary departments. First, there is a body shop, where body panels are brought together and welded into a shell that will eventually provide the structure of the vehicle. This shell is known as the "body in white." Next is a paint shop, where the body is primed and painted and sealer is put on to prevent water entry and to reduce air noise at panel joints. Finally, in the assembly shop, all parts and trim are assembled into the vehicle, and the vehicle is inspected and then prepared for shipment. Some plants also have stamping facilities to stamp the metal parts that make up the vehicle out of sheet metal, engine production and dressing facilities, and plastic molding equipment. However, all high-volume plants have body, paint, and assembly shops, and so, for comparability, that is what we focus on. The types and level of automation used vary dramatically from area to area, and we look at each in turn.

Table 2.7 provides overall automation levels by area. On the surface, there do not appear to be major differences among the Japanese plants, the transplants, and the U.S. plants. The body shops are generally the most automated section of the assembly plant, with the majority of spot and arc/seam welds placed via automated equipment. Paint shops are less automated, with some processes fully automated and others completely manual. Very few fully automated processes are found in assembly areas.

While automation levels are quite comparable across the different plants, there are some significant differences between the Japanese-owned plants and the U.S. plants when one looks more closely by department at the actual equipment in place and how that equipment is utilized. Table 2.8 shows body shop automation by type. The primary difference between the U.S. plants and their Japanese counterparts lies in the use of flexible automation. Not only do the Japanese-owned plants automate a greater portion of their weld processes (both spot and seam welding), but a larger fraction of that automation is flexible (i.e., robotics). Indeed, almost 80 percent of spot welds at the Japanese-owned plants are placed robotically, compared to about 65 percent at Big Three plants. Not only do Japanese owned plants have more robot welding, but they are more likely to use robots to hold and place parts, as well. As a result, the Japanese-owned plants have an average of twice as many robots on a per-vehicle basis as U.S.-owned plants.

The higher levels of flexible automation at the Japanese plants makes sense, given the theorized links between automation and high-involvement work practices (cf. Adler, 1988; MacDuffie & Pil, 1997; Susman and Chase, 1986; Parthasarthi and Sethi, 1993). By combining flexible automation with high-involvement work and HR practices, plants can handle greater product variety and undertake rapid model changeovers with fewer productivity and quality penalties than would be the case if one were present in the absence of the other.

While, on the surface, the Japanese-owned plants have higher levels of flexible automation as well as overall automation than their U.S. counterparts, there are some intercompany differences in how automation is actually deployed in the Japanese automobile companies. There are two main areas of difference. The first is in the types of robots used and their placement, and the second is in the framing section of the plants where the main components of the body are brought together. It is important to note that the differences described here are company differences, rather than differences between plants in Japan and the transplants. The company differences found in Japan are also present at the transplants.

Talbe 2.7 Automation

Automation Levels	Japan (%)	Transplants (%)	United States (%)	Test JP vs. T	Test T vs. U.S.
Total automation (% direct production steps)	35.5	40.2	33.7	*	
By area					
Body shop	86.1	89.2	77.7		
Paint shop	41.8	60.8	47.0	*	
Assembly shop	1.8	2.0	1.4		

Mann-Whitney t tests done using two-sided confidence interval levels: * = .1; ** = .05; *** = .01.

When it comes to robot type and placement, Toyota, for example, utilizes fairly standardized robots that it deploys, four to six to a work station. Honda, on the other hand, designs and produces its own robots in-house and designs them for the specific function they are intended to perform within the line. As a result, it achieves much higher robot density in a given station. Because the Japanese companies produce a large number of vehicle variants within their plants, they need to rely on flexible framing systems to bring together the main components (e.g., underbody, sides, and roof). This is generally achieved through a system of rotating jigs, with a different jig for each model and body type. Even here there is some variance. For example, while

Table 2.8 Body Shop Automation

Automation	Japan	Transplants	United States	Test JP vs. T	Test T vs. U.S.
% flexibly automated weld spots	71.0	72.5	52.9		**
% hard automated weld spots	18.9	18.4	29.0		
% total automated weld spots	89.8	90.9	81.1		
% automated seam welding	55.7	58.4	14.6		**
Weld robotic index (no. of robots/vehicle/hour)	5.9	5.5	2.8		**

Mann-Whitney t tests done using two-sided confidence interval levels: * = .1; ** = .05; *** = .01.

Nissan follows the Toyota model in most areas of the body shop, it utilizes a different approach to bring together and weld the different subcomponents of the body into the body. In a traditional framing system, between fifty and 100 clamps are used to hold together the pieces that will eventually form the main body shell. These clamps vary by model and help ensure the dimensional accuracy of the final product. The flexible framing stations are found at all the transplants, as well as many U.S. plants. However, at the latter, the flexibility is underutilized because of their simple model mix.

Nissan takes the notion of flexible framing systems a step further by utilizing thirty-five tiny position robots to adjust the position of clamps for different models (at other companies, the clamps are fixed into one position), while sixteen robots weld the pieces together. This system of robots, called the Intelligent Body Assembly System (IBAS), is capable of handling all of Nissan's car models. The robotic clamps can be reprogrammed between each body to accommodate different models. The software for a new model can be debugged at one location and then used in any of Nissan's plants. Toyota's flexible body line and Mazda's circulation body assembly line have similar goals but use different equipment to achieve them. Where the Japanese companies exhibit differences in the actual technology used in their body shops, these differences are also transferred overseas. Not all companies in Japan have invested in such elaborate automation, but those that operate overseas generally have.

Most plants, regardless of location, automate the electro-coating process, which protects the vehicle from rust. Most plants in the United States and Japan also automate the application of the top-coat paint. However, there is greater variance when it comes to applying sealer and to painting the vehicle interior. While there are differences across the transplants, Japan plants, and Big Three plants in these domains, they are generally driven by how new the paint shops are. Investments in paint shops are generally nonreversible (although robots can be added, for example, to do sealer application), and because of the expense involved, the investments are generally long-term. In the Japanese plants, older paint shops generally result in lower levels of interior paint automation. Several of the transplants purchased new systems and have moved to water-rather than solvent-based paint—a move that benefits them in the area of emission regulations.

The assembly area of automobile plants represents the most labor intensive portion of automobile production, and few processes are automated. Indeed, the average assembly plant automates only six assembly steps—mostly for tasks that are easy to automate and where automation enhances quality (e.g., windshield installation) or where tasks are very strenuous or physically demanding (e.g., engine mounting, spare tire insertion). In the early 1980s, companies in both the United States and Europe undertook extensive and expensive efforts to automate their assembly areas. Examples include VW's Hall 54 and Fiat's Cassinno plant. However, companies have since realized that automation in the assembly area is very expensive, is prone to breakdown, and requires extensive maintenance support. As a result, many have pulled automation out of existing plants and refrained from putting it into new ones (e.g., Fiat's Melfi plant).

In the late 1980s and early 1990s, a decline in the Japanese labor force, as well as a reduction in the number of working hours, induced Japanese companies to look more closely at the automation of assembly work (Fujimoto, 1997; Tanase et al., 1997). By utilizing automation to make their factories more "human friendly," the companies hoped to be able to attract workers who were increasingly shunning careers in manufacturing. The companies also hoped to reduce their dependence on labor. Cheaper capital costs also helped. However, assembly automation is quite space intensive, and a lack of space constrained the rapid expansion of assembly automation. High levels of model mix complexity in Japan further limit the extent to which automation could be added.

Mazda, in Hofu, went quite far in designing a modular approach to vehicle assembly whereby the plant could absorb model variety impact off-line and a higher degree of automation could be used on line (Kinutani, 1997). Similarly, Nissan designed its new assembly plant in Kyushu to be able to accommodate extensive automation. However, the enthusiasm for assembly automation in Japan also appears to be waning. Expected labor savings did not materialize (labor reductions on the direct side were offset by increases in indirect labor), up-time was lower, and the automated equipment generally restricted product design and the mix of products that could be produced on a given line. Toyota, for example, reduced its emphasis on automation at its new Kyushu plant and its retrofitted RAV4 line at the Motomachi plant. During the period when the Japan plants were experimenting with assembly automation, the Japanese transplants were not experiencing any labor shortages and did not feel the same need to implement high levels of automation in their assembly shops—especially in light of the poor performance of such automation in Japan and elsewhere.

While there has been a shift away from fully automated equipment, some interesting differences among the Japanese companies have emerged—particularly when it comes to the location of automated equipment in the assembly line. At Mitsubishi, lines are laid out so that automated equipment is focused in so-called automation islands. Indeed, at its Mizushima plant, the line is laid out so that the automated portion of the assembly area is concentrated in two sections that are adjacent to each other. These areas contain highly complex forms of assembly automation, and the concentration of automation permits a clear demarcation and separation of the automated section of the line from the remainder of the line. The automated portion falls under the responsibility of the maintenance workers. In contrast, at Toyota's new plant in Kyushu, conscious efforts have been made to integrate automation into the line. Rather than rely on sophisticated fully automated equipment, it relies instead on equipment that finishes tasks that workers start. For example, a worker places under-body bolts, which are then tightened by a piece of equipment that moves in sync with the line and that does not need the sophistication to select and place bolts, since it only tightens them to the required torque. The worker who places the bolts is also the first line of defense against the equipment going down and handles basic repair and preventive maintenance. These company differences in approaching complex automation are also evident at the transplants.

While fully automated assembly processes are on the wane, the Japanese companies are continuously expanding their use of "automation assist" (MacDuffie & Pil, 1997). Automation assist consists of tools that help the worker but do not replace him or her. Unlike full automation, automation-assist tools do not perform full assembly tasks. Rather, they place parts, or deliver tools for workers to use, or finish off a task started by production workers. These tools serve two purposes: they help alleviate ergonomic strain, and they reduce nonvalue-added movement. Automation assist can take various forms, including robotic arms that lift a worker into a vehicle to install carpet, platforms that move with the line on which a worker can sit while performing under-body work, and lifter tools to help workers with heavy parts or subassemblies. The most prominent form of automation assist is carts that move with the line, carrying tools and parts. These are generally very simple affairs that move with a vehicle, holding parts and tools that the worker needs. The carts roll with a vehicle from the point where it enters a work area to the end of that work area before returning back to roll with the next vehicle. By making tools and parts available to the worker where he or she is working on the vehicle, the carts significantly reduce nonvalue-added time.

Automation assist tools are generally quite simple. For example, the tool and parts carts are generally pushed along by the assembly line conveyor, until they are retracted by a simple retractor mechanism or returned to their starting place by hand. Automation assist is generally designed in-house by teams of production workers and engineers, using relatively cheap parts. When production workers are involved in their design, workers feel a greater degree of ownership of the tools and are more likely to use them and find incremental ways to improve them.

Automation assist is used extensively in both the Japan plants and in the transplants. While it is gaining adherents at the Big Three plants, automation assist is not as prevalent as at the Japanese-owned plants. In part, the greater use at the Japanese plants reflects a different philosophy with regard to the division of labor between human and machine. It is also evidence of a broader philosophy of worker involvement and participation in the work place overall. As Zuboff (1988), noted, the same basic technology can play very different roles—controlling and deskilling workers or empowering and upskilling them. The goal at the Japanese-owned plants is to strive for the latter. The worker involvement in the design of automation assist also reflects a view held in both Japan and the transplants in North America: the greater the worker involvement and interaction with the technology at its design phase, the more flexible its ultimate use. This view manifests itself in the design not just of automation assist tools but of automation at the transplants and Japan plants more generally. For example, when Mitsubishi recently purchased a new assembly line for its transplant facility (a joint venture with Volvo) in the Netherlands, it sent more than 400 workers to Japan to test the new equipment and to find ways to improve it before it was even delivered to the plant.

While technology is generally viewed as a substitute for labor, we saw that flexible automation can serve as a complement to flexible work and HR practices. Furthermore, we saw that, while aggregate indicators of technology may appear similar, how that technology is utilized can differ dramatically, even among Japanese companies. While the Japanese companies have transferred their technology to the United States, company variations in the types of technology are quite prominent.

Supplier Relations

Organizations encompass "systems of coordinated and controlled activities that arise when work is embedded in complex networks of technical relations and boundary spanning relations" (Meyer and Rowan, 1977). These networks are very important for Japanese companies and are a key source of strategic advantage for them (Clark and Fujimoto, 1991; Cusumano and Takaishi, 1991; Dyer, 1996). Let us look at relationships with suppliers as one indicator of how this network operates.

Suppliers are important for successful automobile production. An average vehicle contains approximately 15,000 parts. Of these 4,000 to 5,000 are nonstandard and model specific. Problems with more critical components, whether a result of quality concerns or of tardy delivery, can shut down a whole assembly plant—especially in the face of low buffers. We have been told numerous stories of plants chartering helicopters, jets, even the Concorde in the case of one British plant, to bring in parts when those parts were either out of stock or defective. We have also observed plants build cars without seats and with mismatched facia because of missing parts, the parts to be installed when they became available. Defective parts reduce the quality of the overall vehicle and adversely impact public opinion of the vehicles affected. Suppliers are important, not only in ensuring quality parts and on-time delivery but also in speeding up the vehicle design process (Clark, 1989). Suffice it to say that the capabilities of a plant reside to some degree in the strengths of its relationships with suppliers and in the abilities of those suppliers (Kogut 1991; Oliver & Wilkinson, 1992).

As mentioned earlier, the Japanese automobile producers are successful at building close cooperative ties with suppliers—ties that lead to advantages in product design, product cost, parts quality, and delivery assurance. Many reasons have been proffered for the successful relationships between assemblers and suppliers in Japan. Some argue for the importance of partial financial ownership of suppliers (Klein, 1980). A recent study found that Nissan and Toyota own an average of 23 percent of the stock of their partner suppliers (Dyer, 1996). The suppliers in Japan are able to more easily finance their operations if they have close ties with an automobile assembler (Dyer, 1996). Interfirm employee transfers also help maintain trust and foster communication between assembler and supplier (Dyer and Ouchi, 1993). Bank-centered enterprise groups help regulate the alliances between assemblers and suppliers, and supplier associations help reduce the likelihood of assembler transgression (Gerlach 1992; Nishiguchi, 1994). Many of the factors that are associated with the superior supplier relations at Japanese plants are believed to date back to the immediate post–World War II period, when the Japanese auto companies lacked the financing to meet demand and resorted to developing a supplier network (Nishiguchi 1994).

With the exception of the joint ventures, the transplants set up operations in the United States with no supply base in place.[12] Initially, the transplants placed heavy reliance on imported parts. Over time, however, they have shifted to local production to increase local vehicle content. Initially, most of the sourcing went to Japanese suppliers that moved to the United States, and eventually to U.S. suppliers (Kenney and Florida, 1993). Given that organizations are subject to institutional influences in managing their supply base (Roberts and Greenwood, 1997), we would expect that the relationships developed in the United States by the transplants would be at least somewhat similar to those found between Big Three plants and their suppliers.

Looking at Table 2.9, we see that the relationships between the transplants and their suppliers in the United States is quite similar to the relationship between assemblers and suppliers in Japan. First, the transplants have very few suppliers, despite the fact that they outsource a greater number of parts and subassemblies than do their U.S. counterparts. Having fewer suppliers is beneficial because it reduces the logistical problems associated with dealing with a larger number of suppliers. It also reduces the number of small-volume purchases, which do not help in building strong relationships with suppliers.

Table 2.9 Supplier Relations

	Japan	Transplants	United States	Test JP vs. T	Test T vs. U.S.
No. of parts	10,290	3,078	2,753	***	
No. of suppliers to assembly area	195	164	503		***
% of parts single sourced	92.6	93.6	98.1	*	
Inventory level (in days, avg. of 8 parts)	0.6	0.8	1.4		

Mann-Whitney t tests done using two-sided confidence interval levels: * = .1; ** = .05; *** = .01.

While the transplants have a small number of suppliers, they nevertheless double-source a subset of key parts at the plant level. In contrast, the Big three double-source very few parts. Despite the fact that many of the transplants had been in North America for less than a decade at the time of data collection, they nevertheless have succeeded in building successful ties with their suppliers, as evidenced by the fact that they have very low inventories, which generally requires tight coordination and information flow between supplier and assembler. They also do virtually no inspection of incoming parts, evidencing their confidence in suppliers of key components.

Despite the fact that they have little of the relationship history or the institutional factors, like *keiretsu* ties or supplier associations, that are credited with the strong supplier relations in Japan, the transplants' supplier relations are very similar to those found in Japan. One potential factor explaining their similarity is the support systems that the transplants have put in place for their suppliers. Honda, for example, has a team of fifty employees who, in conjunction with engineers and managers from different parts of Honda, provide support and assistance to its suppliers in the form of its BP system (best process, best productivity, best partners—see MacDuffie and Helper, in this volume). Similar processes are in place at other Japanese transplants (Dyer, 1996). However, while the supplier support systems are modeled on similar systems in Japan, they are different in some ways. For one, they are free. Honda's BP system, for example, costs suppliers in Japan 2 percent of sales, whereas it is free in the United States. Another difference is that in the United States it is provided to all suppliers that could benefit from it, even if those suppliers also supply other companies.[13] This is further evidence of strong efforts by the Japanese transplants to recreate the same relationships with suppliers that are important for supporting the production system in Japan.

Performance

We have discussed how the Japanese transplants resemble their Japanese peers in many ways. However, it is still the case that the transplants operate in a very different institutional and cultural environment from that found in Japan. The workforce is much less homogenous, the educational and legal systems are different, and there is no legacy of cooperative relations with suppliers. Many theorists argue that congruence between organizational practices and culture or values bears a strong relation to performance (Erez, 1986; Morris and Pavett 1992). The question then arises as to whether the transplants are capable of achieving the same levels of performance as their Japanese counterparts, given that they utilize the same work and HR practices, have similar buffer levels and technologies, and have tried to develop supplier relations similar to those found in Japan.

To explore the performance of the transplants, we look at two measures of performance: productivity and quality. First, we provide a brief overview of how each of these is measured:

Productivity

The productivity measure is the number of labor hours it takes to build a vehicle. It is based on a calculation procedure developed by John Krafcik (1988) and further refined by MacDuffie and Pil (1995).[14] Krafcik's procedure had as its goal to create a measure that would permit an "apples to apples" comparison between different automobile plants in all regions of the world. The measure takes into account differences in vehicles produced, vertical integration, and working hours. Appendix A provides an overview of the specific adjustments made. Because three of the transplants did not provide all the data we need to calculate their productivity, our figures reflect productivity for only five of the eight transplants discussed in this chapter.

In Table 2.10 we see that the overall productivity levels at the transplants are fairly close to the levels found in Japan. Indeed, there are no statistically significant differences. However, as Winter (1991) noted, while competitive pressures affect an organization as a whole, suboptimal arrangements may nevertheless exist and persist within those organizations. We have the advantage of actually being able to examine performance across departments to study whether the transfer of Japanese practices and policies overseas has resulted in pockets of suboptimal performance. By looking at performance

Table 2.10 Productivity

Productivity (Labor Hours per Vehicle)	Japan	Transplants	United States	Test JP vs. T	Test T vs. U.S.
Overall productivity	16.2	17.3	21.9		**
By area					
Body shop (direct)	2.3	2.8	3.2		
Paint shop (direct)	2.1	2.7	2.4	*	
Assembly shop (direct)	5.0	5.2	8.7		***
Indirect	3.2	4.6	5.2		
Salaried	2.0	1.8	2.0		
Part-time + seasonal	1.5	0.1	0.3	**	
n	12	5	25		

Note: These figures are *not* weighted by plant volumes.

Mann-Whitney t tests done using two-sided confidence interval levels: * = .1; ** = .05; *** = .01.

across departments, we can explore whether technology-intensive areas, such as the body shop, perform relatively better or worse than labor-intensive areas such as the assembly line.

In paint shop performance—an area that is both technology- and labor-intensive—there are small statistically significant differences between transplants and plants in Japan. The transplants use more indirect employees (a category that includes material handling, quality control, and maintenance). This is offset, however, by significantly lower use of part-time and seasonal employees at the transplants. While the Big Three plants have productivity levels that are lower than the transplants, they exhibit slightly better performance in the paint shop. The biggest difference between the transplants and the Big Three is in the assembly area, where the Big Three require almost two-thirds more labor. We suspect this difference is explained in part by the more traditional work practices in use at the Big Three plants.

Quality

It is important to have a quality measure that does not confound quality problems over which the plant has direct control with those that tend to lie outside its domain, like supplier- or design-related problems. This measure is based on J. D. Power and Associate's New Quality Survey. Every February J. D. Power randomly selects new car owners based on vehicle registry the previous November and asks them to fill in a survey about their experience during the first three months with the vehicle. Detailed questions capture the full range of problems that the owner could have encountered. J. D. Power very generously provides us with this information in disaggregated form. We use the data from these surveys and aggregate across vehicles by plant of origin all the problems that are under direct control of the assembly plant, on the basis of a classification scheme developed by Krafcik and further refined by MacDuffie and Pil. We measure things like paint finish, fit of body panels, and water leaks. We exclude all problems that could be supplier or design related. These include different kinds of electrical problems, engine problems, problems related to how much the customer likes the design, and so forth. This provides us a metric that is standard across all plants that sell vehicles in the United States. We also calculate a supplier quality measure that captures the problems that generally originate at suppliers. Because we have data only for products sold in the United States, we do not have data for four of the twelve Japanese plants discussed in this chapter, and thus our quality figures for Japan reflect only the remaining eight. We do have quality data for all plants in Japan that export to the United States, as well as all U.S. plants and transplants, and also report those.

In terms of quality, we see no statistical differences between the performance of the transplants and their Japanese counterparts (see Table 2.11; note that the figures reported here are straight averages rather than averages weighted by plant volume). The U.S. plants perform worse, although their performance has improved dramatically in this area over the last few years

Table 2.11 Quality for 1993–1994

Quality (Defects per 100 Vehicles	Japan	Transplants	United States	Test JP vs. T	Test T vs. U.S.
Quality for plants in sample	52	48	71		***
By area					
Body	8.5	7.8	13		***
Paint	12.8	11.2	16.6		**
Assembly	30.7	29	41.3		**
Supplier quality	21.8	19.1	27.3		***
n	10	8	25		
Quality for all plants selling in U.S.	58.7	54.7	64.7		
By area					
Body	9.0	9.4	11.0		
Paint	14.9	12.2	15.2		
Assembly	34.8	33.1	38.5		
Supplier quality	23.7	21.8	26.4	*	
n	21	11	32		

Note: The figures in this table are *not* weighted by plant volumes.

Mann-Whitney t tests done using two-sided confidence interval levels: * = .1; ** = .05; *** = .01.

(MacDuffie and Pil, 1998). There are also no differences in terms of quality performance by department. This is true for the plants represented in this chapter, as well as for the broader group of plants that export or sell their products in the United States. Looking at supplier quality, we see that, again, the transplants perform on par with Japan-based plants. While U.S. plants have been improving in this area, our fieldwork suggests that a portion of the quality improvement at the Big Three plants has come through inspectors and end-of-line repair.

Product Variety

While the transplants achieve very good productivity and quality performance, it is important to note that they follow a different product strategy from the plants in Japan—strategies better adapted for their role in the North American environment, where they target the domestic markets rather than overseas exports. While there is some adaptation of styling and vehicle dimensions for the U.S. and Canadian markets, the interesting difference in terms of plant-level product strategies lies in the low level of product mix complexity at the transplants. While it would be possible to produce more variants at the transplants given the technology employed, as well as the flexible work practices and high skill levels, the transplants have relatively low model-mix complexity, producing few different models and body types in their plants. Furthermore, as can be seen in Table 2.12, the transplants deal with significantly lower parts complexity. This is true for the number of engine/transmission combinations and wire harness variants in the products produced. It is also true for the number of exterior colors used in the plant, a figure that serves as an indicator of facea and trim variations. In part, the lower variation is the result of the transplants' serving fewer export markets. However, it nevertheless remains true that, while the transplants are able to achieve great productivity and quality levels using tools and methods transferred from Japan, it is not yet clear whether they can achieve those performance levels at higher levels of variety. But we should note that they are operating at higher levels of complexity than typically is the case at their Big Three counterparts. For example, Toyota in Georgetown is building the Sienna minivan on the same line as the Camry.

Conclusion

As we have seen, the transplants have undertaken extensive transfer of the operating practices and principles found in Japan. However, this transfer did not occur blindly, and some adaptation was needed. The external environment played a role in determining what was transferred and what adaptation occurred. For example, the compensation systems at the transplants matched those used by other Big Three plants, rather than the Japan plants. Similarly,

Table 2.12 Product Characteristics

Complexity Measure	Japan	Transplants	United States	Test JP vs. T	Test T vs. U.S.
Model mix complexity (0 = simplest, 100 = most complex)	39.5	24	20		
Engine/transmission combinations	100+	35	28	**	**
Wire harness part numbers	100+	24	12	***	**
Exterior colors	34	12	11	***	
No. of export markets	17.8	5.7	5.5		
% of output for export	44.9	33.2	7.9		**

Mann-Whitney t tests done using two-sided confidence interval levels: * = .1; ** = .05; *** = .01.

the transplants chose to follow their local environment when it came to deciding team tasks. However, the transplants also undertook measures to reduce the impact of their being in a different institutional and cultural environment. These measures included comprehensive employee selection methods as well as training and socialization. They further included the development of proxies for Japanese institutional practices such as lifetime employment and enterprise unionism.

In the area of technology, we also see some, albeit fewer, influences of the external environment. We discussed, for example, how some automation efforts in assembly at the Japan plants was driven in part by environmental factors related to labor supply and cheap capital availability. These external factors were not present in the United States, and as a result the transplants have less fully automated assembly equipment. In contrast, the technology in the body shop is less influenced by external factors, and here we see almost complete transfer. However, because the external environment has less influence on body shop technology, we also see more intercompany variance in that technology.

Perhaps the most interesting developments were on the supplier side, where, despite a lack of the institutional influences and historical precedent for support, the transplants have succeeded in developing supplier relationships that are in many ways similar to those found in Japan. The development of these relationships is ongoing, and, while the transplants have been slow in shifting to U.S. suppliers some of the product development tasks that the Japan suppliers take on, it is nevertheless interesting to note that the transplants have been able to mimic at least in part the relational supplier networks found in Japan.

While there have been instances where the transplants have stumbled (see, e.g., Fucini and Fucini, 1990; Graham, 1995; Rinehart, Huxley, and Robertson, 1997), their performance on the whole has been very good. Despite being in a very different cultural and institutional environment, the transplants have succeeded in achieving many of the performance characteristics of plants in Japan. Their productivity is almost as good, and their quality reaches the same high standards. The performance levels of the transplants are good across the board, including labor-intensive and technology-intensive activities, as is the quality achieved through the supply network. The caveat does remain, however, that the transplants do not yet handle the levels of product variety found in Japan plants. As demand for niche products and small-volume specialty models increases, they may need to increase their levels of variety.

While the transplants have certainly learned a lot from their counterparts in Japan, they are also learning from their new host environment. For example, while the Japanese companies have homogenous workforces in Japan, that is by no means the case in North America. As this diversity manifests itself in new ideas and opportunities, the transplants may become a source of innovation for the Japan plants as these try to deal with new organizational and social challenges in their home country.

Given the remarkable performance of the transplants, will the demonstration influence of the transplants help induce change in practices in place at plants of the Big Three? In other research, we have discussed the difficulties inherent in fundamentally altering an organization's practices (Pil, 1996; Pil and MacDuffie, 1996). However, the Big Three are experimenting with new work practices at various locations, particularly in the United States, and they have also been rethinking some of the ways in which they utilize their technology (MacDuffie and Pil, 1997). The long-term effect of the transplants remains to be seen. What is clear, however, is that the transplants have succeeded in transferring and adapting many of the practices found in Japan and are finding ways to reduce the impact of their new environment on their internal operations. They are achieving performance levels that are approaching those of their sister plants in Japan and thus show that national, cultural, and institutional boundaries are not insurmountable obstacles.

Appendix

The following adjustments are made to ensure comparability of productivity figures across plants.

Actual Effort

Because we are using this to measure the performance of plants in an international sample, problems arise with accounting for differences in conventions for relief time, acceptable absenteeism levels, and so forth. To eliminate this as a problem, absenteeism is factored out of the labor time required to build a vehicle on the assumption that, when a worker is not in the plant, he or she is not contributing to the building of vehicles. The methodology also adjusts for differing amounts of relief time by standardizing all plants to a world average relief time.

Vehicle Differences

Vehicle size.   Larger vehicles, like a Ford Taurus, may require more work than small vehicles, like a Honda Civic. They generally require either more, or larger parts, resulting in a greater workload. There is an adjustment to the labor hours required to build a vehicle that reflects the size of the average product produced in a plant in relation to the average size of vehicles in the world. There is also an adjustment for recreational trucks to reflect the decreased workload required by the truck bed. These adjustments are important because they capture fundamental differences in product characteristics between the U.S.-owned plants and their Japanese-owned counterparts. Big Three plants, for example, produce a greater preponderance of trucks, sport utilities, and minivans than their Japanese competitors.

Option content.   Higher levels of options result in increases in the time it takes to build a vehicle. The Japanese vehicles generally have a higher option content compared with their U.S. counterparts.

Design difference.   Some vehicles have more work designed into them than others. Adjustments are made for differences in weld and joint sealer content. Japanese vehicles, for example, generally have higher sealer content than the products produced by the Big Three.

Vertical Integration

We identified a key set of activities that most assembly plants perform, and employee data and other information were collected only in relation to those key activities. These are the major operations that occur within the body shops, paint shops, and assembly shops. Stamping and engine dress are excluded because many assembly plants do not do these in-house. The same holds true for various subassemblies and for many support tasks. When a plant does not perform one of the key activities, an adjustment is made in the labor hours per vehicles to reflect this. The Japanese plants are significantly less vertically integrated than the Big Three plants.

Notes

1. Surveys were translated to Japanese. Translations were translated back to English, as well as reviewed by a Japanese academic who specializes in the automobile industry to ensure they captured the same information as the English version of the surveys. Japanese plants received Japanese surveys, and transplants received both versions.

2. North America reflects a very different cultural environment from that found in Japan. Japan is generally classified as being culturally distinct—not just from North America but also from all other countries considered in culture studies (Hofstede, 1980; Ronen and Shenkar, 1985).

3. Indeed, the desire to go to an enterprise union model is evident from a Japanese transplant in Europe. Nissan UK refused to set up operations unless there was an up-front agreement to permit the plant to be organized by a single union—something unprecedented in the UK.

4. Because the transplants and Japan plants belong to the same companies, it is possible that there are significant differences between the transplants and the Japan plants that are not captured because of large company-driven variation in both regions. For example, if the intraregional variation were great but plants belonging to any given company were consistently lower in one region than another, Mann-Whitney statistics would find no significant differences across regions because they do not consider company membership. To test for the possibility that interregional differences do exist when company differences are considered, an aligned ranks test (Lehman, 1975, 138–141), was performed.

5. Some of the homogeneity sought by the transplants can at times go to extremes—Cole and Deskings (1988), for example, found that they are less likely to hire minorities than their U.S. counterparts. However, we did find that they had a greater number of women on their workforce than either their Japanese or U.S. counterparts (19.2% compared to 12.6% for U.S.

plants and only 2.1% for Japanese plants in Japan). In part, the latter may reflect the recency of these hires.

6. While the presence of expatriates on staff could be seen as a means to ensure that practices get replicated in overseas subsidiaries, Edstrom and Galbraith (1977) make the reverse hypothesis, suggesting that, as the number of expatriates increases, there is increased capacity in the communication channels between headquarters and the overseas subsidiaries, which would "allow greater local discretion and responsiveness" (p. 251).

7. The high level of training for experienced employees may reflect in part the fact that the transplants are all relatively new, and even experienced workers have relatively few years of experience.

8. Thinking of buffers as evidence of loose coupling within organizations also draws out other implications of buffers. Loosely coupled systems reduce conflict between the different systems being coupled together. These systems do not need to coordinate with each other, adapt to each other, or even interact much with each other (Meyer and Rowan, 1977). This reduces conflict. However, it also results in reduced communication and thus reduces joint efforts at optimizing the overall systemic framework, rather than its element systems.

9. While low buffers increase the visibility of problems, they also serve other purposes. In particular, buffers represent a nonproductive capital investment. Reducing such investments releases capital and makes that capital available for other, more productive purposes.

10. The Japanese companies built plants that were significantly smaller than the norm in the United States. The average area needed per vehicle/year is 5.4 sq. feet at the transplants, compared with 7.7 sq. feet at Big Three plants and only 3.9 sq. feet at plants in Japan.

11. Parts are: wheels, wire harnesses, steering wheels, tires, instrument clusters, headlights, interior carpet sets, and batteries.

12. An exception is Honda, which was already producing motorcycles in the United States prior to setting up automobile production facilities.

13. Companies like Honda do, however, work hard to convince their suppliers to provide dedicated plants for their parts.

14. Some of these changes include accounting for part-time employees, making a size adjustment for minivans, using actual world average installation times to adjust for option content rather than proxies derived from dealer option prices, including adjustments for sealer content, and applying the option adjustment to assembly and indirect and salaried employees, rather than making a blanket adjustment across all employment categories.

References

Abegglen, James, and George Stalk. 1985. *Kaisha—The Japanese Corporation*. New York: Basic Books.

Adler, Paul. 1988. "Managing Flexible Automation." *California Management Review* 30(3): 34–56.

Adler, Paul. 1992. "The Learning Bureaucracy: New United Motor Manufacturing Inc." In B. Staw and L. Cummings, eds., *Research in Organizational Behavior*. Greenwich, Conn. JAI Press.

Aldrich, Howard E., and Jeffrey Pfeffer. 1976. "Environments of Organizations." *Annual Review of Sociology* 2: 79–105.

Almeida, Paul, and Bruce Kogut. 1999. "The Location of Knowledge and the Mobility of Engineers in Regional Networks," *Management Science*.

Aoki, Masahiko. 1990. "Toward an Economic Model of the Japanese Firm." *Journal of Economic Literature* 28: 1–27.

Bartlett, Christopher A. 1986. "Building and Managing the Transnational: The New Organizational Challenge." In Michael E. Porter, ed., *Competition in Global Industries*, pp. 367–401. Boston: Harvard Business School Press.

Bigoness, William, and Gerald Blakely. 1996. "A cross-National Study of Managerial Values." *Journal of International Business Studies*" 27(4): 739–752.

Brown, Claire, and Michael Reich. 1989. "When Does Union-Management Cooperation Work? A Look at NUMMI and Van Nuys." *California Management Review* 31: 26–44.

Buckley Peter, and Mark Casson. 1976. *The Future of the Multinational Enterprise*. London: Macmillan.

Caves, Richard. 1982. *Multinational Enterprise and Economic Analysis*. Cambridge, Mass.: Cambridge University Press.

Clark, Kim. 1989 "Project Scope and Project Performance: The Effect of Parts Strategy and Supplier Involvement on Product Development." *Management Science* 35(10): 1247–1263.

Clark, Kim B., and Takahiro Fujimoto. 1991. *Product Development Performance*. Cambridge, Mass.: Harvard Business School Press.

Cole, Robert. 1979. *Work, Mobility, and Participation: A Comparative Study of Japanese and American Industry*. Berkeley: University of California Press.

Cole, Robert, and Donald Deskins. 1988. "Racial Factors in Site Location and Employment Patterns of Japanese Auto Firms in America." *California Management Review* 31(1): 9–22.

Cusumano, Michael A., 1985. *The Japanese Automobile Industry*. Cambridge, Mass.: Harvard University Press.

Cusumano, Michael, and Akira Takeishi. 1991. "Supplier Relations and Supplier Management: A Survey of Japanese, Japanese-Transplant, and U.S. Auto Plants." *Strategic Management Journal* 12(8): 563–588.

Dimaggio, Paul J., and Walter W. Powell. 1983. "The Iron Cage Revisited: Institutional Isomorphism and Collective Rationality in Organizational Fields." *American Sociological Review* 35: 147–160.

Dore, Ronald. 1973. *British Factory, Japanese Factory: The Origins of National Diversity in Industrial Relations*. Berkeley: University of California Press.

Dore, Ronald. 1986. *Flexible Rigidities: Industrial Policy and Structural Adjustment in the Japanese Economy, 1970–1980*. Stanford, Calif.: Stanford University Press.

Dyer, Jeffrey. 1996. "Does Governance Matter? Keiretsu Alliances and Asset Specificity as Sources of Japanese Competitive Advantage." *Organization Science* 7(6): 649–666.

Dyer, Jeffrey, and William Ouchi. 1993. "Japanese-Style Business Partnerships: Giving Companies a Competitive Edge." *Sloan Management Review* 35: 51–63.

Edstrom, Anders, and Jay Galbraith. 1977. "Transfer of Managers as a Coordination and Control Strategy in Multinational Corporations." *Administrative Science Quarterly* 22: 248–263.

Erez, Miriam. 1986. "The Congruence of Goal-Setting Strategies with Sociocultural Values and Its Effect on Performance." *Journal of Management* 12: 585–592.

Fucini, Joseph, and Susan Fucini. 1990. *Working for the Japanese—Inside Mazda's American Auto Plant*. New York: Free Press.

Fujimoto, Takahiro. 1997. "Strategies for Assembly Automation in the Automobile Industry." In Takahiro Fujimoto and Ulrich Jurgens, eds., *Transforming Auto Assembly—International Experiences with Automation and Work Organization.* Frankfurt: Springer-Verlag.

Gerlach, Michael L. 1992. *Alliance Capitalism: The Social Organization of Japanese Business.* Berkeley: University of California Press.

Graham, Laurie. 1995. *On the Line at Subaru-Isuzu: The Japanese Model and the American Worker.* Ithaca, N.Y.: Cornell University Press.

Hannan, Michael T., and John Freeman. 1989. *Organizational Ecology.* Cambridge, Mass.: Harvard University Press.

Hofstede, Geert. 1980. *Culture's Consequences: International Differences in Work-related Values.* Beverly Hills, Calif.: Sage.

Hymer, Stephen Herbert. 1976. *The International Operations of National Firms: A Study of Direct Foreign Investment.* Cambridge, Mass.: MIT Press.

Kenney, Martin, and Richard Florida. 1993. *Beyond Mass Production: The Japanese System and Its Transfer to the U.S.* New York: Oxford University Press.

Kinutani, H.. 1997. "Modular Assembly in Mixed-Model Production at Mazda." In Takahiro Fujimoto and Ulrich Jurgens, eds., *Transforming Auto Assembly—International Experiences with Automation and Work Organization.* Frankfurt: Springer-Verlag.

Klein, Benjamin. 1980. "Transaction Cost Determinants of 'Unfair' Contractual Arrangements." *American Economic Review* 70(2): 356–362.

Klein, B. G. Crawford, and A. Alchian. 1978. "Transaction Cost Determinants of "Unfair" Contractual Arrangements." *American Economic Review* 70(2): 356–362.

Kochan, Thomas, Harry Katz, and Robert McKersie. 1986. *The Transformation of American Industrial Relations.* New York: Basic Books.

Kogut, Bruce. 1991. "The Permeability of Borders and the Speed of Learning among Countries." In J. Dunning, B. Kogut, and M. Blomstrom, eds., *Globalization of Firms and the Competitiveness of Nations.* Sweden: Lund University Press.

Kogut, Bruce, ed. 1991. *Country Competitiveness and the Organization of Work and Technology.* London: Macmillan.

Koike, Kazuo. 1989. *Understanding Industrial Relations in Modern Japan.* Transl. Mary Saso. New York: St. Martin's Press.

Krafcik, John F. 1988. "Comparative Analysis of Performance Indicators at World Auto Assembly Plants." M.S. thesis, Sloan School of Management, Massachusetts Institute of Technology, Cambridge.

Lawler, E. E., III. 1992. *The Ultimate Challenge.* San Francisco: Jossey-Bass.

Lawrence, Paul R., and Jay W. Lorsch. 1967. *Organizations and Environment.* Boston: Harvard University Press.

Lehman, E. L. 1975. *Nonparametrics: Statistical Methods Based on Ranks.* San Francisco: McGraw-Hill, Holden-Day.

MacDuffie, John Paul. 1995. "Human Resource Bundles and Manufacturing Performance: Organizational Logic and Flexible Production Systems in the World Auto Industry." *Industrial and Labor Relations Review* 48: 197–221.

MacDuffie, John Paul, and John Krafcik. 1992. "Integrating Technology and Human Resources for High-Performance Manufacturing: Evidence from the International Auto Industry." In Thomas Kochan and Michael Useem, eds., *Transforming Organizations.* New York: Oxford University Press.

MacDuffie, John Paul, and Frits K. Pil. 1995. "The International Assembly Plant Study: Philosophical and Methodological Issues." In Steve Babson, ed., *Lean Work: Empowerment and Exploitation in the Global Auto Industry*, pp. 181–198. Detroit: Wayne State University Press.

MacDuffie, John Paul, and Frits K. Pil. 1997. "Flexible Technologies, Flexible Workers." In Takahiro Fujimoto and Ulrich Jurgens, eds., *Transforming Auto Assembly—International Experiences with Automation and Work Organization*. Frankfurt: Springer-Verlag.

MacDuffie, John Paul, and Frits K. Pil. 1998. " 'High-Involvement' Work Systems and Manufacturing Performance: The Diffusion of Lean Production in the World Auto Industry." Working paper, Department of Management, Wharton School, University of Pennsylvania.

Meyer, John, and Brian Rowan. 1977. "Institutionalized Organizations: Formal Structure as Myth and Ceremony." *American Journal of Sociology* 83(2): 340–363.

Morris, Tom, and Cynthia Pavett. 1992. "Management Style and Productivity in Two Cultures." *Journal of International Business Studies* 23(1): 169–179.

Nishiguchi, Toshihiro. 1994. *Strategic Industrial Sourcing: The Japanese Advantage*. New York: Oxford University Press.

Oliver, Nicholas, and Barry Wilkinson. 1992. *The Japanization of British Industry*. Oxford: Blackwell.

Orlikowski, Wanda J. 1992. "The Duality of Technology: Rethinking the Concept of Technology in Organizations." *Organization Science* 3(3): 398–427.

Parker, M., and J. Slaughter. 1988. "Managing by Stress: The Dark Side of Team Concept." *ILR Report* 26(1): 19–23.

Parthasarthy, Raghawan, and Prakash Sethi. 1993. "Relating Strategy and Structure to Flexible Automation: A Test of Fit and Performance Implications." *Strategic Management Journal* 14(7): 529–549.

Perrow, Charles. 1983. "The Organizational Context of Human Factors Engineering." *Administrative Science Quarterly* 28: 521–531.

Pil, Frits K. 1996. *The International and Temporal Diffusion of High-Involvement Work Practices*. Ph.D. diss., Wharton Business School, University of Pennsylvania.

Pil, Frits K., and John Paul MacDuffie. 1996. "The Adoption of High-Involvement Work Practices." *Industrial Relations* 35(3): 423–455.

Pil, Frits K. 1997. "Country and Company Influences on Organization Work Practices." Working paper, University of Pittsburgh; presented at the National Academy of Management, August.

Pil, Frits K., and John Paul MacDuffie. 1999. "The Japanese Automobile Transplants: Managing the Transfer of Best Practice." *Journal of World Business*.

Pil, Frits K., and John Paul MacDuffie. Forthcoming. "Organizational and Environmental Factors Influencing the Use of High-Involvement Work Practices." In Peter Cappelli (ed.), *Employment Strategies: Understanding Differences in Employment Practices*."

Ralston, David A, David Holt, Robert Terpstra, and Yu Kai-Chen. 1997. The Impact of National Culture and Economic Ideology on Managerial Work Values: A Study of the United States, Russia, Japan, and China. *Journal of International Business Studies*. 28(1): 177–207.

Rinehart, James, Christopher Huxley, and David Robertson. 1997. *Just Another Car Factory? Lean Production and Its Discontents*. Ithaca, NY.: Cornell University Press.

Roberts, Peter W., and Royston Greenwood. 1997. "Integrating Transaction Cost and Institutional Theories: Toward a Constrained Efficiency Framework for Understanding Organizational Design Adoption." *Academy of Management Review* 22(2): 346–373.

Ronen, Simcha, and Oded Shenkar. 1985. "Clustering Countries on Attitudinal Dimensions: A Review and Synthesis." *Academy of Management Review* 10(3): 435–454.

Saltzman, Gregory. 1994. "Job Applicant Screening by a Japanese Transplant." *Workplace Topics.* 4(1): 61–82.

Shan, Weijian, and William Hamilton. 1991. "Country-Specific Advantage and International Cooperation." *Strategic Management Journal* 12: 419–432.

Shimada, Haruo. 1985. "The Perceptions and Reality of Japanese Industrial Relations." in Lester Thurow, ed., *The Management Challenge: Japanese Views.* Cambridge, Mass. MIT Press.

Smith, P., and J. Misumi. 1989. "Japanese Management: A Sun Rising in the West?" In C. L. Cooper and I. T. Robertson, eds., *Annual Review of Industrial and Organizational Psychology,* 4: 329–369.

Stiglitz, Joseph E. 1987. "Learning to Learn. Localized Learning and Technological Progress." In Partha Dasgupta and Paul Stoneman, eds., *Economic Policy and Technological Performance.* New York: Cambridge University Press.

Susman, Gerald, and Richard Chase. 1986. "A Sociotechnical Analysis of the Integrated Factory." *Journal of Applied Behavioral Science* 22(3): 257–270.

Tanase, K., T. Matsuo, and K. Shimokawa. 1997. "Production of the NSX at Honda." In Takahiro Fujimoto and Ulrich Jurgens, eds. *Transforming Auto Assembly—International Experiences with Automation and Work Organization.* Frankfurt: Springer-Verlag.

Thompson, James, D. 1967. *Organizations in Action.* New York: McGraw-Hill.

Weick, Karl E. 1976. "Educational Organizations as Loosely Coupled Systems." *Administrative Science Quarterly* 21 (Mar.): 137–158.

Westney, Eleanor. 1987. *Imitation and Innovation: Transfer of Western Organizational Patterns to Meiji Japan.* Cambridge, Mass.: Harvard University Press.

Westney, Eleanor. 1993. "Institutionalization Theory and the Multinational Enterprise." In Sumantra Ghoshal and D. Eleanor Westney, eds., *Organizational Theory and The Multinational Corporation.* New York: St. Martin's Press.

Womack, James, Daniel Jones, and Daniel Roos. 1990. *The Machine That Changed the World.* New York: Rawson Associates, Macmillan.

Young, Mark. 1992. "A Framework for Successful Adoption and Performance of Japanese Manufacturing Practices in the United States." *Academy of Management Review* 17: 677–700.

Zipkin, Paul H. 1991. "Does Manufacturing need a JIT Revolution?" *Harvard Business Review* Jan. Feb.: 40–50.

Zuboff, Shoshana. 1988. *In the Age of the Smart Machine.* New York: Basic Books.

Zucker, Lynne G. 1988. *Institutional Patterns and Organizations: Culture and Environment.* Cambridge, Mass.: Ballinger.

3

Hybridization

Human Resource Management at Two Toyota Transplants

Paul S. Adler

There is broad consensus that the superlative efficiency and quality performance of Japanese auto "transplants" in the United States is in large measure due to their combination of the "lean" production systems and distinctive human resource management (HRM) practices (Womack, Jones, and Roos, 1990). While the production system has been well documented, there is considerable uncertainty over the nature of these human resource management practices. Some researchers see them as essentially Japanese in origin (e.g., Johnson, 1988; Kenney and Florida, 1993). Others argue that Japanese overseas subsidiaries, like those of companies headquartered in other countries, typically hybridize the parent companies' management approaches, adapting them at least in part to fit the host country conditions (e.g., Beechler and Yang, 1994; Elger and Smith, 1994; Milkman 1991; White and Trevor 1983; Yuen and Kee, 1993).

This chapter reports the results of a pair of case studies of two Toyota auto assembly transplants in the United States—Toyota Motor Manufacturing, Kentucky (TMMK), located in Georgetown, Kentucky, and New United Motor Manufacturing, Inc. (NUMMI), located in Fremont, California—with the aim of better understanding the causes and consequences of their HRM choices. Comparison of these two plants is instructive since they were very similar in all but a few, crucial respects. In both plants, organization and management were under Toyota control: TMMK was a wholly owned Toyota subsidiary, and, while NUMMI was a joint venture of GM and Toyota, its day-to-day operations were under Toyota control. They both produced relatively high-volume, standardized products (NUMMI produced Geo

Prizms, Toyota Corollas, and Toyota compact pickup trucks, while TMMK produced Camrys and Avalons). They were both thorough in their adoption of the Toyota production system (as described by Monden, 1983, and Schonberger, 1982). They were both sizable operations (in 1996, NUMMI employed some 4,300 people, and TMMK about 6,000). And they were both "world-class" operations in quality and efficiency. However, their HRM systems had been adapted to the American context, and adapted in significantly different ways. Most notably, NUMMI was unionized, while TMMK was not, and this difference had ramifications for several facets of their respective HRM policies.

The next section reviews relevant prior research and elicits from it a set of hypotheses concerning the degree of hybridization of these plants' HRM systems. I then outline a conceptual framework for characterizing the two plants' HRM approaches, identifying four broad HRM domains and eighteen components of these domains. The following two sections describe my research methods and provide brief overviews of the two plants. The core of the paper examines the eighteen HRM components in each of the plants. A discussion section synthesizes the results of this analysis and contrasts them with the hypotheses drawn from prior research. With a sample of only two, it would be inappropriate to seek to test these hypotheses, but the discrepancies between the hypotheses and the empirical findings highlight some issues in need of theoretical clarification. A conclusion summarizes and suggests some directions for future research.

Hybridization: Theoretical Background

Early generations of research on multinationals assumed that overseas subsidiaries could adopt headquarters' HRM approaches or instead adopt approaches prevalent in the host country (Doz, Bartlett, and Prahalad, 1981; Perlmutter, 1969; Prahalad and Doz, 1987.) More recent research has recognized that subsidiaries can also "hybridize" parent approaches with host-country approaches (Abo, 1994).

Hybridization in the broad sense in which I am using it here refers to any of a number of forms of adaptation. First, approaches to specific facets of HRM can be said to be hybridized when they share some features with host-country approaches and other features with home-country approaches. Second, the overall configuration of HRM approaches of a given organization can be said to be hybridized if some or all of its components are hybridized or if some components are adopted from the home country while others are directly patterned on local approaches.

Characterizing HRM practices as more or less hybridized is a conceptually complex task, since we must distinguish the practice from its objective function and from its subjective meaning. We sometimes observe the same function being expressed in different, more locally appropriate practices. A U.S. practice might thus serve as the "functional alternative" or functional equivalent of a Japanese practice (Cole, 1972). On the other hand, identical practices can serve different functions (Cole, 1972, labeled this possibility "structural modeling with environmental effects"). Moreover, independent of their objective "function," the same practices can also have different subjective meanings in different contexts. Brannen (1992) and Brannen, Liker, and Fruin (this volume) analyze this as "recontextualization." In the present study, I focus on the hybridization of practices themselves and comment on their function and meaning where appropriate.

Research on multinationals has shown that control is typically more decentralized and approaches are more likely to be hybridized in HRM than in production and marketing, while finance is the most centralized and least hybridized domain of all (see reviews by Martinez and Ricks, 1989, and Goehle, 1980). A considerable body of empirical research has described the adoption/hybridization patterns in HRM approaches found in Japanese firms' overseas subsidiaries (see Yang, 1992, for a selective review of pre-1992 research on Japanese subsidiaries in the U.S.; see also Kenney and Florida, 1993). Abo and his colleagues (1994) have described in some detail the patterns of hybridization found in Japanese transplants in the United States, but, like many of the empirical studies of hybridization, they offer no theoretical rationale for these patterns.

Alongside these empirical studies, a number of researchers have proposed a variety of theoretical perspectives for explaining the extent of hybridization. A "rational design" strand argues that, given their industry and technology, subsidiaries will tend to adopt whatever organizational forms and HRM policies optimize their business performance (Kujawa, 1986; Womack et al., 1990). The "culturalist" strand of international management research predicts that adaptation will be necessary when, as in the case of Japanese subsidiaries in the United States, the home and host cultures are very different (Hofstede, 1980; Ishida, 1986; Wilms, Hardcastle and Zell, 1994).

Several other theoretical strands are more sensitive to the specific issues posed by multinationals. A "strategy" strand points to the variability across firms in their international business strategies—ethnocentric, polycentric, or geocentric, to use Perlmutter's (1969) classification—and in their "administrative heritage" (Bartlett and Ghoshal, 1980), and to the implications of these differences for the way parent organizations design and control subsidiaries. An "institutionalist" strand argues that the structures and processes of foreign subsidiaries are pulled in different directions by competing isomorphic forces from the parent and from the local environment (Westney, 1993). A "resource dependency" strand has argued that the relative influence of parent and local environment is a function of the relative dependencies that characterize the parent/subsidiary/local-actor triangle (Beechler and Yang, 1994; Martinez and Ricks, 1989). Resource dependency theory has also been invoked in opposition to contingency, culturalist, and institutional theories to argue that subsidiaries may be able to resist adaptation pressure by actively changing their local environments, for example, by changing host-country supplier practices (Kenney and Florida, 1991).

These theories offer alternative explanations of why the HRM domain should be relatively more hybridized than other management domains such as production or finance. Institutional theory, for example, explains this relative propensity to hybridize HRM by invoking the difficulty of clearly defining this function's "technology" and its "outputs." Applying the typology of societal sectors proposed by Scott (1987) to distinguish functions within the firm, we would say that HRM is relatively strongly influenced by legitimacy pressures and relatively weakly influenced by efficiency pressures. A second, possibly complementary explanation comes from a resource-dependency perspective: while production practices typically have little salience to external parties, practices in the HRM domain govern the organization's relation with external actors—employees, unions, and regulators—who often wield considerable power. A third, strategic management perspective might remind us that headquarters is far more interested in the subsidiary's financial results than in the means used to achieve them (see, for example, Kujawa, 1971).

These theories have also been used to ground propositions concerning the relative degree of hybridization of subsidiaries in different contexts. Table 3.1 summarizes the propositions advanced in this research, clustering them according to the nature of the causal factors invoked: the differences between home and host country, the nature of the corporate parent, and the specific situation of the subsidiary. The first five studies (Yang, 1992; Beechler and Yang, 1994; Taylor, Beechler, and Napier, 1996; Beechler and Taylor, 1994; Martinez and Ricks, 1989) are based primarily on resource dependency theory. The sixth through the eighth studies (Rosenzweig and Singh, 1981; Rosenzweig and Nohria, 1994; and Hannon, Huang, and Jaw, 1995) are grounded primarily in institutional theory. The ninth study, by Schuler, Dowling, and De Cieri (1994), is theoretically eclectic. The final study, by Banks and Stieber (1977), is a summary of the results of research prior to that time. I have sequenced the propositions under each of the three main headings in logical order: (1) propositions common to at least some of the papers in the different theoretical perspectives, (2) propositions from the resource dependency perspective, and (3) propositions from institutional theory.

Table 3.1 reveals, first, that hybridization can be influenced by a rather broad range of determinants, some common to the different theories and some theory-specific. Second, it shows that the different perspectives lead to broadly compatible propositions. In only one case (A1) do the different theoretical starting points lead to opposing propositions: from a resource dependence viewpoint, cultural differences between home and host country make the adoption of home-country practices more difficult; from an institutional theory viewpoint, cultural differences make it more likely that the isomorphic attraction of the home-country model will pull the subsidiary's approach away from the prevailing host-country pattern. But even in this case, the two propositions will both be satisfied if subsidiary approaches are hybrids reflecting both home and host country influences.

The last column of Table 3.1 translates these propositions into hypotheses concerning the average and relative degree of hybridization of NUMMI and TMMK (sketches of the two plants that justify these interpretations are given later in this chapter). Seven hypotheses predict that both plants will adopt Japanese HRM approaches, while three predict that both will adopt local approaches. Two of these latter three, A2 and C13—the differences between Japanese and U.S. legal contexts and the degree of dependence on institutional legitimacy—seem difficult to refute and do indeed lead us to expect considerable adaptation. The third of these three (B6) is, however, based on a more dubious assumption, namely, that cost-focused organizations are too concerned about labor costs to implement a sophisticated HRM approach. While this may be true of some cost-focused companies, it does not ring true of Toyota, whose assembly plants see both low cost and high quality as high strategic priorities and see sophisticated HRM approaches as critical to achieving both priorities. All eleven propositions that discriminate between NUMMI and TMMK suggest that TMMK's HRM approach will be more Japanese than NUMMI's.

With a sample of only two subsidiaries, the present study can hardly aim to test these hypotheses. But when the cases are analyzed through the lens these hypotheses provide, inconsistencies can legitimately be used to prompt us to reconsider the underlying theoretical reasoning.

Far less research attempts to predict which specific components of HRM are more likely to reflect home versus host country patterns. In Table 3.2, I summarize what is available. Resource dependency and institutional theories both predict that facets governed by legal imperatives will be correspondingly adapted to local conditions. Resource dependency also attributes a role to the parent company's philosophy of control: those components of HRM that are seen by headquarters as more critical to the subsidiary's success presumably will be more closely controlled (ceteris paribus) by the parent. Institutional theory also argues that the balance of competing isomorphic pulls from parent and local actors will be influenced by the visibility of a given practice to the respective actors.

So far, research has not clearly articulated a theoretical foundation for discriminating among HRM components along such dimensions. I therefore refrain from formulating specific hypotheses. But these propositions can serve to sensitize us in interpreting the pattern of findings reported below.

Framework and Methods

In order to compare HRM policies at NUMMI and TMMK with policies in Toyota's Japanese operations and with the patterns observed in U.S. industry, I have grouped HRM under four broad headings: work organization, individual and organizational learning, employment relations, and HRM administration (see Table 3.3). In the absence of any compelling theory, these intuitive groupings will suffice.[1] The rationale of the employment relations

Table 3.1 Propositions and Hypotheses Derived from Prior Research on the Extent of Subsidiary HRM Hybridization

Subsidiaries Will Adopt Japanese HRM Approaches to the Extent That	Source[a]										NUMMI /TMMK[b]
	1	2	3	4	5	6	7	8	9	10	
A Host- vs. home-country contexts											
1 The cultural distance between home and host countries is lower		*	*	*		R	R			*	?
2 The legal environments of home- and host-country are similar (vs. different)			*						*		neither
B Corporate context											
1 The parent requires a high degree of cross-unit integration and communication		*	*	*		*	*			*	both
2 The corporation pursues a global (vs. multidomestic) strategy		*	*			*	*	*		*	both
3 The subsidiary's performance is of greater importance to the parent		*	*		*						TMMK
4 Prior experience leads the parent to believe transfer of Japanese approach is feasible (vs. too difficult)		*	*	*							?
5 The corporation believes that its HRM system represents a distinctive competency		*		*							?
6 The corporation pursues a differentiation (vs. cost) strategy				*							neither
7 The parent has less (vs. more) international experience							*		*	*	TMMK
8 The home-country culture displays a low degree of tolerance for uncertainty						*		*			both
9 Ownership stake is higher					*				*		TMMK

C   Local subsidiary conditions

Local subsidiary conditions	1	2	3	4	5	6	7	8	9	10	
1. The subsidiary relies on corporate technology, know-how, and resources rather than on its own						*	*	*	*	*	both
2. The subsidiary is a greenfield operation rather than acquired	*			*		*	*	*			TMMK
3. The subsidiary has more power vis-à-vis local actors	*					*	*	*			TMMK
4. The subsidiary is not unionized	*	*				*	*	*			TMMK
5. The subsidiary has more expatriates representatives from the parent	*				*	*	*		*		TMMK
6. The subsidiary is more recent and thus uses more advanced management ideas	*					*					TMMK
7. The subsidiary's strategy focuses on quality and efficiency, rather than on attracting scarce local talent	*										both
8. The nature of the subsidiary's business demands and allows the development of an organizational culture	*										?
9. The subsidiary relies on integrated process technology, rather than on individual contributors	*										both
10. The subsidiary is located in a more rural region more accepting of Japanese paternalism and egalitarianism	*										TMMK
11. The subsidiary's workforce is more homogeneous	*										TMMK
12. Local labor market conditions allow lower turnover rates											TMMK
13. The subsidiary is less dependent on institutional legitimacy in the host country						*	*		*	*	neither
14. The subsidiary is smaller							*				both

a. Sources of these data are from the following: (1) Yang 1992; (2) Beechler and Yang 1994; (3) Taylor, Beechler, and Napier 1996; (4) Beechler and Taylor 1994; (5) Martinez and Ricks 1989; (6) Rosenzweig and Singh 1991; (7) Rosenzweig and Nohria 1994; (8) Hannon, Huang, and Jaw 1995; (9) Schuler, Dowling, and De Cieri 1993; (10) Banks and Stieber 1977.

b. Entries in this column indicate whether the proposition suggests that NUMMI and/or TMMK should adopt Japanese home-country practices.

* signifies that the proposition was advanced in the study. R signifies that the reverse proposition was advanced.

Table 3.2 Propositions Derived from Prior Research on the Extent of Hybridization in Different HRM Domains

In Any Given Subsidiary, Some HRM Domains Will Be More Localized Than Others to the Extent That They . . .	Source[a]					
	1	2	3	4	5	6
1 Are subject to more legal imperatives	*			*	*	*
2 Are seen by headquarters as less critical to organizational control			*			*
3 Are more visible and salient to locals					*	
4 Involve less interaction with the parent					*	*

a. Sources of these data are from the following: (1) Yang 1992; (2) Beechler and Yang 1994; (3) Taylor, Beechler, and Napier 1996; (4) Rosenzweig and Singh 1981; (5) Rosenzweig and Nohria 1994; (6) Banks and Stieber 1977.

Table 3.3 A Framework for Analysis

Domain	Component
Work organization	Job classification
	Production teams
	Job rotation
	Roles of supervisors
Individual and organizational learning	Education and training
	QC activities
	Suggestion system
	Information sharing
Employment relations	Symbols of unity
	Employment security
	Labor relations
	Grievances
	Discipline
	Personnel selection
	Promotion
	Wages and benefits
	Health and safety
HRM administration	Role of HR department

category is to group those components of HRM where conflict of interest between workers and employer is particularly salient. This chapter focuses on HRM as it affects blue-collar workers: I leave for another occasion the analysis of white-collar and managerial personnel.

My characterization of NUMMI and TMMK draws primarily on company documents and more than 120 interviews with NUMMI employees and managers, conducted between 1989 and 1994, more than thirty interviews at TMMK, conducted in 1992 and 1993, and twenty-four interviews at Toyota facilities in Japan, conducted in 1992. I interviewed individuals from all ranks of the two transplants, including production workers, skilled trades workers, Team Leaders, Group Leaders, Assistant Managers, Managers, and senior executives. At NUMMI, I also interviewed union officials of UAW Local 2244, included members of both the Administration and the People's Caucuses. In Japan, my interviewees included staff and plant managers, engineers, union officials, and production workers.

Particularly valuable secondary sources on similarities and differences between Toyota and Toyota's U.S. transplants include Grønning (1992) on NUMMI and Abo (1994, pp. 186–188 for NUMMI and 188–190 for TMMK). Sources on the specific features of Toyota's operations in Japan include Cole (1979), Grønning (1992), and Shimizu and GEMIC (1993), and Shimizu and Nomura (1993).

To characterize these plants' HRM systems, they need to be compared against not only Japanese but also U.S. HRM policies and practices. Here I rely on several recent surveys. Starting with the most general, Lawler, Mohrman and Ledford (1995) surveyed *Fortune* 1000 companies in 1987, 1990, and 1993. Osterman (1994) surveyed a U.S. national sample of manufacturing and nonmanufacturing establishments in 1992. MacDuffie (1996) summarizes extensive surveys of auto assembly plants in 1989 and 1993.

Since some of transplants' policies resemble those found in nonunion American firms (as noted by Milkman, 1991), I also compare the transplants with Foulkes's (1980) sample of twenty-six large nonunion companies. While Foulkes's study avoided what he called the "militantly antiunion" companies, the firms he sampled differed in their response to the possibility of unionization. Some companies pursued what could be called a strategy of "union indifference": they paid little attention to the union threat when they set wages or established their employment relations. Others pursued what Kochan (1980, pp. 183–191) and Holley and Jennings (1994: 108–109) call a "union substitution" strategy, a strategy characteristic of firms that Mills (1982) calls "better-standard nonunion employers." TMMK, as we will see, followed a systematic union substitution strategy, so Foulkes's sample will provide a useful reference point.

After presenting an overview of each plant, I discuss each of eighteen HRM components, comparing NUMMI and TMMK approaches to those found in comparable Toyota[2] and U.S. Big Three plants. The main goal is to assess whether the transplants' practices are closer to the practices prevailing in the home country or to those in the host country. The secondary goal is to assess possible differences in these practices' functions and meanings; however, in the interests of brevity, I raise these issues only when they appear particularly salient.

An Overview of NUMMI

New United Motor Manufacturing, Inc., opened in 1984. It was created as a joint venture between Toyota and GM. Its mission was to produce small cars for sale by both partners. Toyota invested $100 million in cash, supplied the cars' designs, and managed the factory, while GM provided the building and marketed half the cars. Each partner was a half-owner of the new company.

The company took over the GM-Fremont plant that had been closed in 1982. Unexcused absenteeism at GM-Fremont had often run over 20 percent. Both quality levels and productivity had been far below the GM norm, which itself was falling ever further behind the world-class standard then being set in Japan. Labor relations were highly antagonistic.

It was politically impossible for the plant to reopen without UAW involvement. So, although Toyota was initially reluctant to work with the UAW, it agreed to recognize the union and to give priority to rehiring the laid-off workers. The employee selection process was done jointly by the union and management. Notwithstanding the three full days of interviews and tests, few workers who went through the selection process were rejected. The entire union hierarchy was rehired, and of the 2,200 workers hired by late 1985, more than 95 percent of the assembly workers and 75 percent of the skilled trades workers were former GM-Fremont employees.

The initial 1985 collective bargaining contract embodied a very different role for the union than it had in the Big Three plants. The introduction stated that the union and management "are committed to building and maintaining the most innovative and harmonious labor-management relation in America." Innovative features of the plant's human resource policies supported this commitment

By 1986, with largely the same workforce and comparable equipment, NUMMI had achieved productivity levels almost twice those of GM-Fremont in its best years, 40 percent higher than those at the typical Big Three assembly plant, and very close to the levels at its Toyota sister plant in Takaoka. It was also producing the highest quality levels in the industry. In 1989 Toyota announced that it would invest another $350 million to expand the plant and begin production of pickup trucks. This led to the hiring of an additional 700 workers—this time selected from an applicant pool of 9,000—bringing total employment up to 3,700. With the addition of an axle line and a plastics plant, by 1995, employment had risen to 4,200.

Through the early 1990s, the plant continued to excel in quality and productivity. In 1995, J. D. Power and Associates ranked the Prizm the best-built car in North America, the Corolla was number two in the small-car segment, and the Toyota HiLux was the best compact pickup truck built in North America.

Worker satisfaction and commitment were also high. Researchers who asked NUMMI workers whether they would switch jobs if there were a Big Three plant across the street received responses that were uniformly negative (Adler, 1993; Holusha, 1989; Krafcik, 1989). According to a biannual Team Member survey at the plant, the number of workers who said they were "satisfied with [their] job and environment" increased progressively from 65 percent in 1985 to 90 percent in 1991, 1993, and 1995. Throughout the 1980s, the absence rate (excluding only scheduled vacations) hovered around 3 percent, compared with an average of nearly 9 percent at Big Three plants in that period. Turnover remained under 6 percent through 1996.

An Overview of TMMK

In Toyota's strategy for building capacity in the United States, Toyota Motor Manufacturing, Kentucky, was a successor to NUMMI, leveraging some of the lessons Toyota managers felt they had learned there. Whereas NUMMI was a joint venture, Toyota managers now felt they knew enough about the U.S. environment to operate as a wholly owned subsidiary. And whereas GM had imposed the choice of NUMMI's location and in doing so had made union recognition a de facto requirement, Toyota now chose to locate TMMK in a rural area in the South and not to invite the union into the venture.

According to TMMK's senior vice president (an American), in designing its HRM policies, "We really began with a blank sheet of paper. [A Japanese expatriate] came to us from NUMMI as our first HR coordinator, but we really invented our own policies." This "blank sheet of paper" approach minimized the transfer of ideas from NUMMI. This approach reflected the fact that TMMK had a different "mother" plant (Tsutsumi) in a different division from NUMMI. In part, it also reflected Toyota's policy of giving challenging assignments to new people to enhance their development, rather than relying on experienced people who become specialists (White and Trevor, 1983).

Plant construction began in 1986, and volume production began in 1988. Plant expansions were made in 1988, 1989, and then again in 1993. By 1994, total investment had reached more than $4 billion. The plant's productivity is reputed to be close to that of its world-class Japanese mother plant. It has won a string of J. D. Power and Associates award for overall quality: the gold award in 1990, the silver in 1991, the bronze in 1992, and the gold again in 1993.

Hiring began in 1987. Compared to NUMMI's initial round of hiring, TMMK's was highly selective. There were some 50,000 applicants for the initial 3,000 jobs. Applicants were screened through a total of eighteen hours of tests and interviews as well as through reference checks. By 1994, total employment reached 6,000, and the total number of applicants since hiring began was more than 200,000. All the blue-collar and white-collar employees had at least a high-school diploma, and more than 50 percent had some college education. On the other hand, only 2 percent had any auto background.

The evidence suggests a rather high level of job satisfaction and commitment. The last employee opinion survey on which I have data was conducted in 1992. The response rate was 69 percent (compared to around 95 percent at NUMMI, where the surveys are conducted on work time during the model changeover periods). Some 95 percent of respondents describe TMMK as a good place to work. Turnover in 1992 was 2.7 percent, lower than at NUMMI because of a much younger workforce and correspondingly fewer retirements. Participation in the suggestion program that year was 93 percent with an average of 8.57 suggestions received per employee.

HRM Policies Analyzed

Using the framework presented in Table 3.3 as a guide, this section reviews each HRM policy domain in turn. Under each heading, I characterize Toyota's approach in its Japanese plants, then compare the practices observed in the two transplants with both the Toyota approach and available U.S. models.

Interviews with senior managers at NUMMI and TMMK revealed that, at Toyota, the differentiation between adoption/adaptation choices was a matter of corporate strategy. Toyota distinguished between the Toyota Production System (TPS) and the other components of the management system that complement and buttress TPS. Local management was tasked by corporate headquarters with the faithful implementation of TPS, as embodied in an integrated set of policies: just-in-time production, production leveling, continuous improvement, visual control, errorproofing, the team concept, and standardized work. In contrast, the other management systems, and in particular human resource management policies, were deliberately tailored to the local conditions. The former president of TMMK, Fujio Cho, described the policy in these terms: "I told people here that the [Japanese] coordinators were teachers on production issues and TPS, but that they were the students in the office areas such as Legal, Human Resources, and Public Affairs." This strategy shaped the overall pattern observed: HR domains that overlap with TPS—work organization and learning—were very "Japanese," while others were hybridized.

HRM policies at NUMMI and TMMK were rather stable over time. In part, this reflected a frequently encountered imprinting effect (Stinchcombe, 1965), but it also reflected the fact that the policies initially selected fitted their tasks reasonably well. This paper therefore treats hybridization as an outcome state, and I leave for another occasion discussion of the processes that led these outcomes.[3]

Job Classifications

Worker multifunctionality is a key element of TPS: it allows for greater flexibility in operations, and it broadens workers' understanding of the production process and thus strengthens their ability to contribute improvement ideas. As a result, Toyota had only one production worker classification and one skilled trades classification, and the line between them was very blurred as production workers progressively acquired selected trade skills. Moreover, among production workers, six skill grades with corresponding pay levels were distinguished. Production workers were responsible for some facets of quality control, simple maintenance, and line-side housekeeping. By contrast, in Big Three U.S. auto plants there were often more than eighty production worker classifications and more than eighteen skilled trades classifications; production workers' tasks were narrowly defined; and there were no skill grades within classifications.

Both NUMMI and TMMK were closer to Toyota's approach. Both had three Team Member classifications: production, tool-and-die, and general maintenance. Production workers' responsibilities were broadened with the goal of achieving a breadth similar to that found in Japan. TMMK had plans for the complete cross-training of all skilled trades personnel.

Two nuances are worth noting, however. First, neither transplant had skill grades with different pay levels. Second, the division of labor between production workers and skilled trades was much sharper than was found in Toyota's Japanese plants. While this division may well be optimal from an industrial relations point of view in the U.S. context, it is hard to believe that it did not have a negative effect on performance: unscheduled equipment downtime was reputedly significantly higher at the U.S. transplants.

While Foulkes (1980) made no mention of job classifications, the practice of broadening job descriptions seemed to be growing in the United States, particularly in nonunion facilities. Lawler et al. (1995) documented the spread of self-inspection practices and the use of statistical control methods by frontline employees. Moreover, the use of intraclassification skill grades and skill-based pay systems was spreading. However, relative to the auto industry norms, NUMMI and TMMK appear to have been relatively closer to the Toyota model.

Production Teams

Toyota's team concept was the means by which worker multifunctionality yielded operational flexibility; it was also seen as an important social mechanism for maintaining commitment. Toyota workers were thus organized in production teams of five to seven workers under a Team Leader (*hancho*). Four or five teams composed a group under a Group Leader (*kumicho*). The Team Leader was usually responsible for some lower-level administrative responsibilities, for training, and for filling in for workers absent for health, training, or other reasons.

NUMMI and TMMK followed this Toyota practice rather closely, with all production and skilled trades workers organized into small teams. As in Toyota, these teams had little autonomy. Production work teams could not pace their work, since they were tied to the pace of the assembly line, nor did they play any role in hiring or firing. They were, however, the key structure for job rotation (see later discussion) and process improvement.

Team Leaders at NUMMI and TMMK were hourly workers, and at NUMMI they were UAW members. They were paid a modest wage premium. Unlike the practice of many U.S. organizations using "self-directed teams," Team Leaders at Toyota, NUMMI, and TMMK were not selected by the Team Members as "team representatives" but played an essentially technical role akin to a "lead hand." To quote the TMMK Team Member handbook, they were supposed to play a role more like that of a "basketball coach." At NUMMI, Team Leaders were initially chosen by management, but, after growing complaints of favoritism, a new procedure was negotiated with the union in which Team Leaders were chosen by a joint union/management selection committee. At TMMK, Team Leaders were selected by management, but peer evaluation is one of the selection criteria (see discussion of promotion and wages).

The use of teams in the transplants contrasted with the practice in the Big Three, but was consistent with broader trends in U.S. industry. MacDuffie (1996) found that the percentage of workers organized in teams among the U.S. auto manufacturers was very low and actually declined from 10 percent in 1989 to 6 percent in 1993. In U.S. industry as a whole, however, "self-managed work teams" were growing in popularity. Lawler et al. (1995) used a definition of self-managed teams that would probably exclude Toyota plants because teams in these plants had too narrow a range of decision-making autonomy. Lawler et al.'s (1995) survey nevertheless found that 68 percent of the *Fortune* 1000 sample used self-managed teams for at least some employees, although in most cases for less than a quarter of the workforce (p. 28–29). Osterman's survey (1994) found that 32 percent of manufacturing plants used some kind of teams for more than 50 percent of their core workforce (i.e., the largest group of nonmanagerial employees involved in producing the establishment's main products).

While data are lacking, anecdotal evidence suggests that teams at Toyota and the transplants were much smaller (five to six people) than teams in U.S. firms (often fifteen to twenty-five people) (Eads, 1987: 724). In part, that was because Toyota and the transplants were more attentive to the influence of the social dynamics of small groups on commitment and on such important outcomes as absences. It also reflected the primarily technical role attributed to the Team Leader under the Toyota production system. In many U.S. plants, the ambiguous authority of the Team Leader would be unstable; it would rapidly resolve into either a supervisory role or a team spokesperson role—more likely the former, given management's lack of interest in the latter and its considerable interest in ensuring cost-effective spans of supervisory control. (See Grønning, 1997, for a comparison of teams at TMMK and Ford's Kentucky Truck Plant.)

Overall, I conclude that both the transplants followed a policy close to Toyota's. We should note, however, that the subjective meaning of this teamwork was a little different. Authority relations in Japan appeared to be less problematic and conflictual than in the United States, and the social power of the group over the individual was typically stronger. As a result, teamwork in the United States brought with it the connotations of both team autonomy and consensus-based decision making that it did not have in Japan. This recontextualization created an undercurrent of tension around the team concept in the U.S. transplants.

Job Rotation

In order to create multiskilled workers who could provide both flexibility and improvement ideas, Toyota trained workers in different jobs within their team and group and encouraged periodic rotation. By contrast, traditional American unionized plants rarely allowed rotation, if only because of the extensively differentiated job classifications. However, MacDuffie (1996) found that the mean frequency of rotation in Big Three had increased significantly in the early 1990s.

Both NUMMI and TMMK had even more rotation during the working day than Toyota plants. The aims of rotation in both plants were to encourage multiskilling for operational flexibility, to alleviate boredom, and to reduce ergonomic strain. Toyota paid little attention to the demotivating effects of boredom and used rotation to lighten the ergonomic load of only the most difficult jobs, fearing the quality and efficiency cost of rotation. Toyota had more systematic planning for longer-term rotations that could add to the worker's "deep knowledge" of the production process. (We should also note that in Japan, auto workers typically rotated shifts, whereas in the United States, shifts were fixed and workers transferred individually between them as a function of seniority.)

Foulkes noted that some nonunion companies used job rotation to broaden workers' skills and thus created greater flexibility. This flexibility was considered useful in dealing with business downturns, since personnel could be reassigned and could replace a buffer of part-time workers (1980, p. 109). Osterman (1994) found that 37 percent of manufacturing establishments used job rotation for at least 50 percent of their core workforce. Lawler et al. found that 13 percent of the *Fortune* 1000 sample had cross-trained more than 60 percent of their employees during the past three years, and 69 percent had cross-trained more than 20 percent of their workforce over the same period (1995, p. 14, 16). Anecdotal evidence suggests, however, some more subtle differences between U.S. practices and those found at NUMMI and TMMK. In many U.S. plants, particularly in the Big Three, rotation created only limited task variety, it was mainly done at the worker's request, and it was rarely part of a systematic strategy of building flexibility and knowledge.

Overall, I rate the two transplants' practice as close to Toyota's. Their greater emphasis on intraday rotations reflected a recontextualization of rotation as a quality of worklife issue; Toyota's greater emphasis on longer-term mobility reflected a more strategic focus on skill building.

Role of Supervisors

At Toyota as at other Japanese manufacturers, supervisors were responsible for tasks that in the United States typically remained staff industrial engineering responsibilities. Historically, this pattern derived from Toyota's commitment to the "Training Within Industry" (TWI) philosophy. In the immediate post–World War II years, Toyota found itself with the same dearth of engineers as U.S. industry had faced during the war. Toyota adopted the solution developed by TWI and formalized in the TWI "Job Methods" program: delegate methods engineering and line balancing tasks to the foreman, and encourage the foreman to collaborate with experienced workers in these tasks. The TWI program was embraced by numerous Japanese firms during the Occupation years and continued to hold sway in Japan (Robinson and Schroeder, 1993; Schroeder and Robinson, 1991). The Big Three—like most of the rest of U.S. industry—lost interest in the TWI program at the war's end; since then, the role of supervisors in the Big Three has become less technically oriented and more focused on labor management and discipline.

NUMMI and TMMK inherited the TWI practice from their parent company. Group Leaders in the transplants were responsible for job methods (which at Toyota is called standardized work and figures as a key element of TPS) and troubleshooting production problems. I rate the two transplants as close to the Toyota practice. Modest steps in a similar direction appear in U.S. industry, with a growing interest in work process redesign by shop-floor personnel (Lawler et al., 1995, p. 41).

Training

In order to create multiskilled workers, Toyota trained workers for different jobs within their team and group and encouraged workers to broaden their skills by moving from one area of the plant to another over a period of years. By contrast, opportunities for job changes in U.S. unionized plants were typically determined on a seniority basis, and few unionized companies encouraged, let alone planned, such development (Brown and Reich, 1995).

NUMMI and TMMK followed Toyota's pattern of intensive investment in training. In this, Toyota and its subsidiaries resembled other Japanese plants and transplants: MacDuffie and Kochan (1995) found that newly hired auto assembly plant production workers received on average forty-two hours of training in their first six months in U.S. firms, 225 hours in Japanese transplants, and 364 hours in Japanese plants. Workers with more than one year's experience received thirty-one hours in the U.S. companies, fifty-two in the transplants, and seventy-six in Japan.

As part of the Training Within Industry program, Toyota also adopted "Job Instruction," TWI's formalized technique for on-the-job training. JI had four steps, each of which had defined component activities: (1) prepare the worker to receive instruction, (2) present the operation, (3) try out performance, (4) followup. The rigor of the TWI approach contrasted with the more casual, "watch Joe" approach common both then and now in U.S. industry. Both TMMK and NUMMI trained workers and managers in Toyota's version of Job Instruction.

Unlike NUMMI and TMMK, Toyota skilled trades workers did not begin with a concentrated apprenticeship. Instead, they acquired a broad range of skills over a period of ten years and more, moving from assignment to assignment with short classroom courses interspersed with work experience and on-the-job training. NUMMI maintenance and skilled trades followed certified apprenticeships. At TMMK, the skilled trades program did not seek external certification but maintained a clear demarcation of job responsibilities and was even more aggressive than Toyota in its plans to develop fully multifunctional skilled trades workers.

Foulkes (1980) made no mention of training, except for a brief reference to retraining to avoid layoffs. Kochan mentioned as one characteristic of the union substitution model a "high rate of investment per worker in human support programs such as training and career development" (1980, p. 185). Overall, I rate the transplants' training practices close to Toyota's.

Suggestion System

A key principle of the Toyota production system is continuous improvement (*kaizen*). Ongoing *kaizen* efforts occurred through both top-down (management-led) and bottom-up (employee-driven) processes. By contrast, in Big Three plants, the UAW contract usually specified that outside a 120-day period following a model changeover, there could be no unilateral change of methods, and, in practice, methods changed rarely outside this window. MacDuffie (1996) found that in 1993, whereas Japanese auto manufacturers received on average 51 suggestions per employee per year with an acceptance rate of 84 percent, the comparable figures for U.S. companies was 0.3 suggestions per year of which 41 percent were accepted. The average Japanese transplant had 3.6 suggestions per year, and 65 percent were accepted.

As a part of the bottom-up *kaizen* process, Toyota put great emphasis on individual and team suggestions. Toyota managers saw productive, educational, and attitudinal benefits to the suggestion program. Unlike U.S. managers, they were therefore less focused on a few high-value suggestions and more concerned to encourage universal participation, with many small suggestions (Yasuda, 1991). Group Leaders and Assistant Managers were evaluated in part on participation rates. Participation thus often had a "mandatory voluntary" character (Grønning, 1992).

The suggestion systems at NUMMI and TMMK were very similar to Toyota's. As at Toyota, the focus was on encouraging a large number of small-scale suggestions from a high proportion of the workforce. By 1994, over 90 percent of workers at both transplants were participating. As at Toyota, accepted suggestions were given considerable symbolic recognition but only modest financial rewards. At TMMK in 1992, for example, where 98 percent of submitted suggestions were implemented, the average suggestion yielded total estimated first-year savings of $601, of which $108 was in "hard" savings as distinct from cost avoidance, and the value of the average reward per suggestion was $22.

Foulkes (1980) did not mention suggestion systems. Kochan noted that union substitution efforts often included "informal mechanisms for, or encouragement of, participation in decision making about the way work is to be performed" (1980, p. 185). Lawler et al. (1995) found that 85 percent of their *Fortune* 1000 sample had some kind of suggestion system; they did not, however, measure the activity level.

NUMMI and TMMK rated close to the Toyota model in this domain. We should note however, some interesting recontextualization effects. On the one hand, as mentioned earlier, suggestion activity was more truly voluntary in the transplants. On the other hand, according to several interviewees, Japanese supervisors' pressure on subordinates to submit suggestions did not appear to Japanese workers as so external a form of control as comparable pressure would be in the United States. In Japan, the broader culture encourages a more "devotional" attitude to work, and supervisors pressure could leverage this predisposition. In the United States, workers often saw their involvement as a sign and reflection of mutual respect between management and workers and of their joint commitment to quality. Suggestion activities thus had a somewhat different significance in the two countries.

Quality Control Circles

Consistent with its *kaizen* philosophy, Toyota devoted substantial resources to supporting Quality Control circles. Each work team also met as a circle, typically twice a month on overtime. Like suggestions, QC circle activity at Toyota had a "mandatory voluntary" character (Grønning, 1992). Extensive engineering and administrative support ensured responsiveness to the circles' suggestions. Training courses for managing QC circle activity were long: nine days for Group Leaders and Team Leaders, and a further eight days for Assistant Managers. In contrast, American companies often seemed to underestimate the support required for an effective QC program, which is probably why the "mortality rate" of American QC programs was very high (Lawler and Mohrman, 1985). For the auto sector, MacDuffie (1996) found that in 1993, 90 percent of workers in Japanese plants participated in some kind of employee involvement group; the comparable figure for U.S. manufacturers was 26 percent, and for the Japanese transplants in the United States it was 25 percent.

NUMMI's QC circle program (called "problem-solving circles") was relatively new, having begun in 1991. Toyota managers thought of QC circles as an advanced practice, requiring deep production knowledge that took years to acquire; they thus waited several years before establishing PSCs at NUMMI. NUMMI's PSCs were more truly voluntary than those at Toyota, although participation was expected of workers hoping for promotion to Team Leader positions. PSCs were structured as standing committees based on work groups (not teams, as in Toyota). In an average month during 1994, 14 percent of NUMMI workers participated in the PSC program.

TMMK started its quality circle program in 1989, sooner after plant startup than NUMMI. According to a manager I interviewed, "Mr. Cho had planned to wait five years before launching QCs, since he was skeptical of their value before we understood our processes. But the Team Members forced the pace. They heard about plans for QCs in the future during their assimilation training and urged us to get going on it. So the program was launched in 1989." At TMMK as at NUMMI, participation in QCs was voluntary. QCs usually meet monthly on paid overtime. In an average month in 1993, about 40 percent of the eligible people participated in a QC.

Given Toyota's extensive expertise in QC circles, it interesting to note that, before TMMK launched its program, managers visited several American companies to learn how they managed their own programs. An interview with one of the American managers most closely involved with TMMK's QC program generated a list of Japanese and American features of this program and revealed a modest but not insignificant degree of hybridization.

The TMMK system takes some elements from the Japanese approach. We take a practical problem-solving approach—less theoretical than many U.S. programs. QCs here are not "another program"—they are part of TPS and rely on real buy-in from line management. So the program has to connect with management goals and TMMK/Toyota needs. First-line supervisors are actively involved in QC support—running interference, getting data, etc.—in contrast with the more common American approach where QCs are an "off line" activity. Management suggests a list of possible themes, rather than leaving it completely to the QC itself. Line managers [Assistant Managers] act as program administrators—in contrast with most American programs that have a dedicated program administrator for each ten to twenty QCs. We couldn't afford that, and we wouldn't want to, philosophically.

The TMMK system takes some other elements from the American approach. Managers suggest possible themes, but workers chose them— as opposed to management handing them down. Our facilitators really facilitate—versus the more directive Japanese style. Our tools are more American—we don't use Paretos much, for instance. The Japanese are more patient and sometimes seem to go in for overkill in their analysis. In the United States, we have a bias towards action. Now the QC

members themselves are asking for more advanced tools. And participation is voluntary—not mandatory or pseudovoluntary.

TMMK's approach differs from Toyota's in some other ways too.
Unlike Toyota, TMMK has cross-team QCs. Unlike Toyota, we has
QCs in office areas—about twenty-five of them. Toyota has actually
asked us to take the world-wide lead in developing this activity. Toyota
is starting some now. And compared to Toyota, we have far less for-
mality in QC presentations. (interview with TMMK manager)

These modest differences in the transplants' QC circles practices—in particular, the roles of managers and workers in picking topics to work on—reflected an equally modest recontextualization by which U.S. workers saw
circles as somewhat more like a "voice" opportunity, whereas Japanese workers saw them as more like a technical problem-solving mechanism.

Although the idea of QC circles originated in the United States, few American companies had them until the Japanese successes in quality forced American manager to rethink their approach to quality. Foulkes (1980) made no
mention of anything resembling QC circles. In the years since Foulkes's survey, QC circles grew in popularity. In 1993, some 65 percent of Lawler et
al.'s (1995) sample of 1,000 used them, and in more than half these cases,
they covered more than 20 percent of the workforce. Many more organizations use other kinds of temporary employee participation groups. Osterman
(1994) found that 29.7 percent of manufacturing plants he surveyed used
QCs for more than 50 percent of their core workforce.

Overall, the transplants clearly were trying to emulate Toyota's practice
in Japan, but the gap remained considerable.

Information Sharing

Toyota, like other Japanese firms, provided workers with considerably more
information about business performance and its various determinants than
did comparable American firms. Both NUMMI and TMMK followed the
Toyota approach. There was an extensive system of monthly group meetings,
company newsletters, and information memos. TMMK also had its own internal TV system to broadcast information in locations such as the cafeteria.
Workers in both transplants received an impressive amount of sales and quality information, sensitizing them to the strengths and weaknesses of the
plants' performance.

Foulkes (1980) noted that one of his sampled American nonunion firms
held an annual "jobholders' meeting." In another case, "personnel meetings"
were conducted every twelve to eighteen months, sometimes more frequently.
Otherwise, his account had little to say on the subject of information sharing.
Kochan (1980) noted that companies pursuing a union substitution strategy
often deployed "advanced systems of organizational communications and information sharing." Lawler et al. (1995) asked their respondents what kinds
of information were disseminated to more than 60 percent of their employees;

84 percent said they communicated the company's overall results, 66 percent their unit's operating results, 31 percent information concerning new technologies that might affect them, 54 percent business plans and goals, and 25 percent competitors' relative performance. These proportions all increased over the period from 1987 to 1993.

NUMMI and TMMK both rated closer to Toyota than to the Big Three on this point.

Symbols of Unity

MacDuffie (1996) found that U.S. auto companies were moving toward reducing status differentiation but on average still had far more than the Japanese companies, which in turn had more than their transplants. NUMMI and TMMK went further than Toyota and much further than the U.S. Big Three in their symbolic efforts to create a sense of unity. Unlike senior managers in the Big Three and in Toyota's Japanese operations, managers at these transplants had neither separate parking nor cafeterias and more often than not wore uniforms rather than suits

Foulkes's (1980) sampled U.S. companies varied greatly in this dimension. Some had no executive perks: no separate dining rooms or parking spaces, free coffee and doughnuts for everyone, no closed offices. Some even shunned different benefits or bonuses for managers. And some were described as keeping executive salaries relatively low to maintain a sense of unity. Kochan noted that the union substitution strategy typically involved the "development of a psychological climate that fosters and rewards organizational loyalty and commitment."

Overall, NUMMI and TMMK appeared to have gone beyond the Toyota model, by imitating the most egalitarian of the nonunion U.S. firms.

Employment Security

Toyota, like other large Japanese manufacturers, offered its regular employees a degree of employment security that stood in stark contrast with its American peers' aggressive pursuit of numerical workforce flexibility. This security was the material counterpart of symbolic unity, and in this respect NUMMI and TMMK were similar to the parent company.

NUMMI's collective bargaining agreement made an explicit commitment to employment security. NUMMI lived up to this commitment in 1987–88, when capacity utilization fell to under 60 percent but no one was laid off. Workers were put into extra training programs and were put to work on *kaizen* projects and facilities maintenance jobs previously contracted out.

TMMK's commitment was more nuanced. Fearful of the legal consequences of an explicit commitment, and perhaps hoping to reserve for management a greater margin of flexibility in hard times, the TMMK Team Member handbook described "career employment" as a "goal" but emphasized that it is "not a legal commitment nor a contract." In this approach, TMMK resembled Toyota, where the union contract does not specify the kind of guarantees formalized in the NUMMI contract and where, instead, the commitment was primarily a matter of trust.

Unlike Toyota, neither transplant used temporary employees. Transplant managers feared that the use of temporaries would undermine the sense of unity they strove to maintain. In Japan, Toyota had to deal with far larger and more frequent fluctuations in demand.

While employment security, at least for "core" employees, is frequently cited as a distinctive feature of Japanese employment practices, Foulkes (1980) found that almost all the U.S. companies in his sample went to considerable lengths to avoid layoffs. Like Toyota, nonunion American firms surveyed by Foulkes saw important benefits to this policy: better employee morale because of reduced insecurity, less employee resistance to change of methods or technology, lower unemployment insurance costs, savings in hiring and training costs, and an improved corporate image. Since Foulkes's study, however, a growing enthusiasm for downsizing suggests that many nonunion U.S. firms have shifted their philosophy on this issue.

NUMMI rated close to Toyota on this dimension, although its more formalized commitment and its lack of temporary workers suggest a significant degree of hybridization. TMMK's more nuanced position resembled that found both in Toyota and in the (older) union substitution model, but here, too, the absence of temporary workers suggests some degree of hybridization.

Labor Relations

Toyota, like other Japanese auto companies, had an enterprise-based union. All blue-and white-collar employees, as well as managers up to the middle ranks, were union members. Since the major conflicts of the early 1950s, relations between union and management had been very cooperative, with a comprehensive structure of union/management consensus building, consultation, and informational forums at the corporate, plant, and workplace levels. Senior union leaders often moved into senior management roles. The contrast with the arm's-length and often adversarial relations between the Big Three and the UAW was striking. Supervisors were barred from union membership in the United States.

While UAW Local 2244 retained its affiliation with the International union, the local's leadership cooperated with NUMMI management through an extensive structure of joint committees. As in many Big Three plants, there were weekly meetings between management and the union bargaining committee, weekly safety committee meeting, weekly meetings between section managers and union committeepeople, and quarterly three-day off-site meetings between union and company leadership. Unlike those at many Big Three plants, these meetings often allowed the union to have real influence over policy decisions. Recent shifts in the leadership of the local from the Administration caucus to the People's caucus and back again did not significantly reduce the high level of dialogue and cooperation. The combination of an industrial union with extensive involvement of the local in planning and joint forums suggests that NUMMI represented a hybrid of Toyota and American union traditions.

TMMK was nonunion and followed a conscious union substitution strategy. The analysis offered by a senior TMMK executive (an American) was very similar to that found by Foulkes (1980) in many of his sampled non-union companies:

> Sure, I'd pay $27 a month to have someone represent me—if I didn't trust management. But we try to create and maintain that trust. And a union would create many problems for us because the U.S. labor laws combined with the union structure would encourage an adversarial relationship. . . . We need our workers' trust, and the risk of unionization is just an index of how poorly we are managing. We should be offering all the safeguards of a union contract.

This substitution strategy imposed real constraints on the plant, since the UAW threat is real. In the words of one worker I interviewed:

> I don't hear much talk about a union here. Mind you, the UAW in Georgetown do hand out leaflets occasionally. And I stop to read them. They usually show up when a Team Member calls them when the pressure gets too much, like when we're doing excessive overtime. Some people in the plant obviously want a union. You even see people wearing UAW T-shirts in the plant. I suppose I see some benefit if you're injured. But otherwise, what's the point? The union wouldn't change our pay or benefits.

Indeed, TMMK maintained wage levels very close to those of the Big Three and created numerous forums for employees to voice their grievances and concerns (discussed in next section).

Overall, I rate NUMMI as representing a hybrid of the Toyota and the UAW models. TMMK resembled more closely the union substitution model.

Grievances

Toyota, like other Japanese firms, resolved most grievances through the supervisor and the next levels of management. The union was involved for more serious cases, but even then, their involvement was typically in an informal, joint problem-solving mode. By contrast, grievances in American unionized auto plants were resolved through a formal, quasi-juridical, multistep process that was separate from the day-to-day administration of the plant.

NUMMI's "problem resolution procedure" resembled Toyota's in its emphasis on joint problem solving in the first step, but subsequent steps brought it into closer conformance with the traditional UAW model, including third-party arbitration as the final step. It is, however, noteworthy that the collective bargaining agreement specified that there would be no strikes over health and safety issues. Instead, in case of unresolved disputes in these matters,

"Either party may call upon the UAW Regional Director and W. J. Usery for final resolution of the problem" (1994 Collective Bargaining Agreement, p. 163). (Bill Usery was a mediator instrumental in forging the initial agreement with the UAW.)

In the absence of a union but the presence of a strong union threat, TMMK put into place an extensive set of mechanisms to identify grievances. A "concern resolution process" paralleled NUMMI's problem resolution procedure, but without union involvement. TMMK also had a twenty-four-hour-a-day message system, called the Hotline, where workers could register complaints, anonymously if they desired. All complaints and responses were posted. There were also regular employee opinion surveys (as at NUMMI), roundtable meetings between Team Members and senior management, and managers' "lunchbox meetings." Consistent with its overall labor relations strategy, TMMK devised policies for grievances that fit the union substitution model. This included the traditional limitations of that model (McCabe, 1988): employees filing a concern had no dedicated expert assistance in making their case; there was no final arbitration step; there was no provision for peer review (unlike for discipline cases—see next section); and TMMK was explicit that all concerns had to be presented as individual ones (to avoid the protections afforded "concerted action" under sections 8(a)1 and 7 of the Wagner Act).

Here, as with labor relations, NUMMI represented an innovative hybrid of Toyota and UAW models, while TMMK closely resembled a well-established union-substitution model.

Discipline

The formal process for discipline at NUMMI was similar to that found in UAW plants. It allowed the worker representation by a union committeeperson and included a final arbitration step. I have found no evidence of any Toyota influence in the design of this process.

TMMK's discipline process, the "corrective action program," was described in the employee handbook as one based on "positive discipline." This approach, including the penultimate step of one day of "decision-making leave," was patterned after the policy found in several progressive nonunion U.S. companies (Campbell, Fleming, and Grote, 1985; Cameron, 1984). The final step (for all cases but those that involved serious misconduct) was a voluntary peer review panel made up of three Team Members and two managers. Membership on the panel was voluntary and rotating. Its judgment was only advisory, and there was no external arbitration available to the worker.

The most common discipline problems at both NUMMI and TMMK were due to absences. In Toyota plants, considerable supervisory and peer pressure was applied to keep the absence rate very low. American unionized auto plants were traditionally much more lenient in this domain. NUMMI's absence policies were very formalized and strict. For example, there was no official distinction between excused and unexcused absences outside annual vacations and other officially sanctioned leaves of absence. TMMK had even fewer absences than NUMMI. The team member handbook defined no specific policy on absences. The Group Leaders' policies and procedures manual stated: "Under usual circumstances, we will have a Corrective Action conference if a Team Member accumulates more than five absences within 12 months."

Here again, NUMMI represented a hybrid of Toyota and UAW models, while TMMK resembled the union-substitution model. We should recall, however, that both of these plants also relied on peer pressure from team members to create an informal, lateral discipline regarding absences.

Personnel Selection

It is often asserted that Japanese firms rely on a relatively "homogeneous" workforce in order to maintain a sense of unity, integration, and flexibility. This homogeneity was easier to ensure given the Japanese population characteristics. Moreover, the major auto companies offered highly prized jobs for production workers (at least, until the early 1990s), and Toyota screened applicants very carefully. In contrast, the Big Three plants' workforce was very ethnically diverse, and their traditional selection criteria were very loose.

With the exception of NUMMI's first round of hiring of GM-Fremont veterans, NUMMI and TMMK screened their recruits very carefully. As mentioned earlier, NUMMI interviewed 9,000 people to hire 700 for its truck-line expansion, and TMMK's workforce of 6,200 was selected from a total applicant pool of more than 200,000. Whereas the ethnic and gender diversity record of some Japanese transplants has been lamentable (Cole and Deskins, 1988), Toyota's North American transplants were better than average. NUMMI's workforce was 19 percent African American and 28 percent Hispanic, and, whereas minorities represented 7 percent of Kentucky's workforce, they represented 15 percent of TMMK's production Team Members and 15 percent of the section managers.

At both NUMMI and TMMK, "work ethic," teamwork ability, flexibility, and willingness to learn were the key factors in the selection of new hires. Some 73 percent of workers at TMMK had at least some college education. College education was far less common in NUMMI, perhaps reflecting differences in local labor market opportunities. Interestingly, while TMMK had hired a sizable number of managers from both U.S. auto companies and transplants, it had not sought actively to attract production workers or skilled trades people with prior auto industry experience. (In part, this was due to the incentive package given TMMK by Kentucky, which specified that Kentuckians had hiring priority.)

My interviewees' accounts of TMMK's choice of location in Kentucky were consistent with the arguments advanced by Kenney and Florida (1993) and others that the transplants favored rural labor forces because they were reputed to have lower absence rates. This location, combined with the extensive screening of job applicants, might also have served to reduce the likelihood of hiring people with union sympathies. (For a broader discussion of screening for union sympathies by transplants, see Saltzman, 1995).

GM did not give Toyota any choice of plant location. Moreover, the UAW was a partner in the plant startup at NUMMI and threatened to take to arbitration any refusal to rehire GM-Fremont veterans. As a result, even though applicants went through three days of testing and interviews, only 300 out of 3,000 applicants were turned down. Later rounds of hiring associated with the start of the truck line were highly selective and based on criteria similar to those used at TMMK.

In their early years, both TMMK and NUMMI relied extensively on expatriate advisors from Toyota. NUMMI began operations with 400 Toyota trainers on site. Every American manager was paired with a Japanese counterpart. While NUMMI relied extensively on the Takaoka plant for this assistance, TMMK relied just as much on Tsutsumi. Over time, however, the number of these advisers was greatly reduced, and by 1995 NUMMI had only twenty-five Toyota "coordinators" and managers. Their primary responsibility was facilitating communication with headquarters and with the mother plants in Japan. In both organizations, the executives were mostly American, including the vice presidents for human resources. The presidents of both plants, however, were Japanese.

Foulkes (1980) made only one mention of screening at nonunion U.S. companies. One sampled company centralized all hiring at the corporate level because it thought of itself as hiring for a career, not for a specific job. This was indeed somewhat similar to the Toyota approach that prevails at NUMMI and TMMK. Lawler et al. (1990) noted that new high-involvement plants put considerable emphasis on screening and selection. Kochan pointed out that the union substitution strategy often involved the "location of new production facilities in rural or other weak union areas wherever possible, and in some cases, use of employee selection devices to avoid workers most likely to be pro-union" (1980, p. 185).

Overall, and with the exception of NUMMI's original hiring of GM-Fremont veterans, the two transplants seem close to the union substitution model.

Promotion

There was a considerable difference between Japanese and Big Three policies concerning promotion, both within various worker categories (such as from grade to grade or from Team Member to Team Leader at Toyota or across classifications at the Big Three) and from worker to supervisor. At Toyota, almost all positions were filled from within, and promotions were based on seniority, confidential evaluations, and direct recommendations by superiors. There was neither job posting nor formal testing. In the Big Three, supervisors were often recruited from outside, and changes within worker categories were determined strictly by seniority, with a formal system of job posting.

At NUMMI and TMMK, promotions to Team Leader and Group Leader were almost all from within. Unlike Toyota, NUMMI had a system of job posting. People who wanted promotion undertook training on their own time (twenty hours for promotion to Team Leader), and selection was based on their performance in these classes and in their current jobs. After complaints in NUMMI's early years about favoritism in Team Leader selection, management negotiated a more formal process in which the evaluation and final selection were conducted by a joint union/management committee. Seniority was used only as a tiebreaker. TMMK's system was very similar. Seniority was used as a tiebreaker there, too. One notable difference was that TMMK but not NUMMI included peer evaluation in the selection criteria.

How novel were these practices? Foulkes (1980) summarized the results of his survey in these terms: "Promotion from within is an important cornerstone of the personnel policies and practices of all the companies studied. . . . The majority of companies . . . also have job posting for hourly employees. . . . [But] job posting does seem to tend to drive a company toward giving considerable weight to seniority in promotion decisions" (pp. 143–44). Kochan noted that U.S. companies pursuing a union substitution strategy typically were characterized by "rational wage and salary administration, performance appraisal, and promotion systems that reward merit, but also recognize the relevance of seniority" (1980, p. 185).

In this domain, NUMMI seems to have created a hybrid of Toyota and UAW models, and TMMK a hybrid of Toyota and U.S. union substitution models.

Wages and Benefits

At Toyota, wages and bonuses were based on skill grades, seniority (*nenko*), group performance indices, and personal performance evaluations (*satei*) conducted by supervisors and closed to workers. Since the late 1980s, Toyota had given progressively less weight to group performance and more to individual skill and effort (Grønning, 1995; Shimizu and GEMIC, 1993; Shimizu, 1995). Overall wages and benefits had historically been seen as attractive relative to the available alternatives but still low enough to ensure that workers welcomed regular overtime. In contrast, in the Big Three, wages were determined by a rigid and detailed job classification system, bonuses were based on company-wide profit-or gain-sharing programs, and, overall, auto workers' income was high compared to alternative jobs, especially compared to similarly skilled nonunion jobs.

Neither NUMMI nor TMMK had individualized workers' pay. There was no seniority/age component, no personal assessment, and no group or team performance bonus. Neither plant had differentiated worker skill grades. Both transplants had gain-sharing type programs based on plant performance. At NUMMI, the program paid all workers identical amounts. At TMMK, there were two programs tied to different performance indicators, one based on a percentage of the worker's pay and the other paying identical amounts to all workers.

NUMMI was tied to the Big Three/UAW wage rates. NUMMI workers were also paid for their lunch (thirty minutes), which was very unusual. At GM-Fremont, workers would often leave the plant at lunch and sometimes get a couple of drinks at one of the local bars. NUMMI management feared the quality consequences and created this incentive to keep workers in the plant.

TMMK, too, followed the Big Three/UAW pattern regarding wage levels, a practice Foulkes (1980) found to be common in the union substitution strategies of firms operating in unionized industries. Indeed, TMMK management regularly distributed comparisons of its Team Member wage rates with the Big Three rates. As of 1993, TMMK ranked second—after NUMMI—for both production and skilled trades workers.

Toyota's commitment to training and development led it to distinguish several skill grades and corresponding wage rates within each of the two main classifications. By contrast, neither TMMK and NUMMI distinguished skill grades within production worker, maintenance/skilled trades, or Team Leader ranks. The concern was often expressed at the transplants that such distinctions would be divisive, at least in the current state of the plants' development and culture. However, in a very limited way, "grow-in" periods at TMMK and NUMMI served as a functional equivalent to skill grades. Whereas at GM-Fremont, newly hired production workers started at 92.5 percent of full pay and progressed to the full rate after ninety days, at TMMK and under NUMMI's initial agreement they came in at 85 percent and grew in over eighteen months. In 1991, NUMMI changed this to 75 percent and twenty-four months, then, in 1994, to 70 percent and thirty-six months. Although these changes paralleled changes in the national GM-UAW contract, they raised tensions on the shop floor, where many workers were unhappy working alongside peers who were earning such different rates for the same jobs.

The reluctance to individualize workers' pay more extensively at TMMK appeared similar to the pattern at American nonunion firms. Foulkes (1980) noted, "While merit pay plans are common in the entirely nonunion companies studied, for a variety of reasons they are frequently not administered as the stated policies would have one believe. Instead, the principles of seniority, automatic progression, and equal treatment seem to be given much weight" (p. 185). Unlike many of the nonunion companies surveyed by Foulkes, neither TMMK nor NUMMI put production workers on salary.

Overall, it appears that, in the structure and process of wage determination, NUMMI followed the UAW model with very little Toyota influence, and TMMK followed the union substitution model—and as a result resembled closely the UAW model—with little Toyota influence. Benefits followed the same pattern: whereas Toyota benefits were very comprehensive and extended far into workers' nonwork lives (the company operated its own housing, associations, sports activities, and hospitals for its workers), benefits at

NUMMI and TMMK were more American in their scope and form and much less intrusive of workers' private lives.

The lack of individualized bonuses is in striking contrast not only to the practice at Toyota but also to the practice at a growing number of U.S. nonunion firms, notably ones that fall into the union indifference rather than the union substitution category. Insofar as individualized material incentives might be thought to be functional prerequisites for ensuring workers' ongoing willingness to contribute discretionary effort, rewards for suggestions and (over the longer term) increased opportunities for promotion to Team Leader and beyond might be interpreted as functional equivalents, albeit only weak ones.

Health and Safety

An important set of HR policies in an auto plant is directed at health and safety. In U.S. industry as a whole, underreporting of occupational illnesses and injuries was frequent until the federal Occupational Safety and Health Administration (OSHA) stepped up pressure in the mid-1980s. As a result of this pressure, the OSHA-recordable incidence rate in the motor vehicle industry (SIC code 3711) climbed from 5.5 per 100 employee-years in 1985 to 32.3 in 1992. Underreporting in Japan was even more extreme. Middle managers in Japanese auto companies were under pressure to report as few occupational injuries and illnesses as possible, and workers often concealed their disorders for fear of embarrassing their work group or disrupting their group's or factory's perfect "no accident" ratings (Wokutch, 1992, pp. 104).

The assessment of a number of knowledgeable interviewees at NUMMI and TMMK was that ergonomic problems were relatively less frequent in Toyota plants than in the transplants (Adler, Goldoftas, and Levine, 1997; studying another company and its U.S. subsidiary, Wokutch, 1992, reached a parallel conclusion). One positive factor appeared to be the greater resources dedicated to health and safety. Each section within the Japanese plants had a dedicated safety person and a dedicated health person—a per-worker staffing ratio some five times greater than NUMMI's. Ergonomic problems appeared to be further reduced in Toyota's Japanese plants by an all-male, physically homogeneous, younger production workforce. (Older workers were rarely found on the assembly line, where the jobs were the most physically demanding—they were either promoted or moved into physically easier off-line jobs, or they quit.) The smaller variance in height, weight, and strength among Japanese workers made it easier to ensure optimal processes, tools, and layouts.

At NUMMI, several rounds of workstation evaluation focused on trouble spots, but, until 1994, ergonomics did not appear to be a high priority for the plant. In January 1993, California's Occupational and Safety and Health Administration (Cal-OSHA) issued three citations against NUMMI, of which two were rated "serious." NUMMI appealed, and, in January 1994, a settlement was reached that obligated NUMMI to higher levels of ergonomics monitoring, evaluation, training, and staffing. A separate agreement with the UAW local created a union ergonomics representative position alongside the existing health and safety representative position. These changes brought NUMMI close to the ergonomics approach of the Big Three. In 1994 NUMMI management made ergonomics improvement a strategic priority, and in 1995 ergonomics results started to improve significantly.

At TMMK, a surge in repetitive strain problems a few months after plant start-up prompted management to give ergonomics a high priority. Several rounds of work station evaluation focused on trouble spots, and those problems that were uncovered were systematically addressed. TMMK's health-and-safety-staff-per-employee ratio was nearly twice as large as NUMMI's but still half that of comparable Toyota plants. Unlike Toyota or NUMMI, TMMK hired a qualified ergonomist and installed sophisticated ergonomic testing equipment. TMMK was also distinctive in designing ergonomically balanced rotation sequences. Under a "work-hardening" program, new hires were allowed a slow ramp-up in their work intensity over the first five weeks. They had to learn two jobs in the first four weeks to ensure that they could rotate. TMMK had a program that allowed a gradual, planned reintegration of returning injured workers. Their QC and suggestion programs had at various times made ergonomics a priority, but, unlike those at NUMMI, workers at TMMK had no independent voice on ergonomics issues. The net effect, according to a TMMK HR manager, was notable: "Our injury rate is now down to one-third its peak 1989 level, and about one-fifth the industry average rate."

In health and safety, NUMMI and TMMK both seem to have taken some elements from Toyota but hybridized them with UAW and union substitution practices, respectively.

HRM Administration

Consistent with Toyota's corporate policy of giving its U.S. transplants substantial control in the HR arena, the key HR executives at both plants were U.S. nationals. NUMMI's vice president for human resources, Bill Childs, was recruited from the personnel department at General Dynamics. Alex Warren, senior vice president at TMMK until 1996 but originally responsible for its HR and administration areas, had a background in labor relations at U.S. Steel and at Rockwell and in HR at Leaseway Transportation. TMMK's vice president for human resources, Sam Heltman, came from the HR department at Ford's New Holland plant. In its reliance on local personnel in the HR function, Toyota followed the standard practice of U.S. and European multinationals abroad, and, in particular, the practice of the U.S. Big Three (see Kujawa, 1971).[4]

Notwithstanding the key roles played by these U.S. managers, NUMMI and TMMK gave their HR departments a breadth and influence similar to that enjoyed by HR departments in Toyota's home-country operations. The HR department in many large Japanese firms, like Toyota, was a political "heavyweight," whereas the HR department in corresponding American firms was typically a minor player (Inohara, 1990; Pucik, 1984). One NUMMI manager who had formerly worked in a large unionized American company in a related industry described the differences in these terms:

> At NUMMI, HR takes responsibility for the whole individual. We exercise what you might call "stewardship" over all aspects of the employees' involvement with the company. I can give you many examples of where HR at NUMMI takes responsibility where at an American company the responsibility belongs to another function. For example, HR is "budget responsible" for headcount and overtime. HR holds manufacturing managers to account for their budget expenditures. That's the Toyota approach. At an American firm, it's Finance that plays this role. Payroll here is in HR, not under Finance. Benefits and Pension Plan Accounting is in HR, rather than under Finance or Accounting. All travel approvals go through HR rather than Finance. We have a "team member involvement" group within HR that manages activities such as the suggestion program, ride sharing, and the company picnic. At an American company, these activities would have been dispersed in different departments. HR also has a significant say in things that elsewhere would be the sole province of the manufacturing people, like takt time [line speed] changes. On the other hand, there are some things that we share with line management here that in an American firm would be the sole province of HR, such as training. But, overall, I'd say that in power and influence ranking in the organization here at NUMMI, number one is Production Control, and HR is number two and not far behind. At an American company, it's all power to Finance!

TMMK followed Toyota even more closely in this dimension. The HR department followed Toyota practice and established "HR representatives" who had desks both in the plant and in the HR area. Each HR representative serviced between 250 and 450 employees.

American nonunion firms were, however, rather similar in this emphasis on HR. Mills (1982, p. 148) noted, for example, how "better-standards" nonunion firms often have HR representatives that function somewhat analogously to union representatives as channels for grievances. Foulkes (1980) made a more general argument:

> Personnel departments of nonunion companies have and exercise great power. . . . Much of their clout comes through their close relationship to top management and their delegated audit-and-control role. . . . Line managers are not free to ignore their advice. . . . Perhaps it is accurate to say that the personnel departments in the great majority of companies studied are analogous to those found in Japanese companies. (pp. 95–96)

Notwithstanding this similarity in underlying philosophy and in some specific practices, overall, the role of the HR department in the transplants resembled most closely that found in Toyota's home-country operations. The contrast with the Big Three was huge. Top management saw HRM as a critical ingredient of their success. While headquarters saw the need to hybridize HRM with local approaches, this was the result not of seeing HRM as unimportant, but, on the contrary, of the high priority accorded by top management to the task of forging an HRM system that both complemented the Toyota Production System and fit with the local context.[5]

Discussion

The previous section reviewed the key HRM components at NUMMI and TMMK; this section attempts to synthesize. The key findings of the previous section are summarized in Table 3.4.

First, we can see some commonalties across the plants. Notably, the Toyota model predominated in the domains of work organization, learning, and HR administration, whereas hybridization and adoption of indigenous American models prevailed in the domain of employment relations.

These patterns are consistent with the propositions summarized in Table 3.2. Components of HRM that were closest to the Toyota Production System—work organization and learning—were hybridized the least. Toyota saw the implementation of TPS—a technology that Toyota saw as a source of competitive advantage—as critical to the subsidiaries' effectiveness and control. Consistent with proposition 1, those HRM components that were the most directly related to TPS were the most directly modeled on Toyota. Conversely, and consistent with propositions 1, 3, and 4, components of HRM that fell most directly under local law, custom, and scrutiny—components I have grouped under "employment relations"—were hybridized the most. Employment relations were particularly subject to hybridization pressure since this domain is most strongly influenced by the legal environment (Edelman, 1990): it encompasses those components where conflicts of interest between workers and managers are most likely, and labor and employer groups have mobilized considerable political resources over many decades to create a dense fabric of laws and regulations to govern this domain. The effect of these laws and regulations can be seen rather directly in Cal-OSHA's citation of NUMMI and, more indirectly, in the considerable investment in ergonomics made by TMMK.

Second, we can compare the two plants. Overall, NUMMI adopted many Toyota features and hybridized some with features of the UAW model and the American union substitution model; the total influence of the parent company seems to have been considerably larger than the combined effect of the two host-country models. TMMK showed somewhat less Toyota influence than NUMMI; it developed some interesting hybrids, but it seems to have relied more on the union-substitution model than NUMMI did on the UAW model.

These patterns are only partially consistent with the hypotheses presented in Table 3.1. Yes, on balance, both plants adopted numerous facets of the

Table 3.4 Summary: Primary Influences on HRM Practices

Domain	Component	NUMMI			TMMK	
Work organization	Job classifications	Toyota			Toyota	
	Production teams	Toyota			Toyota	
	Job rotation	Toyota			Toyota	
	Roles of supervisors	Toyota			Toyota	
Individual and organizational learning	Training	Toyota			Toyota	
	Suggestion program	Toyota			Toyota	
	QC circles	Toyota			Toyota	
	Information sharing	Toyota			Toyota	
Employment relations	Symbols of unity	USM			USM	
	Employment security	Toyota-UAW			Toyota-USM	
	Labor relations	Toyota-UAW			USM	
	Grievances	Toyota-UAW			USM	
	Discipline	Toyota-UAW			USM	
	Personnel selection[c]	UAW-USM			USM	
	Promotion	Toyota-UAW			Toyota-USM	
	Wages and benefits	UAW			USM	
	Health and safety	Toyota-UAW			Toyota-USM	
Administration	Role of HR department	Toyota			Toyota	
Overall	Total scores[b]	Toyota 12.0	USM 1.5	UAW 4.5	Toyota 10.5	USM 7.5

a. Coding: Toyota = close to Toyota's practices in its Japanese operations; USM = close to the practices characteristics of the American union substitution model; UAW = close to the progressive union model of the United Auto Workers; Toyota-UAW = a hybrid between Toyota and UAW models; Toyota-USM = a hybrid between Toyota and the American union substitution model.

b. Scoring: Each mention of a model as the sole influence is scored as 1 point, and each mention as a shared influence (hybrid) is scored as 0.5 points. The overall pattern of the results is not changed by the use of alternative plausible scoring schemes.

c. Personnel selection at NUMMI was originally conducted like a recall under strong UAW influence. In later rounds of hiring, the union played only a minor role.

Toyota model. But, TMMK showed less, not more, Japanese influence than NUMMI. Notwithstanding the fact that TMMK produced considerably more cars and profits than NUMMI (*pace* B3), that TMMK was established when Toyota had more international experience (*pace* B7), that NUMMI was a joint venture while TMMK was wholly owned (*pace* B9), that TMMK was a greenfield and NUMMI a brownfield site (*pace* C2), that TMMK disposed of more power vis-à-vis local government and workers (*pace* C3), that TMMK was not unionized (*pace* C4), that it had more expatriates than NUMMI (*pace* C5), that it was formed more recently (*pace* C6), that it was located in a more rural area (*pace* C10), that it had a more homogeneous workforce (*pace* C11), and that the local labor market offered fewer alternatives (*pace* C12)—notwithstanding all this, TMMK appears to be more, rather than less, localized than NUMMI.

Why should this be the case? We need to go back to the reasoning underlying this part of Table 3.1. The original studies assume that, in defining its HRM approaches, the subsidiary is pulled by competing forces from the parent and from the local environment. The underlying assumption is, therefore, that *ceteris paribus* the parent would prefer that the subsidiary adopt its policies and that it is the technical and institutional constraints of the local environment that stop that adoption. But what if the parent interprets its overseas expansion as an organizational learning process, where it discovers not only constraints but also resources in the subsidiaries' local environments? The history of both NUMMI and TMMK seems to support such a view: entering the United States, Toyota invented ways of working effectively with the UAW at NUMMI and sought out proven effective union substitution-style policies at TMMK. Such a "strategic" view of subsidiary organizational design is also supported by the apparently disconfirming pattern found in Japanese subsidiaries established in the United States in the prior period. Prior to the 1980s, Japanese transplants in the United States almost always adopted North American practices, but this was the result not of local constraints so much as of a decision by Japanese firms: "Japanese firms were not as confident in the 1970s as they are now regarding the merits of their work systems" (Cutcher-Gershenfeld et al., 1994, pp. 54–55).

Prior research has tended to exclude this active organizational learning hypothesis by its interpretation of theories of resource dependence, of institutional, and of culture. First, theories of resource dependency assume that all actors seek autonomy and therefore that subsidiaries fight for local control, while headquarters fights for central control (Pfeffer and Salancik, 1978). This appears to be too cynical a view, at least when applied to a company like Toyota that appears to have been rather effective at maintaining the salience of superordinate goals.

Second, much institutional theory implies that isomorphism is based on a process in which taken-for-granted values and schemas are absorbed into the new organization (e.g., Zucker, 1987). Our analysis of two plants has shown, however, that this view of the process of isomorphism is too passive. Institutionalization, as Scott (1991) has argued, should not be construed so as to preclude all elements of strategic choice. Some multinationals might indeed set the goal of subsidiaries' human resource management as minimizing labor costs while avoiding labor relations and regulatory strife—as suggested by Kujawa's (1971) study of the Big Three in Europe; if so, and if labor unions and regulations were powerful, then we would hypothesize that HRM would be strongly conditioned by institutional legitimacy considerations and only weakly influenced by technical efficiency considerations. Toyota, in contrast, appears to have seen HRM as a more critical, strategic issue, just as important as its production system in ensuring competitive performance; under such circumstances, HRM would be subject to intense pressure of both legitimacy and efficiency kinds—which, indeed, seems to have been the case in the two transplants.

The view of hybridization afforded by these two cases also undercuts the credibility of simplistic conceptions of culture. Researchers in international management have argued that national cultures are important constraints on management practices (e.g., Erez and Early, 1993; Ishida, 1986). Japanese culture is said to differ from American by being relatively high on tolerance for uncertainty and on masculinity and relatively low on individualism (Hofstede, 1980). Some practices in Toyota's American subsidiaries appear consistent with this view—such as the absence of seniority-based pay—but others appear anomalous—such as the successful use of production teams and symbols of unity. It is difficult to see how generalized views of national culture could generate strong predictions concerning the more concrete and specific practices analyzed here (see also Jackson and Schuler, 1995). The subtly nuanced portrait of cultural hybridization at NUMMI drawn by Wilms, Hardcastle, and Zell (1994) shows something of the challenge that faces theorists of culture.

Conclusion

This chapter has examined the HRM approaches of two Japanese transplants. The main empirical findings are these: (a) overall, these subsidiaries' HRM approaches were neither purely Japanese nor purely American but, rather, hybrids; (b) Japanese approaches were adopted in policies that addressed work organization, learning, and administrative process, whereas localization or hybridization was the norm in the various components of employment relations domain; (c) this hybridization drew not on one homogeneous host-country model but, rather, on diverse models available in the host country—both a progressive union model and a union substitution model; and (d) under rather different HRM approaches, Toyota's Japanese plants and its two U.S. subsidiaries all achieved world-class levels of productivity and quality.

These findings resemble those of White and Trevor (1983) in their study of Japanese subsidiaries in the United Kingdom. In both the U.S. and in the U.K., the different HRM components were designed in a spirit of "piecemeal pragmatism," rather than wholesale adoption of Japanese approaches, but this pragmatism was quite the opposite of following local practice "in purely passive way"; it reflected the "serious interest taken by senior management" in HRM.

The main theoretical conclusion is that we must avoid seeing hybridization in terms that are too generic. Not only are different components of a subsidiary's HRM system subject to different pressures, but the pressures coming from the local environment are neither entirely homogeneous nor entirely deterministic. Foreign subsidiaries in the United States (or elsewhere) operate within a complex cultural, social, and institutional context that affords—indeed, demands—interpretation, choice, and learning.

Some caveats should be noted. In particular, these two plants' HRM approaches may yet change. Institutional theory suggests that once "imprinted" with a viable set of HRM policies, organizations will only change under the impact of major disruptions in the external environment; but such disruptions are hardly inconceivable. In 1987–88, when NUMMI's capacity utilization fell below 60 percent, it was politically unthinkable that Toyota allow its first transplant, a plant created in large measure to defuse trade pressures, to lay off workers; but what will happen when these subsidiaries mature and when, as is likely to happen one day, economic conditions deteriorate again? It is not inconceivable that such a change could happen under global business conditions that limit the support that Toyota could offer its transplants. In this scenario, the sense of unity between plant management and workers may either crumble or come to appear less salient than the conflict of interests between the global corporation and its local workers. HRM policies could change in ways difficult to predict.

This study suggests some directions for future research. First, we might usefully seek to explore through more systematic surveys the determinants of hybridization. Second, if, indeed, overseas subsidiaries engage in a process of organizational learning in defining and refining their operations, future research might also explore more closely the microprocesses by which this learning takes place. Third, these subsidiaries' HRM approaches appear to have been very stable over time; it would, therefore, be useful to analyze the ways in which multinationals shape the HRM choices of their subsidiaries in their initial planning phases. Finally, it is important to understand how firms that engage in a process of globalization—such as Toyota has done in recent years—learn over time how to make better organization design choices in the startup of new subsidiaries.

While research into the specific features of transplants' HRM and production systems and on the forces that shape them needs to be pursued and rendered more systematic, we should be careful not to lose sight of the forest for the trees. Some researchers (e.g., Kenney and Florida, 1993) see these Japanese approaches as the core of a profoundly new model of management. According to an old proverb, "When the master points at the moon, the fool looks at the finger." Given that there is some—perhaps extensive—hybridization when the Japanese approaches are exported overseas, future research should keep in sight the bigger question: what is the resulting vector of change in the broader, overall pattern of management practices in U.S. industry?

Notes

1. Since the present study focuses on manufacturing workers, in developing this categorization I adopted the perspective of the operations function. It can be compared to Tichy et al.'s categorization (1982)—selection, appraisal, rewards, development—which adopts the HR function's point of view and ignores the work organization and administration domains and the industrial relations components. Beer et al. (1984) adopt a general management point of view, leading them to distinguish employee influence, human resource flows, reward system, and work system.

2. Unless otherwise specified, Toyota refers to Toyota's operations in Japan.

3. For an analysis of stability and change at NUMMI, see Adler, Goldoftas, and Levine 1998. In contrast with the two Toyota transplants, HRM policies at the Mazda Flat Rock plant were poorly adapted and have evolved considerably (see Babson, 1994).

4. Toyota's approach differed from the one Yoshino (1973) found in a sample of Japanese-owned companies in Thailand. There, more than half the personnel managers were Japanese nationals. Compared to subsidiaries of companies based in other countries, the Japanese subsidiaries in Thailand and in other Asian countries relied far more on expatriates. However, Toyota's approach to its U.S. affiliates was not unusual: in his study of nine Japanese transplants in the U.S. (including Honda motorcycles but none in the auto industry), Kujawa (1986) found that all of them had U.S. nationals heading their personnel functions.

5. I would hypothesize that, at NUMMI and TMMK, the ratio of HR department staff to total plant headcount was much higher than at comparable Big Three plants. However, there are no such comparable plants because Big Three plants relied on their corporate staff for much of their labor relations and some of the other HRM domains, whereas NUMMI and TMMK were more like stand-alone businesses in these regards.

References

Abo, Tetsuo, ed. 1994. *Hybrid Factory: The Japanese Production System in the United States.* New York: Oxford University Press.

Adler, Paul S. 1993. "The New 'Learning Bureaucracy': New United Motors Manufacturing, Inc." In Barry Staw and Larry Cummings, eds., *Research in Organizational Behavior,* pp. 111–194. Greenwich, Conn.: JAI Press.

Adler, Paul S., Barbara Goldoftas, and David I. Levine. 1997. "Ergonomics, Employee Involvement, and the Toyota Production System: A Case Study of NUMMI's 1993 Model Introduction." *Industrial and Labor Relations Review* Apr.: 416–437.

Adler, Paul S., Barbara Goldoftas, and David I. Levine. 1998. "Stability and Change at NUMMI." In Robert Boyer, Elsie Charron, Ulrich Jürgens, and Steven Tolliday, eds., *Between Imitation and Innovation: Transfer and Hybridization of Production Models in the International Automobile Industry,* pp. 128–160. New York: Oxford University Press.

Babson, Steve. 1994. "Mazda and Ford at Flat Rock: Transfer and Hybrid-ization of the Japanese Model." Paper prepared for the GERPISA con-ference, Berlin, Wayne State University, Oct.

Banks, Robert F., and Jack Stieber. 1977. "Introduction." In Robert F. Banks, and Jack Stieber, eds., *Multinationals, Unions, and Labor Relations in Industrialized Countries.* Ithaca, N.Y.: New York State School of Indus-trial Relations.

Barley, Stephen R., and Gideon Kunda. 1992. "Design and Devotion: Surges in Rational and Normative Ideologies of Control in Managerial Dis-course." *Administrative Science Quarterly* 37: 363–399.

Bartlett, Christopher, and Sumantra Ghoshal. 1989. *Managing across Bor-ders: New Organizational Responses.* Boston: Harvard University Press.

Beechler, Schon, and Sully Taylor. 1994. "The Transfer of Human Resource Management Systems Overseas: An Exploratory Study of Japanese and American Maquiladores." In Nigel Campbell and Fred Burton, eds., *Jap-anese Multinationals: Strategies and Management in the Global Kaisha,* pp. 157–185. New York: Routledge.

Beechler, Schon, and J. Z. Yang. 1994. "The Transfer of Japanese-style Man-agement to American Subsidiaries: Contingencies, Constraints, and Competencies." *Journal of International Business Studies* 3: 467–491.

Beer, M., B. Spector, P. R. Lawrence, D. Q. Mills, and R. E. Walton. 1984. *Managing Human Assets.* New York: Free Press.

Brannen, Mary Yoko. 1992. " 'Bwana Mickey': Constructing Cultural Con-sumption at Tokyo Disneyland." In J. Tobin, ed., *Remade in Japan: Everyday Life and Consumer Taste in a Changing Society.* New Haven: Yale University Press.

Brown, Clair, and Michael Reich. 1995. "Employee Voice in Training and Career Development." Paper presented at the IRRA meetings, Washing-ton D.C., Jan.

Cameron, D. 1984. "The When, Why and How of Discipline." *Personal Journal* July: 37–39.

Campbell, D. N., R. L. Fleming, and R. C. Grote. 1985. "Discipline without Punishment at Last." *Harvard Business Review* July–Aug: 162–178.

Cole, Robert E. 1972. "Functional Alternatives and Economics Develop-ments." *American Sociological Review* 38: 424–38.

Cole, Robert E. 1979. *Work, Mobility, and Participation: A Comparative Study of American and Japanese Industry.* Berkeley: University of Cali-fornia Press.

Cole, Robert E., and Donald Deskins. 1988. "Racial Factors in Site Location and Employment Patterns of Japanese Automobile Firms in America." *California Management Review* 31(1): 9–23.

Cutcher-Gershenfeld, Joel, and Associates. 1994. "Japanese Team-Based Work Systems in North America: Explaining the Diversity." *California Management Review* 37(1): 42–64.

Doz, Yves L., Christopher A. Bartlett, and C. K. Prahalad. 1981. "Global Competitive Pressures and Host Country Demands: Managing Tensions in MNCs." *California Management Review* 23: 63–73.

Doz, Yves, L., and C. K. Prahalad. 1984. "Patterns of Strategic Control within Multinational Corporations." *Journal of International Business Studies* 15(2): 55–72.

Eads, G. C. 1987. "Comments and Discussion." *Brookings Papers on Eco-nomic Activity* 3: 720–725.

Edelman, Lauren B. 1990. "Legal Environments and Organizational Gover-nance: The Expansion of Due Process in the American Workplace." *American Journal of Sociology* 95(6): 1401–1440.

Elger, Tony, and Chris Smith, ed. 1994. *Global Japanization: The Transnational Transformation of the Labour Process.* New York: Routledge.

Erez, Miriam, and P. Christopher Early. 1993. *Culture, Self-Identity and Work.* New York: Oxford University Press.

Foulkes, Fred. 1980. *Personnel Policies in Large Nonunion Companies.* Englewood Cliffs, N.J.: Prentice Hall.

Goehle, D. G. 1980. *Decision Making in Multinational Corporations.* Ann Arbor: University of Michigan Research Press.

Grønning, Terje. 1992. "Human Value and 'Competitiveness': On the Social Organization of Production at Toyota Motor Company and New United Motor Manufacturing, Inc." Ph.D. diss., Ritsumeikan University Graduate School of Sociology.

Grønning, Terje. 1995. "Recent Developments at Toyota Motor Co." In Åke Sandberg, ed., *Enriching Production: Perspectives on Volvo's Uddevalla Plant as an Alternative to Lean Production,* pp. 405–426. Aldershot: Avery.

Grønning, Terje. 1997. "Technical, Social and Political Dimensions of Labour Groupification: A Comparison of the Ford and Toyota Plants in Kentucky, USA." Paper presented at the 17th International Labour Process Conference, Edinburgh, Mar.

Hannon, John M., Ing-Chung Huang, and Bih-Shiaw Jaw. 1995. "International Human Resource Strategy and Its Determinants: The Case of Subsidiaries in Taiwan." *Journal of International Business Studies* 3: 531–54.

Hofstede, Geert. 1980. *Culture's Consequences: International Differences in Work-related Values.* Beverly Hills, Calif.: Sage.

Holley, William H., and Kenneth M. Jennings. 1994. *The Labor Relations Process.* Chicago: Dryden Press.

Holusha, John. 1989. "No Utopia, but to Workers It's a Job." *New York Times,* Jan. 29, Section 3: 1.

Inohara, Hideo. 1990. *Human Resource Development in Japanese Companies.* Tokyo: Asian Productivity Organization.

Ishida, Hideo. 1986. "Transferability of Japanese Human Resource Management Abroad." *Human Resource Management* 25(1): 103–120.

Jackson, Susan E., and Randall S. Schuler. 1995. "Understanding Human Resource Management in the Context of Organizations and Their Environments." *Annual Review of Psychology* 46: 237–264.

Johnson, Chalmers. 1988. "Japanese-style Management in America." *California Management Review* 30(4): 34–45.

Kenney, Martin, and Richard Florida. 1991. "Transplanted Organizations: The Transfer of Japanese Industrial Relations to the U.S." *American Sociological Review* 56: 381–398.

Kenney, Martin, and Richard Florida. 1993. *Beyond Mass Production: The Japanese System and Its Transfer to the U.S.* New York: Oxford University Press.

Kochan, Thomas A.. 1980. *Collective Bargaining and Industrial Relations.* Homewood, Ill.: Irwin.

Koike, Kazuo. 1984. "Skill Formation Systems in the U.S. and Japan: A Comparative Study." In ed., Masahiko Aoki, *The Economic Analysis of the Japanese Firm,* pp. 47–75. New York: Elsevier/North Holland.

Krafcik, John. 1989. "A New Diet for U.S. Manufacturing: The Auto Industry Enters the 1990s." *Technology Review* Jan. 28–35.

Kujawa, Duane. 1971. *International Labor Relations in the Automotive Industry: A Comparative Study of Chrysler, Ford and General Motors.* New York: Praeger.

Kujawa, Duane. 1986. *Japanese Multinationals in the United States: Case Studies*. New York: Praeger.

Lawler, Edward E., III. 1990. "The New Plant Revolution Revisited." *Organization Dynamics* 19(2): 5–14.

Lawler, Edward E., III, Susan A. Mohrman, and Gerald E. Ledford Jr. 1995. *Creating High-Performance Organizations*. San Francisco: Jossey-Bass.

Lawler, Edward E., III and Susan A. Mohrman. 1985. "Quality Circles after the Fad." *Harvard Business Review*, 85(1): 64–71.

MacDuffie, John Paul. 1996. "International Trends in Work Organization in the Auto Industry." In L. Turner and K. C. Wever, eds., *The Comparative Political Economy of Industrial Relations*, Madison, Wisc.: Industrial Relations Research Association, pp. 71–113.

MacDuffie, John Paul, and Thomas A. Kochan. 1995. "Do U.S. Firms Invest Less in Human Resources? Training in the World Auto Industry." *Industrial Relations* 34(2): 147–168.

Martinez, Zaida L., and David A. Ricks. 1989. "Multinational Parent Companies' Influence over Human Resource Decisions of Affiliates: U.S. Firms in Mexico." *Journal of International Business Studies*, 1: 465–487.

McCabe, Douglas M. 1988. *Corporate Nonunion Complaint Procedures and Systems*. New York: Praeger.

Milkman, Ruth. 1991. *Japan's California Factories: Labor Relations and Economic Globalization*. Los Angeles: Institute of Industrial Relations, UCLA.

Mills, Daniel Quinn. 1982. *Labor-Management Relations*, 2nd ed. New York: McGraw-Hill.

Monden, Y. 1983. *Toyota Production System*. Atlanta, Ga.: Institute of Industrial Engineers.

Oliver, Christine. 1991. "Strategic Responses to Institutional Processes," *Academy of Management Review* 16(1): 145–179.

Osterman, Paul. 1994. "How Common Is Workplace Transformation and How Can We Explain Who Adopts It?" *Industrial and Labor Relations Review* Jan.: 47: 175–188.

Osterman, Paul. 1995. "Skill, Training, and Work Organization in American Establishment." *Industrial Relations* 34(2): 125–146.

Perlmutter, Howard V. 1969. "The Tortuous Evolution of the Multinational Corporation." *Columbia Journal of World Business* 4: 9–18.

Pfeffer, Jeffrey, and Gerald R. Salancik. 1978. *The External Control of Organizations*. New York: Harper and Row.

Prahalad, C. K, and Yves L. Doz. 1987. *The Multinational Mission: Balancing Local Demands and Global Vision*. New York: Free Press.

Pucik, Vladimir. 1984. "White-Collar Human Resource Management: A Comparison of U.S. and Japanese Automobile Industries." *Columbia Journal of World Business* Fall: 87–94.

Robinson, Alan G., and Dean M. Schroeder. 1993. "Training, Continuous Improvement, and Human Relations: The U.S. TWI Programs and the Japanese Management Style." *California Management Review* Winter: 35–57.

Rosenzweig, Philip M., and Nitin Nohria.1994. "Influences on Human Resource Management practices in multinational corporations." *Journal of International Business Studies* 2: 229–251.

Rosenzweig, Philip M., and Jitendra V. Singh. 1991. "Organizational Environments and the Multinational Enterprise." *Academy of Management Review* 16(2): 340–361.

Saltzman, Gregory M. 1995. "Job Applicant Screening by a Japanese Transplant: A Union-Avoidance Tactic." *Industrial and Labor Relations Review* 49(1): 88–104.

Schonberger, Richard J. 1982. *Japanese Manufacturing Techniques.* New York: Free Press.

Schroeder, Dean M., and Alan G. Robinson. 1991. "America's Most Successful Export to Japan: Continuous Improvement Programs." *Sloan Management Review* Spring: 67–81.

Scott, W. Richard. 1987. *Organization: Rational, Natural and Open Systems,* 2nd ed. Englewood Cliffs. N.J.: Prentice Hall.

Scott, W. Richard. 1991. "Unpacking Institutional Arguments." In Walter W. Powell and Paul J. DiMaggio, eds., *The New Institutionalism in Organizational Analysis,* pp. 164–182. Chicago: University of Chicago Press.

Schuler, Randall S., Peter J. Dowling, and Helen De Cieri. 1993. "An Integrated Framework for International Human Resource Management." *International Journal of Human Resource Management* 4, (4): 717–764.

Shimizu, Koichi. 1995. "Humanization of the Production System and Work at Toyota Motor Co. and Toyota Motor Kyushu." In °Ake Sandberg, ed., *Enriching Production: Perspectives on Volvo's Uddevalla Plant as an Alternative to Lean Production,* pp. 383–404. Aldershot: Avery.

Shimizu, Koichi, and GEMIC. 1993. "Toyota." *Actes du GERPISA* 8: 69–198.

Shimizu, Koichi, and Masami Nomura. 1993. "Trajectoire de Toyota: Rapport Salariale and Système de Production." *Actes du GERPISA* 8: 29–68.

Stinchcombe, Arthur L. 1965. "Social Structure and Organization." In James G. March, ed., *Handbook of Organizations,* pp. 142–193. New York: Rand McNally.

Taylor, Sully, Schon Beechler, and Nancy Napier. 1996. "Toward an Integrative Model of International Human Resource Management." *Academy of Management Review* 21(4): 959–985.

Tichy, N., C. J. Fombrun, and M. A. Devanna. 1982. "Strategic Human Resource Management." *Sloan Management Review* 2: 47–61.

Westney, D. Eleanor. 1993. "Institutionalization Theory and the Multinational Corporation." In Sumantra Ghoshal and D. Eleanor Westney, eds., *Organization Theory and the Multinational Corporation,* pp. 53–76. New York: St. Martin's Press.

White, Michael, and Malcolm Trevor. 1983. *Under Japanese Management: The Experience of British Workers.* London: Heinemann.

Wilms, Wellford W., Alan J. Hardcastle, and Deone M. Zell. 1994. "Cultural transformation at NUMMI." *Sloan Management Review* 36, (1): 99–113.

Wokutch. Richard. E. 1992. *Worker Protection, Japanese Style: Occupational Health and Safety in the Auto Industry,* Ithaca, N.Y.: ILR Press/ Cornell University Press.

Womack, James, Daniel Jones, and Daniel Roos. 1990. *The Machine That Changed the World.* New York: Rawson Associates, Macmillan.

Yang, John Zhuang. 1992. "Americanization or Japanization of Human Resource Management Policies: A Study of Japanese Manufacturing and Service Firms in the United States." *Advances in International Comparative Management* 7: 77–115.

Yasuda, Yuzo. 1991. *Forty Years, Twenty Million Ideas: The Toyota Suggestion System.* Cambridge, Mass.: Productivity Press.

Yoshino, Michael Y. 1976. *Japan's Multinational Enterprises*. Cambridge, Mass: Harvard University Press.

Yuen, Edith C., and Hui Tak Kee. 1993. "Headquarters, Host-Culture and Organizational Influences on HRM Policies and Practices." *Management International Review* 33(4): 361–383.

Zucker, Lynne G. 1987. "Institutional Theories of Organization."20 *Annual Review of Sociology* 13: 443–464.

4

Recontextualization and Factory-to-Factory Knowledge Transfer from Japan to the United States

The Case of NSK

Mary Yoko Brannen

Jeffrey K. Liker

W. Mark Fruin

One of the biggest concerns for managers with respect to international technology transfer is the fit between what they are transferring—a nexus of work, technology, and organizational practice—and a new environment. As many researchers have noted, moving technology into new user–operations often leads to a degree of misalignment between the technology and a new environment (see, for example, Busche, 1988; Leonard-Barton, 1992, 1995). Most of the research on internationalization in organizational studies has focused on strategic fit or finding the right corporate strategy to match products and technologies to foreign markets (for useful literature reviews, see Ghoshal, 1987; Kogut, 1989). In addition, these studies have typically concentrated on the tangible or "hard" side of the technologies being transferred. Such work is important in helping us understand and assess the various modes of foreign entry and management available to firms, but its selective view of internationalization as exportation or transnational transmission leaves out an important and increasingly hard-to-ignore part of the story.

As internationalization moves from being export-oriented to concentrating on foreign direct investment (FDI) and transferring abroad whole organizational systems, the tacit, intangible or "soft" side of technology transfer has become more and more important. A fuller account of internationalization needs to examine the host country's response and to include equal scrutiny of the accompanying process of importation or what might be termed cross-cultural acquisition of intangible firm and factory assets (Fruin, 1997; Hall, 1993). Some of the current writings on global strategy have shifted to reflect these changes by concentrating on how the global firm should structure flows of tasks within its world-wide value-added system (Ghoshal and Nohria, 1989). But, by emphasizing the importance of rationalizing task flows that govern the transfer of products and technologies, the importance of internal processes—such as information flows, work practices, organizational culture, and other aspects of the social system in which the products and technologies are embedded—is deemphasized.

Misalignment occurs when technology, work, and organizational fit in one environment prove maladapted to a new environment. The lack of complementary support systems in a new environment precipitates adjustment, adaptation, or some sort of realignment in order for technology to "fit" and be productive in the new setting. Therefore, rather than conceptualizing technology transfer as rational flows of equipment and expertise that are "handed off from one user to another," in this chapter we use the concept of recontexualization (Brannen, 1992; Brannen and Wilson, 1996) to address issues of system embeddedness (both organizational and social) and the iterative and interactive processes of realignment in a new environment.

Recontextualization and the Transfer of Technology

Recontextualization is the transformation of the meaning of firm offerings (e.g., technologies, work practices, and products) as they are uprooted from one cultural environment and transplanted to another. By "cultural environment" we refer both to the organizational culture internal to the firm and to the larger, societal culture external to the firm. Figure 4.1 illustrates the recipient host environment's role in transforming firm offerings.

Every cultural environment is embedded with its own system of organizational signification involving distinct work-related assumptions, behaviors, and practices. Given this reality, misalignments easily occur between what is sent from abroad and how it is perceived locally. Recontextualization involves how firm offerings are initially understood, as well as how meanings evolve in a new environment. Transferred offerings go through a preliminary round of recipient cultural sense making in which they are assimilated into preexisting meanings. Then, as they are implemented, acted on, and interacted with, they continue to undergo recontextualization.

As depicted in Figure 4.1, recontextualization can have positive or negative effects on a firm's internationalization. Successful recontextualization, if the process is properly understood, can become a source of organizational learning and, in turn, become a competitive advantage. Unsuccessful recontextualization, on the other hand, will result in lost opportunities for site-specific

New Cultural Environment

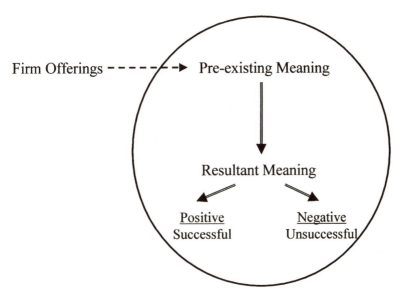

Figure 4.1 Recontextualization of firm offerings.

learning and strategic realignment and may seriously hinder transfer efforts in the most severe cases.

Yet, planning for and monitoring recontextualization are not simple matters. In most cases, managers are initially unaware of all but the most obvious aspects of recontextualization, such as differences in company language, organizational structure, shop floor layout, and industrial and supplier relations. Furthermore, much of recontextualization happens in situ and cannot be planned for. At best, managers become aware of recontextualization as they are confronted with organizational barriers to implementing technology transfer. What they are aware of is only a small part of what is.

Such was the case for NSK, Ltd., as it attempted to transfer technology from Japan to its U.S. plants. Although NSK's Ann Arbor, Michigan, plant has turned out to be somewhat of a success story, success has by no means been realized in a linear fashion, as the story of quality improvement in Ann Arbor will attest. Over a one-year period, 1984–1985, Ann Arbor cut scrap from 5 percent to 2.5 percent. This was remarkable, but it should be said that quality had not improved in thirty years prior to this time. With further efforts, the scrap rate was reduced by a factor of five—to just under 0.5 percent. In other words, the scrap rate moved from 1 out of 20 parts to 1 out of 200 parts during a ten-year period. Compared to NSK's plants in Japan, which run at 0.09 percent scrap, Ann Arbor is still generating more than five times the scrap rate of its Japanese counterparts.

We attribute much of the performance variance to recontextualization, and, in the course of the chapter, we examine both the positive and the negative consequences of recontextualization on the transfer of NSK's Japanese management system (JMS) to Ann Arbor. More generally, we use this case to induce a framework for understanding how recontextualization affects technology transfer. Although the direction and amount of recontextualization cannot be gauged in advance, our framework can help managers anticipate initial misalignments, monitor ongoing adjustments, and take advantage of local innovations in new user environments.

Understanding recontextualization requires a baseline. In the case of NSK, a convenient baseline is the parent plant (*oya-kojo* in Japanese, also called "mother" and, more recently, "sister" plant) in Japan that is assigned to each overseas factory. NSK has three bearing plants in the United States: Ann Arbor, Michigan; Clarinda, Iowa; and Franklin, Indiana. Each has a parent factory in Japan that provides technological, operational, and personnel support for offspring plants. Matches are based primarily on similarity of product lines. In this study we compared one matched pair—NSK's factory in Ann Arbor, Michigan, and its parent factory in Ishibe, Japan. Our research team consists of two business professors, both fluent and literate in Japanese, one in organizational behavior and one in corporate strategy, and an engineering professor with expertise in JMS and technology transfer. Data were collected in both English and Japanese and were mostly qualitative in nature, relying heavily on observation, semistructured interviews, organizational documents, and other secondary data.

Preliminary interviews with the plant manager and his Japanese assistant plant manager in Ann Arbor uncovered a set of core practices and technologies that NSK wished to transfer. We immediately noted a disparity in what the company wanted to transfer and in what was actually transferred. In comparing intended and actual transfer, we noticed that some core aspects of NSK's operations were transferred largely intact, while others were significantly altered. Many of NSK's standards and technical processes, for example, were transferred relatively unaltered, although some were modified. Most notably, the structure and meaning of work teams and teamwork differed significantly between Ann Arbor and Ishibe.

In early interviews, NSK articulated its philosophy of technology transfer. It is necessary to provide technical assistance, particularly in the early stages of overseas operations, to get equipment running in accordance with NSK's standard operating procedures (SOPs), NSK explained. NSK managers claimed that it was not their business to interfere in overseas personnel management issues, or what they called the "people side" of management. It was as if technical standards and SOPs were independent of the social and cultural aspects of their system.

Technology is always coupled with social and cultural systems, and if these linkages are left unmanaged, unexpected outcomes occur, frustrating successful transfer. Japanese managers may say they do not wish to change personnel management practices in America, yet there is a great deal of cultural information being communicated to American plants through Japanese expatriates and by regular visits of American plant members to Japan, as this quotation shows: "We tell our American managers that who is at fault is not important. If you criticize workers they may feel embarrassed" (assistant to plant manager, Ann Arbor plant, 6/14/95). While this statement is consistent with Japanese norms with regard to work responsibility and social sanctions, an emphasis on "face-saving" is not the rule in the United States, where blaming individuals is more common.

The goal of our study was to understand why some, but not all, aspects of NSK's system underwent major transformations when brought to Ann Arbor. In short, we wanted to understand why recontexutalizations occurred in some cases more than in others. The organization of this paper follows our experience trying to answer this question. First, we sketch the company's background, including its general strategy of internationalization. Second, we present an historical account of the development of the Ann Arbor plant. Third, we analyze examples of the management system that NSK wished to transfer and provide a framework for understanding which aspects of it did and did not undergo major recontextualization. We conclude with implications of NSK's case for general issues of overseas technology transfer.

NSK's Internationalization Strategy

NSK has articulated an explicit three-stage strategy for how the company's internationalization efforts will progress. Like that of most firms, NSK's strategy starts with the establishment of overseas sales operations and joint ventures. Its first manufacturing plant overseas was built in São Paulo, Brazil, in 1970. In Ann Arbor, NSK began selling its ball bearings to the Hoover Ball Bearing Company in 1958. This led to a subsequent joint venture with Hoover in Ann Arbor, in 1973, and to the founding of manufacturing facilities in Clarinda, in 1975, and in New Castle, England, in 1976. All of these early internationalization moves were motivated by a desire to be close to important markets, not only because it was troublesome to supply them from Japan but also because ball bearings are intermediate goods. Ball-bearing manufacturers need to be closely involved with their customers early on, in design and development activities that precede production. Obviously, it is far easier and more efficient to supply intermediate products locally than at long distance from Japan.

A second stage of internationalization, the current stage of NSK's progression, is one of factory-to-factory technology transfer and parenting of overseas operations. This strategy can be seen as a nested model of parent-led change at three intraorganizational levels: firm, factory, and shop floor. At the firm level, NSK assigns a mother plant to each overseas plant matched by product and process. Since one mother plant might parent several overseas plants, a separate organizational unit at the mother plant is created for each overseas offspring. This unit is called the overseas management team, and it reports directly to the overseas management department at headquarters. The plant manager and an overseas project manager are included in the administrative core. At the factory level, technical specialists, including an international technology transfer manager, product line managers, engineers, and quality managers, are assigned to the transfer. Finally, the shop floor level is made up of multiskilled workers in Japan who are matched with skilled-trade persons abroad.

The second stage of internationalization may be divided in two: an initial period of direct tutelage when the parent's manufacturing and operating systems are transferred one-to-one to the child, as described earlier, and a later period where what has been transplanted takes on a life of its own as it adapts and is adapted to the social and organizational environment. In NSK's mind, the gap between the two stages may be hardly noticeable or quite substantial, depending on the complexity of what is being transferred and the maturity or sophistication of the receiving body. Although NSK's factory-to-factory approach to technology transfer provides a very strong model, including a strategic vision (the "ball-bearing culture") and a pragmatic strategy listing the technologies, tools, and techniques to be transferred, we found that the model was altered in practice. Our efforts to map why these modifications occurred are represented in Figure 4.3, discussed later in the chapter.

The third stage of internationalization, in NSK's view, is a global network culminating in the technical and organizational independence of four regional manufacturing systems, namely, North America, Europe, Japan, and the rest of Asia. This vision includes a concept of competition and cooperation between the four regions. In other words, the four corners of NSK's global network compete against as well as complement one another.

NSK's Internationalization in the United States

Like many Japanese companies, NSK got its manufacturing start in the United States through a joint venture, in this case with Hoover Corporation. Hoover started as a steel ball company making bicycle bearings in two factory sheds in Ann Arbor in 1913. It gradually moved into making auto bearings, and in 1935 it became the Hoover Ball and Bearing Company. In 1958 Hoover moved to a modern, 180,000-square-foot plant in Ann Arbor and entered into a fifteen-year agreement with NSK in Japan to import and sell NSK bearings in the United States

In 1973, the Hoover-NSK Bearing Company was formed as a joint venture with equal ownership. At this time, NSK saw Hoover as a big, successful American firm and the stronger partner. NSK management still speaks respectfully of how much it learned from Hoover. In 1975, NSK Ltd. acquired Hoover's 50 percent stock ownership and retained the Hoover-NSK name. Also in 1975, Hoover-NSK expanded by building a new bearing plant in Clarinda. In 1985 the name was changed to NSK Corporation, and an additional greenfield plant was added in Franklin, Indiana. Plant expansions at the original plant in Ann Arbor, totaling more than 67,000 square feet, took place in 1987, 1988, and 1990. Clarinda and Franklin are nonunionized greenfield ventures. Ann Arbor, by contrast, is a unionized brownfield venture. The Ann Arbor plant is represented by the United Auto Workers.

The Ann Arbor plant sits on thirty-five acres of land about ten miles south of the University of Michigan and Ann Arbor. About 300 hourly and fifty salaried employees work in the plant, which runs a three-shift operation. The average age of employees is just over forty, and average seniority over ten years. The plant makes bearings for water pumps, magnetic clutches, and wheels and also "single-row" bearings for various uses. "Single-row bearings," as the name suggests, have a single row of bearings, whereas two-row bearings (used for products like automotive air compressors and air conditioners) are more complex, more expensive, and more effective in reducing friction. Single-row bearings are made in much higher volumes at Ann Arbor.

Product variety is much greater than the four lines suggest, as there are about forty or fifty variations within each line. In total, the Ann Arbor plant makes 600 to 700 bearings with different part numbers. In fact, Ann Arbor boasts lower volume, higher variety, and more flexible assembly lines than NSK's plants in Japan and the larger plant in Clarinda. Other than a dedicated water pump line, bearings are run in batches ranging from a few thousand to 20,000 or 30,000. Ishibe, Ann Arbor's parent plant, runs larger batches of the same product, using similar equipment, and there is a good deal of overlap in their product lines. Ishibe makes 7.5 million bearings per month, while Ann Arbor makes about 2.5 million bearings per month.

The plant in Ann Arbor focuses largely on automotive customers while the Clarinda plant concentrates mainly on electrical motor applications. A typical car has more than 200 bearings. So, a major reason NSK wants to maintain a plant in Michigan is to be close to the high concentration of Big Three auto manufacturing in Michigan, Ohio, and Canada. NSK is a first-tier supplier, shipping bearings directly to the auto makers, mainly to the transmission and engine plants.

Core Systems NSK Intended to Transfer

As the largest bearing manufacturer in Japan and the second largest producer of bearings worldwide, NSK is a highly respected company. Fitting with its lead position in the industry, NSK has many excellent manufacturing practices characteristic of top Japanese manufacturers. NSK's plants, both in Japan and abroad, proudly display awards granted by industry such as the ISO/QS 9000 certification, and customers such as Toyota, Nissan, Chrysler, and Ford have given NSK awards for excellence in delivery, performance, and quality. Mr. Ueno, the plant manager of NSK's Ishibe plant—Ann Arbor's parent plant—explained that these practices are integral parts of NSK's "bearing culture" that must be transferred to make high-quality products efficiently. "Bearing culture" is the way things are done within NSK to make high-quality bearings, he intoned; "bearing culture" can be transferred and used universally throughout NSK's global enterprise.

These sentiments were echoed by the vice president of corporate planning, as well as engineers and managers in the overseas project division both at Ishibe and at the Tokyo headquarters. NSK believes very strongly in its engineering standards as essential to high-quality operations. High precision is what drives bearing culture. Tolerances of plus or minus three microns are common. At this level of precision, even a speck of dirt can throw off a bearing's functioning. Follow-up interviews with Mr. Ueno and with members of the internationalization division at headquarters suggested that the formal standardized processes, techniques, and procedures that have evolved within NSK over decades are what they mean by "culture." This was what they wanted to transfer one-to-one.

There are human resource requirements that accompany the successful transfer of NSK's technical system. For example, machine operators need to be flexible, oriented toward problem solving, and capable of maintaining the discipline needed to produce high-quality bearings with a minimum of waste. This, in turn, assumes a shared work culture among employees. However, NSK's teams that were sent overseas were not charged with changing work culture. Rather, their assignment was to set up production equipment and machinery and to teach SOPs to supervisors and operators.

Overview of NSK's Technical Production System

The process for producing bearings is to cast the outer and inner rings in steel (typically done by a separate casting plant), fire the rings at high temperatures to harden them (a process called "heat treat"), grind the inner and outer rings in several phases, grind the grooves ("raceways") in which the steel balls sit (the balls themselves are outsourced), and then assemble the inner and outer rings with the balls in the raceways (see "Phase 2," Figure 4.2). This is a relatively simple process, but the precision required is very high (e.g., tolerances in microns) and there are many individual steps in grinding and assembly.

The "hard side" of the production system (what NSK calls "hardware")— the equipment, technical process flow (such as heat treat and machining), automation, and flexible assembly—has been transferred largely intact from Japan to the United States. In fact, NSK develops and builds some of its own production technology in-house and buys larger pieces of equipment from a small number of Japanese vendors. NSK's general approach to overseas transfer of production technology is to design and build equipment in Japan, set it up and debug it in a Japanese parent facility, bring representatives of the overseas operation to Japan for training on the equipment, and then disassemble and ship it to the overseas facility. It arrives with a complement of Japanese production engineers who help with the local installation and debugging.[1]

The "soft side" of NSK's production system (what NSK calls the "software") has many common features associated with Japanese manufacturing: a strong system of quality assurance, now known as Total Quality Management (TQM), a clean and orderly workplace, very well maintained equipment with thorough preventive maintenance programs, continuous flow production wherever possible, flexible lines to reduce set-up times, and extensive inventory control. A significant portion of NSK's business is automotive, and its largest customer in Japan is Toyota. Despite JMS's many similarities to the Toyota Production System (TPS), NSK engineers in the United States and Japan make it clear that they do not strictly follow TPS. NSK builds in batches, does not use a strict pull system, and tends to have more inventory than plants that follow TPS. A brief summary of the main technical features of NSK's production system follows.

Extensive standardization. NSK has its own "NSK engineering standards" (NES), which are consistent with U.S. and Japan national standards and with I.S.O. standards. As one NSK manager put it: "There are volumes of these standards." They identify all critical dimensions of parts and how to measure them. There are standard tolerances, standards for settings on major operations (e.g., temperature ranges for the heat-treat furnaces), standards on how to transfer production equipment from Japan, and so on. Standards are maintained by a Standards Committee in the Tokyo headquarters. The quality systems are based on NSK's engineering standards, such as NES gauge maintenance programs and NES defect classification schemas, and include appropriate ways to respond to different classes of defects. Standards are created and maintained at corporate headquarters with input from manufacturing facilities.

Quality procedures. Part of the NES are detailed standards for quality procedures. This includes management by eyesight (*me de miru kanri*) (Fruin, 1997; Grief, 1991); statistical process control (used selectively); charting key measurables of cost, quality, delivery, and safety on visible shop floor bulletin boards; and sophisticated metrology labs in each plant to calibrate gauges, test parts, and test alternative product designs. NSK proudly talks of its highly redundant inspection procedure, referred to as 300 percent quality checks, meaning every part is checked multiple times. These checks include automated checkers built into the process, visual checks by operators, and *bakayoke*, also known as *pokayoke*, or mistake proofing. Whenever a bad part is kicked out at any stage, there is 100 percent inspection of all parts by a human inspector. Workers keep inspecting 100 percent of parts until they find three consecutive batches free from defects. One might think this would lead to a huge staff of inspectors. But quality in Ann Arbor has improved so much that the number of dedicated inspectors has gone down to a fraction of what it once was, from fifty-one to ten. In addition, many "inspections" are now automated, and operators are responsible for checking their own quality.

Workplace organization. This is emphasized in many prescriptive books on Japanese manufacturing (cf. Suzaki, 1993). NSK's translation of the famous "5 Ss" is: (1) housekeeping, (2) cleanliness, (3) sweeping/wiping, (4) everything in its place, and (5) discipline.

Equipment maintenance. NSK considers good equipment maintenance to be a subset of TQM. As a form of visual control, large charts in each area list maintenance items for each process, with a schedule represented by columns. Blue stick pins are put in appropriate columns when tasks are done. In this way it is obvious when maintenance is behind schedule. A surprise was the relatively small size of the skilled trades workforce assigned to maintaining equipment in Japan. For example, at the largest production complex in Tamagawa (outside Tokyo), where 550 production workers build almost 11 million bearings each month, there were only ten people assigned to maintaining equipment. In the case of Ishibe, eight people are responsible for maintaining more than 2,500 machines. Equipment maintenance is viewed as a very routine task. NSK expects production workers to do their own routine checking of equipment and most routine preventive maintenance. In its view, production engineering should focus on major equipment upgrades, equipment installation, and some new equipment design.

Continuous flow and inventory control. Continuous flow of materials is central to the philosophy of the Toyota Production System, and, in general, Japanese plants are known to have relatively low levels of work-in-process inventory. Traditional U.S. manufacturers group machines by function, while Japanese manufacturers prefer to organize product flows. A major part of the 1986 renovation of the Ann Arbor plant (discussed in a later section) was focused on shifting from a functional layout to product lines. Work-in-process inventory is not controlled by *kanban* at NSK as it is in Toyota plants, but there are maximum acceptable levels, and inventory is carefully managed. Inventory control is closely related to set-up times. NSK has significantly reduced set-up times but seems to have bottomed out at about two hours in Japan (and far longer in Ann Arbor). A substantial part of that time is spent making the fine adjustments needed to achieve tolerances in microns.

Transferring NSK's Production System

As NSK increased its direct overseas investment in production in the 1970s and 1980s, there was a growing need to support their overseas factories. NSK focused on direct factory-to-factory technology transfer. Since Ishibe is the main NSK producer of automotive components and since Ann Arbor serves the American auto industry, Ishibe was a natural mother plant for Ann Arbor. But in cases where a particular production technology that needs to be transferred is located in one of NSK's other plants, that plant will support Ann Arbor for that technology. The only plant that occasionally supported Ann Arbor was the former Tamagawa plant near Tokyo.

As mentioned earlier, a special team devoted to overseas plant management is set up in each NSK plant. In Ishibe this department is directed by a former production engineer who spent three years in Ann Arbor—Mr. Yano. Mr. Yano was the lead engineer on the Japanese project management team in charge of the renovation. Mr. Yano's title at the Ishibe plant is overseas project senior manager, a staff position that reports directly to the Ishibe plant manager. He is in charge of technology transfer from Ishibe to overseas plants, including the transfer of equipment and people, as well as centralized development and testing of equipment for overseas transfer. As such, Mr. Yano has local staff reporting to him in Japan and expatriates reporting to him from overseas (though day-to-day management of expatriates is handled by Japanese managers on site). The Japanese staff reporting to him at Ishibe have regular line responsibilities, as well as special overseas project team responsibilities.

NSK's typical expatriate is someone with direct production experience (engineering or management) with the particular technologies being transferred who accompanies the equipment to get it running. NSK believes expatriates should go overseas to provide technical assistance, including setting up new equipment and debugging it, making improvements to existing equipment, and training operators. Expatriates should not be placed directly in line management positions; these are left to locals, although there are several plants with Japanese "assistant plant managers," including Ann Arbor. Typical overseas stays are one to five years. There is a strong belief that after five years, expatriate employees might get out of touch with Japanese life, and, perhaps more important, their children might get out of step with the Japanese educational system.

Personnel managers have a significant role in the selection of expatriates and in planning their overseas stay. At Ishibe, Tamagawa, and NSK headquarters, there are similar views of what NSK wants in selecting individuals for overseas assignments. Certain personality characteristics are associated with overseas success, such as openness and the ability to listen. NSK does not believe that expatriates should be skilled as change agents and have responsibility for cultural change in overseas operations. People management should be handled by local plant managers. NSK expatriates should act primarily as technical assistants but should have personal qualities acceptable to locals and that help them fit in. As expatriates are mostly young engineers, their stay abroad will help NSK become a more global company when they return home.

Developing a production system in Ann Arbor that matched the performance of Ishibe was fraught with setbacks and difficulties, as we discuss in the next section. We hypothesize that NSK would have been more successful in its efforts to get Japanese-level performance and could have gotten there more quickly if it had overtly recognized the need for recontextualization and for considering the cultural level along with the technical level. While we cannot prove this hypothesis on the basis of one case study, we will provide examples of recontextualization at Ann Arbor and suggest how cultural barriers to change impeded the transformation process.

Background and Case History of Technology Transfer at the Ann Arbor Plant

We divide our description of the historical development of the Ann Arbor plant into three phases, though the process was continuous and not as clear-cut as this model suggests. We begin at the time NSK decided to make a major investment in renovating the plant, then talk about parent-led renovation, and finally discuss locally led incremental improvement. A summary of the key events in these phases is presented in Table 4.1.

Phase I. History and Context up to 1985

As previously mentioned, Ann Arbor was a U.S.-owned facility until 1973, when NSK and the Hoover Corporation merged as Hoover-NSK. The joint venture lasted two more years, after which time NSK bought out Hoover's share. Hoover was interested in selling because the plant was inefficient and unprofitable. In fact, Hoover got out of the bearing business altogether because the bearing division was not making the 30 to 40 percent profit margin expected for divisions to remain viable. NSK, on the other hand, had a long-term outlook and saw the Ann Arbor plant as an opportunity to expand U.S. auto industry sales. The plant already had some equipment, trained personnel and an existing customer base and was located in Michigan, near the nerve center of the automotive industry.

During this period, the product line was limited to two of the current four lines, and production technology was rudimentary—hourly workers were literally hand-assembling the bearings one by one. NSK did not immediately invest a large amount of money in bringing the plant up to Japanese technological standards. From 1975 to 1985 there were only minor improvements made at the plant. NSK has a numbering system for significant technological improvements in its overseas plants. Each project is given a number, and a group led by a production engineer from Japan is assigned to carry out the project. Over the ten-year period between 1975 and 1985, the Ann Arbor plant underwent six projects, UA1 to UA6 (UA = U.S., Ann Arbor), each involving incremental improvements to the grinders.

Why would a company like NSK, with a long-term outlook, an aggressive globalization strategy, and a desire to break into the Big Three auto business, buy a troubled plant and then let it run at low levels of efficiency and profitability for ten years? This is a question that we asked repeatedly in Ann Arbor and Japan. Numerous answers were given, and they were all subject to the limitations of people's retrospective sense-making abilities. Our best analysis of what happened follows. First, in 1975, at the time NSK bought out Hoover's share, it built a brand-new greenfield plant in Clarinda, Iowa,

Table 4.1 Key Events at NSK–Ann Arbor

Time Period	Events
Phase I: History–1985	
1958	Subcontractor of bearings to Hoover
1973	Joint venture in Ann Arbor, called Hoover-NSK
1975	NSK buys out JV from Hoover; still called Hoover-NSK
1975–84	Modest improvements to equipment
1982	Began quality circle program (QTIPS)
1983	Ford threatens to drop NSK as supplier if quality does not improve
1984–85	Scrap Reduction Team installed; Scrap reduced from 5% to 2.5%
1985	Abandoned QTIPS because of lack of results
1985	NSK concludes Ann Arbor must make major improvements or be closed
Phase II: Parent-Led Change	
1985	Decision in Japan to invest in renovating Ann Arbor plant
1985	Reopened union contract to reduce job classifications and provide flexibility
Oct. 1986	Three-week meeting of Ann Arbor engineers/managers and NSK personnel in Japan to plan renovation
1986–87	Ann Arbor plant renovation
1987–90	Incremental improvements to Ann Arbor plant
Phase III: Locally Led Improvement	
1990–94	Incremental improvements to production equipment
1994	Early contract negotiations with open financial books led to modern operating agreement
1995–97	Designed and implemented product line organization structure and self-directed work teams jointly with UAW
	• Jan.-May 1995—Strategic plan
	• June 1995—Trained top leadership on CI process
	• July 1995—Started CI process with staff team
	• Oct. 1995—First team on the floor
	• May 1996—Teams expanded to other products
Summer 1996	Larry McPherson named to NSK board of directors

and in 1976 it opened another new plant in Peterlee, England. All three plants—at Clarinda, Peterlee, and Ann Arbor—were big ones requiring money, engineering resources, and significant expatriate support. Resources were in scarce supply, so they were focused on getting the new (greenfield) plants up and running. Second, there were internal debates within NSK's board of directors in Tokyo as to whether or not Ann Arbor was a good investment. Without a consensus on this, NSK Japan was slow to invest in Ann Arbor. Third, since the Ann Arbor plant was a unionized brownfield plant with a well-established culture—and not one entirely consistent with NSK's "bearing culture" vision—NSK felt it needed to go slow before making major changes.

In 1982, an NSK team from Japan visited the Ann Arbor plant to consider modernizing the plant. A member of the team was Hajime Otsuka, a grinding engineer who was ultimately given quality assurance responsibility at Ann Arbor and ended up as a pivotal figure in the plant's transformation. He believes that the slow preparation prior to renovation was essential for its success: "We were preparing for the NSK system. At least 95 percent of the work is preparation. Putting in equipment is just 5 percent." When he first arrived in 1982, he tested a sample of parts and found that more than 80 percent were out of NSK's specifications. He showed the test results to American managers, but they did not believe the data and dismissed them. In fact, at one point there was so much resistance to Otsuka's presence that there was a move to send him back to Japan.

But, in 1983, parts procurement managers at Ford Purchasing bluntly said, "We don't want any more of your junk parts." If Ford pulled its business, which was 30 percent of output, the plant would be forced to close. Otsuka reacted. He suggested the plant send NSK employees to Ford plants to sort out the bad parts. Otsuka formed scrap-reduction teams, and defects were reduced from 5 percent to 2.5 percent (see Table 4.1). The American employees realized Otsuka was right and began listening carefully to his advice. When Otsuka was reassigned to Japan in 1989, there was such an emotional reaction to losing their mentor that Ann Arbor employees used their own funds to purchase and plant a Japanese maple tree in his honor at the factory entrance.

During this period of transfer, NSK ran up against many social and cultural barriers to the successful implementation of technology. Many of Hoover's production practices were shocking to the Japanese, including sluggish maintenance, quality not being seen as a line function, and poor housekeeping standards. Moreover, Ann Arbor was saddled with an adversarial union-management relationship. NSK management worked hard to maintain good informal relations with the workforce, believing that more stringent shop floor discipline would upset the fragile peace between management and labor.

Prior to renovation, the technological conditions and management of the plant were nothing short of dismal. There were 500 to 600 employees, with regular layoffs and rehiring as business fluctuated. The plant was dirty and grimy. "The place was in a perpetual oil fog. No one could see each other's face," as one engineering manager explained. Grinding equipment broke down regularly; ball bearings were assembled by hand. There was an army of inspectors. Materials were being picked up and set down seventeen times during the assembly process. Such conditions were far from the excellent state of NSK's manufacturing plants in Japan.

Phase II. Parent-Led Plant Renovation and Improvement, 1985–1990

Renovation made Ann Arbor into a showcase plant—visually, technically, and operationally. By the time the renovation was completed, the total number of employees was down to 220. Under the old system, when bearings were assembled by hand, on "a good day" the plant produced 1,000 pieces per person, with thirty-five assemblers working three shifts. With the new automated lines, the plant often exceeds 1,750 pieces per person, with only two people operating each of the five lines. The job category of "assembler" has now been replaced with "builder" and "packer" in charge of set-up and running the lines. Currently, there are thirty shopfloor workers in total.

When NSK decided to renovate the Ann Arbor plant, Larry McPherson, the plant manager at the time, announced that the union contract should be renegotiated. At the time, business was down and people were being laid off, so the UAW was willing to make concessions in exchange for NSK investment. One major concession was a reduction in job classifications. There had been forty job classifications; that number was halved. Set-up of equipment and operation were done by two different people with two different classifications; after contract negotiations, one job classification could perform both roles, do its own quality inspections, and perform maintenance checks— a system strikingly similar to the one at the parent plant in Ishibe. But in spite of these similarities, there are still fundamental differences. Ann Arbor boasts a history of individualism and contentious union-management relations, while at Ishibe there is a company union, and workers seem willing to follow management's lead (we discuss these differences in greater detail in a later section).

The renovation plan (eventually realized as projects UA7–9) was implemented by a binational team of Americans and Japanese working together. Americans at the Ann Arbor plant were asked to prepare their best plan and to bring it to a three-week working session in Japan, while a Japan-based team developed another plan independently. The U.S.-based team, used to minimal plant expenditures ($30,000 was "big time"), worked to keep down the cost of renovations. It drew four quadrants representing machining, grinding stage 1, grinding stage 2, and assembly and kept these operations in separate parts of the plant, organized by function. It kept the old batch concept shown in Figure 4.2 (first diagram). It did not propose any construction, except some demolition, and did not propose changes in the plant's physical conditions referred to by some as "creature comforts," such as lighting and floor renovation. Nonetheless, the U.S. plan totaled $8 million, and

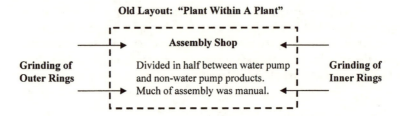

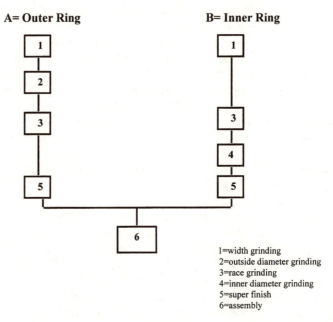

Figure 4.2 Old versus new grinding and assembly layout for Ann Arbor plant.

the U.S.-based team was very nervous enroute to Japan, thinking that its plan would be rejected on cost alone.

When the U.S. team members saw the Japanese plan, they were shocked. The Japanese plan had an initial price tag of $17 million, with more expenditures coming at later phases. The main feature of the Japanese plan was a shift from a functional layout to a product line layout, as represented in Figure 4.2 (second diagram). In the original layout, the grinding machines were all grouped together, with inner rings done on one side of the shop and outer rings on the other. These were then fed into final assembly lines in the center of the plant, creating an inner assembly area within an outer machining plant (or a "plant within a plant," as they call it). The new layout required gutting the plant, moving and adding equipment, and arranging the grinding and final assembly into twenty-nine product lines, not counting some empty space for adding lines when extra capacity was needed. Even with the new layout, there was not a completely smooth flow, since the inner and outer rings go through different operations (Figure 4.2). Heat treat was still done in batches in a separate part of the building in large furnaces.

The product-oriented layout proposed by the Japanese led to buying more machines than the American approach, but NSK was willing to invest in the long-term benefits of organizing for improved flow and better quality. The Japanese plan called for gutting the plant, digging out noxious storage, and improving the physical environment. It also sought to improve lighting, refurbish the ceiling, and create a new auxiliary support system (e.g., for recycling oil used for machining and grinding). It called for replacing almost all the old equipment and adding new automation. Japanese and American teams met for three weeks to work through their proposals, with the result that the Japanese plan was accepted almost intact. The biggest change was an American suggestion to make the final assembly equipment much more flexible than the Japanese plan originally called for. Japanese engineers at Ishibe developed the technical solutions to actualize the design.

By the start of renovations in 1986, a major downsizing had reduced the number of employees from 500 in the mid-1970s to 290. Downsizing was motivated by loss of business in part, but increasing automation and reduction of product lines contributed, as well. Downsizing techniques included attrition due to retirements, job terminations (voluntary and nonvoluntary), and decreases in hirings. The Japanese plan (including bearings for water pumps) could only support only 199 people. Bringing back some single-row bearings into production bumped the figure to about 215. So, as a direct result of the renovation, another seventy-five people needed to be downsized. This was accomplished through normal attrition and early retirement.

Despite continued downsizing, there was broad support for renovation for three reasons. First, as the former plant manager put it, "it was our opportunity to go from [what we had] to a showcase plant." Second, the plant has had no layoffs since 1985; since the renovations were completed, employment has been stable. Finally, it was clear that Japanese auto transplant companies were coming to America, and this gave Ann Arbor hope for a new and growing customer base. During renovation, twenty-two Japanese expatriates, mostly production engineers, were assigned to the Ann Arbor plant to assist in reorganizing the plant and launching the new lines.

During the initial three weeks of planning for the renovation, the American team in Japan realized that Ann Arbor did not have sophisticated production engineering capabilities for upgrading plant and equipment. Plant layout engineers were on corporate staff, but there were no day-to-day, hands-on production engineers at Ann Arbor. Returning to the United States, they put together a five-person manufacturing engineering group composed of one Japanese expatriate, an American from plant maintenance, and several people from R&D. There was no special training program for the role; the group learned on the job by assisting in technology transfer from Japan, installing equipment, debugging, teaching shop floor people how to run equipment, and working on technology upgrades. The emergence of internal production engineering capabilities became a very important force in moving Ann Arbor toward local autonomy.

Phase III. Locally Led Incremental Improvement, 1990–Present

It is not clear when parent-led incremental improvements end and the transfer to locally driven improvements begin. At the time of our interviews in 1996, there was still a crew of eight Japanese expatriates in Ann Arbor, including an influential Japanese assistant plant manager. The large overseas production department in Ishibe continues to work on upgrading technology at Ann Arbor, although, on the other hand, there is a large group of Americans who have been back and forth to Japan and have developed a deep understanding of NSK's production system. Ann Arbor managers have helped set up systems in other American plants in place of Japanese managers. Over time, there has been a shift in the locus of technological improvements toward more American-led initiatives. Ann Arbor now has its own R&D center with some product development capability, though product testing is the main focus.

On the management and organization side, Americans have triggered significant human resource initiatives to break down barriers in operating the "software" and "hardware" of NSK's production system. Among these were self-directed work teams (SDWT) and several collective bargaining agreements involving seniority, shift rotation, job bidding, overtime, and housekeeping. Other changes included a new approach to working with union representatives, opening the books to union inspection in 1994, and instituting new performance review procedures.

One of the clearest indicators that NSKs U.S. subsidiaries are developing autonomy is that Larry McPherson, president and chief operating officer of NSK's U.S. subsidiary, was named to NSK's board of directors in the summer of 1996. While NSK is not the first company to place an American on the headquarters board, it is certainly one of the first. A less obvious, yet equally significant indication in the shift toward local autonomy is the increasing use of the phrase "sister plant" to refer to Ishibe. This breaks down the "mother-child" distinction, putting the paired plants on more of an equal footing.

Understanding Recontextualization at the Ann Arbor Plant: Method of Analysis

As the previous account shows, some aspects of NSK's production system were transferred fairly intact, while others met significant barriers to implementation. To better understand why this occurred, we found it useful to sort the technologies. We first sorted processes by whether they were "hard" or "soft" technologies. The sorting was motivated by NSK's own custom of distinguishing between "hardware" and "software" when referring to trans- ferred processes. However, the distinction is supported by recent theory in research on technology transfer that distinguishes between physical and social technologies (Tornatzky and Fleisher, 1990).

Our informants at NSK did not really elaborate what they meant by either term, but it was clear they were using "software" as a shorthand for tech- nologies that were heavily people-dependent. In analyzing "hard" and "soft" technologies and processes, the distinction is clearly based on the extent to which technologies and processes rely on accompanying organizational sys- tems. We therefore named this dimension "system embeddedness" and de- fined it as the degree to which technologies and processes were more or less tightly integrated with other technical and social systems.

Tornatzky and Fleisher (1990, p. 10) defined technology as "tools and tool systems by which we transform parts of our environment, derived from hu- man knowledge, to be used for human purposes." Using this broad definition, a second categorical dimension became evident—the knowledge base asso- ciated with the technology. By knowledge base we mean something akin to what Kogut and Zander (1992) call "know-how" associated with imple- menting and operating technology. "Know-how" was well articulated and codifiable in some cases, but not in others.

This led us to think about technologies in terms of the distinction between their explicit and their tacit knowledge base (Doz et. al, 1996; Nonaka and Takeuchi, 1995; Polanyi, 1966). Whereas the former type of knowledge is articulable and relatively easy to document, the latter is not. Rather, tacit knowledge is the taken-for-granted understandings associated with tech- niques and processes that are learned over time through socialization (inter- acting within an organization and with society at large). Tacit knowledge is deeply embedded in a member's consciousness and is therefore difficult to access. These dimensions, induced by case data and supported by theory, gave way to the following model of recontextualization in transferring technology (both physical and social) to new user environments.

Model Relating Technology Characteristics to Recontextualization

After identifying the two salient dimensions for categorization, we mapped transferred technologies and processes on a grid, with the x-axis as the degree of system embeddedness and the y-axis as the degree of tacit or explicit knowledge base (see Figure 4.3). This mapping indicated that some technol- ogies and processes were recontextualized to a greater extent than others. Processes with high embeddedness and a large tacit knowledge base were recontextualized to a greater extent than were those with low system embed- dedness and high explicit knowledge. We therefore introduced a third axis

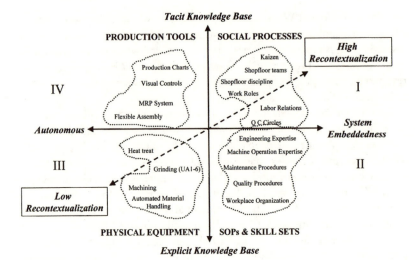

Figure 4.3 Model relating Japanese technology characteristics to recontextualization.

(the z-axis) to represent the degree of recontextualization as a function of system embeddedness and tacit versus explicit knowledge. Figure 4.3 models these technical characteristics and recontextualization.

With regard to recontextualization—how much the technology was transformed as it was transplanted in Ann Arbor—we observe the following. There was less recontextualization for autonomous equipment with an explicit knowledge base (what we have called "physical equipment") and a lot more recontextualization for social technologies that required considerable tacit knowledge (what we have called "social processes"). The off-diagonal quadrants—"production tools" and "SOPs and skill sets"—are between these extremes.

Examples of Recontextualization at the Ann Arbor Plant

Looking at the four quadrants of Figure 4.3, we see an interesting pattern: as technologies and processes have been implemented, Ann Arbor has become increasingly system-embedded and reliant on tacit knowledge. Minor modifications to existing equipment (shown in Quadrant III) made during Phase One (1975–1985) were low on system embeddedness and tacit knowledge. Phase Two changes (1985–1990), including new complex equipment (Quadrant III) and flexible assembly (Quadrant IV) and many of the accompanying standard operating procedures (Quadrant II), were much more system-embedded and required greater amounts of tacit knowledge. Finally, the social processes listed in Quadrant I that have become central in Phase Three, especially since the push for shop floor teamwork that started in 1994, are the highest in system embeddedness and tacit knowledge. We discuss each of these quadrants, from the least to most recontextualized.

First, we tried to sort equipment for each major production process by system embeddedness and knowledge base. For the former, we classified technologies as "hardware" or "software" and then considered the degree to which they were interconnected with other organizational or social systems. We used Perrow (1967) to guide our thinking about the analyzability of technology and knowledge. For tasks high in analyzability, standard operating procedures can be applied to solve problems that arise in a straightforward manner. Tasks low in analyzability, by contrast, require novel problem solving, demanding deeper levels of experience or socialized "know-how."

Physical Equipment: Quadrant III

We expected that highly automated equipment would be less people dependent and require less tacit knowledge than more manual operations because the automation would basically run itself. We were told just the opposite. Deborah Reinhart, Ann Arbor's systems manager, observed that automated manual processes, such as material handling and assembly, were more, rather than less, dependent on social systems support. She attributed this to (1) the increased coordination needed to operate the processes and (2) the increased responsibilities of hourly workers who set up equipment, monitored processes, checked for quality, and solved problems when there were defects. (Persistent problems may require skilled-trade persons, but even then operators participate in problem solving.) What looked like autonomous physical technology was not, once it was coupled with social processes that underpinned successfrul implementation.

Automated materials handling and machining.   The most autonomous physical technologies were the automated materials handling and machining equipment brought over during the earliest stages of technology transfer. These technologies underwent the least recontextualization because they were the least technically complex and required the least experiential knowledge for operation.

Grinding (UA1–6).   Machining adjustments and minor modifications in grinding (UA1–6), from 1975 to 1984, were improvements that did not change the basic functioning of equipment or operator roles. Given no basic changes, we found little recontextualization. However, in comparison with machining or automated material handling, grinding requires a greater degree of system dependence, chiefly with respect to the social organization of work. Grinding (especially outer diameter, or "OD," grinding) was described as the most demanding process for operators. They work as a team on three tandem machines (one finish operator and one rough end operator), doing their own set-up and running the equipment at required quality levels. "OD is probably the most challenging department in the plant; [it involves]-setting up, grinding, checking OD size—taper, waviness, roundness, roughness, and square-ness—and inspecting for grind burns," according to the (assistant plant manager). Each bearing must meet 100 percent specifications. When one does not, operators must perform additional manual tolerance checks. Given these characteristics, we placed grinding further toward the center of the system-embeddedness axis than the more autonomous equipment already discussed.

Heat treat.   Although the heat-treat operation appears straightforward to an untrained observer, apparently it is the most technically complex physical process in ball-bearing production. If parts are not heated precisely, as specified, they must be scrapped. Testing and adjusting the heat-treat equipment are highly complex procedures that require a good deal of training and experience. For these reasons, we placed heat treat further along the tacit knowledge dimension than the other technologies in this quadrant.

Production Tools: Quadrant IV

We labeled this quadrant "production tools" because its technologies are physical mechanisms and software that aid production. Whereas quadrant III's technologies represent the key physical processes necessary to produce bearings, those in quadrant IV are technologies, both "hard" and "soft," that support them.

Flexible assembly.   Perrow states that task uncertainty derives from unanticipated ways that systems fail and require novel problem solving. The flexible assembly equipment (used to assemble bearings brought to Ann Arbor) had more moving parts and customized technologies and software than any of the other production technologies. It was quite common to see this assembly line kick out bad parts. The Ann Arbor equipment was particularly complex since it ran smaller quantities of a wider variety of bearings than did comparable equipment in Japan. Given all this, we classifed the assembly equipment as higher on tacit knowledge than the other equipment in quadrant III. Yet the equipment was set up and debugged in Japan, brought to Ann Arbor by Japanese, and then further debugged in situ, so there was not a lot of recontextualization of the physical hardware or computer software. However, in the shifting work behaviors of operators, skilled-trades persons, and production engineers who were charged with maintaining, repairing, and upgrading the equipment, a fair amount of recontextualization unfolded.

Material requirements planning system.   Material requirements planning is the system NSK uses for planning purchases of raw materials and scheduling production. This contrasts with the Toyota Motor Company's world-renowned Kanban pull system. However, NSK Japan seems to use MRP very effectively to keep up stable production with strictly maintained maximum standards for both in-process and supplied-parts inventories. The technology uses less explicit knowledge than some of the physical equipment discussed in Quadrant III because it runs on company-specific software. Norms and understandings for using the software are as important as the software itself. The MRP system was recontextualized to a lesser extent than we saw for other social processes, although there was less discipline in maintaining buffer sizes and controlling inventory to match system requirements in Ann Arbor.

Production charts and visual controls.   Production charts and visual controls are part of what NSK calls its quality system's "software." By production charts we mean graphs that compare actual and planned performance. The physical charts and visual controls (e.g., color-coded bins, stack lights) are tangible objects that lend themselves to being transferred by means of explicit knowledge exchange. But how they fit into shopfloor design and, more important, how they are used in new settings require deeper tacit knowledge.

For example, these tools are used for continuous improvement and making immediate process adjustments. Immediate response is needed when performance is below what is planned. Visual controls are designed to indicate deviations from a standard; for example, a lot of rejects in a red bin indicates problems. How an organization responds to such signals is what counts more than the specific design of visual controls.

The Ann Arbor plant duplicated the physical substance of NSK's production charts and visual controls, but the way in which they were used underwent substantial recontextualization. Production charts, though placed near shop floor work stations, were not consulted on a regular basis. The color-coded bins were often left empty while the floor around them was crowded with waste and rework.

Standard Operating Procedures and Skill Sets: Quadrant II

Standard operating procedures (SOPs) categorized in quadrant II are a basic means to ensure the successful transfer of "bearing culture" because they are the detailed procedures needed to operate the plant and equipment at exacting quality standards. When expatriates were sent to Ann Arbor, their primary responsibilities were to set up equipment, debug it, and teach the SOPs for running and maintaining the equipment.

There were clearly difficulties in doing this, according to the stories we heard. For example, one American manager explained:

Our workers [before renovation] were mainly doing manual work using wire and bubble gum to keep machines running. They did not know how to deal with the new precise, expensive equipment. Before you could just given them a whack, but when they did that to the new equipment they had Japanese screaming at them. Other rules were imposed. In the past you could drink coffee and smoke on the shop floor. Under the new rules that was not allowed. The Japanese could not believe they were smoking with oil around.

To the extent that proper execution of procedures depends on individuals who have "bought into a system," SOPs are quite social systems-dependent. Even so, NSK tries to control for variance in execution by making SOPs as explicit as possible.

SOPs: Workplace organization, maintenance and quality procedures.   Explicit directions for carrying out maintenance, quality, and organizational procedures are posted at each work station. Sometimes the explicitness of these directions are a bit too much from an American point of view. One worker recounted a recent experience in using the company car. "I was driving the company car and in the glove compartment [I found] a detailed set of operating instructions, including keeping the tank half full, what to do in case of an emergency, etc."

Despite NSK's emphasis on stardards, getting operators to follow them regularly has been a key complaint of Japanese expatriates. NSK attributes this to a lack of shop floor discipline (discussed further under social processes). The use of NSK standards regarding workplace organization around scrap reduction is a good case in point. NSK has a color-coded bin system for sorting nonstandard parts. Red containers are for scrap, yellow for rework, and white for parts or materials that are out of place (e.g., parts found on the floor). At Ishibe the white buckets were almost empty, whereas in Ann Arbor they were large and well used (despite the fact that one still finds occasional parts on the floor).

There were also difficulties in getting Americans to follow the rigid time schedules that were normal in Japan. Japanese expatriates wanted to keep lines running continuously as much as possible, and to do so they wanted to reduce lunch time from thirty to twenty minutes. But the American operators said they could not eat so quickly, and lunch stretched back to thirty minutes. It is common to bring a box lunch to work in Japan, but at Ann Arbor employees commonly went to the cafeteria during lunch.

The new schedule also called for keeping lines running continuously between shifts. In the old batch operations, first-shift operators felt it did not matter if second-shift operators came on time as long as they built up enough inventory. Today's product-oriented lines are set up to run in a continuous flow, and each operation is dependent on earlier ones to keep things running smoothly.

The form of SOPs has been transferred more or less intact from the vantage point of recontextualization, but their actual functioning has not. We believe this is because SOPs have been severed from the underlying beliefs and values so ingrained in Japanese behavior. We discuss the roots of these behaviors under shopfloor discipline later.

Machine operation expertise.   NSK believes and invests in its people. For NSK, machine operators are critical for maintaining efficient, quality operations. Machine operators are expected not just to operate machinery but also to manage a process—generally, a complex and highly automated process.

Knowing what a machine should sound like, spotting defects quickly, and knowing how to make minor repairs—all of these on-the-job-skills require a deep contextual understanding of the product and manufacturing process. Such expertise depends on a social system that encourages learning and continuous improvement.

We put machine operation expertise toward the middle of our grid because, even though a lot of an operator's expertise relies on tacit knowledge, a good deal of it can be made explicit. At Ann Arbor, operators had lengthy operating manuals with clear, precise directions on how to execute each of the production steps. To help transfer some of the tacit knowledge associated with operator expertise, several American operators were sent to Japan for training, and others were trained at the hands of Japanese engineers, supervisors, and operators who came to Ann Arbor. The expertise of American operators was less broad and deep than that of their Japanese counterparts because their work roles were more circumscribed in Ann Arbor than in Japan. On-the-job training served as a means of transferring tacit knowledge without having to first make it explicit.

Engineering expertise.   Transferring engineering expertise is similar to transferring machine operation expertise because NSK believes that engineers are not useful unless they "get their hands dirty." They need to understand the manufacturing process at a deep level, including the operation of production equipment. Engineers should also be able to improve the technology. Like other Japanese companies, NSK values contextual knowledge over formal knowledge.[2] NSK expects university graduates to have a background in physics and basic sciences, but it expects to train new graduates (even engineering graduates) to become "true" engineers through hands-on experience under the mentorship of in-house senior engineers. NSK believes that its main competitive advantage comes from its ability to train engineers and to give them experience in designing production technology specific to bearing manufacture. The needed expertise is primarily tacit and learned on the job, not explicit and written down. Production engineers need to understand how to operate equipment, as well as how to design and build equipment. So they have an even stronger tacit knowledge base than operators, and their expertise is therefore shown in Figure 4.3 further up the tacit dimension of the graph.

When American engineers went to Japan in 1986 to propose their version of the plant renovation, they came back with an awareness that Hoover did not really have production engineering expertise like what they saw in Japan. Their engineers were not on the shop floor but in R&D, specifying new advanced processes and working with outside vendors to purchase equipment. At NSK Japan, production engineering was in the plant, designing and building its own machines, and working on equipment upgrades to improve processes. As a result, Ann Arbor selected four individuals to become production engineers closer to the NSK-Japan model.

Social Processes: Quadrant I

The social processes categorized in Quadrant I of our model experienced the greatest amount of recontextualization. These are processes characterized by high system embeddedness and tacitness in their application.

Quality circles. The first team concept that was transferred to Ann Arbor was quality control circles. NSK Japan has an active quality circle program, and, although there is no written policy saying so, all employees are expected to contribute suggestions. The first attempt by Ann Arbor to institute an employee involvement program was modeled directly, one-for-one, on NSK/Japan's quality circle program. The program was called QTIPS, and it began in 1982, but by late 1985 it was disbanded—a full year before plant renovation.

QTIPS is considered a dismal failure by NSK personnel in America and Japan and is often referred to as an example of what not to do in the area of quality circles and problem-solving groups. There was relatively little involvement of top management in QTIPS, and the small group sessions quickly turned into complaint sessions that focused on "creature comforts" (things that would make their work life easier). Japanese managers explain QTIPS' failure as a result of allowing American workers to choose their own problems to work on. In Japan, management "suggests" topics for problem solving. As one group leader put it: "In Japan you don't choose who is on the team. . . . In Ishibe team members expect that it is up to managers to determine the direction of the team. Since overseas members choose, they also expect to have a voice in what the teams do instead of following the leader's direction as would be the Japanese practice."

An American middle manager explained that, in retrospect, a major error with QTIPS was bypassing the authority of middle management. The QC circles were allowed to choose their own leaders, who were often not foremen. This led to resistance by lower middle managers, who felt left out. As Robert Cole (1979) has noted, quality circles in Japan often strengthen the power and influence of foremen. Cole (1979, p. 201) writes about the highly publicized job redesign of the Toyota auto body shop:

> . . . The emphasis is not on participation per se, but rather on achieving the consent of workers for policies which management wants to pursue, as well as guiding workers in the direction in which management would like to see them move. We have here a carefully controlled participation in which management often takes the lead informally or formally in initiating policies that workers are then guided to accept and pursue.

The Japanese found confusing the coupling of quality circles in America with Western notions of worker participation and workplace democracy. Quality circles were introduced in America at a time when there was a shift from top-down, autocratic management to bottom-up, participative management. Training typically included quality tools and problem-solving methods, as in Japan, but with a heavy emphasis on group dynamics and consensus decision making. So, quality circles in America were not just a tool for improving quality and productivity but were part of a broader movement toward worker participation and empowerment, although quality circles were a relatively weak form of participative management, since their activities took place off the job. Lawler (1986) called this a parallel participative structure acting in concert with a traditional, top-down functional organization.

Labor relations.   It is well known that large Japanese companies have enterprise unions that are fundamentally different from American industry-based trade unions. The NSK union represents almost all NSK employees (white and blue collar), and its fate is tied wholly to NSK's fate as a company. Thus, union members participate enthusiastically in productivity improvement programs to help their company's competitiveness. The UAW, in contrast, represents a fraction of employees in Ann Arbor, and it has historically taken an adversarial position with managers in order to effectively represent the interests of the workers.

The most recent strike in Ann Arbor was in 1977. Given the plant's dismal performance during the 1970s, the union was not in a strong position to resist the mid-1980s efforts to revitalize the plant. So, when Larry McPherson came back from Japan in 1985 and said that the union contract needed renegotiation and that fewer, broader job classifications would be created as a result, there was not much resistance. It was time to change or close down the plant.

In spite of a new contract, the (Japanese) assistant plant manager explained that job flexibility was still not what was needed to achieve Japanese productivity levels. He explained:

> In Japan if the operator is working on a machine and it malfunctions, maybe they can fix it by themselves on the spot. Here the operator must ask the foreman who calls maintenance, and there are limited maintenance people. We are trying to eliminate this issue—by negotiating with the union. . . . Some operators are frustrated. They want to produce more and fix minor problems. But others do not want to change.

Another problem was that Americans equate seniority with special privileges. The same expatriate explained:

> We have a three-shift operation in Ann Arbor. Senior people want to work the first shift. Sometimes the second shift is very weak because there are only new workers on the second shift. In Japan, we put senior people on each shift. Here it is strictly by seniority. We cannot have influence. In Japan we think people should shift monthly or weekly. Here people stay in one shift.

He then went on to explain the quality and productivity problems caused by a lack of experienced workers on the later shift. In Japan, groups, along with their supervisor, stay intact and rotate as a group across shifts every other week.

Overtime was another issue. In Japan, overtime is handled by a supervisor who asks the most qualified employees to stay over, although he also tries to spread the work around. The person asked to work overtime is expected to agree. In fact, how operators cooperate with overtime requests is an item on the performance appraisal form. But in the United States, "the supervisor asks the most senior people first, even if they can't do the job"—another example of the American preoccupation with individuality that struck the Japanese as incredibly inefficient. The numbers support the Japanese: quality problems and lower productivity were endemic during the second and third shifts in Ann Arbor.

Differences in work and union role definitions extended to office staff and supervision. A Japanese expatriate explained:

> There is a difference in attitude between office staff and supervisors toward the shop floor in Japan and America. In America salary and hourly are very separate and different. In Japan, they have more in common. There is less distinction between office and the shop floor. Here only shop floor people are in the union. In Japan most employees, shop floor and office, are in the union. The benefit structure is the same, so there is a common bond. Here it is like [fists together] a strong clash. A honcho makes a decision, but does not know in detail the shop floor and it may be a bad decision. Shop floor people have much more knowledge of the shop floor. Sometimes operators on the floor make more money than supervisors because of a shift premium or more overtime.

In America, middle managers do not have a lot of experience on the floor and do not have a lot to contribute to shop floor efficiency. In Japan, supervisors always know all the jobs in detail, and they are generally selected as supervisors because they were the best operators. Eighty percent of a supervisor's job is efficiency improvement on the shop floor at Ishibe. At Ann Arbor, supervisors spend a large part of their time adjusting overtime schedules or responding to operator complaints, and they do not think about operational improvements. According to one expatriate, "When we came to the United States we were expecting to see a lot of improvements to the equipment and efficiency, but actually the launch was very slow, and some people didn't care about improvement."

A turning point in the relationship between the UAW and management came in 1994, when management decided to open the books, and the UAW had a financial consultant do an analysis. The union thought that NSK was making money hand over fist. But by the time NSK had put $130 million into Ann Arbor, based on profitability trends at the time, the plant would not recover the investment for a long time. A new "modern operating agreement" was signed as part of a three-year contract on June 17, 1994, three months before the old contract was due to expire. The agreement allowed for relaxing job classifications and union work rules and the beginning of a movement toward self-directed work teams (SDWTs). This paved the way for unprecedented union-management cooperation at Ann Arbor.

While the new union agreement seems like a convergence between the American and the Japanese systems, the process and underlying dynamics are different. Job classifications are broader and blur somewhat between skilled trades and equipment operators, for example, but boundaries are still very real and rigid in Ann Arbor. Biweekly shift rotations of intact work groups and their supervisors, routine practice at NSK in Ishibe, are unthinkable in Ann Arbor. And the focus on worker autonomy and control in Ann Arbor is completely unlike the active collaboration of workers in company initiatives in Japan.

Work roles. In Japan, job responsibilities are said to be broad. A more accurate statement would be that individuals take on roles and are willing to stretch those roles as necessary. In fact, below a certain level of management, there are neither job titles nor job descriptions. For production workers, this means their role is to maintain efficient, high-quality production by whatever means, as well as to make suggestions for improvement. If minor maintenance is needed to keep equipment running, workers gladly do it, even though their primary job is to run production.

The introduction, in 1986, of new technology at Ann Arbor changed basic assumptions regarding job categorizations and responsibility. The number of job classifications went from forty to twenty and the number of inspectors from fifty-one to ten. The lion's share of the technologies and processes transferred, such as flexible assembly, automated material handling, work teams, and quality circles, depend on broadly defined jobs with lots of overlap between tasks. As the (Japanese) assistant plant manager described it:

> We put more responsibility on the operators. Before they were paid by piece rate. We had a two classifications of hourly worker—a set-up person and an operator to run the machine. We also had two quality-class workers—a GIC (general inspector checker) and a bench inspector. The GIC would audit the parts and then, if they found any bad ones, the bench inspector would sort the bins for that defect. At one time we had fifty-one such GIC inspectors. Now, we've gone from quality control to quality assurance where, rather than having so many quality checkers, the operator himself is responsible for product quality.

As new, complex equipment was debugged in Japan and set up in Ann Arbor, there was a shift from Ann Arbor's traditional narrow and specialized job roles to the broader, more flexible job roles characteristic of Ishibe. This looks like a one-to-one transfer of the technology and its associated work roles. Yet, upon closer inspection, it is clear that there are significant differences between Ishibe and Ann Arbor. At Ishibe, shop floor workers feel obliged to do whatever it takes to keep the process running at high levels of quality and productivity. The small size of the skilled trades workforce is a result of workers' willingness to do their own maintenance. In Ann Arbor, while there was a blurring of job responsibilities between maintenance and shop floor workers, these continued as clearly separated roles. Shop floor workers were willing to do some routine preventative maintenance, but it would be a violation of union principles for shop floor workers to do maintenance workers' jobs. At Ann Arbor, there were still clearly delineated "jobs," though with broader boundaries, and continuous improvement activites were limited. At Ishibe, there was no clear conception of "my job," and continuous improvement was a way of life.

Shop floor discipline.   Despite NSK's emphasis on standards, a lack of shop floor discipline in following standards at Ann Arbor has been a major complaint of Japanese expatriates. They were especially critical of difficulties in getting Americans to clean up after themselves. The stereotype that Japanese plants are so clean you can eat off the floor describes well the Ishibe plant. At first glance, this is also true of the Ann Arbor plant. But, on closer inspection, there are a lot of little things and piles of stuff on the floor that do not belong there. The Japanese expatriates could not understand how Americans could function in such a mess. They shuddered physically when they spoke of Americans throwing used gloves and towels onto the shop floor.

As mentioned earlier in our discussion of SOPs, we believe that much of the variance in operator discipline stems from differences in underlying beliefs and values. Japanese schoolchildren as young as six are responsible for keeping their classroom clean (there are no janitors in Japanese schools), serving lunch, organizing classroom equipment, and so on. While disorganization and dirt are considered bad in and of themselves, they are seen as particularly bad for plants that operate high-precision machinery. Beliefs and values such as these are not yet evident in Ann Arbor.

Shop floor teams.   The movement toward SDWTs was part of the modern operating agreement after the failure of the earlier organized QTIPS. In December 1994, both parties agreed to hire "Workplace Transformation" as an outside consulting firm. A planning team was put together, half from management and half from the union, and with the help of Workplace Transformation a UAW/NSK strategic plan was developed. The plan called for a shift from a functional organization (e.g., one manufacturing department or one quality department) to product-based units (e.g., water pump or auto bearings), with a unit manager in charge of each.

The plan was taken to the plant employees in a general presentation in April 1995. The union had already agreed to self-directed work teams in the 1994 contract, so this was mainly for the purposes of information sharing. Learning from QTIPS, staff and middle management were encouraged to participate in the process. Beginning with pilot efforts between 1995 and 1997, key measures for quality, safety, productivity, and delivery were defined for each business unit, and continuous improvement forms were created for garnering operator input. Teams ranged in size from seven to eighteen members for each shift; a twelve-hour training program for teams was launched.

From the perspective of recontextualization, the key issue in bringing teams to Ann Arbor was fostering understanding of what a team is. Even in Japan, we experienced difficulty in defining what was meant by the word "team." While the English word "team" (*chiimu* in Japanese) is used at Ishibe, its use is reserved for special activities that are set up on a temporary basis, like task force teams. The only formal group categories are QC circles and *han* (work groups).

On the shop floor, work teams are called *han*, and team supervisors are called *hancho* (literally, "group leader"). *Han* include forty to fifty members at a maximum. These large groups are then broken down into lines (called *ra-in*, a borrowed approximation from English) of about ten workers led by "line leaders." Line leaders are hourly employees who do not have formal authority over team members. They know all the jobs in their line area and are expected to fill in when group members are absent. Pay is based on seniority, and line leaders are not paid a bonus for their efforts. However, they can expect to become a *hancho*, which is impossible without first serving as a line leader.

Work is done in concert in Japan—it is hard to conceive of work not done in teams. Lively discussions with several levels of managers finally led to a uniform view of teams at NSK Japan. Teams mean "teamwork." Central to teamwork is team consciousness that comes from informal activities such as drinking and playing softball together. Beyond that, teamwork is doing what is needed to get the job done well. Lines of demarcation are notably absent. According to a young member with several years of overseas experience: "In Japan, the concept is that we are in the same boat together and less a collection of specialists. We can all pitch in and do what it takes. In Japan we do not enter the firm with the idea that we are trying to achieve individual rewards and it is expected that if the goal is clear we will all chip in and work together to achieve the organizational goal . . . so teamwork happens quite naturally." Another member who had lived in England explained: "The whole idea of the factory system is very different in Japan. . . . In England, my children would raise their hands in school, and when they came home they would raise their hands and be self-assertive but in Japan this is not encouraged . . . Japanese are socialized into following the lead—going along."

Given this view of teamwork, NSK employees found Western work life confusing. On one hand, they could not understand why Westerners questioned authority so much and maintained clear boundaries around "jobs." On the other, they were surprised by all the hoopla around "teams" when American firms first tried to organize small group-based programs and activities. All of that contrasted vividly with the more natural, day-to-day teamwork they are used to.

Although NSK's official stance is not to interfere with human resource practices in overseas subsidiaries, NSK's influence on human resource management in Ann Arbor is profound and evident in a number of ways:

1. Over the years there have been more than forty Japanese advisers in Ann Arbor, and inevitably they offer their opinions about human resource management issues.
2. American managers from Ann Arbor often visit Japan, and they try to emulate NSK's high-performing plants.
3. Managers from Ann Arbor are exposed to "best-practice models" of Japanese manufacturing in the United States through outside consultants and customer contacts.
4. A common performance measure in all of NSK's plants is the number of employee suggestions. Hence, any good plant manager works to encourage employee involvement, at least to the point of getting a minimum number of suggestions from the shop floor.

At Ann Arbor, SDWTs were instigated and directed by local American management. There were no Japanese representatives on the planning team. American managers felt strongly enough about ownership that "Japanese were pretty much kept out of the loop on this." Although those leading the effort believe that it is an American-led agenda, they also acknowledge that their approach is consistent with the Japanese philosophy "that people are the most important resource." But at the same time they recognize that their self-directed teams are quite different from Ishibe's teams. In America, teamwork does not come naturally but has to be specifically structured and encouraged. The main lesson of QTIPS was that American workers are not happy to let management define projects and goals for small groups activities, unlike NSK's employees in Japan. American workers want to choose whether or not to be involved and what to work on.

Those familiar with workplace democracy movements in Europe and with sociotechnical system approaches in manufacturing will recognize Ann Arbor's self-directed team structure. Ann Arbor's approach marries Western conceptions with Japanese approaches in a number of ways. In self-directed work teams, quantitative measures are not typically a central driving force. But, in Ann Arbor, key measures were developed in the areas of quality, safety, productivity, and delivery.

Debbie Reinhart, a former quality manager who was put in charge of the SDWT movement, described the process as top down. The top, she explained, has to fully understand what is expected and cascade this understanding down. For the SDWT process, staff were trained in using forms and in calculating key measures. Measures were used as indicators of problems, and then staff members were encouraged to get down to the "nitty-gritty of identifying root causes." As part of the SDWT process, jobs classifications were further broadened, and a "4S" campaign (speed, service, spirit, system) was instigated in each production area.

Developing and training employees in standardized procedures has also been central to the SDWT process. The first stage was defined as developing a continuous improvement process. The second phase focuses on identifying job skills and operator guidelines—not common in sociotechnical system approaches but central to Japanese manufacturing (Adler and Cole, 1993). The emphasis on key measures, continuous improvement, and standardized work is characteristic of NSK Japan. Notions of "natural process owners" and "team autonomy" are clearly not. We regard the blending of Japanese and Western conceptions of employee involvement and teamwork in Ann Arbor as recontextualization.

Kaizen. *Kaizen* is a philosophy and a process rather than a specific set of tools and methods. It includes the belief that many tiny improvements can add up to competitive advantage and that everyone's job is to contribute to the day-to-day improvement of the enterprise. *Kaizen* also requires that employees be clear on the goals of the firm and that these goals cannot be reduced to explicit instructions to "continually improve." *Kaizen* is inherently a system feature or process that is broadly shared at the level of beliefs and assumptions.

In Ann Arbor, it was clear to Japanese expatriates that the *kaizen* philosophy was not shared by the Ann Arbor workforce. Workers were not striving to improve continuously, and they were not working every day to do their best on the job; indeed, when the Japanese tried to structure employee involvement in improvement through QTIPS, the effort failed because employees wanted to choose creature comforts over business priorities. The Ann Arbor incarnation of *kaizen* is "*kaizen* teams," which meet regularly to improve work processes; they are a lot like quality circles but with an explicit shop floor focus. *Kaizen* teams are trained in problem solving, and there are facilitators to help run meetings. They emphasize performance measures to track progress over time. So this tacit, embedded philosophy from Japan is being transformed into a set of explicit tools and methods at Ann Arbor.

Discussion and Conclusion

In physical technologies, production tools, and much of the standard operating procedures, Ann Arbor looks like a replica of Ishibe. There is also a good deal of organizational similarity between NSK's parent plant in Ishibe and its offspring in Ann Arbor. This isomorphism is partly a result of direct influence by Japanese expatriates and partly a consequence of imitating models of "best practice" from Ishibe and some of their American customers. Because of isomorphic forces, moreover, it is no coincidence that NSK tried to implement quality circles when this was a fad in the 1980s and is now moving toward self-directed work teams as this becomes faddish in American industry.

But Ann Arbor is not like Ishibe in some critical ways. Only a limited amount of technical innovation has been attempted in Ann Arbor, and almost all of NSK's R&D still takes place in Japan. Ishibe has learned little from

Ann Arbor, and this judgment covers not only the physical and social aspects, of NSK's production system but its mental and motivational aspects as well. In all these respects, Ishibe has been a parent mentoring a child, notwithstanding the fact that the child is growing up. Ann Arbor was NSK's first manufacturing facility in America when it forged a joint venture with the Hoover Ball Bearing Company in 1973. Surely in that quarter-century of experience, not to mention long experiences elsewhere, NSK could have learned from its overseas operations.

Ample and varied recontextualization are among the many lessons to be learned. Recontextualization is most apparent in Ann Arbor's social processes that support the physical and engineering technologies. It is apparent, as well, in Ann Arbor's approach to teamwork. Ann Arbor's self-directed teams are influenced partly by consultants who were acceptable to both union and management, partly by Western traditions of workplace democracy, and partly by the autonomous work group models taken from the sociotechnical systems approach and Japanese philosophies of continuous improvement.

What has been transferred to Ann Arbor lacks the full functionality of the Japanese original, but that is to be expected. It is obviously impossible to transfer whole systems and sets of organizational routines easily or quickly across national and cultural boundaries. Decades of accumulated engineering and shop floor experience cannot be readily transferred, either in the short or the long term. So less than full functionality in NSK's international operations, relative to Japan, is not surprising.

How experiences and influences will blend and evolve remains to be seen, but clearly recontextualization happens. Understanding that it occurs and that it is inevitable should not lead one to assume that it can be unerringly foreseen and managed. NSK's case illustrates the degree to which transplanted systems and procedures are transformed in selective adaptation to a foreign environment. Recontextualization advances as the meanings and assumptions attached to techniques and procedures in one context are stripped away, negotiated, and transformed in a new context. They are a part of the culture of management, especially transnational management, but not of the management of culture.

Although recontextualization cannot be planned for, managers can consider and weigh local context in transfer. But thinking through how practices will change when they are transferred overseas is not yet manifest in NSK's internationalization strategy. NSK predicts a more or less homeostatic, four-fold division of labor between Japan and its non-Japanese operations. One could argue that NSK is sticking its head in the sand with this stance or, more generously, suggest that NSK is measuring its progress one small step at a time. Since NSK is in the early phases of stage two of its internationalization strategy, the company is not yet pushing for local autonomy in international operations. When that happens, NSK may significantly alter its internationalization strategy.

For now, NSK has recognized the role of its Japan-based parent factories as learning factories (Fruin, 1997). It transfers, monitors, and implants NSK's proprietary technology abroad. Managers, engineers, and workers in Ann Arbor are able to learn firsthand from their counterparts in Japan, both by going there and by hosting NSK's Japanese employees in Ann Arbor. Stage two, the current stage of NSK's internationalization strategy, is earmarked as a time when overseas factories are explicitly paired with Japanese parent factories. The pairing and parenting functions are a recognition of the role of NSK Japan's facilities as knowledge-creating organizations.

NSK's transfer and development of a production system in Ann Arbor was pragmatic and, in many respects, successful. The plant is producing at productivity and quality levels that appeared impossible a decade ago, and even now consistent improvement is more the rule than exception. All of this has been accomplished in a UAW plant that was initially concerned with quid pro quo concessions but became in time infused with genuine labor-management cooperation. There have been no layoffs since plant renovation. Sales are pushing capacity. Incremental yet continued introduction of new technologies is the norm.

NSK's philosophy of advancing core technologies and technical standards but leaving people management to the locals seems to have merit. Nonetheless, we cannot help but wonder about the length of the transformation process; could it have been accomplished in less than the twenty years since NSK's original purchase? If NSK had thought more about how core features of its production system are embedded, would NSK have accomplished its goals more quickly and efficiently? We suspect the answers are yes. By doing so, perhaps more of the taken-for-granted, tacit aspects of NSK's technologies and capabilities would have been apparent and lent themselves to explicit knowledge transfer.

We end by emphasizing that technology transfer takes place in a historical progression that lends itself to phased evolutionary analysis. Recontextualization, as part of the technology transfer process, unfolds along a dynamic path that requires endless, yet logical, changes in the pace, form, and content of what is being transferred. Recontextualization is a process of cultural give-and-take, trial-and-error, and, although it cannot be systematically planned for, it can be anticipated, probably monitored, and perhaps facilitated. At NSK Ann Arbor, a step-like progression from "hard" to "soft" recontextualization characterized technology transfers. Practices that required the least amount of selective adaptation were the first to appear. Today, core underlying assumptions that require significant adjustments on both sides of the Pacific are being recontextualized, confirming that recontextualization is an important part of managing the fit between international technology transfer and evolving work, technology, and organizational practices.

Notes

1. One exception to this was at NSK's Peterlee plant in Newcastle, England, which was one of its oldest and biggest overseas production operations. For one flexible assembly line that was being transferred to Peterlee

from Ishibe, NSK brought to Ishibe Peterlee engineers who were to train on the equipment and then go back home and set up and debug the equipment on their own. This was a major step forward for NSK in creating autonomous regional operations.

2. This finding is consistent with Barley's observations in regard to the importance of contextual knowledge for technicians: "The substantive knowledge that proved most critical came from neither courses nor books, but from doing. Thus, by experience technicians did not simply mean years of practice. Instead, they meant a situated, rather than a principled knowledge of materials, technologies, and techniques" (Barley, 1996: 425). Although, distinct from Barley's observation that the rise in importance of contextual knowledge is leading towards horizontally structured work, at NSK contextual expertise has not displaced hierarchical relations.

References

Adler, P., and Cole, R. 1993. "Designed for Learning: A Tale of Two Auto Plants." *Sloan Management Review* Spring:

Barley, S. R. 1996. "Technicians in the Workplace: Ethnographic Evidence for Bringing Work into Organization Studies." *Administrative Science Quarterly* 41: 404–441.

Brannen, M. Y. 1992. " 'Bwana Mickey': Constructing Cultural Consumption at Tokyo Disneyland." In J. Tobin, ed., *Remade in Japan: Everyday Life and Consumer Taste in a Changing Society.* New Haven: Yale University Press.

Brannen, M. Y., and J. M. Wilson III. 1996. "Recontextualization and Internationalization: Lessons in Transcultural Materialism from the Walt Disney Company." *CEMS (Community of European Management Schools) Business Review*, vol. 1, 1st ed.

Busche, G. R. 1988. "Cultural Contradictions of Statistical Process Control in American Manufacturing Organization." *Journal of Management* 14: 19–31.

Chesborough, H. W., and D. J. Teece. 1996. When is Virtual Virtuous? Organizing for Innovation." *Harvard Business Review* Jan.–Feb.: 65–73.

Cole, R. 1979. *Work, Mobility, and Participation.* Berkeley: University of California Press.

Daft, R. L. 1978. "A Dual-Core Model of Organizational Innovation." *Academy of Management Journal* 21: 193–210.

Damanpour, F. 1987. "The Adoption of Technological, Administrative, and Ancillary Innovations: Impact of Organizational Factors." *Journal of Management* 13: 675–688.

Damanpour, F. 1991. "Organizational Innovation: A Meta-analysis of Effects of Determinants and Moderators." *Academy of Management Journal* 34(3): 555–590.

Damanpour, F. 1996. "Organizational Complexity and Innovation: Developing and Testing Multiple Contingency Models." *Management Science* 42(5): 693–716.

Damanpour, F., and W. M. Evan. 1984. "Organizational Innovation and Performance: The Problem of 'Organizational Lag.' " *Administrative Science Quarterly* 29: 392–409.

Doz, Y., Asakawa, K., Santos, J., and Williamson, P. 1997. "The Metanational Corporation." INSEAD Working Paper No. 97/60/SM, Fontainebleau, France.

Evan, W. M. 1996. "Organizational Lag." *Human Organizations* 25(Spring): 51–53.

Fiol, C. M. 1996. Squeezing Harder Doesn't Always Work: Continuing the Search for Consistency in Innovation Research." *Academy of Management Review* 21(4): 1012–1021.

Fruin, W. M. 1997. *Knowledge Works: Managing Intellectual Capital at Toshiba*. New York: Oxford University Press.

Greif, M. 1991. *The Visual Factory: Building Participation through Shared Information*, Portland, Ore.: Productivity Press.

Ghoshal, S. 1987. "Global Strategy: An Organizing Framework." *Strategic Management Journal* 8(5): 425–440.

Ghoshal, S., and N. Nohria. 1989. "Internal Differentiation within Multinational Corporations." *Strategic Management Journal* 10: 323–337.

Hall, R. 1993, November. "A Framework Linking Intangible Resources and Capabilities to Sustainable Competitive Advantage." *Strategic Management Journal* 14(8).

Kogut, B. 1989. "Research Notes and Communications: A Note on Global Strategies." *Strategic Management Journal* 10: 383–389.

Kogut, B., and U. Zander. 1992, August. "Knowledge of the Firm, Combinative Capabilities, and the Replication of Technology." *Organizational Science* 3(3): 383–397.

Lawler, E., III. 1986. *High Involvement Management*. San Francisco: Jossey-Bass.

Leonard-Barton, D. 1992. "Core Capabilities and Core Rigidities: A Paradox in Managing New Product Development." *Strategic Management Journal* 13: 111–125.

Leonard-Barton, D. 1995. *Wellsprings of Knowledge: Building and Sustaining the Sources of Innovation*. Boston: Harvard Business School Press.

Lyles, M. A., and C. R. Schwenck. 1992. "Top Management, Strategy and Organizational Knowledge Structures." *Journal of Management Studies* 155–173.

Nonaka, I., and H. Takeuchi. 1995. *The Knowledge Creating Company*. New York: Oxford University Press.

Perrow, C. 1967. "A Framework for the Comparative Analysis of Organizations." *American Sociological Review* 32: 194–208.

Polanyi, M. 1966. *The Tacit Dimension*. New York: Doubleday.

Suzaki, K. 1987. *The New Manufacturing Challenge: Techniques for Continuous Improvement*. New York: Free Press.

Tornatzky, L. G., and Fleischer, M. 1990. *The Processes of Technological Innovation*. Mass.: Lexington Books.

Westney, D. E. 1987. *Imitation and Innovation*. Cambridge, Mass.: Harvard University Press.

Winter, S. 1987. *Skill and Knowledge as Strategic Assets*. In D. Teece, ed., *The Competitive Challenge*, pp. 159–431. Cambridge, Mass.: Ballinger.

5

Creating Lean Suppliers

Diffusing Lean Production through the Supply Chain

John Paul MacDuffie

Susan Helper

The existence of supplier-customer relationships, particularly among Japanese companies, that fit neither "market" nor "hierarchy" categories has drawn sustained attention in recent years (Cusumano and Takeishi, 1995; Dyer and Ouchi, 1993; Helper, 1991, 1992; Nishiguchi, 1994; Smitka, 1992). Such arrangements are integral to the structure of Japanese business networks (Gerlach, 1993), and they have also been a companion to Japanese direct investment in overseas manufacturing facilities. In the auto industry, Japanese companies initially used parts from Japan in the new assembly plants built in North America in the 1980s. But, since then, they have steadily increased the percentage of parts purchased from U.S.-located suppliers of both U.S. and Japanese ownership (Kenney and Florida, 1993; Mair, 1993). In the process, some of these Japanese companies have taken the unusual step of working extensively with their suppliers to teach them "lean production"— often by sending their own employees into supplier plants for weeks or months to redesign work stations, reorganize process flow, modify equipment, and establish problem-solving groups.

This level of involvement with the internal operations of externally owned firms is unprecedented and raises the question, Why create lean suppliers? One answer is that Japanese companies have not been able to continue supplying their U.S. assembly plants from Japan-based suppliers because of political pressure to source parts locally (due to Japan's persistent trade surplus with the United States) and the strong economic incentive to move production overseas that was provided by the strength of the yen throughout much of the 1980s and 1990s. Yet, as we discuss later, this is not sufficient to explain the intensity of the supplier support activities undertaken most extensively by Honda, Toyota, and Nissan (Bennet, 1994; Florida and Jenkins, 1996).

In this chapter, we examine Honda's supplier support efforts in particular, drawing on extensive field work at six Honda suppliers; Table 5.1 identifies their key characteristics. We spent a total of eight days at Honda and from one to two days at each of the supplier sites.[1] We asked respondents (who included purchasing and supplier support staff at Honda, as well as managers, shop floor workers, supervisors, union officials, production engineers, and corporate staff at the suppliers) to tell us about key events in the business relationship with Honda but also about "problems, issues, and opportunities for improvement" that had emerged over the course of their relationship with Honda.

We begin by considering the question raised earlier—Why *create* lean suppliers? Next, we review Honda's philosophy of supplier relations and introduce the "BP" program, perhaps Honda's central supplier support activity. "BP" has many meanings—best practices, best process, best profits—and a distinctive approach to transferring technical knowledge related to lean production. At the heart of the chapter are the six BP case studies that reveal the complex dynamics accompanying this mechanism for knowledge transfer. We then analyze the impact of BP on supplier capabilities along various dimensions. Finally, we utilize concepts from research on organizational learning to draw out the general implications of Honda's BP—for customers who want to boost the performance of their supply chain by providing technical assistance; for suppliers who must try to absorb this knowledge while coping with customers who want access to their internal operations; and for understanding what sorts of "mediating mechanisms" for knowledge transfer are most likely to yield suppliers who are self-sufficient and capable rather than dependent on their customer for ongoing support.

Why *Create* Lean Suppliers?

If one thing is clear from half a century of management research (and the experience of countless companies), it is that organizational change is difficult to bring about and even more difficult to sustain (Dosi and Kogut, 1992; Nelson and Winter, 1978). Given this, it is by no means obvious that a company should undertake to bring about organizational change at its suppliers.

Lean production in the auto industry, as described by M.I.T.'s International Motor Vehicle Program (with which we are both affiliated), involves far-reaching organizational and technological changes. Within a firm's own manufacturing operation, it involves reducing buffers through just-in-time inventory systems, producing only what is needed by downstream "customers," whether internal or external; pushing down responsibilities for quality inspection and the specification of work tasks to motivated, multiskilled

Table 5.1 Characteristics of Supplier Companies

Company	Capitol	Progressive	Tower	Donnelly	SEWS	GTI
Product	Plastic moldings	Stampings	Stampings	Door mirrors; window modules	Electrical distribution systems	Plastic moldings
Ownership Plant location	U.S. Ohio	U.S. Ohio	U.S Indiana	U.S. Michigan	Japan Kentucky	U.S./Japan Ohio
1992 annual sales (in millions)	$30	$13	$84	$271	$151	?
1995 annual sales (in millions)	$28	$29	$222	$383	$303	?
Total no. of U.S. employees (1992)	300	95	525	2,000	1,900	240
No. of employees at plant (1992)	300	95	145	270	1,900 (3 plants)	240
Year plant opened	1960	1954	1985	1987	1987	1987
Year began sales to Honda	1979	1989	1982	1987	1987	1987
% of total U.S. sales to Honda (1992)	60	25	30	15	80	95–100
% of total U.S. sales to Honda (1995)	70	65	36	14	60	?
No. of significant non-Honda customers (>5% sales) for same product line (1992)	2	6	1	0	1	?
No. of significant non-Honda customers (>5% sales) for same product line (1995)	2	5	1	2	1	?

workers organized into teams; and eliciting a steady stream of ideas for process improvement (*kaizen*) from employees at all levels (Womack, Jones, and Roos, 1990). Added to this, customers are likely to demand that suppliers assume substantial responsibility during product development; accommodate customer requests for engineering changes in their product or manufacturing process; be highly reliable with respect to quality and delivery; and have the ability to respond quickly in case of problems. These requirements are difficult for a supplier to meet unless it has adopted lean production practices itself. Thus, a lean customer is likely to find it more productive to work with lean suppliers.

However, the adoption process can be risky, since it is common for improvements on one dimension (e.g., reducing inventory levels) to have the *initial* impact of reducing performance on another dimension (e.g., delivery reliability or responsiveness to customer schedule changes). Thus, if an automaker possesses an important capability, such as lean production, that it wants to establish in its supply base, several alternatives might appear more appealing than trying to develop those capabilities among not-lean suppliers.

Do it yourself. Vertical integration was once the clear preference when manufacturing firms wanted to ensure that they controlled the output of upstream processes. Presumably, the firm understands its input requirements better than anyone else, already has manufacturing capabilities, and can ensure through administrative fiat that input prices will not be monopolistic. More recently, vertical integration has fallen out of favor, partly because of the advantages of long-term relationships with separate supplier companies demonstrated by Japanese companies (Nishiguchi, 1994; Smitka, 1991). If parts are single- or dual-sourced, suppliers may be able to achieve substantial economies of scale. The customer can help the supplier with technical assistance while not bearing full investment costs and can still benefit from any supplier improvements because of the stipulation that productivity gains will be shared. By focusing on a single product line, suppliers can develop innovations that are beyond the customer's ability to achieve. Extensive tacit knowledge can develop in the supplier-customer relationship, facilitating coordination of the respective expertise of the parties, particularly with respect to complex, value-added tasks such as product development.

Switch to a lean supplier. If a lean customer can arrange to do business with suppliers who are already lean, what are the advantages of helping existing suppliers learn to be lean? The strongest argument against switching suppliers to get new capabilities is that all the benefits associated with long-term supplier relationships might be lost. As Sako (1992) has pointed out, trust between supplier and customer is essential to achieve these benefits, so switching suppliers can hurt not only the relationship with the supplier that lost business but also with other suppliers that observe this event. In addition, the best lean suppliers may have prior commitments to other customers, so they may be less responsive to a newcomer. Finally, the customer has fewer sourcing options if it waits for competitive forces to generate a larger pool of lean suppliers than if it acts to improve the capabilities of its existing suppliers.

Steer your supplier to a good consultant or partner. The assumption here is that a customer should encourage a supplier to develop lean capabilities on its own or to seek help from consultants or partners rather than interfering directly with the supplier's internal operations. Yet, the knowledge underlying lean production is not necessarily easy to transfer across organizations. It seems to require a primarily "hands-on" approach in which key principles are taught by observing how certain problems are handled in real-life context (MacDuffie, 1997). Also, a large customer (who has the power to directly affect a supplier's sales) may have more leverage to convince the supplier to continue to put forth the high levels of effort necessary for success (Celeste and Sabety, 1993). Thus, a lean customer may conclude that, compared with most alternatives, it has superior knowledge about lean production and a greater ability to motivate suppliers to learn.[2]

Thus, the decision to create lean suppliers is driven by multiple concerns. There can be substantial diseconomies of vertical integration outside the core business. Switching to lean suppliers may entail considerable costs (economic, political, and reputational). Helping suppliers become lean potentially enlarges the pool available for sourcing choices. Finally, customers may be more effective than outside parties in teaching suppliers to be lean.

Honda's Philosophy of Supplier Relations

History

Honda's approach to supplier relations is rooted not only in the common Japanese practice of long-term supplier relationships but also in its own history in the auto industry. Unlike Toyota and Nissan, which were building cars before World War II and developed strong and loyal supplier groups in the postwar era (Cusumano, 1984; Nishiguchi, 1994), Honda was founded only in 1948 and began as a motorcycle company. When Soichiro Honda decided to begin building cars in the early 1960s, he had to develop a supply base from scratch, drawing on three sources: (1) suppliers of motorcycle parts, who were already familiar with Honda but had to learn to make automobile parts; (2) other small suppliers in the surrounding area, who needed to be persuaded to invest in new production capabilities for Honda, on the basis of an implicit promise of future business; and (3) larger companies that were already supplying other auto companies.

Each of these sources of suppliers posed different problems for Honda. The motorcycle suppliers who were already in the Honda "family" were easiest to help, since channels for coordination and technical assistance were already established. The small local suppliers were eager to establish an affiliation with Honda but technologically backward and unfamiliar with the high reliability in quality and delivery required by an export-oriented automaker. The larger suppliers were primarily oriented toward their dominant customer, so Honda had to struggle to get them to be responsive. However, because they had more sophisticated technology and superior production expertise, Honda was forced to go to them for certain parts (authors' interviews at Honda in the U.S. and Japan; Mair, 1994).

There are parallels between these early experiences in Japan and Honda's early years of developing a supply base in the United States. Honda's decision to come to the United States reflected a long-term strategy of "make our products where we sell our products" and its corollary for purchasing—"buy our parts where we make our products." When Honda started its U.S. manufacturing operations in 1978 (again with motorcycles), it was initially supported by a core of Japanese suppliers that were already part of the Honda "family," a number of which established satellite plants near its Ohio manufacturing complex. Honda also began trying to identify small local suppliers in Ohio and surrounding states to take on certain parts. Many of these suppliers were eager to work with Honda but needed considerable assistance to meet Honda's cost, quality, and delivery requirements. Finally, Honda approached some of the larger auto suppliers whose primary customers were the U.S. "Big Three." While these firms had superior capabilities, they were typically not as responsive to Honda's requirements as the smaller suppliers.

Philosophy

This history helps explain key aspects of Honda's philosophy of supplier relations. Honda wants suppliers who can be "self-reliant," with a sufficiently diversified customer base that they will not be at risk if Honda's orders drop due to demand fluctuations. The importance of self-reliance was a lesson learned from painful experience during recessions in Japan, when Honda's commitment to its "child" suppliers (small local companies highly dependent on Honda) became an immense financial strain.

Honda also selects suppliers on the basis of whether their management is willing to be responsive to Honda's needs. These managerial attitudes are more important to Honda than the supplier's technical expertise. Examples of the "right" attitude, from Honda's perspective, include (1) a willingness to take risks, consistent with the "racing spirit" that Mr. Honda worked hard to maintain in Honda's culture;[3] (2) investments in new technologies in advance of competitors; (3) investments also in organizational and human resource capabilities (e.g., advanced engineering and production control staff; sophisticated management systems; worker training); and (4) doing all of these things without explicit contractual commitments.

To a self-sufficient supplier willing to offer this kind of responsiveness, Honda offered a great deal in return. A supplier to Honda would have a lifetime relationship—a marriage—in all but the most unusual circumstances. While specific commitments for future business would not be made, suppliers could count on receiving at least as much business as in the most recent year past and possibly much more.

Furthermore, due to Honda's sustained growth, suppliers who were willing to keep up with Honda's strategic direction and production requirements would often be asked to take on new parts they had never made before—and even new production processes. It was clear Honda felt it was easier to teach the technical knowledge associated with a different product or process technology than to find a technically capable supplier who possessed the combination of risk-taking attitude, motivation to improve, responsiveness to future needs, and overall competence that it valued so highly.

The importance of understanding Honda's supplier development activities in the context of this broad vision of mutual responsibility and obligation between supplier and customer cannot be overstated. In the words of Rick Mayo, the Honda engineer who directs these activities, "We are a philosophy-driven company. We do supplier development as a way to teach our philosophy, to put it into action. It's how we try to help suppliers get past their old way of thinking and understand our way of thinking. For me, it's a mission, not a job."

BP at Honda

BP is the core supplier development activity at Honda of America Manufacturing (HAM). HAM has a supplier development group, with fifty staff members in its purchasing department, that oversees BP and other supplier improvement activities (Celeste and Sabety, 1993). Once a supplier is chosen for BP (see below for more discussion), a few staff members from this group, along with employees from other Honda departments (e.g., vehicle quality, process engineering), form a BP team with supplier employees (including shop floor workers) to work for several weeks at the supplier's facility. The BP team focuses on improvements at a few specific work areas and initially avoids projects that would require extensive capital investment ("hard" BP) or extra personnel. Instead, BP tries to cover all aspects of a narrowly defined project—technology, work organization, problems with second-tier suppliers, or workforce issues (e.g., motivation, training, compensation, employment security).

The narrow scope allows quick results, which provides motivation for BP participants and data to convince skeptical managers to continue backing the effort. BP's deep analysis (only feasible for a narrowly defined project) helps teach systemic thinking, which can then be applied to other areas within the supplier's plant. For the lines on which the BP team focuses, performance improvements are large: Honda reported productivity increases averaging 50 percent at the fifty-three Honda suppliers participating in BP as of 1994, and seven firms interviewed for a report on BP reported productivity gains of 25 percent and quality gains of 66 percent (Celeste and Sabety, 1994, p. 34).

The goals of BP are consistent with Honda's production philosophy for its internal operations:

1. Encourage fresh thoughts about production processes.
2. Gather better data to allow for more thorough, fact-based problem analysis.
3. Seek "common-sense," low-cost solutions by following the "five whys."
4. Know the context by examining the "actual part, actual place, actual situation" (the 3As).
5. Create a smooth flow of production with no waste.

The first BP goal of "encouraging fresh thoughts" acknowledges the need to shake an organization out of its routine ways of looking at its production process or a particular problem. Each BP team contains members from various departments and levels in the supplier's organization to ensure varied perspectives. The second goal of gathering extensive data also helps with breaking away from past routines, particularly since Honda has found that many suppliers don't keep records about their processes in ways that make it possible to determine whether or not a change leads to improved performance.

The third goal involves "root cause" analysis. Here Honda teaches the process of asking "why" five times, established by Toyota's Taiichi Ohno.[4] To do an effective "root cause" analysis requires considerable contextual knowledge. The fourth goal of BP is to develop that knowledge by going to see the "actual part in the actual place and in the actual situation." Honda's BP representatives try to demonstrate this principle at all times, insisting that BP team members go to the actual spot on the shop floor whenever a problem needs to be explored—not sit in their offices and analyze the problem abstractly.

Finally, the fifth goal of BP is the elimination of "muda" or waste wherever possible. Waste is defined as anything that interferes with the smooth flow of production. For example, if tools or components in a given work area don't have a specified storage place, workers may have to hunt for them. Even if this takes only a few seconds, the time wasted can be substantial if multiplied across weeks and months of production activity. The effort to achieve a smooth production flow reveals many upstream and downstream problems (e.g., with other operations in the plant, with suppliers, with the customer order process, or with the distribution system). When each of these is pursued to its "root cause" and remedied, huge amounts of "muda" can be eliminated.

Honda required only a few things from the supplier companies participating in BP. A supplier did not have to pay for the time of Honda's BP team members but was responsible for the cost of tools and materials required for improving core production processes; as noted earlier, for most BP projects, these costs were minimal. The supplier also had to agree not to carry out any employee layoffs as a result of BP activities. Finally, Honda required ready access to information about a supplier's cost structure and technology, the ability to move about freely within the supplier's production facility, and the cooperation of management in efforts to involve front-line employees in BP improvement projects.

BP Case Studies

We turn now to case studies of BP projects at the six suppliers we visited between 1992 and 1994. They are organized around pairs of suppliers that are similar in many ways yet have had somewhat different experiences with BP. We pay particular attention to the overall relationship between the supplier and Honda, because it so greatly influenced the BP process.

Donnelly Corporation and Tower Automotive

These two suppliers have a common history in the auto parts industry of Western Michigan. This area was settled by Dutch immigrants in the early nineteenth century and has strong religious traditions that are grounded in the Dutch Reformed church. It is known for a strong work ethic and progressive employers. Social ties among managers and employees are common outside work. Firms in this area have long been innovators in employee involvement and gain-sharing plans, and they typically make a strong commitment to avoiding layoffs.

Honda found these suppliers congenial from the start. The older plants near corporate headquarters in Western Michigan were crowded and cozy, reminding some Japanese managers at Honda of their older plants in Japan. The progressive management policies, the "no layoff" commitment, and the loyal workforce were characteristics that Honda valued and hoped to encourage in all its suppliers. Honda began to work with both Donnelly and Tower in the early to mid-1980s and expanded its business with each company dramatically over time.

Yet, despite this high comfort level, Honda wanted much that was difficult for these firms to provide. Both were technically competent, dependable, long-time suppliers to the U.S. Big Three auto makers, accustomed to the "boom or bust" cycles of the industry and to keeping costs low to avoid being undercut on price by competitors. Fundamentally mass producers of commodity products, they exploited economies of scale while also relying on unique technical enhancements to achieve price and performance advantages over competitors. They were not, when they began working with Honda, particularly familiar with lean production. Instead, they were successful enough as mass producers to have little reason to change their approach.

Donnelly Corporation

Following a strategic decision to try to win business with the Japanese transplants, Donnelly sought Honda's business actively, in part to learn about

Japanese production methods. It assigned a newly hired (and junior) manager, a native of Ireland who had studied in Japan and then worked for Nissan in Tokyo, to the job of managing the relationship with Honda. After several approaches, Donnelly was invited to submit a bid.

Honda had a long-time relationship with a mirror and glass supplier in Japan, Matsuyama, and wanted to keep that firm involved during the transition to production in the United States. Furthermore, Honda believed that Matsuyama's design for rearview mirrors was superior to Donnelly's, even though Donnelly had a 60 percent share of the world market for this product. While Donnelly's mirrors for the Big Three were glued to the windshield, Matsuyama's mirrors were more securely (and expensively) bolted to the car's headliner. Therefore, Honda kept much of its rearview mirror business with Matsuyama and asked Donnelly to make door mirrors—a new product for the company but one that combined their production knowledge related to mirrors and plastic molding.

Donnelly was an eighty-year old company that, following World War II, began to implement a variety of progressive management policies. Its governance structures, which allowed for employee "voice" with respect to wages and grievances and for innovative profit-sharing plans, had been the focus of frequent articles in the business press. But Donnelly had little experience extending its participative culture into the realm of production-related decisions, which were dominated by long-tenure engineers and manufacturing managers. And, as noted earlier Donnelly's production philosophy was strictly mass production.

Honda took a step-by-step approach with Donnelly, first having it copy the designs from Matsuyama and use the same tooling and materials, in order to minimize sources of variation. This clearly grated on the long-time production chiefs and lead engineers at Donnelly, who were highly confident of their own capability. For Honda, the presumption of superior performance at Donnelly was annoying because the supplier was not always meeting its quality, cost, and delivery goals. Despite their junior rank, the few people at Donnelly who spoke Japanese became a crucial communications link as the two companies worked through these tensions.

Ultimately, Donnelly decided to build a dedicated plant for Honda products. ("Honda would never ask," said one manager, "but we knew this was what they wanted.") It was located in the town of Grand Haven, thirty to forty minutes away from Donnelly's other factories in Holland, and a place where prevailing wage rates were 28 percent lower. Donnelly built the plant in just nine months, the fastest it had ever brought a new plant into production. While the plant was completed by December 1987, it took six months of "debugging" to achieve the quality levels Honda was seeking. At first, according to many Donnelly respondents, dealing with Honda was a "pain in the neck." They didn't understand Honda's insistence that they use Matsuyama designs and tooling in order to minimize variation in Honda's operations. After meeting Honda's aggressive schedule for starting up the Grand Haven plant, they found it frustrating that Honda kept bringing them long lists of production problems and rejecting many batches of product, contrary to the Big Three practice of giving a new plant a chance to work out the bugs over time. The following quote reveals just how difficult it was for even a well-managed and experienced American supplier to understand Honda's continuous improvement philosophy:

> Honda people were out here every week. Eventually no one was surprised if they would just come up and start working next to you. At first, there was a lot of fear—people thought Honda was out to find problems and get rid of people. Also it was pride—who are they to tell us what to do? When they walked in, you knew that "good is never good enough." This was tough on people, because it felt like a kind of negativity. And when the targets kept on changing, people got offended.

Initially, the new plant made only unpainted mirrors, but Honda decided to offer painted mirrors on its new models and encouraged Donnelly to equip the plant accordingly, even though painting was a process that Donnelly had never done. In keeping with its philosophy, Honda would not guarantee Donnelly any business but instead asked for Donnelly's trust that the auto maker would act in good faith. The Grand Haven plant began producing the first painted mirrors—for the Gold Wing motorcycle—in 1989. These mirrors were painted in small batches, hand-sprayed and then rolled on racks into a simple oven. There were major quality problems with paint in the first few months, straining relations between the companies.

Late in 1989, Donnelly learned that Honda was planning to source the door mirror for the Civic with another supplier—contradicting Donnelly's expectation that building the Grand Haven plant would ensure its getting this business. After a tense meeting, Honda reversed this decision, agreeing to work with Donnelly to solve the problems with paint. One month later, Honda proposed that Donnelly invest in a full paint shop, with a moving line, automated spraying, and sophisticated paint booths—a total expenditure of $5 million. For Donnelly, this proposal was a tremendous stretch—something that forced it to probe deeply the nature of its relationship with Honda and its vision of the future. One senior Donnelly manager told us about a dinner at this time with Honda's VP of purchasing, Dave Nelson: "We had already had a tough time convincing our board to make the investment for the Grand Haven plant, and we hadn't shown a profit yet. Now Honda wants us to invest another $5 million for a paint line, and they won't give us a contract. I remember looking into his eyes and thinking, 'Can I trust this guy?'" For another manager, this proposal was nearly the last straw: "I was pretty close to the position that we should get out of the transplant business."

Ultimately, Donnelly's board did approve the investment for the new paint line. With the new technology in place, Grand Haven took on a small portion of the volume of painted door mirrors for the 1990 Accord. Again, initial production was plagued with problems. Honda's pressure for improvement continued to intensify, and soon both companies decided that Donnelly should receive technical assistance through BP. As one Donnelly manager told us, "Throughout this period, we were testing each other's will to make it a partnership. It was incredibly stressful but also a tremendous growth experience for us."

During 1991, most problems with the new paint line were resolved. Donnelly now had responsibility for nearly all the painted door mirrors for the Accord, as well as for unpainted door mirrors for the Civic. Its overall investment in the Grand Haven plant now totaled $10–12 million. By 1992, the plant was winning productivity improvement awards from Honda and was beginning to attract considerable interest from other car companies, such as Ford and Toyota. So, after deciding to learn a new process capability, making major investments without a contractual commitment from its sole customer for that product, struggling through repeated difficulties during new product launches, enduring repeated expansions and additions of new technology, and boosting corporate sales from $20 million in 1990 to $30 million in 1992, Donnelly found itself regarded as one of the premier manufacturers of painted door mirrors in the United States—a product that five years earlier, it didn't even make.

It is against this backdrop that Donnelly's involvement in Honda's BP process must be understood. Donnelly was the first U.S. supplier to get BP attention from Honda. According to one Donnelly manager:

Honda had BP in Japan but it wasn't clear what it would be here. When they started, the focus appeared to us to be cost. "Let's get into your books." It was the worst fear we had about the transplants. We persuaded them to shift focus. When they decided to focus on process improvement, they wanted to achieve some small, short-term successes to show people what could be done. We wanted them to focus on the paint process at Grand Haven.

According to a Honda employee who was a member of the first BP team at Donnelly,

They had so many problems with quality and volume at first that it really forced us to work closely with them. Paint is really tricky. You bake metal parts at 300+ degrees, plastic parts at 180 degrees. When it was a batch process, they had the base for the door mirror on a different rack from the housing and the colors wouldn't always match up. There are so many variables with paint, and the only way to learn is to do it. We had lots of people up there. At Grand Haven, they called it "snowflakes"—something would go wrong and a whole flock of Honda people in white uniforms would descend on you.

A quality control associate at Grand Haven picks up the story:

We had never done painted product, and at first we just had two people doing batch painting. Honda came in and taught us how to paint and how to flow material. We tried to reduce inventories of parts going to off-line buffers, partly by having some small in-line buffers that we could manage ourselves. We went from triple handling of some parts to single handling. Then we went to Honda and sat in on QC circle meetings. They're very big on digging to find the answer. Very demanding, but they teach you what you need to know. Now Honda will train our workers in our first QC circle. We've resisted until now, because we've got our own culture.

Thus, BP became a way for Honda to convey technical knowledge about painting and process flow but also to show Donnelly how to couple participative processes with production-level problem solving.

Despite the eventual success of the move into painted door mirrors and Honda's apparent willingness to continue expanding its business, one persistent concern that Honda expressed in our interviews was whether or not Donnelly could maintain and extend the gains made at Grand Haven in 1991–1992, as well as transfer the lessons learned to its other divisions.

Donnelly, in turn, admired Honda's systematic approach to improving manufacturing processes but felt that with rapid growth, not all of the Honda employees who interacted with Donnelly understood that approach equally well; "we end up teaching Honda employees the Honda Way," said several respondents. Furthermore, not all Donnelly managers felt it was necessary to follow the Honda approach, believing that their own technical capabilities, participative culture, and emphasis on autonomous divisions could be just as successful. To some degree, therefore, each company drew different lessons from the Grand Haven experience—for Honda, it proved the value of the BP process for building supplier capabilities, while, for Donnelly, it proved how quickly it could learn a new process capability and achieve strong results.[5]

Tower Automotive

Honda learned about Tower Automotive in the late 1970s, when it sent a team to visit more than 100 U.S. stamping firms listed in the directory of the Precision Metal Forming Association. For Tower, which was accustomed to seeing a Big Three buyer only once every five years, the fact that it was visited by the president and members of the board of Honda of America made a strong impression. One Tower manager in particular became a strong internal advocate for the advantages of working closely with Honda.

Tower's experience with Honda moved through a set of small, steady steps, each of which impressed Tower's initially skeptical management. First, the tools that Honda provided from Japan worked extremely well from the start. Then Honda provided some steel from a Japanese supplier that proved very easy to work with. Eventually, the steel Tower received from Inland Steel—a major U.S. supplier to Honda—began to show the same attributes as Honda worked with Inland on process improvements. While Honda and Tower had very different attitudes toward tool design and maintenance, the two companies were able to work out agreements on acceptable modifications in tooling relatively quickly.

Satisfied by these early experiences, Honda began to give Tower more business. As volume grew, Honda asked Tower to build a dedicated plant for Honda. Tower refused at first but in 1987 did agree to put Honda production into a plant, in Auburn, Indiana, that had been initially built for Ford in 1985. Tower then expanded the Auburn plant four times in the next few years to accommodate the higher volume for Honda.

Tower managers were not always comfortable with Honda's policy of having suppliers provide lots of detailed information about their plans and operations. Said one: "With BP, at first there was a lot of nervous tension. We didn't want to give away the farm. Eventually we realized that Honda's wish to know everything is not because they are trying to steal our good ideas or because they want to be snoopy. They want a partnership and want to be able to help you find the best way to do things."

Honda's zeal for results, attention to detail, and wish for involvement on the shop floor stood in contrast to Ford, the other primary customer at the Auburn plant. Honda's BP people visited Auburn twice a week during the BP project. In addition, quality control people came from Honda twice a month, and Tower people went to Honda in Ohio twice a month. As one manager told us, with Ford you "never" see the buyer in the plant—just the quality control people once a month. "We go to Ford as little as possible—it is our plant's turn once a quarter."

The flip side of Honda's attention was the strong pressure it applied when problems occurred. Tower (like other Honda suppliers) gets a written report any time there is a quality or delivery problem and has to give a written response detailing what "countermeasures" it will take to remedy the problem. Honda keeps track of the number of parts that are defective or delivered late. If a shipment is one part short, the entire number of parts in that shipment is counted as defective. As one manager explained, Ford, in contrast, is more likely to "call us up" when it sees a problem and even then only if it occurs often enough to appear to be a pattern. If a shipment is a few parts short, Ford will tell Tower to "throw a few more" in the next shipment.

Tower managers differed on the merits and shortcomings of Honda's and Ford's approach. One manager preferred Ford:

> Ford has focused on systems. They believe that if you have good quality control systems in place, you'll have good parts. After the systems are in place, they leave you alone as long as you're performing. With design, we're more involved at an earlier stage with Ford. They give us CAD [computer-aided design] data as the master specification and then let us work from there. When there are problems, they handle them informally, over the phone. They get a quicker response that way than if they write us up and "ding" us.

This manager also felt that Honda had benefited from Tower's adherence to Ford's SPC system: "Ford really dragged their supplier base up. Ford was the first to teach us SPC. Seventy-five percent of our salaried people went through their program at the American Supplier Quality Institute. When Honda saw we had Ford's system, they urged us to use it."

Another manager found value in Honda's obsession with eliminating defects:

Honda cares about making the part fit the car, while Ford cares about making the part fit the blueprint. During product launch, Honda takes parts as soon as they are made and runs back to try them on the car. Then they tell us to change this, change that. Ford usually isn't here during our trials. They just want to be sure that we are meeting the spec. If there is a problem, they eventually issue an engineering change. But at Honda, the changes happen in a matter of days. At first we thought they were nuts. But theirs is a great way to do business. You get what you want—a part that works on the vehicle—right away. Everything else—like whether the blueprint is up-to-date—is secondary. Initially, it was incredibly frustrating because Honda was so detail-oriented and wanted responses from us immediately. But I find they are almost always right.

While we were in the plant, we saw an example of how Tower combined Ford's emphasis on procedures with Honda's focus on an attitude of continuous improvement. We had asked to see a statistical process control chart, a type of documentation required by Ford but not by Honda for this product. The manager accompanying us noticed that the process was heading out of control on a key dimension; he and the operator quickly engaged in a discussion of what might be causing the problem and how to stop it.

BP started at Tower in late 1989 with the arrival of a team of three people from Honda—from the welding, quality, and purchasing departments. The team proposed starting with "soft" BP (simple projects with low investment)—organizing all steel blanks in one area, painting floor spaces to indicate where steel coils are to be placed, attaching new bins to stamping machines that are more accessible and can be repositioned. Next came a project involving "hard" BP (i.e., investment in new equipment)—reengineering the work cell for the center pillar (i.e., a stamped part located between the front and rear passenger doors that connects the roof to the side panels). Initially, Tower's work cell utilized dedicated automation, designed for a given center pillar and able to produce 63 parts per hour. Honda encouraged Tower to invest in robotic technology, but of a particular sort. Rather than having the robots move around the part to apply welds, the welding gun was on a pedestal with a fixed location and welding position. Simple, low-cost, and reliable "pick and place" robots could then be used to move the parts around so that each weld could be applied. Automatic sensors were used to check whether all welds were completed successfully. With this new cell design, productivity rose to 125 parts per hour. The life of weld tips was also increased dramatically, from 50,000 welds before tip replacement to 250,000 welds, because the fixed position of the weld gun meant less wear and tear on the tips.

Over time, Tower was able to influence Honda's manufacturing approach. In the words of a manager at Donnelly, as Honda came to trust a firm's technical capabilities, a supplier could "earn the right to disagree." For example, the initial equipment that Tower used to make stampings for Honda was from Japan, provided by Honda's supplier there. Tower engineers noticed a small difference in how holes were punched in a stamping. While Tower used a "button" of metal underneath the part that the punch would strike, ensuring that the punch would always go to the same depth, the Japanese equipment did such a punch without a button underneath. Tower argued that, without a button, the risk of splintering around the hole and the maintenance required for the punch tool increased. Honda agreed and authorized Tower to install easily changeable buttons made of hardened steel to reduce maintenance.

Despite acknowledging that they learned a lot from Honda, Tower managers and engineers still resisted Honda's pressure to provide lots of information. When Tower built its Auburn, Indiana, plant, the first that Honda heard of the plan was when the supplier presented Honda with blueprints. While Honda was pleased that Tower was building a new plant, it would have liked more opportunity to comment—a desire that Tower felt was intrusive.

In another case, Tower felt that it had withstood pressure from Honda and had decided to go its own way. At its Greenville Michigan, plant, Tower hired a consultant to implement a "workplace transformation" program that differed from BP. Whereas Tower managers saw BP as focusing on value analysis and process reengineering, they saw the new program—which, once adopted at Greenville, replaced BP there—as focused on the implementation of independent business units within the plant and "self-directed work teams" on the shop floor. The move to self-directed teams also had an explicit role for the union (the Greenville plant was organized by the UAW, whereas the Auburn plant was nonunion) and emphasized efforts to improve job design. While Tower felt that Honda disapproved of this initiative, Honda disagreed. As one Honda manager explained, "Our first question whenever a supplier proposes something is 'why'? We just want to see if it makes sense. We find that if the supplier doesn't have a good answer, it's a sign of potential problems. But the supplier reaction is often 'Honda doesn't like it.' "

What struck us about this incident was how unfamiliar and uncomfortable the suppliers were with the idea of talking over their internal plans with a key customer. Clearly, suppliers are most accustomed to a situation in which a meeting with the customer is a time for receiving orders.

After the workplace transformation program was launched at Greenville, efforts began to bring it to the Auburn plant as well. This took the Auburn plant manager away from the plant in order to help train other managers, right at the time of the 1994 Accord launch. Honda was concerned that the program's implementation, coming at the same time as a major product launch, was drawing attention away from persistent quality problems with 1994 Accord parts.

Tower also asserted its own wishes in some investment decisions. The quality problems alluded to earlier were concentrated in parts for the Accord station wagon. Because the volume for this product is relatively low, Honda and Tower agreed that investment costs should be kept low and that dedicated welders should not be installed. However, when problems persisted,

Honda pressed Tower to invest in automatic sensors that check for missing welds or nuts on subassemblies. Tower refused, insisting on all-manual processes. In another case, Tower insisted on automating processes that were performed manually by suppliers who made the same parts for Honda in Japan, despite Honda's concerns about the impact on overall costs.

One factor that has affected Tower's relationship with Honda in recent years is Tower's acquisition by Hidden Creek Industries and its consolidation with several other medium-size stamping companies in the area. Tower Automotive, the consolidated firm, has made a determined bid to acquire lots of new business from Ford, Toyota, and Nissan. With Ford reducing its stamping suppliers from 400 to fewer than 50, Tower was determined to stay in that select group. Ford was also increasingly willing to give Tower major design responsibility. Furthermore, Tower was building a new plant in Kentucky to serve Toyota and Nissan. Thus, while the Auburn plant remained dedicated to Honda (as it had been since 1990), managerial time and effort for the newly consolidated firm were pulled in many different directions.

So, despite a strong and long-lasting relationship, Tower has struggled with Honda in many ways. Honda continues to press Tower for performance gains and for continued investments in improved capabilities. Faced with pressures from two major customers—Ford and Honda—Tower's senior managers seemed to be finding Ford's more "hands-off" approach more appealing. With Ford's emphasis on getting good systems in place, Tower was able to satisfy Ford's expectations on a regular basis, while Honda's insistence on responsiveness for each new defect or delivery problem was more annoying. (As one manager explained, "Ford's subliminal message is that a few defects are part of life—get your systems right and you'll basically be OK. Honda is after us with their Supplier Performance Report every month.") Also, Ford seemed more likely to make definite commitments of volume to Tower in advance of investment decisions, while Honda continued to insist that its "partners" continue to make needed investments so they would be ready for whatever new business might be available.

Thus, the Tower case suggests that, even where BP efforts succeed in boosting a supplier's technical skills, capabilities for improvement, and overall performance, the stress of responding to two major customers with different priorities can still prevent a supplier from being as responsive as Honda might like.

Capitol Plastics and Progressive Stamping

These were both very small firms when they began working with Honda. Both had previously supplied Big Three customers, under the traditional "low bid" system. Both made a good impression on Honda because they were willing to be very responsive to Honda's needs, and both welcomed Honda's BP process. But, because of their small size, they had difficulty responding to all of Honda's requirements.

Capitol Plastics

Capitol was one of Honda's earliest U.S.-owned suppliers, going back to the late 1970s.[6] Faced with declining business for the Big Three, Capitol began exploring opportunities to work with Japanese customers. After four years of contacts, Honda made Capital the second supplier of a small motorcycle fender part in 1978, in order to observe its capabilities. The owner, who was also managing the plant at the time of our 1992 visit, recalled how much information Honda asked for in the early days of their relationship: "Other suppliers thought I was crazy to give them so much. But we found out that the dialogue was genuine. First we got an order, then a purchasing agreement. Then our volume began to expand. All very simple, very little written down."

When Honda began to build cars in 1982, it asked Capitol to take on some important console parts for the Accord. At first, the tooling was supplied from Japan. Honda also arranged for Capitol to establish a "technical collaboration agreement" with its supplier of the same part in Japan. This firm, Morioko, began to send technical personnel to Capitol to help with equipment installation and product launch.

Keeping up with Honda's dramatic growth over the next five to seven years was like "trying to keep hold of a tiger," according to the owner. "We showed we'd do whatever they wanted." Capitol's overall sales grew from $7 million in 1979 to $30 million in 1989. But then, in the industry downturn of the early 1990s, Capitol lost a big chunk of business for a Big Three customer because of a design change that eliminated Capitol's part. In the resulting crisis, Capitol went to Honda to find out what improvements it would need to make to continue increasing its share of Honda parts. Honda said that Capitol should get involved in BP.

Despite Capitol's willingness to be responsive, Honda was frustrated with Capitol's inability to resolve persistent quality and delivery problems. It sent a team of four people from the BP group to "live" at Capitol for nine months. Two had engineering backgrounds, and two were former assembly-line workers. This BP team focused, first, on changes at the management level, recommending changes in reporting relationships and redeployment of certain managers in order to get the more people-oriented managers into shop floor positions. Then it undertook three BP projects in the plant, each devoted to a single production line and overseen by a task force composed of operators, engineers, and Honda's BP representatives.

The first two projects took 3 1/2 months each, and the third took two months. The emphasis in each project was twofold: how to evaluate the line and plan improvements and how to get workers involved in the process. Improvements to the line included the redesign of machine layout to reduce walk time and other unnecessary motion, converting parts racks to a "flow" design (in which gravity pulls a new bin of parts down a slanted shelf with rollers once the old bin is removed), constructing circular fixtures to hold parts (height-adjustable for different workers) that can be loaded on one side, spun around for work to be done, and spun again to be unloaded; improving working conditions (e.g., rubber mats on the floor where people stand, better lighting immediately over the work area), and replacing handheld tools with fixed-position tools on movable trollies for better process consistency and less strain on wrists and arms.

During one of the projects, a task force made up of workers from the BP line, organized by Honda's BP staff, uncovered the "root cause" of a mysterious quality problem. On an irregular basis, parts would emerge from the molding machines with "splay" (white spots along the edge of the product) or "short-shots" (a mold not completely filled in). The workers discovered that these conditions resulted from wet, cold particles of plastic resin, which were, in turn, caused by condensation that was falling into the resin container from an exhaust fan in the roof. Once diagnosed correctly, this was an easy problem to fix. Their success inspired great enthusiasm for BP among the task force members. Honda believed it was crucial to teach supervisors and engineers at their suppliers how to be responsive to operator ideas—a difficult cultural change. As one Capitol employee put it, "Their [Honda's] philosophy is to pull the lower skilled people into the job of redesigning the line. They're willing to lose some on the technical side. They're not just after the best process but getting the people motivated, getting their skills involved."

This employee then expressed reservations about how well this approach was working at Capitol:

> I don't know that Honda's approach is the most cost-effective short-term. At Honda, the processes are already set and pretty good, so when workers make suggestions, the changes are small. Here and at most small American suppliers, the process is *not* well established. You need to get the process fixed first, and that's a *big* change, which means a lot of fear. Seventy percent of the people would like to participate but 40 percent are afraid to participate. Sometimes the whole process feels too slow—but I'm not sure management or supervisors could do any better.

The three BP projects brought big improvements in throughput time, inventory levels, scrap, rate defects, cleanliness of the work area, and number of injuries. For example, the BP project for a part called the box instrument back produced a 45 percent increase in productivity and a 67 percent reduction in the scrap rate. For one BP project, some subcontracted work was brought back to Capitol for more control over quality and to maintain employment levels as the line grew more efficient.

However, after the Honda BP team left, problems crept back in. Delivery problems were particularly severe because of Capitol's lack of expertise in production planning. Capitol also failed to capitalize on the enthusiasm unleashed by the initial implementation of BP. Two examples were cited by both managers and union officials during our visit. In the first case, the BP team for one line suggested covering the areas where workers stood with rubber floor mats. Though they cost only a few hundred dollars, the mats proved effective in reducing operators' fatigue from standing on a cement floor. Other workers saw the mats and asked if they could be installed on their lines, too. However, they were told that any changes had to wait until BP came to their line—a time that was subject to many delays. In the second case, workers on another line could not find out how much money their improvement efforts had saved the company. Disclosing this figure (an amount which turned out to be $250,000) was a standard part of the Honda methodology and a key motivator for participants, who wanted to know that their extra effort had produced something worthwhile. However, the owner did not want to disclose financial information to workers because he feared that the union would use it to win wage increases.

Capitol's difficulty in keeping the BP process going and the persistence of quality and delivery problems concerned Honda, as well as the firm's owner. Under guidance from Honda's BP advisers, managerial assignments were re-structured, new staff were hired, and new intensive projects (e.g., a delivery improvement project with another staff group at Honda) were undertaken. Honda's investment in helping Capitol improve was now quite high; Capitol managers estimated that Honda's technical assistance had cost the automaker more than $1 million. But it remained unclear whether Capitol had the re-sources for the investments in both physical and human capital that would be necessary to meet Honda's continuously increasing demands. By the time of our visit, Capitol was actively exploring purchase offers, and, several months later, it was purchased by a large, diversified company that makes many different kinds of parts.

Progressive Industries

Progressive is a small stamping firm that had a long history of second-tier contracts with the Big Three before it began to work for Honda. It is a family-run business now headed by Ruston Simon, son of the founder.[7] His father was an experienced tool-and-die engineer, but Ruston went to college at Northwestern, worked a few years in banking in Boston, then got an M.B.A. before taking over the family business. This combination of education and experience gave him a nontraditional (and more sophisticated) perspective on how a small auto parts firm should be managed.

Progressive was founded in the 1950s as a "die shop" that built tools for bigger stamping companies. To test the tools it was building, it bought an old stamping press. Then a customer asked it to take on the stamping of a small part. It found the steady work associated with an auto contract to be more appealing than the "feast-or-famine" cycle of the tool and die industry and added more and more presses. Many small stampers—tagged by some in the industry as the "smash-and-ship" bunch—had similar histories. Keep-ing costs low was paramount, so physical plant was kept small and spartan, wages were low, presses were old, and high capital utilization was critical. Companies like Progressive that were able to use their tool-and-die skills to keep machines running had some slight advantage over other commodity stampers, but price competition was fierce, and customers were willing to switch suppliers with each new low bid.

When Simon took over Progressive in 1984, the company had moved away from the automotive business to avoid its cyclicality and price competition, but it was not particularly profitable. He decided to move back into the auto industry but discovered that Progressive had fallen considerably behind the performance levels needed to win contracts. He began approaching other small stampers in the area who were facing capacity constraints, offering to make their most difficult part for them. In addition, Progressive was able to help these firms improve the performance of their tools.

When Progressive decided to pursue major auto contracts directly, it found that the Big Three were shedding suppliers speedily. Then, in the fall of 1986, Simon spotted a Honda ad in a metalworking magazine, with the headline "WANTED: Competitive Stamping Sources" (see Figure 5.1). Honda sent an extensive questionnaire asking about the firm's history, equipment, profits, "everything." Then, as it had in the late 1970s (when it found Tower), Honda

WANTED

COMPETITIVE STAMPING SOURCES

Honda of America Mfg., Inc. is investigating stamping sources to increase domestic content of substructure components.

REQUIREMENTS

LOCATION: OH, IN, KY, MI, PA, WV, WESTERN NY; CAPABILITY TO SUPPLY AUTOMOTIVE PARTS; COMPETITIVE IN INTERNATIONAL MARKETPLACE; EFFICIENT, FLEXIBLE PRODUCTION METHODS; DIE MAKING, DIE MAINTENANCE AND SECONDARY EQUIPMENT MAKING CAPABILITY; HIGH QUALITY, ZERO DEFECT PARTS — CONSISTENTLY; JIT PRODUCTION AND DELIVERY CAPABILITY.

Interested manufacturers should contact the North American Procurement Project in the Purchasing Department for further details no later than October 20, 1986.

HONDA OF AMERICA MFG., INC., MARYSVILLE, OH

513/642-5000

Figure 5.1 Honda of America manufacturing 1986 advertisement for U.S. stamping suppliers.

sent a team of three or four American and Japanese purchasing associates to visit 120 stampers in a five-state area. Progressive was one of seven stampers chosen through this process, and the smallest. Honda was impressed with Progressive's quality systems and even more so with the management team's openness to using Japanese tools and learning Honda's production methods.

Progressive's experience with Japanese tools is instructive, because the design philosophy for dies differs dramatically between the United States and Japan. U.S. dies are typically engineered with very hard steel, in anticipation of a long life cycle for a given car model. Hence, they are both expensive to buy and need a long lead time to build. Japanese dies are typically cheaper and made of softer metal, and they require a shorter lead time to develop; however, they also need frequent maintenance. This fits well with the shorter life cycle for most Japanese-designed autos, since extra maintenance costs are easily offset by the quicker development process and cheaper raw materials.

By using Japanese tools, Progressive's tool-and-die makers gained exposure to this very different philosophy of die design and maintenance. As a result, they developed ideas about potential improvements in the Japanese dies and, after producing successfully with these tools for a few years, persuaded Honda to switch to U.S.-designed dies that incorporated these ideas. Thus, Progressive was able to show that it was receptive to new ideas but also able to contribute its own innovations.

Progressive was particularly innovative in the use of die sensing—mechanical and electronic gauges on the surfaces of dies and edges of presses that monitor whether the stamping equipment is operating within certain critical parameters. For many traditional stampers, this monitoring process was done by assessing the sound of the machine and the shininess of the areas where die surfaces meet. With Progressive's home-grown sensors (and the accompanying software, developed with outside vendors), presses could be calibrated more precisely, to use the "minimum pressure required," which reduces wear, saves energy, and allows more precise matching of jobs to the tonnage of the equipment. Also, sensors can quickly shut down machines as soon as they detect a problem, similar to the "jidoka" philosophy associated with the Toyota Production System.

The information generated by die sensing became important in one of the BP efforts Honda carried out at Progressive: the development of very detailed technical standards and operating procedures for each press, to systematize production processes, limit variance that could lead to defects, and allow the accumulation of process knowledge that could lead to further innovations.

While Honda was relatively satisfied with Progressive's technical capabilities as a stamper, it pushed the firm to move to the next "value-added" step of welding and assembly of stamped parts to produce a finished subassembly. Unlike U.S. automakers, who were more likely to build such subassemblies in their own plants, Honda has long preferred to give responsibility for subassemblies to suppliers. At Honda's small stamping suppliers in Japan, roughly two-thirds of the workforce is devoted to welding and assembly tasks. These were new areas for Progressive, but adding these capabilities was appealing to Simon, who wanted to move the company away from being viewed as a mere "commodity" producer. "We needed to earn our spurs with them" on welding and assembly, he admitted, "and we were given more leeway at first than the bigger guys. They started us off on small, simple tasks and we were able to show good results early." Increasingly, Honda is pushing Progressive to take on more complex parts and weld patterns, moving toward multiple welds along multiple axes. Progressive's tool shop heritage has been applied to in-house development of customized welding equipment for the Honda parts it makes, including robotic cells.

The BP projects at Progressive unfolded against this backdrop of increasing responsibility, technical challenge, and expansion into new processes. According to Progressive managers, "there was no single, critical event that was plant-changing. It was a steady learning process. Honda brought us along very slowly." One BP project developed a color-coded priority system for die maintenance. Another BP project took a single press and made a series of small improvements:

1. The control panel was moved from the side of the press and put onto a rotating arm so that it could be moved close to the operator while he or she observed press operation.
2. Small welded compartments to hold tools during maintenance were attached to the press.
3. Oil needed for press maintenance was piped from a central storage location, rather than being hauled in barrels and poured into line-side storage containers.
4. A staging area for steel coils was created upstream from the presses, to speed changeovers.
5. Simple metal dividers were installed to ensure that scrap pieces would fall automatically into scrap containers without having to be handled.
6. Three bins for finished parts were put onto a rotating stand so that one bin could be filling while another bin was being unloaded into shipping containers.
7. The floor area around the press where incoming materials or outgoing parts are stored was painted to indicate precise placement locations for each item.

Complementing Progressive's BP efforts on the shop floor was a human resource system that was consistent with Honda's values and, in many cases, influenced by Honda's policies. Progressive has had only one layoff in its forty-year history, so the firm had no problem accepting Honda's no-layoff condition for BP. To absorb volume fluctuations, Progressive established a work schedule of forty-five hours (four ten-hour days and five hours of scheduled overtime) so that it could cut back to forty hours when times were lean or add overtime in boom periods. Besides their relatively low base pay ($8 for operators and $15 for skilled trades), employees received profit sharing based on meeting targets in each quarter, plus a discretionary bonus ($980 in 1993) at year's end. Progressive also provided full reimbursement for out-side education and boosted its training significantly, often using training ma-terials developed by Honda.

As with Capitol, Progressive's early responsiveness to Honda brought a steady growth in orders—sales to Honda that more than doubled from 1992 to 1995 and an increase in first-tier and second-tier parts produced from be-tween ten and twenty in the late 1980s to between 125 and 130 by 1994. Unlike Capitol, Progressive has been able to manage this growth effectively, while also taking on additional responsibilities. More money for investments, a more technically sophisticated staff, and more attention to human resource development all appear to be part of Progressive's success. The Progressive case is a good example of Honda's preference for giving additional business to suppliers who have demonstrated responsiveness, good performance, and the willingness to take on new challenges.

Sumitomo Electric Wiring Systems (SEWS) and Greenville Technologies Inc. (GTI)

Both Sumitomo Electric Wiring Systems (SEWS) and Greenville Technologies Inc. (GTI) were subsidiaries of Japanese-owned companies that had long his-tories of selling to Honda in Japan. Each established U.S. operations at the request of Honda and, for a time, had Honda as its only U.S. customer. Both companies were confident of their lean production capabilities and felt secure in their relationship with Honda. However, both had some initial problems that prompted Honda to conduct BP at their plants. Given this background, the main effects of BP were different from those in the other cases we've examined. Both firms already were familiar with the techniques of continuous improvement. Instead, they needed to learn how to manage in the U.S. con-text.

Sumitomo Electric Wiring Systems (SEWS)

SEWS is a subsidiary of Sumitomo Electric, a 400-year old company that had supplied Honda for decades. SEWS came to the United States in 1986 and, at the time of our visit in 1994, did 80 percent of its business with Honda of America Manufacturing (HAM). However, it had ambitious plans to ex-pand its customer base; by 1997, it expected that HAM's share of its business would be down to 53 percent.

SEWS's parent company was highly regarded by many observers for its lean production capabilities. In fact, the parent company, Sumitomo Electric, had done some technical assistance of its own, spending six months instruct-ing a supplier to NUMMI (the GM-Toyota joint venture) in continuous-improvement techniques. The instruction was so successful that the supplier went from being among NUMMI's ten worst suppliers (out of 400) to among the ten best (Gillett, 1993). This raises a question: Why does such an expe-rienced, powerful supplier need BP?

For Honda, the reason for initiating BP was a set of problems that SEWS encountered during its adjustment to the U.S context. The problems were in three areas: quality, responsiveness to Honda requests for engineering changes, and management policies that led to tensions with the company's American workforce. For SEWS, participating in BP was one way to show responsiveness to Honda while picking up some potentially useful technical knowledge. BP also offered easy access to Honda's *cultural* knowledge about managing in the U.S. environment.

The first SEWS plant chosen for BP was located in Edmonton, Kentucky. The plant was started in 1988 and assembled wiring harnesses, the bundles of wires that distribute electrical signals throughout the car. The plant initially went through some tough years; in 1990, it was among HAM's engine plants' twelve worst suppliers, with 8.4 claims per month against it. By 1992, claims per month were down to 1.25. This success came after much intervention by HAM, including BP. Subsequently, SEWS quickly transferred BP within the Edmonton plant. The first BP project at Edmonton began in June 1992; by April 1994, BP projects had been finished in nineteen of the plant's twenty production areas. All but the initial project were carried out entirely by SEWS personnel.

This quick technology transfer was made possible by the fact that HAM was not trying to teach principles of *kaizen*; these were already well understood by SEWS managers. Instead, the function of BP was mainly to improve communication, first between SEWS and HAM management. According to a SEWS engineer: "The best thing about BP was getting to know Joe and Doug [the HAM associates who worked on BP]. They're part of SEWS now . . . they're a way to get information we'd never get through sales or purchasing. This lets us get a jump-start on a design change. Also, they'll call us about a change HAM is thinking about to say, 'How will this affect you'?"

In turn, SEWS felt that BP was a way to educate HAM about the fragile nature of SEWS's product. On a visit to HAM's engine plant, arranged through BP, a SEWS employee saw a HAM associate using a harness as a handle to swing an engine around. This could cause wires to pull out of their connections and SEWS to be charged with a defect. In addition, the BP interactions with HAM allowed SEWS to communicate potential cost-quality tradeoffs in wire harness design. For example, having slightly longer (and thus more expensive) wires could make a harness easier to assemble, thus reducing the potential for defects.

Honda's presence also improved communication between workers and managers at SEWS. SEWS's training manager was proud of how BP activities and related "on-the-job training" allowed a particular subset of the workforce—"smart women who made one bad decision" (e.g., a failed marriage that left them with children to support and limited labor market opportunities)—to achieve more of their potential. Honda continually emphasized the importance of involving associates in the problem-solving process during BP. According to a SEWS BP coordinator: "We learned from Honda that you never try to sneak anything by the associates. In our morning meetings, we always ask them, 'What's your biggest problem?' Or if we're proposing something, we'll ask, 'Do you think you'll like this change?' *[Interviewer: What if they say 'No'?]* Well, if they say no, we'll say, " 'Give it a chance anyway.' " As the quotation suggests, employee involvement, in Honda's mind, did not mean that workers had veto power. For example, in one work area, the BP team wanted to move machines very close together for better visual control. The machines were moved one day while the workers in that area were at lunch. When workers were asked for their reaction, they complained that the machines were too close, so the team moved them further apart. Even though the machines were still much closer together than before, managers felt that everyone was happy with the compromise.

This advice from Honda was one factor that allowed the Edmonton plant to avoid some of the problems experienced with *kaizen* efforts at its Morgantown plant. Morgantown, opened in 1987 was Sumitomo's first U.S. plant. Acting cautiously, Sumitomo decided to turn labor relations over almost entirely to Americans. According to current SEWS management, Sumitomo hired managers who were experienced in the classic paternalistic Southern strategy for union avoidance. They put a great deal of effort into knowing employees personally (including having frequent social events at the president's house), they did not put much pressure on employees to work hard, and they had few management systems. For example, people would schedule themselves to work overtime when they needed extra money, regardless of whether or not output was needed.[8]

With the growth in business with Honda, the Morgantown plant grew far beyond Sumitomo's original expectations. As Honda's demands for quantity and quality also increased, the original management approach no longer worked. Without consulting workers, management speeded up the line and installed more controls. Production volume lost due to *kaizen* meetings had to be made up by working faster during the rest of the shift. These actions led to a vote, in September 1992, on whether to join the United Steelworkers. Management won this vote but saw it as a clear signal that problems were severe. At the time of our visit, Morgantown management was working to revive the *kaizen* program and to build on its very high participation in the individual suggestion program. (In March 1994, management had received almost half of a suggestion per worker and had implemented more than 75 percent of them by mid-April). It was also beginning to train team leaders to be intermediaries between management and labor. Finally, it was in the early stages of implementing BP, with the help of HAM and the Edmonton plant.

Despite improvements, SEWS management saw the potential for continued problems in labor relations. Some felt the main issues were cultural. According to this view (expressed by American managers), American workers lacked a work ethic and were too individualistic. In contrast to workers in Japan, they would refuse to sacrifice (e.g., "give up scheduled breaks") for the good of the company. Other managers (mostly Japanese) felt that the problem was rooted in the history of the Morgantown plant. "Japanese workers have had the experience that if they do something extra for management, management will do something extra for them," they said. SEWS's U.S. employees had not yet experienced this give-and-take.

Other challenges also remained. One was communication between SEWS plants. For example, a *kaizen* group from Edmonton was trying to fix a problem in which tape sometimes slipped off a joint because one type of tape stretches more than the other. The group had been working on the problem for five months and was scheduled to present their findings at Honda the week following our visit. However, the group had been unable to get SEWS engineers to explain why triple taping of that joint was necessary, since the tape didn't slip if there were only two layers. Double taping was easier to pierce, so the group needed to know more about the product's function in order to understand the tradeoff. SEWS engineering seemed unwilling to share that sort of knowledge. The group had gone ahead and recommended as a long-term countermeasure getting the SEWS plant a few miles away in Scottsville to use stickier tape, but Scottsville had not paid much attention. When we asked about this issue at Scottsville, we were told, "We don't see it as a big problem. Edmonton doesn't have alternatives; they have to come to us. We have consulted with our other customers; it's OK with them, and we don't want to make a different product just for Edmonton."

A second issue was uncertainty about the long-term future of the Kentucky operation. SEWS thought that its costs in Mexico were about 15 percent lower than those in the United States (although claims for quality defects were two to five times higher). This uncertainty was taking its toll on the *kaizen* programs, since 20 percent of U.S. employees were temporary, and key quality and training people were spending a quarter to half of their time in Mexico.

To come back to the original question, Why did SEWS do BP? The answer seems to be that the events of 1992 at Morgantown had made Honda nervous and SEWS humble. On the customer side, Honda responded not only with BP but also by introducing a second source for SEWS's product in 1992. On SEWS's part, the management at Edmonton became willing to try BP, because it saw it as a good way to meet Honda's pressure for low costs and high quality while also learning to avoid the problems with workforce management that had plagued Morgantown.

Both parties seem to have benefited considerably from the BP effort. Of all of the suppliers we visited, SEWS had done the best job of diffusing BP— first throughout the entire Edmonton plant and then by enlisting BP coordinators at Edmonton to help carry out BP projects at Morgantown.[9] For Honda, BP at SEWS provided a way to stay in close communication with a highly competent supplier who was growing in sales, volume, and number of customers. This was one way for Honda to be sure that its status as a "principal customer" would be respected and that SEWS would stay responsive to its needs, even when less dependent on Honda business.

Greenville Technologies Inc. (GTI)

Greenville Technologies Inc. (GTI) was a joint venture among Morioko (a Japanese injection molding company that had a long history of selling to Honda in Japan), Honda (a small stake), and the owner of Capitol Plastics. Management control resided firmly with Morioko. GTI was established when it became clear that Capitol Plastics was not going to be able to meet all of Honda's volume requirements or all its demands for improvement. The operation was set up as a joint venture to minimize Morioko's risk. GTI's plant opened in Greenville, Ohio, in 1987 and had doubled in size by the time of our visit in 1992. The plant's 230 employees worked with the very latest in plastic-injection molding equipment. The factory was airy and brightly lit; the machinery fairly gleamed. GTI prided itself on its ability to paint plastic parts and to build complex assemblies.

The plant was located in a rural part of southwestern Ohio. This location was less than three hours away from the Honda of America Manufacturing (HAM) complex in Marysville, close enough for frequent deliveries (ten times per day), but with disadvantages as well. It was not close enough to a community college for employees to receive training there. Also, it was a three-hour drive to the nearest die maintenance shop. Since this delayed die repair, the firm kept an extra day of work-in-process inventory on hand.

The first BP project was carried out in 1989. The focus was the timing belt cover. GTI's evaluation of the outcome was mixed. On the one hand, Honda "helped us by being very systematic"; on the other, "they treated us as if we didn't know what we were doing." Although "some companies would think they're invasive, we've grown up with it, and we needed their help—we're only five years old."

This relationship was not without frustration. GTI engineers failed to see the relevance of statistical process control to their product, "because molds don't produce bad parts once they are in operation—it's the first ten parts you've got to watch. Besides, our machines are new, so they hardly ever cause us problems." They also felt that HAM personnel were under too much pressure to come up with a permanent countermeasure when they found a quality problem: "They don't want to leave without a plan. Sometimes we have to explain to them that their plan won't work. For example, there just may not be enough steel in the mold to make the change they want." But things were improving; the same engineer also felt that "increasingly, Honda is relying on us, considering us the experts in plastic trim parts."

GTI's confident attitude was often justified by performance. An example comes from one of GTI's later BP projects, carried out by GTI personnel exclusively. In 1991 Honda found that consumers preferred a continuously adjustable heater vent control instead of the initial design, which allowed the vent to be only on or off. A team of engineers and operators at GTI realized that it could achieve adjustability with the existing design if it could tighten the tolerances enough so that the plastic louvers could come to rest anywhere in their range of motion, not just at their endpoints. Implementing this insight, however, meant modifying the production process at five or six places. Operators contributed many of the suggestions, based on their understanding of the interactions between different steps in the process. GTI's expertise meant that Honda was able to implement the change quickly and with minimal cost for redesign and new tooling.

An unresolved issue was how to make parts compatible around the world. GTI pointed out several instances in which a HAM request for an engineering change made the part incompatible with the one Morioko was producing for Honda in Japan; if one of the Accords shipped to Japan by HAM needed a replacement, the Morioko part would not fit. GTI often refused to make such changes, a source of tension with HAM, which expected responsiveness to engineering change requests from its suppliers.

Relations among managers at GTI seemed smooth. In contrast to some Japanese transplant suppliers, GTI held only one set of meetings—in English. Both Japanese and American managers seemed comfortable with the complex process by which Morioko tooling designs were modified in Japan to fit U.S. conditions (e.g., higher volume per part, newer machinery). At the time of our visit, 80 percent of the tooling came from Japan; this figure was to fall to 60 percent in two years, when the next Honda model came on line. According to the Japanese resident engineer, the goal is to become "an American company, although Japanese owned. This will occur when GTI no longer depends on the parent for support." Already, GTI claimed to outperform the mother company in every area of production.

However, relations were not always smooth with the hourly work force. Training was done haphazardly. While engineers and managers participated actively in *kaizen*, functioning quality circles were rare. Managers felt that some of these problems could be traced to a lack of attention to employee motivation in the past. They described a key incident in which some managers received large bonuses, while line workers got much smaller bonuses. While senior managers felt the differential was justified by the difference in contribution, employees felt that it violated the egalitarian spirit of the plant. After considering, and ultimately rejecting, a change in compensation policy, managers decided that these tensions could be avoided in the future by better communication about how bonuses were determined.

Yet, other than encouraging more employee participation in quality circles, Honda did not make much effort to influence GTI's management of the workforce. Indeed, BP at GTI seemed more a way to keep a friendly eye on a strong and confident supplier than a means of teaching lean production. Through the regular communication involved in BP, Honda could assess whether GTI would be able to handle substantially higher production volume; how much design responsibility to give GTI; and whether the confidence of GTI's management team was at any risk of crossing the line to arrogance or hubris. As GTI began to add other customers (as its managers, as well as Honda, hoped it would do), it seemed clear that Honda hoped involvement with BP might also be a way to ensure that ties remained strong and that

GTI would continue to display a "principal customer" responsiveness to Honda's needs.

Analyzing BP's Effectiveness and Supplier Capabilities

We start our analysis of the six supplier cases by evaluating the effectiveness of BP and the development of new supplier capabilities (see Table 5.2). First, we assess the scope and sustainability of the organizational learning associated with BP at each supplier and the absorption of the *kaizen* philosophy of continuous improvement. The two Japanese transplants (SEWS and GTI) were most successful at implementing the lessons of BP, because of their prior knowledge of lean production methods. The primary challenge at these plants was training U.S. employees in lean production and persuading them to share the commitment to *kaizen*. For the U.S.-owned suppliers, however, the adoption of a *kaizen* philosophy represented a significant change in their organizational culture. For a small company like Progressive, whose owner became a quick adherent, this culture change occurred relatively quickly. Small size did not help at Capitol, where control-oriented management thinking and limited staff capabilities hindered the prospects for *kaizen*. The move toward *kaizen* was slower at Tower and Donnelly than at Progressive, yet there were more resources to sustain change once it occurred.

Next, we consider the extent to which each supplier took on the responsibilities and developed the capabilities for being an effective long-term supplier partner for Honda. This set of suppliers was quite effective in meeting Honda's basic cost, quality, and delivery requirements, with the possible exception of Capitol. In addition, virtually all of these suppliers had "earned the right to disagree" with Honda with respect to manufacturing processes, particularly the stamping firms that persuaded Honda to modify aspects of die design and maintenance practices.

There was more variation in the extent to which these suppliers made major investments in new technologies and new facilities in order to keep up with Honda's future requirements. The larger U.S. suppliers made major investments, while the smaller U.S. suppliers did not—clearly a function of the larger firms' easier access to capital. (Both Japanese transplants had recently built new facilities with new equipment, thus reducing the need for additional capital spending during this period.) It was also U.S. suppliers who agreed to take on new products and production processes in order to be responsive to Honda's future needs—most prominently Donnelly, learning to paint door mirrors, and Progressive, adding subassembly tasks. Finally, it was only Donnelly that was beginning to take on major design responsibilities for the parts made for Honda.

We believe that the experience of the firms we visited provides can be useful for customers and suppliers thinking of embarking on a program of

Table 5.2 BP Effectiveness and Supplier Capabilities (Based on 1992–94 Plant Visits)

	Capitol	Progressive	Tower	Donnelly	SEWS	GTI
Main product	Plastic molded parts	Small metal stampings	Small metal stampings	Painted door mirrors	Wire harnesses	Plastic molded parts
Scope of BP's influence	Individual work areas	Entire plant	Entire plant	Entire plant	Multiple plants	Entire plant
Sustained after Honda leaves?	No	Yes	Mixed results	Yes	Yes	Yes
Transfer across plants?	N/A; single plant company	N/A; single plant company	Minimal, but other plants don't make Honda products	BP efforts at window module plant have limited effect	Yes	N/A; single plant company
Kaizen well-established in plant culture?	No	Yes	Varies by product line	Yes, in principle, but still resisted by some	Yes	Yes
Workforce involved in kaizen efforts?	Minimal	Minimal	Minimal	Moderate	Little at some plants, lots at other plants	Moderate to high

Able to meet cost, quality, delivery goals?	Recurrent problems	Mostly	Mostly, but some problems with low-volume parts	Mostly	Mostly	Yes
Influencing Honda on production process decisions?	No	Yes, for die hardness and maintenance	Yes, for die hardness and maintenance	Limited	Yes	Limited
Investing in new technological capabilities?	No	No	Yes—transfer presses	Yes—paint line	No	Yes—molding equipment
Learning new production processes?	No	Yes—doing subassemblies after stamping	No	Yes—painting	No	No
Major design responsibility?	No	No	No	Yes	Yes, but at parent company in Japan	Yes, but at parent company in Japan

knowledge transfer. In the next section, we draw several lessons from our research.

Lessons for Customers

1. *Structure the learning process so that the knowledge is easier to absorb.* Organizational learning and innovation theorists argue that knowledge is particularly difficult to transfer if it involves a technology that has an abstract or complex scientific base; is "fragile" (i.e., doesn't work consistently); requires "hand-holding" because of idiosyncrasies that make standardization impossible; is "lumpy," because knowledge transfer would affect lots of people at the same time (Eveland and Tornatzky, 1980); has a "tacit" or "uncodified" nature that is difficult to explain explicitly (Nelson and Winter, 1982); or has a "radical" or "competence-destroying" nature that makes obsolete some of the recipient's existing capabilities (Abernathy, Clark, and Kantrow, 1983).

Honda (consciously or not) designed the BP process to avoid most of the characteristics of technical knowledge that make it difficult to transfer. First, the scientific knowledge underlying the reengineering of production lines was primarily concrete and simple rather than abstract and complex. BP reinforced this by following the principle of "actual part, actual place, actual situation" (the 3As) and by focusing attention on a single problem. Second, the solutions developed through BP were highly reliable. These solutions routinely produced fast, large improvements in suppliers' operations—reinforcing the incentive to continue with the program. Third, standardization of processes was often achievable and was encouraged as part of a continuous improvement cycle that alternated periods of standardization and periods of experimentation with improved methods. Fourth, by beginning BP on a single "pilot" line and then slowly diffusing the same principles to other redesign efforts, the "lumpiness" of broad, sweeping organizational change—and the potential organizational resistance to such change—was minimized.

Furthermore, BP was well suited to the tacit nature of the knowledge underlying lean production and continuous improvement. In addition to practical illustrations of how to reengineer a discrete production line, the entire BP process modeled the behaviors that Honda hoped the suppliers would adopt—utilizing the "3 As," gathering "before and after" data to evaluate countermeasures, emphasizing minimal capital investment until process steps were organized for smooth flow, respecting worker knowledge as a source of ideas for process improvement, and paying attention to (nonwage) factors that dissipated worker motivation.

Lean production mixes old and new ideas in a way that complicates the knowledge transfer process. On the one hand, many of the skills, attitudes, and heuristics developed under mass production (e.g., emphasizing attaining economies of scale and production targets over quality, establishing buffers to keep production running despite defective parts, high turnover, and poorly motivated employees) are obsolete under lean production. Becoming lean requires alternative perspectives on many dimensions of production (e.g., accepting a "quality first" philosophy, understanding the logic of buffer reduction, becoming more open to employee input into production problem solving) that, taken as a whole, represent a radical shift in managerial mindset. On the other hand, lean production is not entirely competence destroying. Indeed, successful implementation of lean production places heavy demands on traditional skills such as production scheduling, workflow planning, and data management. Much of the challenge in learning lean production is understanding which aspects of traditional manufacturing practice provide a necessary foundation and which represent barriers to adoption.

2. *Choose the knowledge recipient carefully, keeping in mind how the recipient's "absorptive capacity" and "identity" will affect the knowledge transfer process.* Honda's choice of BP participants was based on a variety of factors, some of which heavily influenced the success of the knowledge transfer process. All participants were expected to meet the following criteria: highly motivated to learn, willing to make their operations completely accessible to Honda, and willing to commit to the "no layoff" policy that Honda saw as crucial to BP success. Beyond those criteria, there were two predominant paths to being selected for BP. One path (Capitol) was to have performance problems that persisted despite Honda's standard feedback reports and pressures for improvement. Another path (Donnelly, Tower, and Progressive) was to demonstrate strong capabilities in some areas valued by Honda and an attitude of responsiveness about learning new capabilities to meet Honda's current and future needs. A third path (SEWS and GTI) was to be an experienced supplier having some difficulties that prevented it from being as responsive as Honda would have liked.

Two concepts—absorptive capacity and organizational identity—are helpful as a way to characterize what Honda experienced. One key factor in the successful transfer of knowledge, according to Cohen and Levinthal (1990), is the "absorptive capacity" of the recipient. The capacity to absorb new knowledge depends critically on the level of related knowledge that already exists in the recipient firm, since prior knowledge facilitates the assimilation and exploitation of new knowledge. While ultimately grounded in individual learning, absorptive capacity at the organizational level requires effective communication mechanisms between members of the firm and sources of knowledge inside and outside the firm.

The absorptive capacity of a firm is also related to its organizational identity. As characterized by Kogut and Zander (1996), the "identity" of the firm is defined by the organizational boundaries that indicate who is (and is not) a member of the organization, by shared goals and values, and by patterns of interaction among individuals that give rise to a common language and common frameworks for action. A firm's ability to absorb technical knowledge is greatest when both the new knowledge and the firm's prior related knowledge are close to the core of the firm's identity. In contrast, a strong identity creates obstacles to the absorption of radical change, because the firm's identity is typically wrapped up in a stock of previously developed knowledge and organizational routines.

These two factors (absorptive capacity and identity) have different implications for the process of knowledge transfer at large and small suppliers. Larger suppliers should have more absorptive capacity than smaller suppliers, both because they have greater prior related knowledge of the traditional skills on which lean production draws and because they have a stronger identity, based on particular areas of technical expertise, long histories of successful performance, cohesive corporate cultures, and long employee tenure. However, this strong identity might also increase the resistance of larger suppliers to the competence-destroying change of mind-set associated with adopting lean production and make them less responsive to the customer's suggestions than were smaller suppliers. There can be tremendous appeal for a customer who is trying to "create lean suppliers" in building up small firms into intensely loyal medium-size ones. Their motivation is high, and they are likely to mold their "identity" very closely the customer's. However, there is a risk in this strategy that suppliers will become too dependent and have too few resources for developing advanced capabilities. This risk is apparent in the Capitol Plastics case. Capitol's strenuous efforts to be responsive to Honda led at first to its winning a larger and larger amount of Honda's business. When the limitations of Capitol's management team, production expertise, and technology became clear, Honda used BP to try to bolster the company, at considerable effort and expense but to little avail.

The alternative strategy of working with already established firms that have a strong customer base but still have ample room for improvement seems more promising. The early stages can be considerably more complex, since the identity struggles are fierce at the beginning. Picking the right supplier-partner can make a big difference during this stage—for example, the initial "fit" in company cultures between Honda and Western Michigan suppliers such as Donnelly and Tower, even if far from tight, was sufficient to provide a strong basis for their relationship with Honda, even during difficult times. Certainly the fact that the fundamental absorptive capacity is present means that the provider firm can concentrate energy on motivating the recipient firm and minimizing the "stickiness" of the knowledge transfer process. However, even once the initial struggles are past, the responsiveness of larger firms may be limited by the competing demands they face from different customers, as was the case at Tower vis-à-vis Honda and Ford.

Also, the case of Progressive Industries suggests that it is too simple to assume that large suppliers are more capable of learning from a lean customer like Honda. BP's success at Progressive was a result, in part, of the "absorptive capacity" of a key individual—the firm's owner—who saw the need to keep expanding the services his firm could provide Honda and in part of the strong foundation of technical skills developed during the firm's history as a machine shop and a provider of advanced controls to other stampers.

Over eight years of experience with BP, Honda has gained a greater appreciation of the demands the BP process places on a supplier's absorptive capacity. Accordingly, it now makes sure the supplier is in a position to devote the necessary resources to the improvement process before beginning— no major product launches going on for Honda or another customer; willing and able to devote at least one person full time, and with no major problems with its organizational structure, managerial resources, quality and production scheduling systems, or labor relations. According to Rick Mayo, who directs BP for Honda:

> There are three things we look at now to evaluate whether BP will work: first, their infrastructure; second, what else is on their plate; and third, who else is in there [other customers]. What we'd do now if a Capitol Plastics arose would be to do an analysis of their overall management structure and resources. We would see that the problem is much bigger than BP. When you realize it's more than BP, don't try to solve it with BP.
>
> Before, we tried to make BP an answer for all issues. Now, we realize that a basic precondition of BP is having capable people in place. For example, suppose they fired a quality manager and don't have a replacement. If we go in, we become the quality manager. I might send in a BP guy, but to manage quality, not to do BP. After they've got the basic issues under control (we're getting parts reliably, they change dies when they should, they're not promoting unqualified people), then we can do BP.

Honda also felt that it was very important to encourage suppliers to see continuous improvement as part of their identity, by finding a way to make it fit with their organizational structure, culture, and history and by striving for a consistency of approach across customers. According to Mayo:

> We've learned to get BP into their company so it's not seen as a radical change. We used to meet with the top guy and say "do this project." Now we realize that the supplier needs to have their own way of doing BP. So we ask, "what will fit best with your overall plans?" They don't even need to call it BP. Improvement activities need to be part of their culture, their vision. BP is one club in the golf bag—it's probably the driver, and we hit it hard—but it's not meant to be everything to everyone.

Thus, over time, Honda has refined its assessment of which suppliers should participate in BP and, even more important, when and how to undertake a BP project at a supplier.

The Japanese-owned suppliers had somewhat different problems with implementing lean production than did their U.S.-owned counterparts, in ways that are also illuminated by the concept of absorptive capacity. Japanese-owned suppliers had a higher level of prior related knowledge about lean production than did U.S.-owned suppliers, facilitating their absorption of those aspects of BP. But the transplants, by definition, have a lower level of prior-related knowledge about operating in the U.S. context than do U.S. firms, increasing their need for assistance in this area. In fact, SEWS and GTI were more successful, on the whole, in developing the scope and sustainability of their process improvement efforts than were the U.S.-owned suppliers. For these firms, BP became a way for Honda to convey cultural knowledge that was helpful in adjusting to the U.S. context—not a process likely to lead to long-term dependency—and to improve coordination around design changes.

However, developing advanced supplier capabilities locally is likely to be more effective if the customer works with established domestic firms rather than with the overseas subsidiaries of their long-time supplier partners. Japanese firms such as Sumitomo Electric and Morioko are unlikely to move full design capabilities to their U.S. subsidiaries, since this would hollow out their domestic capabilities. There is perhaps more incentive for an established U.S. supplier to develop these advanced design capabilities for a Japanese transplant customer, particularly if it helps the supplier attract more customers.

3. *Once suppliers have been selected, manage the relationship in a way that minimizes long-term dependence and speeds the transition to self-sufficiency.* One risk of a "hands-on" knowledge transfer process is that the recipient firm (the supplier) may come to rely on the support services from the provider firm (the customer) and thereby limit its learning (Attewell, 1992). The cases offer some support for the idea that the suppliers might view BP as a service and become dependent on Honda, thereby reducing their incentive to master lean production on their own. Honda associates may have exacerbated the problem by their intensity about fixing problems, which may have encouraged supplier employees to feel "unworthy" and to defer to the BP staff. (Recall the manager at Donnelly's Grand Haven plant who described in vivid detail the combination of relief and anxiety he felt when the "snow-flakes"—white-uniformed Honda employees—descended on the production lines at his plant.) When Honda withdrew its BP staff, hoping that the supplier would institutionalize these processes, it was frequently disappointed with the solo initiatives that followed.

This was particularly apparent at Capitol Plastics, where performance gains achieved on certain production lines diminished after the BP team left. At Progressive, performance remained strong, subassembly tasks were successfully added, and technological improvements were effectively implemented. But Honda remained somewhat frustrated with the limited depth of Progressive's management capabilities. According to one Honda manager, "We try to tell them they can't stay as just a mom-and-pop shop and do big business. They can't do it all with 'promote-from-within.' At some point, they'll need more professional management." In contrast, dependency was less of a concern at Tower. At the beginning of their relationship, Tower was somewhat dependent on Honda's technical assistance to work with unfamiliar Japanese dies and equipment. Yet this dependence was difficult for Tower, whose identity as a capable manufacturer was well established. The ambivalence about being so dependent on Honda (and about the demands of the BP process) eventually served, we believe, to motivate Tower to become more self-sufficient with respect to lean production capabilities and to synthesize what it was learning from its two major customers. However, as Tower became more self-reliant, it may also have become less receptive to Honda's "hands-on" approach and more favorable towards Ford's "manage-by-the-numbers" approach. These dynamics were similar for Donnelly, though, during the periods of greatest difficulty for the Grand Haven plant, the dependence on Honda was quite high.

That the relationship between supplier and customer during the "learning" period is often characterized by tension and ambivalence is not necessarily a bad thing. It can motivate the supplier to push through the dependency stage and become self-reliant.[10] Honda was willing to tolerate the risk of dependency because of its belief in the value of its hands-on "live in the plant" approach in encouraging the learning of new capabilities. Honda's investment of time and energy in helping suppliers was a visible sign of commitment—something the suppliers could hold on to and use to justify the "leap of faith" required in the absence of contractual commitments. As noted earlier, BP also demonstrated the behaviors Honda hoped the suppliers would adopt on their own.

In summary, reaching self-sufficiency with respect to newly acquired knowledge is more likely when the supplier has a moderate degree of identification with and dependency on the customer. If these are too high, the supplier will be tempted to continue to rely on the customer for assistance. If they are too low, the supplier will feel that the customer has nothing to teach. On the basis of the limited evidence from these cases, we conclude that Honda has achieved the most supplier self-reliance with larger companies, which have an identity as strong, competent actors and thus try to reduce their dependence on Honda as quickly as possible.

4. *Balance "learning" and "monitoring" behaviors, while being sure to generate supplier trust.* Customers who want their suppliers to improve must balance the need to monitor the suppliers' existing performance while encouraging them to learn new skills that in the short term might disrupt that performance (Sabel, 1994). Indeed, if supplier capabilities change sufficiently, it could force changes in the monitoring system. While BP was primarily a mechanism for learning, it did allow some monitoring. However, tensions over monitoring at times seemed to threaten learning, as was the case at Tower. For the most part, Honda seemed willing to let BP to stand alone as a learning mechanism and to deal with monitoring as part of routine interactions between Honda purchasing, financial, and quality functions and each supplier.

While some tension between learning and monitoring is inevitable, the more capable suppliers become, the more they can participate in discussions in which both sides benefit, as occurred in the fruitful combination of U.S. and Japanese die practice at Tower and at Progressive. Honda appeared to recognize the benefits of such discussions, becoming more flexible in its approach to BP over time, with more willingness to blend a variety of activities together, even those not part of the initial BP plan. Honda also came to realize that suppliers might undertake separate initiatives with other customers or outside consultants and that these, too, should be treated as potentially complementary to BP.

5. *Don't worry about knowledge spillover to competitors through a shared supplier. Do worry about the impact of multiple customers on a supplier's responsiveness.* As we argue later, lean production is certainly beneficial in serving other customers besides Honda. Honda managers seemed to take a "rising tide lifts all boats" view of the risk that their rivals might free-ride on their investment in knowledge transfer: "If Ford and GM get better, that's OK. That will push us to get better."

Also, unlike information about future products or specific technological advances (which Honda certainly did protect), Honda managers seemed to believe that efforts to eliminate the spillover of knowledge about lean production to competitors ran the risk that suppliers would not gain all of the benefits that accrue to systemic implementation. Indeed, helping a supplier achieve consistency across all its operations and all its customers was an important component of Honda's strategy for supplier self-reliance. Mayo told us: "Measurement is one of the biggest things we do—measuring everything in the plant in the same way, gathering real data from physical operations. That how we end up working on Ford, GM, and Chrysler lines as well as our own. We try to make continuous improvement part of the supplier's culture."

Honda's emphasis on long-term, "marriage"-like relationships with key suppliers may also mitigate the risks of knowledge spillover. The loyalty generated by a successful knowledge transfer process can mean that suppliers remain more responsive to their teacher even over many decades.[11] According to Mayo: "We want to help suppliers solve their biggest problems, but also to think long-run and to be self-reliant. We train our BP staff to pay attention to issues of philosophy and commitment. That's the strength of BP—it starts in one place and leads to other things."

Honda seemed more concerned about the issue of supplier responsiveness to its needs in the face of competing customer demands. According to one Honda manager, "Some of these suppliers get pressure from many customers and often say yes to everything. But they have limited managerial resources for dealing with all those demands." BP activities are increasingly postponed for suppliers with "too much on their plate," which most commonly occurs when a supplier is launching new products for more than one customer. This concern about retaining suppliers' attention also seemed to be the rationale for Honda's policy of choosing smaller suppliers and then helping them with extensive supplier development activities, despite the greater difficulty in helping them achieve self-reliance.

Lessons for Suppliers

1. *Understand what skills will be taught, how long it will take to learn them, and how applicable they will be to other customers.* Should suppliers be willing to get involved with a customer bent on improvement—*theirs?*

Certain advantages of a knowledge transfer process like BP seem clear—the operational improvements from the BP projects themselves, the development of internal capabilities for transferring these improvements to other plants and divisions, the strengthened relationship with an important customer. Yet a skeptic might argue that it is a mistake for a supplier to make major investments in building capabilities that suit a customer's requirements in the absence of solid long-term contractual agreements about future business.

If a skill is specific to one customer, then a supplier should make sure in advance that customer is willing to assure the supplier of a return on its investment in learning—otherwise, the supplier is vulnerable to a "hold-up," in which the customer does not allow the firm a return on its investment, knowing that it has no alternative use for the asset (Klein, Crawford, and Alchian, 1978). If the skill is general but requires a long gestation period, then the supplier should ensure that it can weather the learning period, either by a commitment from the customer or from retained earnings.

BP seems to fall in this second category; it teaches general problem-solving skills helpful to a variety of customers. Even the BP-related investments in capital equipment that we saw were for general-purpose machines. However, in the short term, the intense focus on one line required by Honda can be a distraction from meeting the needs of other customers. This tension was expressed most clearly by Tower, which was cautious about allowing its intensive relationship with Honda to hurt its position with Ford by diverting too much energy from developing the capability and relationships necessary to obtain a major design role.

2. *Make sure your customer is trustworthy.* Sako (1992) distinguishes among three types of trust: competence trust (a belief that the customer is capable of doing what it says it will do); contractual trust (a feeling that the customer will abide by its agreements), and goodwill trust (a belief that the customer will take initiatives for mutual benefit and refrain from unfair advantage taking). All types of trust are important for the success of an intensive knowledge-transfer project.

First, it is important that the customer be a competent teacher. Even if the customer doesn't charge for instruction, the process of learning a general skill like lean production can still be quite costly in terms of time for supplier managers, engineers, and employees. Regardless of their other reactions to BP, the suppliers were uniform in their respect for Honda's mastery of lean production philosophies and methods—often called the "Honda Way"—particularly as manifested in the skills of the BP coordinators sent to their plants. This sense of Honda's high level of competence was crucial for overcoming the initial skepticism of many suppliers towards the BP process.

Second, contractual trust—which, on the face of it, wouldn't apply to Honda because it rarely provides formal contracts—remains extremely important. Knowing that a customer abides by *unwritten* contracts (e.g., Honda's implicit guarantee of continued annual business for responsive and capable suppliers, at a level that at least matches the previous year's volume) can strengthen a customer-supplier relationship more than seeing an customer in an arm's-length relationship go "by the book" in observing the terms of a formal contract.

Third, because the knowledge transfer process opens up so many unforeseen avenues for improvement (and potential investment), it is crucial that the supplier believe that its customer is trustworthy in a goodwill sense. The intense amount of information sharing and coordination between suppliers and a customer like Honda is often resisted at first, because of fear that this information will be used opportunistically.[12] Yet suppliers often change their views if they see that the customer is merely seeking possible process improvements. Furthermore, as shown in the Donnelly, Tower, and Progressive cases, firms can develop goodwill trust over time, progressively moving toward more and more mutual responsibility, interdependence, and open information exchange. A knowledge transfer program like BP can be an important part of the trust-building process, since the customer's investment in teaching a supplier *is* specific to that supplier; if the firm no longer supplies the customer, the customer loses the benefit of having provided the training.

3. *Provide incentives for all members of the firm to contribute their ideas.* Just as supplier management needs to trust customer management, supplier workers need to trust their managers, on both the competence and the goodwill dimensions. This was a difficult part of the BP process, at least in part because supplier managers underestimated the importance of the changes required in labor-management relations. Capitol unleashed an initial flood of employee enthusiasm, which turned to a trickle when management dragged its feet on the implementation of employee suggestions. At SEWS, workers did not feel initially that the process would have any benefits for them. In contrast, Progressive's management responded more favorably toward suggestions, particularly from its more skilled employees, and reinforced the emphasis on problem solving by providing extensive employee training, both on the job and at outside educational institutions. Overall, we found that Honda's emphasis on the importance of shop floor employee involvement beginning with the very first BP project and its requirement that no workers be laid off due to BP-related efficiency gains helped shift managerial mindsets at the suppliers we studied.

4. *In determining your manufacturing strategy, consider the impact of your decisions on your future ability to learn, as well as on your factor costs.* Lean customers such as Honda want suppliers who both have low costs now and have the ability to learn in the future. These demands can place suppliers in a tricky position. The way that most of the firms we visited responded was to build new plants for Honda in low-wage places outside the traditional auto-producing areas of Detroit and Cleveland. In some ways, this strategy of going to new areas is advantageous for both supplier and customer, because it allows a supplier to be both low-cost and capable of learning new production methods. The people you hire don't have preconceived notions, and you can pay wages that are low by traditional industry standards but high by local standards, so you still get motivated employees. However, going

to new areas may hinder learning if you lose access to traditional skills that are widely available in established industrial agglomerations. Recall that GTI kept an extra day of inventory because of an inability to find a nearby die repair source and had trouble arranging convenient training for its employees. For Donnelly, the decision to move to Grand Haven and to pay the prevailing wage there seems to have been a false economy. Workers there quickly found out that they were making significantly less than their counterparts only a few miles away; their anger at the imbalance probably cost more in terms of managerial time and lost suggestions than it saved.

SEWS initially made a somewhat different decision; by locating its labor-intensive wiring harness production in the United States at all, it bucked the trend toward moving this work to Mexico. Honda supported SEWS in this decision, by initially granting it a 10 percent price premium. Honda felt the savings from proximity would more than offset the increased piece price. One incident from our visit to another Honda supplier of wiring harnesses illustrates why this might be so. This firm had chosen to locate its factory in Juarez, Mexico. Managers described to us an incident in which Honda would intermittently send back its harnesses, saying they didn't meet the specification. The supplier insisted that they did meet the specification. Only when the problem happened while a Honda associate was visiting was it discovered that the two sides were interpreting the specification differently. (It said that one branch in the wire harness should be a certain length, measured from the middle of a plastic component. It turned out that Honda had a different view of what the "middle" was and also of how tightly the wire should be stretched when the measurement occurred.) It took a long time for the two sides to understand their differences because Honda associates rarely visited the far-away plant; the confusion was enough to disqualify the supplier for a Honda Quality Award.

It is hard for suppliers to make these location and wage decisions in a profit-maximizing way. (Firms should also consider the impacts of their decisions on the welfare of local communities.) The savings from the low-wage approach are immediately obvious; the costs in terms of reduced access to specialized services and fewer chances to discuss ideas with the customer, with suppliers, and with workers and managers well versed in manufacturing disciplines are much harder to measure. For a customer like Honda, the choice between choosing suppliers with plants in Greenfield versus existing locations represents a tradeoff between lower-cost responsiveness and easier access to traditional skills—one that shares many similarities with the choice between working with small and large suppliers discussed earlier.

5. *Grow your capabilities as fast as you grow your business—if not faster.* The experience of becoming a supplier-partner for a fast-growing firm like Honda was, for the companies we studied, frustrating and exhausting, as well as stimulating and exhilarating. Proving capable of handling Honda's demands was often a ticket to gaining additional business from the other Japanese transplants and the Big Three. In the face of such opportunities for volume, it could be easy for suppliers to defer investments in future capabil-

ities—whether in process technology, information systems, managerial expertise, or production worker skills. However, such a deferral is, from Honda's perspective, the most serious impediment to continuing an effective relationship with a supplier. According to Rick Mayo,

> We don't want companies to grow their business faster than they grow their capabilities. We tell suppliers to grow at the right pace to be ready when the time comes for the next phase of work together. For example, when we want to get a supplier involved in the "guest engineer" program (where the supplier sends engineers to work on "design for manufacturing" issues with Honda's product designers), they need to have the right kind of engineers already on board and familiar with their operation.
>
> We view self-reliance in suppliers as a means to achieve long-term competitiveness. For most of our competitors, when they do supplier development activities, it's just about today. We care about today, but we also want residual benefit for the future. Some suppliers don't get it, but some get it very well. Those that get it are better suppliers for us and better suppliers for our other customers, which means we know they'll be around.

The larger firms are not necessarily better than the smaller firms at doing this, in Honda's view, but they do possess certain advantages—access to capital, depth of managerial resources, a broader customer base, and, therefore, less vulnerability to fluctuations in Honda's volume. The fact that there is widespread consolidation in the automotive parts industry, primarily through merger and acquisition, indicates that many investors, customers, and supplier managers believe that size is a prerequisite to survival in the global sourcing competition of the future. But we offer a cautionary note about the dangers of suppliers who grow too big too rapidly. [13] Size alone will not guarantee the successful development of the many capabilities required by lean customers like Honda; in fact, growth through diversification into new products and processes may deter the development of those capabilities.

Honda certainly wants suppliers to develop their own capabilities because, as the BP experience shows, they are likely to absorb Honda's philosophy and practical lessons most successfully. But another benefit, from Honda's perspective, is that these self-reliant suppliers more quickly "earn the right to disagree" and thus provide an impetus for Honda's own improvement.

Conclusion

Given the difficulties described in this chapter, should a customer still try to create lean suppliers? Should suppliers agree to work with those customers that are pursuing this goal? We believe that both suppliers and customers can benefit from entering into the kinds of knowledge transfer arrangements described in this study of Honda's BP. However, the specific mechanism chosen by Honda is far from the only way in which such knowledge transfer can take place. We have observed different mechanisms at other companies that are less "hands-on" and time-intensive and less focused on learning from the "actual part, actual place, actual situation." While these mechanisms are arguably less effective at conveying the tacit knowledge associated with lean production, they might also be less costly to the customer and less disruptive in their challenge to the supplier's identity. Some knowledge transfer arrangements seem clearly *undesirable* in terms of imbalances in the risks and rewards that either customers or suppliers are asked to bear. Where knowledge transfer mechanisms require highly customer-specific investments of time and capital without a long-term commitment from the customer, the risk for suppliers may be unacceptably high. On the other hand, if customers agree to detailed, legally enforceable long-term contracts, they will lose much of their potential leverage with respect to getting suppliers to learn new capabilities.

However, even the best transfer mechanism, applied to a highly absorptive and responsive recipient, is not sufficient to guarantee successful knowledge transfer. The fundamental lesson of Honda's BP experience is that a relationship that generates high motivation for learning and high trust between provider and recipient is a crucial condition for any transfer of a complicated, largely tacit body of knowledge like lean production.

Notes

1. We provided Honda with the criteria for supplier selection, and Honda prepared a list of fifteen, from which we chose the final set. Honda informed the suppliers that it supported our project, but we made arrangements for the supplier visits ourselves, and no Honda employees were present during our visit.

2. Honda does steer its suppliers to good partners, in one sense, by asking their suppliers in Japan to assist the U.S. supplier of the same part. While much of this assistance is technical and product-specific, some involves more general advice about the production system. Yet these Japanese suppliers have a limited interest in developing the capabilities of a U.S. supplier who will be competing with them for business. They are likely to provide some assistance for the sake of goodwill in their relationship with Honda, but not the long, intensive tutoring necessary to incorporate fully the principles of lean production.

3. It is striking how often, in the course of our interviews at Honda, employees (from managers and engineers to purchasing staff) would repeat phrases attributed to Mr. Honda as central to the "Honda Way." Examples (from Mair, 1994, p. 45) include: "Proceed always with ambition and youthfulness. Respect sound theory. Develop fresh ideas and make the most effective use of your time. Enjoy your work and always brighten your working atmosphere. Strive constantly for a harmonious flow of work. Be ever mindful of the value of research and endeavor."

4. Ono (1988) found that experienced employees often provide instant diagnoses of problems in a situation that seems familiar, emphasizing "first-level" causes, (e.g., "that machine always breaks down when we run production at this volume") and solutions, (e.g. "we need a new machine"). Going further requires probing for why the machine breaks down: for example, "preventive maintenance not done" (why?); "because maintenance people are busy repairing another machine" (why?); "because the other ma-

chine overheats at high volume levels" (why?); "because it is located in a part of the plant with poor ventilation and no air conditioning" (why?); "because it was moved there to make room for a new piece of equipment that never arrived." The true "root cause" of the observed problem points toward a solution (moving the machine or improving ventilation at its location) very different from that suggested by the original diagnosis (replace the machine).

5. The next few years would reveal that Honda's concerns were justified and that Donnelly's confidence in its own independent capabilities was unwarranted. A recent paper by Liker and Allman (1997) reveals that the successes achieved in 1992 were short-lived. The first sign of trouble was a unionization campaign at Grand Haven in 1993, a function of the continued pay gap between Donnelly employees in Grand Haven and those in Holland who were doing similar work and of problems with an erratic and inconsistent hiring policy in 1992–1993, a time when the number of employees grew by 16 percent. While the union campaign was unsuccessful, the problems created by rapid growth continued. With a 50 percent increase in sales and two new product launches in 1993–1994, Donnelly began hiring many temporary workers at Grand Haven and rushing them onto the job with little training. Defects soared from a low of 444 parts per million (PPM) in 1992 to more than 5000 PPM by 1994, product launches were late, and Honda became very dissatisfied with Grand Haven, calling it a "high-maintenance supplier" and threatening to cut off its business unless things improved. Donnelly's initial response to these problems was to create an internal program called Delta, run by corporate staff and based primarily on the Synchronous Manufacturing Program developed by General Motors. While it did incorporate some ideas from Honda's BP (as well as from the GM supplier development program PICOS), Delta focused primarily on the implementation of U-shaped cells, a remedy not particularly well suited to Grand Haven's problems. Performance did not improve, and employees grew increasingly frustrated. Donnelly's next step was to bring in outside consultants to run "radical" *kaizen* events, emphasizing rapid implementation of process changes. These events did improve performance considerably, but, because of their "top-down" nature, they did not succeed in improving employee morale. Indeed, during this time another unionization drive began, with 90 percent of employees signing union cards by February 1995. Finally, in the summer of 1995, major changes in the management structure at Donnelly, at both corporate and plant levels, were made; a new VP of manufacturing, who had many of years of Toyota Georgetown experience, undertook a more systemic, longer-term approach to performance improvement that emphasized drawing on the expertise of all employees. With the establishment of continuous improvement teams and development of a Donnelly Production System (modeled on the Toyota Production System and emphasizing one-piece flow and the elimination of queues throughout the plant), Grand Haven's performance once again returned to 1992 levels and then surpassed them. Arguably, the Toyota-inspired reforms to the overall production system were more effective than Honda's BP projects, which were focused on individual lines and processes. However, the crisis period of 1993–1995 and the major management changes may also explain why these recent changes appear to be more sustainable than those achieved under BP.

6. At the time we visited this single-plant firm, in 1992, it was owned and managed by an entrepreneur who had purchased it nine years earlier. Since that time, the firm has been acquired by a large automotive components company, given a new name, and put under new management. All of the events in this case study precede the acquisition and did not involve the current management team.

7. In 1996, Ruston Simon sold Progressive to another investor, although he remains as president.

8. Pay was low, even by area standards; starting wages of $4.70 per hour were 21 percent below the county's manufacturing average in 1991 (Milkman et al., 1991). Managerial salaries were also about $5,000 below the regional average.

9. By 1994, SEWS had gone a step beyond BP at Edmonton, establishing an active quality circle program to institutionalize *kaizen* processes. SEWS was the only supplier we visited that had implemented a plant-wide, ongoing quality circle program.

10. Even once achieved, self-reliance could have different meanings. For Honda, self-reliance did not mean substantially less of the intense interactions between customer and supplier. For U.S. suppliers, in contrast, the idea of self-reliance might be best expressed as "now leave me alone."

11. See Odaka, Ono, and Adachi, (1988) for examples of long-term loyalty to Toyota in Japan generated in part by the automaker's technical assistance programs.

12. Szulanski (1995) argues that trust between the knowledge provider and the recipient is a key factor in motivating the recipient to learn what is being taught; this motivation is as important a factor in successful learning as is a more technical factor like the amount of prior related knowledge a recipient has.

13. A similar sentiment has been sounded, of late, by Big Three executives such as Chrysler's purchasing director, Tom Stallkamp: "There is some danger that suppliers are getting overly integrated. We weren't very good when we were vertically integrated. You should stick to what you do best" (Cleveland Plain Dealer, August 18, 1996).

References

Abernathy, William, Kim Clark, and Alan Kantrow. 1983. *Industrial Renaissance*. New York: Basic Books.

Attewell, Paul. 1992. "Technological Diffusion and Organizational Learning." *Organization Science* 3(1): 1–19.

Bennet, James. 1994. "Detroit Struggles to Learn Another Lesson from Japan." *New York Times*, June 19.

Celeste and Sabety, Ltd. 1993. *Honda of America Mfg., Inc.: An Industrial Model of Technology Transfer—Transforming a Network of Automotive Suppliers*. Columbus, Ohio: Celeste and Sabety Ltd.

Cohen, Wesley M., and Daniel A. Levinthal. 1990. "Absorptive Capacity: A New Perspective on Learning and Innovation." *Administrative Sciences Quarterly* 35(1): 128–152.

Cusumano, Michael. 1984. *The Japanese Automobile Industry*. Cambridge Mass.: Harvard University Press.

Cusumano, Michael, and Akira Takeishi. 1991. "Supplier Relations and Supplier Management: A Survey of Japanese, Japanese-Transplant, and U.S. Auto Plants." *Strategic Management Journal* 12: 563–588.

Dosi, Giovanni, and Bruce Kogut. 1992. "National Specificities and the Context of Change: The Coevolution of Organization and Technology." In Dosi and Kogut, eds., *Country Competitiveness, Technology, and the Organization of Work*. New York: Oxford University Press.

Dyer, Jeffrey, and W. Ouchi. 1993. "Japanese-Style Business Partnership: Giving Companies a Competitive Edge." *Sloan Management Review* 35: 51–63.

Eveland, J. D., and Louis Tornatzky. 1980. "The Deployment of Technology." In L. Tornatzky and M. Fleischer, eds., *The Processes of Technological Innovation*. Lexington, Mass.: Lexington Books.

Gerlach, Michael. 1993. *Alliance Capitalism*. Berkeley: University of California Press.

Helper, Susan. 1991. "Strategy and Irreversibility in Supplier Relations: The Case of the U.S. Automobile Industry." *Business History Review* 65, (4): 781–824.

Helper, Susan. 1992. "An Exit/Voice Approach to Supplier Relations." In Gernot Grabher, ed., *The Embedded Firm: On the Socio-Economics of Industrial Networks*. London: Routledge.

Kenney, Martin, and Richard Florida. 1993. *Beyond Mass Production*. New York: Oxford University Press.

Klein, Benjamin, R. Crawford, and Armen Alchian. 1978. "Vertical Integration, Appropriable Quasi-Rents, and the Competitive Contracting Process." *Journal of Law and Economics*, 21 (Oct.): 297–326.

Kogut, Bruce, and Udo Zander. 1996. "What Firms Do? Coordination, Identity, and Learning." *Organization Science* 7(5): 502–518.

Liker, Jeffrey K., and Keith Allman. 1998. "The Donnelly Production System: Lean at Grand Haven." In Jeffrey Liker, ed., *Becoming Lean: Inside Stories of U.S. Manufacturers*. Portland, Ore.: Productivity Press.

MacDuffie, John Paul. 1997. "The Road to 'Root Cause': Shop-Floor Problem-Solving at Three Auto Assembly Plants." *Management Science* 43(4): 479–502.

Mair, Andrew. 1994. *Honda's Global Local Corporation: Japanization the Honda Way*. New York: St. Martin's Press.

Milkman, Raymond et al. 1991. *Economic and Social Impacts of Japanese Investments in the United States: Case Study of Sumitomo Electric Wiring Systems, Inc*. Maclean, Va.: Lazar Institute.

Nelson, Richard, and Sidney Winter. 1978. *An Evolutionary Theory of Economic Change*. Cambridge, Mass.: Harvard University Press.

Nishiguchi, Toshihiro 1994. *Strategic Industrial Sourcing: The Japanese Advantage*. New York: Oxford University Press.

Odaka, K., K. Ono, and F. Adachi. 1988. *The Automobile Industry in Japan: A Study of Ancillary Firm Development*. Oxford: Oxford University Press.

Ono, Taiichi. 1988. *Workplace Management*. Cambridge, Mass.: Productivity Press.

Sabel, Charles. 1994. " 'Learning by Monitoring': The Institutions of Economic Development." In Neil Smelser and Richard Swedberg, eds., *Handbook of Economic Sociology*. Princeton, N.J.: Princeton University Press.

Sako, Mari. 1992. *Prices, Quality, and Trust*. Oxford: Oxford University Press.

Smitka, Michael. 1991. *Governance by Trust*. New York: Columbia University Press.

Szulanski, Gabriel. 1995. "Appropriating Rents from Existing Knowledge: Intra-Firm Transfer of Best Practice." Ph.D. diss., INSEAD, Fontainebleau, France.

Womack, James P., Daniel Jones, and Daniel Roos. 1990. *The Machine That Changed the World*. New York: Rawson Associates, Macmillan.

Part II

Electronics and Related Products

Japanese Quality Technology

*Transferred and Transformed
at Hewlett-Packard*

Robert E. Cole

Enormous uncertainty gripped top managers in large U.S. manufacturing firms in the early 1980s as they came to realize that their Japanese competitors had developed a large competitive advantage over them.[1] There were a great number of competing explanations as to the cause of the problems facing American industry. Was it quality? Was it productivity? Was it low-paid workers, cheap capital, or unfair Japanese government support for their competitors? Was it a combination of factors? Which combination? Over time and with much trial and error, U.S. managers came to accept that quality was one of the significant competitive issues to which they needed to respond, that the Japanese really were doing better, and that the Americans lacked information on how the Japanese did it.

The next step was how to acquire that information. Would firms choose to learn directly from the Japanese? This expectation is rooted in an understanding of the critical role of information in organizational life. Stinchcombe (1990, p. 2) goes to the heart of the matter with his focus on organizations using the *earliest available information* (italics in original) to resolve actor uncertainty. This earliest information, which becomes progressively available in distinct social locations, shows actors what direction they ought to be going because that is the direction that successful competitors have taken. It is crucial, therefore, for an organization "to be where the news breaks, whenever it breaks" (Stinchcombe, 1990, p. 3). Not only do firms want the earliest information available, they also want knowledge about the specific problems they face from real-world practitioners. Such information reduces the costs associated with customization.

Being the first to grasp and to act successfully on knowledge about the new approaches to quality often meant that a firm could gain advantage over competitors. Most Japanese manufacturing companies had yet to establish production facilities in the United States. Therefore, the social location at which good information was available on quality improvement in the early 1980s was Japan, more specifically, it could be obtained by observing the organizational behavior of selected large export-oriented manufacturing firms.

Even if they wanted to learn from the Japanese, could American firms access the needed information, and at what price? There was, in fact, a set of firms that was uniquely positioned to learn reasonably quickly about the new approaches to quality developed by the Japanese. These were firms that had equity shares in Japanese firms, joint ventures with Japanese firms in Japan, or subsidiaries in Japan. If we add to this total the large number of American firms that had long-standing Japanese suppliers in Japan that could be relatively easily "leaned upon" to share information with their customers, we have a very large number of American manufacturing firms that had potential pipelines into Japan. These pipelines, while costly to develop, could be leveraged to allow the firms to enter into a sustained learning relationship for mastering the new models of quality improvement.

In the light of these observations, it is surprising that U.S. managers in fact showed great reluctance to engage in long-term systematic learning from their Japanese counterparts. Relatively few firms can be said to have engaged in such activities. Three nonmutually exclusive explanations seem responsible for that. They are the uncertainty that Japanese practices would work in the United States, the high costs of learning from the Japanese (including the difficulty of unpacking universally applicable information from Japanese cultural artifacts), and the lack of management norms legitimizing learning from the Japanese. One path of analysis is to explore in depth how these factors operated to restrict the learning process.[2] Another, and the one we have chosen here, is to learn more about the processes involved by looking at the exceptional cases.

A small number of firms are noted for their early effective adoption of the new models of quality improvement. These were firms that effectively used a Japanese source to help drive their quality improvement effort. Notable were the following four companies: Florida Power and Light (FPL), using its relationship with Kansai Electric, Ford Motor Company, using its relationship with Mazda; Hewlett-Packard learning from its joint venture, Yokogawa Hewlett-Packard; and Xerox, drawing on its joint venture with Fuji Photo Film, Fuji Xerox. My own reading of the literature, as well as interviews and personal experiences, suggests that, of these three cases, Xerox relied least on its Japanese source, with Ford in the middle and Hewlett-Packard and FPL at the high end of the continuum (Main, 1994, p. 26).

A great deal of learning and change in practices had to take place to achieve substantial and continuous improvements of the kind the Japanese competitors seemed capable of achieving. The Japanese quality challenge was for all practical purposes an exogenous one-time event that burst on the scene in the early 1980s without any gradual accumulation of learning or understanding. Because American managers by and large had misread earlier warning signals, most in effect were blindsided by the challenge. Their existing reward and accounting systems, the great prominence and power of functional groups like finance and marketing, and the resultant low status of manufacturing ill prepared our major manufacturing corporations for quality competition. Consequently, they were not prepared to acquire and effectively use the tools they needed to be successful in this area. In short, they had a lot to learn.

When we talk about learning in this context, we think of how one organization serves as a model for another, but, as we will see, an organization can serve as a model in a variety of ways. Moreover, management is not about learning per se; management is about creating something of value. This requires that learning be turned into practice that yields value. This is something that some of the academics on the "learning organization" bandwagon of the early 1990s seemed to forget. As psychologists learned long ago, learning is not the same as doing. We are interested in how one organization successfully transfers a specific practice or set of practices to another in a way that adds value to the receiving firm. We know from prior research that imitation is often quite difficult under the best of circumstances (Nelson and Winter, 1982). Therefore, we will pay special attention to those modes of transfer that best close the gap between learning and effective practice. Indeed, our working hypothesis is that those organizations that succeed best with technology transfer are those that best bridge the gap between learning and practice.

This chapter is devoted primarily to describing and analyzing the role that Yokogawa Hewlett-Packard (YHP) played in the adoption of elements of the new approaches to quality at Hewlett-Packard.[3] In particular, we look at the specific paths through which the transmission process took place, as well as examine the adoption and adaptation of one specific quality methodology (*hoshin* management) borrowed from the Japanese. *Hoshin* management is a planning and implementation discipline that identifies key breakthrough objectives and seeks to align the organization behind them in the process of deployment. Through this analysis, I hope to show that learning directly from the Japanese about quality improvement was indeed possible.[4] The goal is also to clarify the process by which this occurred. I describe the special set of circumstances that enabled this learning process to proceed as well as it did; simple intent is insufficient to bring about the desired outcome. Using *hoshin* management as my primary example, I also aim to clarify the kinds of adaptations that Hewlett-Packard managers believed they had to make to Japanese practices to get them accepted in a Hewlett-Packard culture suspicious of centrally directed solutions. These adaptations played a major role in bridging the gap between learning and practice.

Senders and Receivers

To assess a process of learning and technology transfer, we need to know the characteristics of the sender and the receiver at the time of the transfer. These characteristics also tell us a great deal about the prospects for success. As comedians and "garbage can" theorists are wont to note, timing is everything.

The receiver here is Hewlett-Packard Corporation, with its headquarters in the United States but with facilities around the world. In 1980, Hewlett-Packard had sales of $3 billion and 57,000 employees. This was a dramatic increase from sales of $365 million and 16,000 employees in 1970. In the early 1980s, consistent with its tradition of rapid growth and change, Hewlett-Packard was undergoing major evolutionary, even revolutionary changes.

The company had prospered with its integrated, multidivisional form structure of autonomous product-oriented divisions. This decentralized form allowed the company to grow rapidly, spinning off new divisions either as product lines achieved self-sufficiency or when an existing division got too large. The rough-cut point at which a new division was created was more than 1,000 people and/or $100 million in annual revenues. Each division functioned more or less as a stand-alone entity, containing all the resources and functional specialties it needed to support its profit-making activities (Beckman, 1996, p. 159; Kanter, 1983, p. 170).

The autonomy of divisions came under increasing pressure in the 1980s in the search for a corporation-wide response to a variety of challenges. By the late 1970s, HP was going through a major transition away from doing batch production using highly skilled, high-priced labor (basically building product by hand) in what was had been their traditional core business, the instrumentation business (electronic test and measuring devices). The new direction was towards high-volume, high-quality production for its emergent computer products businesses. This shift also involved a move from stand-alone instruments to products like computer terminals that had to interact well with whole systems.

These new markets required both higher productivity and quality (Main, 1994, p. 27). Moreover, HP was starting to sell to end users who were not themselves engineers but rather individuals who expected the product to work "out of the box." Success in the consumer market required that HP develop new marketing expertise and a means to tap into individual customer expectations. HP was proud of its "next-bench" method, where design engineers determined what customers might need by seeing what appealed to the HP engineer working at the next bench (Packard, 1995, p. 97). That worked fine when one's customers were all engineers, but it was an increasingly inadequate guide as HP's customer base expanded. All this was occurring in an increasingly competitive environment.

There is some basis for believing that the quality of HP products actually declined in the 1970s as the company shifted from vacuum tubes to highly integrated circuits and as it entered the computer market. At best, quality levels remained stagnant. The traditional iterative test-and-fix cycle that worked with vacuum tubes and batch production was not suitable for the mass production of highly complex products like integrated circuits. Moreover, rapid growth of the company, the creation of new divisions, and the hiring of new employees not steeped in the "HP way" all may have contributed to a decline or at least a stagnation of quality. Managers were struggling to deal with these problems.

It was at the time that all these changes and challenges were buffeting HP that the Japanese quality challenge became apparent. My description suggests that the forces that drove search behavior for new ways of coping with a competitive environment and the actual changes in manufacturing and market expertise among managers at HP were to a large extent endogenous, not exogenous. While the Japanese quality challenge was external, the changes required for an effective response meshed well with the internally evolving pressures to which Hewlett-Packard's top managers were beginning to respond. Thus, they were already searching for new approaches to manufacturing and to quality improvement and for ways to serve consumer markets more effectively. It was a Hewlett-Packard official who shocked the U.S. electronics industry with his public announcement in 1980 that Japanese chip suppliers had vastly superior reliability levels. This widely circulated assessment had a galvanizing effect on U.S. electronics manufacturers.

One can contrast this situation to that of General Motors and many other companies where the challenge was truly exogenous, with managers seeing the changes required for quality improvement as totally at variance with what they knew, what they believed worked well, and where they believed the company needed to go. Denial, not public acknowledgment, was the operative response. Accustomed to working with a mature technology subject only to incremental changes and working from a position of market strength seemingly secure from new entries, General Motors was "fat and happy" when the Japanese quality challenge hit. Unlike the situation at HP, and contrary to popular views, there is no objective indication that automotive quality was declining prior to the Japanese challenge of the early 1980s. Nor was there any indication that automotive managers perceived quality as a matter requiring special attention, much less new approaches, at this time.

Hewlett-Packard managers were already "discontented" and "running hard" to adjust to their changing market circumstances. At the same time, many key elements of total quality control (TQC)—focus on the customer, continuous improvement, and workforce participation—seemed very consistent with HP's deeply held core values and experiences (Packard, 1995). This was a company that, in its relatively short history, had been characterized by rapid growth, change, and adaptation. Thus, if opportunities for learning from the Japanese and YHP in particular could be presented in the right way at this time, they stood a reasonable chance of meeting a friendly reception. The situation described here is quite consistent with the observation of Ralph

Stacey (1996) that organizational creativity occurs when an organization is operating somewhere between stability and chaos.

We turn now to the characteristics of the sender (YHP) as they influenced its potential for transferring ideas and practices about quality improvement to the receiver (HP). YHP was started in 1963 as a joint venture between Yokogawa Electric Corporation (the leading industrial instrument manufacturer in Japan), which owned 51 percent of the new company, and HP, which owned 49 percent. Initially it was largely a distributor for HP's industrial instruments, but over time it shifted to a company that both distributed and manufactured HP computer-related products. In total, Yokogawa sent some 150 employees, including many managers, to the joint venture. These managers came to constitute the core of the YHP management team in the 1980s and included Kenzo Sasaoka, originally an R&D manager. Sasaoka was to become president and CEO of YHP in 1975.

In 1983 HP raised the issue of ownership, given that computer-related products had come to account for the overwhelming majority of the joint venture's activities. The two companies agreed on a new division: 75 percent HP and 25 percent Yokogawa. The evolution has been such that the Yokogawa people came to see themselves as full members of HP. This is critical to understanding the strong motivation that developed among YHP's senior executives to transfer what they had learned about quality to the parent company. It also helps us to understand the strong proselytizing tone of their efforts that developed over time.

These events constituted a most fortuitous factor for HP. Because Yokogawa was a leading manufacturing company, it could attract top-ranking college graduates to the joint venture. The Yokogawa contribution of high-quality human capital to the joint venture in its early years is an important underlying factor that facilitated YHP's ability to develop and apply TQC effectively and to transfer it to HP.[5]

YHP got involved with TQC in the mid-1970s. YHP leaders saw TQC as a particularly effective way to deal with their major business problem. This was the frequent failure of HP products delivered to Japanese customers within a relatively short time after being installed. These products were either designed in the United States and assembled in Japan or designed and produced in the United States and sold through YHP in Japan. The failure of HP products, as well as the failure of those designed and produced by YHP itself, was widely seen by employees as a major impediment to the growth and success of the company.

YHP managers complained to HP throughout the 1970s about the quality of the products being sent to Japan, but they were rebuffed for the most part. They were told again and again by HP managers that "those problems only seem to happen in Japan," implying there was something peculiar about the Japanese market. Since YHP accounted for a small proportion of HP sales for most divisions, YHP found it didn't have much clout with division and production executives. R&D managers would "blow them off," saying "we'll correct that in the next design."

By early 1979, YHP's TQC activities seemed to be bearing fruit. YHP was starting to record dramatic performance improvements, and in 1982 it won the Deming Prize. There is a sense in which the firm won the Deming Prize at just the right time in terms of having an impact on HP. If it had won it much earlier, no one at HP would have appreciated it (the Deming Prize came to the attention of American managers through the "If Japan Can, Why Can't We" TV documentary in 1980). If YHP had won it later, it would not have attracted so much attention, since by the late 1980s, U.S. companies were winning both the Malcolm Baldrige National Quality Award and the Deming Prize. Thus, the timing seems to have been perfect for maximizing the PR impact of YHP's TQC activities on HP itself. In the early 1980s, the Deming Prize was surrounded by a mystical positive aura that seemed to confer almost magical benefits on its recipients.

In the early and mid-1970s, YHP was still a struggling division trying to learn the HP system. It was reporting very modest profits (in the mid-1970s, its profit rate was about 25 percent that of the average HP division). All this changed rapidly in the late 1970s and YHP achieved the highest profit rate of all HP divisions from 1981 to 1984. There can be no doubt that this improved performance had a dramatic impact on the marketability of YHP's approach to TQC within HP.

We should not underestimate the importance of these financial results for making YHP a viable model for HP. To what extent it was, in fact, primarily attributable to YHP's quality initiative is extremely difficult to determine. The perception that TQC produced these results is what mattered. We see here an extraordinary confluence of forces in which the sending and receiving units developed in ways that favored the transfer of quality improvement practices from one to the other. In the late 1970s and early 1980s, the two entities found themselves, for very different reasons, moving in directions that helped YHP become a model for quality improvement at HP. The description here is consistent with the "garbage can" model of decision making, which stresses the serendipitous combinations of problems and solutions in time and space. Decisions and effective action occur when elements from streams of problems, solutions, participants, and opportunities come together. They did indeed come together in ways that led to effective HP-YHP cooperation in response to HP's quality challenge.

Methods and Accomplishments

YHP's first major breakthrough with TQC was achieved in lowering the wave solder rate of nonconformity from 4,000 parts per million (ppm) in 1977 to 40 parts ppm in 1979 and, with the help of quality circles, to 3ppm in 1982. It was a real breakthrough and provided a kind of practical "showcase" that YHP could use to market TQC throughout the company. Wave solder equipment at the time was one of HP's most expensive capital investments, and improvement in its utilization and performance attracted a great deal of attention.

The wave solder improvement was of major importance from a business point of view and understood as such by all YHP employees. From 1975 to 1982, YHP recorded four times fewer product failures and a fourfold increase in shipments without adding space. Production costs were down 40 percent, inventory was down 70 perecnt, development cycle time was down 30 percent, and market share rose to three times the 1975 level, as did profitability levels. These remarkable improvements were part of the reason the company was awarded the Deming Prize in 1982. Particularly powerful was a slide that was to be shown to many HP personnel. It reported the performance on YHP's proprietary product line (PL 36). As shown in Figure 6.1, it conveyed a clear simple message that implied a causal link among falling costs, declining quality failures, and rising profits.

YHP officials attributed their success in large part to the operationalization of six principles of TQC (Mozer, 1984, pp. 30–33):

1. A commitment to continuous quality improvement led by top management
2. The collection of data in analyzing problems (management by fact)
3. Clarification of who was responsible for action in daily work and in problem solving
4. Systematic gathering of feedback from internal and external customers
5. Use of Deming circle (Shewhart's Plan-Do-Check-Act cycle) as generalized problem-solving process to achieve permanent solutions
6. Use of statistics as a management tool

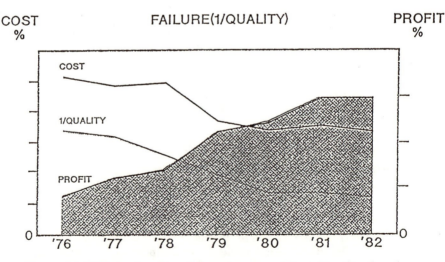

Figure 6.1 YHP product line (36) performance. Note: 1/quality describes quality as a reciprocal of the annual failure rate of YHP's product line.

YHP developed a variety of policies and practices to support the implementation of these principles, including creating quality circles, using *hoshin* management, employing the Presidential diagnostic (a form of audit led by the president characterized by dialogue rather than written responses), training all R&D engineers in and practicing reliability engineering techniques, seeking customer feedback, and instituting problem solving-systems.

The Impact on Hewlett-Packard

Influence from the sending organization can take many different forms. The sender can be seen in those ways:

- A provider of trustworthy information
- A provider of information about what is possible and different from what employees in the receiving organization are already thinking or doing
- A provider of concrete outcome benchmarks
- A provider of a transparent template for concrete processes and practices
- A provider of a broad conceptual template of how an organization should approach major organizational uncertainties

The boundaries among these categories are not always clear, and the categories are by no means mutually exclusive. Our data suggest that YHP's influence on HP operated in all these ways, with the importance of any one factor varying by time period and particular HP division and group.

The importance of trustworthy information in a period of uncertainty cannot be overestimated. Recall that in the early and mid-1980s, U.S. manufacturing managers were very confused about the scope, the significance, and the very nature of the quality problem and how it should be resolved. There were lots of information and opinions on the matter, with little hard evidence. Bad information was mixed with good information, and managers could not distinguish which was which. It was the era of competing gurus and consultants seeking to differentiate their products. Under these circumstances, it is easy to see that it was of great competitive value if firms could identify and access those social locations that permitted them better to separate good from bad information.

This is what YHP provided—a relationship of trust that made its information trustworthy. In response to those employees who responded negatively because of a pervasive "Not Invented Here" (NIH) mentality, proponents of TQC could respond, "We have a testbed right in our own family." As a division of HP, YHP could be assumed not to have pecuniary or other ulterior motive for its claims. Moreover, the practices A[?? 463] identified as worthy could be made transparent, unlike many other claims being advanced at this time. If HP managers wanted more information about a particular practice, they had only to invite a YHP staff member to their unit or to visit YHP operations in Japan.

Katsu Yoshimoto, the YHP quality manager at the time, estimates that, between 1979 and 1989, numerous small convoys of HP managers, totaling upward of 100 managers, came to study TQC at YHP. This is quite apart from those HP managers who came for normal business purposes and got exposed in that fashion. YHP managers visited HP divisions to spread the word, as well. Yoshimoto alone, according to his log, spent 600 days at HP outside Japan, mostly in the United States between 1983 and 1990. The CEO, Kenzo Sasaoka, made some thirty visits to HP U.S. operations between 1980 and 1985 to make presentations about TQC. The effects of this transparency was to increase the trustworthiness of the information being provided by YHP to HP in the eyes of HP managers.[6]

Testimony to the perceived trustworthiness of the information from YHP was the growing support from top management for adopting TQC as practiced by YHP. Quality became a prominent theme in the annual general managers' meetings in the early and mid-1980s. General managers at HP had profit-and-loss responsibility and a great deal of autonomy as to how to run their businesses. These general managers' meetings were a critical communication link for creating common understandings, evaluations, and objectives in this highly decentralized company. Sasaoka was invited to address HP managers a remarkable four times from the period from 1979–1985. This testifies to the importance top management attached to YHP's experiences and the interest of the general managers in what Sasaoka had to say. The significance of featuring quality and YHP's activities at the annual managers' meetings was captured well by John Young, the HP president during these critical years. He observed:

> We used the annual general managers' meeting big time. If you budget the most important premium time you have to this [quality], it says a lot about where it sits on your agenda. There's nothing more influential than your peers standing up at a general managers' meeting, getting to tell how they got the job done and getting psychic rewards for it. (cited in Main, 1994, p. 54)

In positioning quality and YHP in this fashion, HP top management not only showed that it regarded YHP as providing trustworthy information but it also held TQC up as a broad conceptual template of how the organization should approach and resolve some of the major uncertainties facing it at that time.

With YHP in the fold, HP managers had access to comparative data that could be collected and analyzed in response to specific objections raised by nonbelievers. Few other U.S. companies could easily match this access. For example, one way many HP managers found to reject the claims that YHP had found a better way was to argue that the higher reliability of YHP products was explainable in term of the simpler nature of its products. It is much easier to achieve higher reliability if you are producing far less complex products. In response to that argument, the corporate quality staff that worked with YHP produced a chart in 1981 that plotted annual failure rates against list price (using list price as a proxy for product complexity) for the various

HP, YHP, and Yokogawa Electric product lines. This analysis, in effect, "normalized" product complexity. What the staff found was a clear pattern showing the superiority (lower failure rates) of YHP and Yokogawa Electric products across the various price ranges. It was by publicizing these kinds of analyses, which were based on hard data, that HP's leadership was able to break down the denials of many HP managers.

None of this emphasis on trustworthiness and access to objective data is meant to suggest, however, that there was unquestioned acceptance of YHP's message. Despite access to "a member of the family," throughout the 1980s some HP managers continued to deny some combination of the following claims: that quality was a serious problem, that it was a major determinant of corporate-and division-level performance, and that the Japanese had found a better way. These positions should not be dismissed as simply manifestations of irrational resistance. In the very same time period of the biggest push for Japanese-style quality in the early 1980s, customer surveys evaluating hardware reliability in a variety of geographical settings and product markets reported HP to be the very best. Thus, many managers, quite understandably, found it hard to swallow the idea that the Japanese were all that good and they were all that bad. Moreover, notwithstanding YHP's being in the fold, a few HP managers believed that YHP was exaggerating HP's weaknesses because it was in YHP's interest to magnify quality differences to get the company's attention. Some believed that YHP relied on arbitrary and subjective inspection criteria that biased their quality comparisons. Nor did these suspicions simply weaken over time; when YHP's economic performance began to falter after 1985, reservations about the relation between quality and corporate performance were given new life. In keeping with HP's decentralized structure, throughout the 1980s and early 1990s, there continued to be great variation in division managers' consciousness of quality as a problem and in their openness to new approaches.

After YHP won the Deming Prize, John Young, sensing the seemingly good fit between TQC and HP culture, publicly committed to TQC in 1983. The Deming Prize gave Young the final "evidence" he needed. It provided the stamp of approval of Japan Inc. that what YHP was doing was right. In short, the awarding of the Deming Prize legitimated YHP's TQC activities among HP's top managers and removed any lingering doubts that YHP was a source of trustworthy information.

In the early days of the quality initiative, top management did everything it could to ensure that it had early victories and success stories that it could then "merchandise" throughout the corporation. The idea initially was to convince general managers and middle management that lower defect rates paid off in terms of business success (Main, 1994, p. 54). Not only did management merchandise its own success stories; it publicized YHP's, as well. The "marketing" of TQC within the company often took the form of using YHP to show what was possible and doing a before-and-after evaluation of YHP efforts (e.g., comparing figures for 1976 and 1983), documenting the methods the company used to achieve its improvement. The wave solder improvement story took on almost folk status within many HP divisions. It was still used in some HP training programs when I began my interviews in 1996. The fact that the wave solder improvements had been achieved on a second-hand machine shipped from the Santa Clara Division to HP's "backward Japan operation" amplified its impact.

One of the important lessons HP learned and promoted from these observations was the limits of technology in solving quality problems. Ray Demere, former vice president of manufacturing for HP, introduced President Sasaoka at the worldwide general managers' meeting in 1983 with the following observations:

> Let me mention two strategies for improving quality and productivity. One is the automation-driven strategy. . . . The other is the management-driven strategy, which emphasizes the role of people in the context of a well-developed set of management policies, practices, standards, and methods, including statistical tools, aiming at quality. This strategy must precede the automation-driven strategy to achieve significant success. YHP has been most successful implementing a management-driven strategy through the company without extensive automation. Their approach has been to analyze work processes by first measuring and collecting data, using statistical techniques to identify opportunities, taking action to make improvements, and monitoring to control the process. Most improvements have resulted from elegantly simple solutions, scientifically applied to eliminate defects in the process.[7]

These were lessons that GM's top management did not learn until the late 1980s through the experiences of NUMMI and their failure "to leapfrog the competition" through heavy technology investments at Hamtramck and other plants (Keller, 1989, pp. 202–225).

We observed that the sending organization can serve as a model by being a provider of information about what is possible and different from what employees in the receiving organization are already thinking or doing. It is clear that the various examples of YHP success, as exemplified by the wave solder improvement, served just this purpose.

The strongest corporate-wide quality initiative launched at HP in the early 1980s was the "10×" program. Led by John Young, the CEO, this program, announced in 1980, called for a tenfold improvement in hardware quality over the decade. It was based on the recognition that "orders of magnitude" changes were called for within HP to turn quality into a strong competitive factor. While HP still enjoyed a reputation for high quality, it discovered that some 25 percent of its manufacturing costs were being spent fixing quality problems (Young, 1983, p. 10). Those who claimed that quality was not a problem for HP had failed to digest this information. The goal needed to be startling in order to shock employees out of their accustomed belief that HP was a quality leader and to get them to question basic ways of working and improving. At the same time, the program initiators understood that, to be successful, the initiative had to be seen as credible among employees, this required, above all, that it be seen as achievable.

It is highly probable that YHP's achievements, along with other factors such as customer input, contributed to the setting of the 10× objective itself. By 1979, YHP was already showing great improvements under TQC. The initial results of the wave solder improvement effort were coming in. As noted earlier, YHP was able to lower rate of nonconformity from 4,000 parts per million (ppm) in 1977 to 40 ppm in 1979; that meant the number of defects in 1979 was 1 percent of what it was in 1977. This improvement was well in excess of the 10× goal that HP had set for itself (though the wave solder improvements were at the component rather than the product level, the latter being a much more challenging task, combining as it does many interacting components). Sasaoka, reflecting on those days, captured the YHP role as follows:

> We also had a lot of impact on the 10× program. By showing how far behind HP was and how much improvement could take place with concerted effort as we did in the wave solder improvement, we contributed to the ambitious goals that John Young chose to set. Furthermore, the application of TQC approaches was one of the important means by which many managers chose to try to meet the 10× goal.

While acknowledging the impressive achievements of YHP, HP managers who visited YHP increasingly came away with the impression that there was no miracle in TQC, just "basic blocking and tackling." So it appeared doable. In fact, there was an underlying systems logic behind many of the seeming unrelated common-sense practices that would become apparent only through further experience. At the early stages of adoption, however, the belief that it was simply basic "blocking and tackling" gave managers the confidence to move ahead. In this sense, ignorance (failure to realize the larger scope of changes required) was an aid to organizational transformation.

What were the results of the 10× effort? HP declared victory in its internal magazine *Measure* in 1991 (starting the clock in 1981). The standard used by HP to measure progress was the number of failures per $1,000 of product selling price. Using a standardized measure, failure declined from 1.0 in 1981 to almost 0.1 in 1991, just short of the 10× goal. Put differently, product failures under warranty in 1991 were just 10 percent of what they had been in 1981. To be sure, the rate of improvement varied enormously among divisions, reflecting, in part, variation in the seriousness with which the divisions embraced the goal and imperfections in the metric.

Warranty costs were reduced by an estimated $800 million, and huge reductions in inventory, lead time, and labor costs were also recorded. While not directly measurable, one could presume that by reducing customer "down time" with its improved reliability, HP drastically reduced levels of customer dissatisfaction, increased customer loyalty, and increased the probability that existing customers would recommend HP to others. Improved performance, therefore, could be expected eventually to translate into higher sales.

The organizational significance of 10×, however, was that it provided a powerful corporate-wide goal within the quite decentralized culture of HP. It became the foundation for all HP improvement programs in the 1980s. Pressure on managers to meet that goal, in turn, led many managers to embrace some version of TQC. The corporate quality department itself moved from a position of weakness to one in which its directives had a certain obligatory weight vis-à-vis the divisions ("thou shalt do the following"). That is not to say, of course, that it always got its way. Division managers had elaborate methods of passive and active resistance when they disapproved of particular initiatives (Main, 1994, p. 165).

Notwithstanding the pockets of resistance, the overall environment was one in which the 10× umbrella contributed to managerial receptivity to the types of TQC activities being carried out at YHP. As Katsu Yoshimoto, the YHP quality officer, put it, "In the early 1980s, HP's division managers were looking for ways to achieve 10×, and that made them quite receptive to YHP's ideas on process improvement." In summary, YHP's success had an major impact on HP's goal setting in the quality arena and YHP's TQC activities provided a set of concrete processes and outcome benchmarks that served as a template for HP action.

Two Tracks for Transferring Quality Technology

We can think of the diffusion of TQC from YHP to HP as having proceeded along two tracks. The first track was its diffusion in the course of solving ordinary YHP business problems. A second track involved YHP in efforts to consciously spread TQC throughout HP.

The first track was narrow and deep. It did not reach all divisions because it aimed at only those units of HP with which YHP had business relations. While it wasn't as broad as the second track, it was in many ways more effective because YHP modeled the new business practices in its dealing with other HP units. As such, the learning and technology transfer involved was imbedded in normal business problem-solving activities and routines. It is the closest to learning-by-doing of any mode used in the transfer process between HP and YHP and thus was, by far, the most effective method for bridging the gap between learning and practice. Back-and-forth visits by HP personnel to YHP in Japan and by YHP staff to HP to solve specific problems characterized this mode. The practical and iterative character of these exchanges and the clear business purpose of the new practices made the technology transfer involved less threatening, more transparent, more understandable, and, therefore, easier to carry out.

As part of this effort, Yoshimoto, the YHP quality manager, estimated that he did some 200 informal problem-solving diagnostics for HP units during the period 1983–1990. Most of these were done to help YHP solve its business problems by getting HP divisions to do a better job satisfying its Japanese customers. In effect, YHP focused in the 1980s on improving customer feedback and on getting HP personnel to listen to the "voice of the customer." YHP managers believe that this focus on responding to customer complaints contributed to HP's decision, in 1982, to polish up and reinvigorate its traditional corporate objective of customer focus.

YHP targeted what it called the "rainbow division"—the seven worst HP divisions in terms of product quality delivered to YHP—in what later came to be known as the "DOA [Dead on Arrival] problem." One can't help but be aware of the cultural differences here; American managers in a similar situation would have undoubtedly chosen a more aggressive label like "the dirty seven." Yoshimoto, the quality officer, made quarterly visits to the United States to meet with those divisions and to work with those who most needed to improve the quality of their products. He typically met with group general managers and functional managers. Yoshimoto and other YHP personnel conducted joint improvement projects for areas like the DOA products with HP personnel in the rainbow divisions to achieve improvements in product design and manufacturing capability.

Product reliability was also a major continuing focus for YHP, and it often organized joint improvement activities with HP managers. In 1982, for example, YHP formed a joint improvement group with the Desktop Computer Division (DCD) located in Fort Collins, Colorado, to deal with problems YHP was having with products manufactured in both locations. The DCD team members visited Japan in 1982, and a YHP engineer spent six months in Fort Collins. The improvements made by this team led to a 60 percent reduction in the warranty failure rate and lowered manufacturing costs (Mohr and Mohr, 1982, pp. 249–250). It was through these kinds of "hands-on" improvement activities that much of YHP's quality improvement expertise was transferred to HP.

Earlier I noted that YHP's initial complaints were often ignored by HP personnel. With the rising reputation of YHP within HP, however, the joint venture was in a position to have its complaints taken more seriously. Would you want to be the division, group manager, or engineer who resisted its overtures when top management was touting its accomplishments at companywide meetings? YHP learned how to escalate pressure for change. If an engineer in charge was not responsive, it would move up to the division manager, and if he was not responsive it would involve President Sasaoka in putting pressure at the group level. It did what it thought it had to do to get the changes it thought it needed. Of course, matters didn't always come out according to YHK's script, and actual outcomes were the result of a complex of interacting factors.

At the same time, to make HP more aware of customer complaints in a way that would produce action, YHP managers realized that they had to develop more effective feedback to HP. To maximize the probability of a positive HP response, they concentrated on sending the right information to the right person at the right level in the right format. Gradually, the quality of their feedback began to improve. They taught their personnel to analyze each problem to see whether it should be the subject of a "hot-site action" (having a high-level manager meet with the irate customer to assure him or her that everything was being done to solve the problem) and/or whether it should be sent to a quality team or one of the functional units for its disposition and, if the latter, which one and at what level.

YHP mapped the feedback approach to be taken and trained its personnel in the appropriate response. Using TQC, it taught its personnel to no longer just complain to HP or rely on emotional appeals. Instead, the YHP feedback became increasingly characterized by a clear description of the problem and an analysis of its causes. When possible, it recommended a fix (temporary and/or permanent). YHP found the "QC story" format (a series of steps mimicking the actual problem-solving process), with its clear problem statements and data analysis, to be useful for facilitating international communication to resolve specific problems. Basically, it was providing HP with data on end-customer complaints. Increasingly, it was passing on the "customer's voice" in a clear, strong fashion. YHP saw this as critical to getting HP managers to listen. In this way, it used real business problems to spread TQC ideas to selected HP units through its normal business behavior. Learning and effective practice seem to merge using this mechanism.

Success stories grew up around these activities and were marketed through the company. Thus, the Disk Memory Division in Boise became a model of improvement as part of HP's effort to better satisfy its Japanese customers. In 1984, HP hard disk products were at a competitive disadvantage vis-à-vis their Japanese competitors. The HP products operated with a mean time between failure (MTBF) of 8,000 hours, compared to Japanese top products, which operated with a 30,000 hour MTBF. Cooperating with YHP, the Boise operation was able to set the industry standard by increasing its MTBF to 300,000 hours by 1992 and to 800,000 hours in 1995. Notwithstanding this improvement, HP closed this business in 1996. Thus, we are reminded that models of corporate success often have short lives as new events quickly render obsolete past successes.

Predictably, in this loosely integrated company, some HP units were more resistant to the TQC message than others. Some managers were skilled at giving lip service to TQC but did little to change their practices. Often units were reluctant to make a permanent fix to a problem because of the high cost of design change. One YHP manager recalled:

> During my visit to HP units, I could see managers struggling between the need to show short-term profits and their support of long-term business strategies, which included integration of TQC into their practices. Depending on their business background and the signals they were getting from their general manager and the overall profitability of their operations, they tended to emphasize the one or the other.

YHP was the first HP unit to conduct and publicize DOA studies of HP products arriving to be sold in Japan. As they began to study the reasons why installed products were failing at customer sites, they came to realize that many were arriving DOA in Japan. Up to then, this had been something of a taboo subject in the corporation. HP found in its first study, in 1980, that a remarkably high 10 percent of HP products were arriving in Japan DOA (a figure that some HP managers considered inflated because of what they saw as the arbitrary inclusion of cosmetic and other minor defects). Partially through YHP's strong efforts to publicize the problem and the resources it devoted to working with HP on the problem, by 1990 the number of DOAs detected in Japan had fallen to 1 percent. YHP also helped create a more differentiated approach to DOA by adding the category of DEFOA (Defective on Arrival, for reasons including late delivery and missing accessories, kits, and documents). YHP's DOA activities came to serve as an HP performance benchmark. As one veteran HP employee told me, YHP came to be the source for "warranty failure rate" data; the DOA rates for products shipped to YHP were considered the most rigorous measure of outgoing quality.

This DOA campaign by YHP was one of the seeds for the development of HP's global order fulfillment reengineering project in the early 1990s. HP had been weak on the delivery of complex systems products (often with components produced in different locations), leading to delayed delivery and DOA problems (Main, 1994, pp. 166–167). Initially, HP managers had been resistant to YHP's negative interpretations of the DOA studies. The HP European quality manager took the lead in championing the YHP position and used YHP's DOA data as an initial basis for creating a global order fulfillment process. Thus, YHP actions provided the inspiration, and its DOA data the launching pad, for the ensuing development of the corporation-wide effort to improve the fulfillment of orders requiring global coordination of HP units.

After YHP won the Deming Prize in 1982, YHP developed a second track, through which it more consciously sought to spread TQC throughout HP. This track was the opposite of the first track in that it was broad but not very deep. It was more a stage-setting phenomenon involving policy advice, exhortation, and the provision of a broad conceptual template. It was effective only when followed by more specific training and action at the operational level. Nevertheless, one could argue that, by proceeding along both tracks, YHP's TQC activities had a significant influence on developments at HP.

The second track was encouraged by HP's top management and took many forms, including President Sasaoka's presentations to the company's general managers, described earlier. It also operated through Yoshimoto's participation in developing corporate quality policy. Yoshimoto was appointed to membership in the corporate quality council in 1983 and attended quarterly council meetings. The council was composed largely of group quality managers (of both product and geographical groups) and key corporate quality staff. In those days, the council was quite influential in setting corporate directions. It operated as a learning organization, picking study topics like *hoshin* management. The council served as a transmission belt for the rest of the quality managers at HP to move these new ideas into practice.

To be sure, this was by no means a smooth or complete process. The quality managers, armed with their new quality mandate, often ran smack into division-level managers who had their own strong ideas about ingredients for the business's success. The extent of melding and dovetailing of the two depended on the proclivities and the receptivity of division-level management, the cleverness, flexibility, and social skills of the quality managers in packaging the new ideas, the nature of the specific quality practice being advocated, how well the business was doing, and the kinds of pressures division managers were getting from their own bosses.

YHP also provided support for developing the Quality Maturity System, a corporate-wide diagnostic activity, and for implementing "*hoshin* management" (policy planning and policy deployment). We need to understand how the process of adoption interacted with adaptive innovations to bring about the successful institutionalization of these practices. To this end, we turn now to *hoshin* management.

Hoshin Management

Hoshin management (*hoshin kanri*) was a set of practices developed by companies like Toyota, Komatsu, and Bridgestone Tire company that crystallized in Japan in the early 1970s and came to constitute one of the core elements of Japanese TQC or CWQC (Corporate-Wide Quality Control). At HP, like many American companies, management chose to keep the Japanese term *hoshin*. The management system is known at HP as *hoshin* planning, as opposed to management by policy (or policy management), the direct translation favored by the Japanese.

Following Shiba, Graham, and Walden (1993, p. 412), we can describe *hoshin* management as a planning and implementation approach that seeks to align all organizational layers and employees behind key company goals and to do so with a sense of urgency. By focusing and coordinating employee efforts and resources on key company goals whose achievement can make a competitive difference, the firm seeks to create breakthroughs. Careful selection of such objectives is expected to quickly and effectively bring a company's goals and activities in alignment with the firm's changing environment. It provides a systems approach to the management of change in critical business processes and involves negotiated dialogues, both vertically and horizontally, through the organization in the selection and coordination of the means to achieve them (Watson, 1991, pp. xxii–xxxiv). The Japanese refer to this back-and-forth dialogue as *kyatchi boru* (catch ball).

Although *hoshin* management crystallized in the early 1970s as a key element in Japanese TQC practices, it is remarkable how long it took to come to the attention of American managers. Involving planning activities as it did, it was one of those invisible elements of the new approaches to quality improvement that eluded most American companies in the early and mid-1980s. HP was no exception in this regard.

In the early 1980s, the thinking of YHP leaders on how to approach quality improvement at HP was first to get HP managers to understand elementary TQC. That would serve as the building block that would allow YHP to proceed to then introduce them to *hoshin* management. YHP's initial overtures to HP general managers on *hoshin* management, however, were not warmly received. HP managers were committed to their ongoing use of management by objective (MBO), involving individual managerial goal setting and measurement, and didn't see *hoshin*'s advantages over MBO.

In 1985 Craig Walter, head of corporate quality, heard from YHP that it had documented *hoshin* management. At the same time, Katsu Yoshimoto was campaigning for HP's adoption of *hoshin* management as the next most important step in its TQC initiative. Craig saw *hoshin* management as basically an approach to strategic planning. YHP also stressed that it would be an effective mode for stepping up achievement of HP's 10x goal (King, 1989, p. ii). It had the YHP documents translated, and Katsu Yoshimoto came over to help explain *hoshin* management. YHP personnel continued to work with HP corporate and selected divisions to help them understand how *hoshin* management worked. HP corporate staff, as well as selected managers, could and did routinely compare their mode of utilization of *hoshin* management with that of YHP.

Independently, Professor Noriaki Kano, a well-known Japanese quality counselor, had begun working at HP. He had been introduced by a corporate HP manager familiar with his work for Malaysian and Singaporean HP groups. Although his introduction was not through YHP, his work at HP came to be closely coordinated with that of YHP's educational and training activities. The use of a Japanese expert served as a variant on Stinchcombe's admonition to be where the news was breaking. By using Kano, HP in effect, brought the news directly from Japan to its U.S. operations. *Hoshin* management was a major focus of Kano's activities, and he strongly reinforced the idea that *hoshin* management was important. He worked to help HP managers use it more effectively. In particular, he stressed the importance of "catch ball," that objectives could stretch over more than one year, and the importance of the PDCA (Plan-Do-Check-Act) cycle in reaching breakthrough objectives.

In the mid-1980s, HP was struggling. Profits were going down, and divisions were still operating under decentralized controls. This difficult situation fueled the movement for greater coordination and consolidation among divisions (Beckman, 1996). Thus, there was growing interest in finding a better mechanism for coordinating the different parts of the company and for giving the company strategic direction. The de facto bottoms-up planning process resulting from the use of MBO was of little help. *Hoshin* management, however, seemed to fit the bill and came along at just the right time. Again, we find evidence for the garbage can model of decision making.

Nor was *hoshin* planning the only solution to the need to give the company more strategic direction. Not long after *hoshin* planning began, a three-to-five-year ten-step planning process was also successfully championed by the corporate engineering and consulting services organization. This planning process came to be used by the divisions together with *hoshin* planning; it is based on fourteen categories (e.g., strategic direction, competition, customer satisfaction).

The corporate quality office took the lead in getting some managers to use *hoshin* management. This group of managers met regularly to discuss problems they encountered. A forum to showcase what four or five groups had achieved after using *hoshin* for one or two years was held, with an audience of other general managers and interested parties. The Chief Operating Officer at the time, Dean Morton, became involved and began practicing *hoshin* himself. This gave a major boost to his commitment to the process and helped to legitimate *hoshin* management. General managers responded well and seemed to like it—it helped them run their businesses and to focus their energies and resources. They liked its clarity and the sense of control it appeared to give them. Over time, they came to see it as a kind of "turbo MBO," using the PDCA cycle to increase the power of traditional MBO. Traditional MBO was entirely results-oriented but, the overlaying of it with the *hoshin* management system sought to balance that focus with an emphasis on process. Rather than arguing for the superiority of *hoshin* over MBO, *hoshin* was marketed within the company as a "more mature MBO."

Hoshin planning became a widely used annual planning tool and was expected to be implemented in all divisions around 1989 (nothing ever seems to be mandated at HP). Upper management was attracted to it, since it gave structure, coherence, and common language to the company's strategy process at a time when they were looking for greater coordination among its divisions and groups.

Lew Platt, the current HP CEO, has been a strong supporter and user of *hoshin*, even participating in the periodic review process where business units are evaluated as to whether or not they are on target to meet their objectives and, if they are not, what, if anything, needs to be done about any shortfalls. As a user, Platt modeled for other managers what he expected. When Platt took over in late 1992, at his first meeting with the general managers he started out by saying, in effect, "this are my *hoshins* [he then went on to list his three key near-term objectives] and this is how I am going to run the company." It was a clear message of support for *hoshin* management and implicit advice for others to get on board.

This is not to suggest that the path was straight and easily traversed. HP managers struggled mightily and still struggle with getting *hoshin* management to work in a way that meets their needs. At first, HP managers had a tendency to set too many objectives each year, a problem Kano calls "chasing too many rabbits"; it took time to learn that they needed to concentrate on a very small number of breakthrough objectives. It also took time for them to learn that they needed to keep these breakthrough objectives separate from their obligation to meet their ordinary "business fundamentals." Many managers had trouble letting go of their traditional MBO practices, they went through the motions of doing "*hoshins*" but never measured their own progress and would create new *hoshins* each year without reflecting on the previous year's accomplishments or lack thereof. Some managers misused *hoshin* management planning by treating it as a control tool (not using the "catch ball" function). They simply worked out the *hoshin* themselves and then announced as a fait accompli to subordinates. Still others turned it into a bureaucratic enterprise or ignored their periodic performance reviews.

In a report on the preliminary results from his study of *hoshin* planning at one HP division, George Easton identified the following problems: There was a failure to fully resolve the relationship between the ten-step planning process and *hoshin* planning. Process facilitators, typically selected from key staff personnel for top division management, often played such a large role that senior managers in effect delegated their *hoshin* responsibilities. This raises the question of whether *hoshin* operated as effectively as it might have and whether the failure of top division management to model the desired behavior won't have long-run negative consequences. Finally, Easton questioned the importance of *hoshin* planning relative to how the business is run.[8] The extent of the problems posed by the issues raised by Easton appear to vary widely across divisions.

A common problem at many U.S. companies, including HP, was that they were better at doing *hoshin* planning (upfront setting of breakthrough objectives) than they were at doing *hoshin* planning for deployment, the actual deployment itself, and the monitoring of that deployment (implementation and regular reviews).[9] In this sense, the use of the term "*hoshin* planning" at HP is not a misnomer, it reflects the weaker emphasis on implementation and review (though planning is required for implementation, as well).

HP's review process was much less formal than that of the typical Japanese practitioner. At YHP, for example, managers tend to methodically look for deviations from the plan. At HP, management thinks that it can't freeze the plan because a variety of contingent events come into play once the plan has been adopted. This, they believe, requires a more dynamic approach. It does not make sense to spread a lot of time and resources documenting in detail differences from the original plan and then developing and formally committing to countermeasures to reduce the difference between the current trajectory and the plan objectives. *Hoshin* is a success at HP, says Richard LeVitt, the corporate quality manager, because

> it helps us to understand who we are as a business and where we are going. It is the act of planning, itself, that builds consensus and brings about alignment. The process of creating alignment around common breakthrough objectives is what matters. Implementation will of necessity be sloppy and messy.

This discussion feeds into the stereotype of the ritualistic and bureaucratic Japanese versus the dynamic innovative Americans. Yet, Noriaki Kano notes that the most effective Japanese companies are also quite willing to do midcourse corrections to adjust their plan to new circumstances. As many at YHP see it, moreover, a weak review process makes it less probable that managers will formulate an effective recovery plan if they are falling short, and they also forgo root cause analysis of their problems. As a result, managers have a more difficult time understanding the process that actually led to the results. Did a defective process lead to the failure to meet the plan, or was it the introduction of some changes in the environment? Without a careful review process, managers don't know and won't learn from their experience. Thus, they may easily choose the same ineffective methods in the future. Put differently, by not practicing the PDCA cycle, they lose the opportunity to create valuable knowledge. In short, from a Japanese perspective, there is incomplete use of the *hoshin* methodology.

HP modified still other Japanese *hoshin* practices. HP used three forms (planning table, implementation table, and review table) to conceptualize and carry out *hoshin* management. YHP typically used four, adding a performance measure table which included a definition of the specific metrics that were agreed upon in advance to measure progress toward the goals, as well as some other items. HP personnel believed this fourth table didn't add much value. Moreover, befitting their greater emphasis on implementation, YHP typically expected four layers of management to construct their own implementation plan consistent with their responsibilities (division managers, functional managers, department managers, and section managers). At HP, however, the further one went down the management hierarchy, the less likely managers were to create their own implementation tables. HP leaders believed they had to simplify *hoshin* management in order to get it accepted. YHP's approach was seen by many HP employees as overly bureaucratic and ritualistic. As one senior corporate HP manager, reflecting on the potential receptivity by middle management, bluntly put it, if we don't simplify it, "the dogs won't eat it."

Overall, top management and general managers came to believe that *hoshin* management evolved in a way that served the company well. They can cite a number of *hoshin* breakthrough objectives whose achievement was important to the company. Yet, *hoshin* at HP operated at less than optimum fashion from a variety of perspectives, including the relatively weak application of the PDCA cycle to reviewing the progress of implementation. Perhaps, however, these adaptations were the price of getting *hoshin* management accepted at HP.

The foregoing discussion highlights the adaptation process involved in effectively moving from learning about TQC to applying it in practice. It reveals some of the key adjustments that needed to be made for YHP's ideas to effectively become a part of HP practice. Our discussion of *hoshin* management does not exhaust the areas in which YHP's influence was felt at HP. In particular, YHP was very influential in developing HP's quality diagnostic and audit system, the Quality Maturity System. Nor have we discussed quality circles, a central element of Japanese TQC and one practiced by YHP. Circle activity, after getting off to a fast start at HP, did not fare well. Interestingly, it was not high on YHP's agenda for transfer as well, though some HP managers thought that it was.

Ambiguity, Decision Making, and Modeling

YHP's role in diffusing ideas about quality to HP was played out in a relatively short time frame, from about 1979 to 1986. Just as HP's interest in YHP's quality practices rose dramatically with the profitability of YHP, it fell rapidly once YHP profitability sank. In 1985 the value of the yen began rising rapidly and YHP business results of YHP started to decline. Over the next few years, this downward turn was reinforced by a variety of micro and macro factors, including internal HP accounting changes that raised transfer prices for YHP's sales organization (thereby raising the prices of imported products to be sold in Japan), the bursting of the "bubble" associated with Japan's hyperspeculation, the high expenses YHP incurred moving into new facilities, and a very high investment made to break into the IC tester market.

In 1992, the YHP manufacturing division actually reported a loss.[10] This was the low point. It was not until 1995 that it was able to restore a high profit rate again, especially in the test and measurement sector, where it once again achieved the number one position at HP. From a practical point of view, one can argue that this brief window of acceptability from 1979 to 1986 was all that was needed. The "bloom was off the rose" by 1986, but, as one YHP manager put it, "we had already pretty much transferred most of what we had to offer as regards TQC." The negative results of YHP were offset for a while by the continuing popularity among American companies of absorbing things Japanese until the early 1990s. At that time, the impact of the bursting of the Japanese bubble started to be felt, and those who presented Japan as a model to be emulated disappeared rapidly from the popular dialogue.

These events raise a more general point. What is the basis on which managers decide that a given company or a unit within a company is or is not a model to learn from? There is no doubt that success in the marketplace is a powerful predictor of which companies and units come to serve as models. Yet, we can ask, was the astounding success of YHP in the early 1980s clearly a function of TQC? Not necessarily. In the early 1980s, Japanese companies (not all of which were doing TQC) faced an increasingly favorable business climate, and, in that environment, TQC proved extremely effective, but so were some other practices. While certainly a good case can be made for the independent contributions of TQC to YHP success, the causal linkages are in fact not all that clear. We are dealing with complex systems. Yet, HP took YHP's financial success as a clear indicator of TQC's effectiveness.

Similarly, HP managers (and even some YHP managers) increasingly questioned the relevance of YHP quality practices as soon as YHP's profit position dissipated in the mid-1980s; YHP clearly lost its attraction as a magnet for other HP managers after the mid-1980s. Yet, were YHP's TQC activities less effective in 1987–1992 than they were in the early 1980s in terms of their contribution to manufacturing efficiencies, to YHP's quality performance and reputation, and, indeed, to the bottom line itself? Probably not. On logical grounds alone (assuming that YHP's TQC activities had stabilized by the mid-1980s), constants can not explain a variable. Instead of their being a negative factor, one can just as strongly argue, as Kenzo Sasaoka does in his reflections on this matter, that because the company stayed true to TQC practices during the downturn, YHP's business decline was not as steep as it would otherwise have been. Similarly, YHP's rapid recovery from the 1992 low point can be seen as a reflection of its adherence to TQC improvement activities while it gradually installed a new, improved business strategy (Sasaoka, 1996, pp. 19–23).

The point here is not that Sasaoka is right or wrong but rather that managers observing this kind of situation often don't know which position is right or wrong. They don't know the cause-and-effect linkages. Yet, faced with this kind of situation, they invariably make the assumption that a decline in corporate success must mean that the practice(s) being considered for borrowing are not working. Managers tends to equate the maturity of their and others' management systems with their financial performance.

What are the underlying conditions that increase the probability of these kinds of assessments? Under conditions in which the innovative practice challenges conventional wisdom and there is not much hard evidence to support its positive or negative effects, a kind of negative halo effect flows from declining corporate performance. This leads managers to the conclusion that their introduction of a given practice being used by their prospective model does not seem to be affecting the model's most important measure of all, corporate performance. The burden of proof is on those supporting the innovative practice. Under the two conditions described earlier, and taken together with the fact that many other changes are occurring simultaneously, managers will tend to conclude that it is better to err on the side of caution and to drop that model. The focus of management activity will be on finding something else that can turn around corporate performance more quickly and more reliably. In this context, it is hard to stand up in management meetings and argue the case for the innovation. Yet, acting on very little evidence creates a big component of uncertainty and leaves a large chance of being wrong. Quality advocates undoubtedly contributed to these management decisions by exaggerating the benefits of quality initiatives and therefore making it appear that there was a very high correlation between quality performance and short-term corporate financial performance. When that couldn't be shown, the advocates were defenseless.

Conclusion

What have we learned from the description in this chapter about organizational design for learning? Clearly, there were a great many serendipitous factors that contributed to YHP's being able to serve as a model for HP's new approaches to quality improvement starting in the early 1980s. While it was not an accident that HP developed a joint venture in Japan, its managers could hardly have predicted that YHP would be in the right place at the right time with the right solutions regarding quality for the right kind of company. This doesn't mean that going to Japan to learn how to do quality improvement would work only under these circumstances, but, nevertheless, not that many American companies could have duplicated all the propitious conditions in the HP-YHP relationship in the early 1980s. This suggests that strategic intent to learn and our ability to consciously design the learning process is more limited than those who make a living (scholars and consultants) writing on this subject might have us believe. Major constraints that condition a successful technology transfer process are often outside the control of those engaged in organizational engineering.

The benefits to HP of the YHP relationship were enormous. First and foremost, YHP served as a source of trustworthy and transparent information. It raised the sights among HP managers of what was possible in the quality arena by providing outcome benchmarks, a paradigm of a new approach that might resolve major organizational uncertainties and a template for specific processes and practices. These were no small contributions. YHP offered both objectives and the means to reach those objectives. To be sure, there were many other influences on HP as it learned about and put into practice its new approaches to quality improvement. The intent here is only to show that access to YHP gave HP a huge head start over many other U.S. companies and distinctly marked its approach to quality improvement in ways that are still quite visible. Even allowing for enormous differences among divisions, no one familiar with HP practices in the quality arena could fail to identify the visible influences of the long-term association with YHP.

The phenomenal success of HP through the first half of the 1990s, as it continued to grow at a very rapid pace, has many sources. While we can't demonstrate quality's role statistically, throughout this period the company has nurtured a strong quality reputation that cannot help but have been a major business asset. In the 1996 American Customer Satisfaction Survey, HP achieved the highest quality score of any of the firms surveyed in the personal computer industry. Its score of 77 compares to the mean score for the industry of 73 (weighted for market share). Many surveys rank HP first in customer satisfaction in a variety of product lines. For example, for 1995 HP was ranked first on notebook computers and was tied for first in desktop personal computers in the J. D. Power and Associates customer satisfaction studies (Bemowski, 1996, p. 27).

Participating in product lines characterized by recurrent periods of explosive growth (e.g., ink jet and laser printers) as a result of short product cycles and dramatic new advances in technology, HP's leadership in quality improvement practices has been an enormous asset. In such industries, the ability to rapidly "ramp up" production for the mass market with a minimum of quality glitches and with high yields is critical to success; HP has excelled in exactly this area (Moore, 1995, p. 81). YHP's contribution to these achievements has not been trivial, but its contributions have continually been modified and adapted to fit new competitive circumstances. HP found a way to be where the news was breaking and to turn that to competitive advantage.

Another early influential pacesetter in the quality arena that relied heavily on learning form the Japanese was Florida Power and Light (FPL). If we compare HP's experiences with things Japanese with FPL's, it appears that HP's decentralized structure served it well.[11] FPL was a highly centralized company in which most employees worked in the same business. The firm was not a particularly dynamic environment compared to HP, and, when changes did occur, they were likely to be felt equally by all employees. FPL employees were accustomed to a strong top-down management hierarchical system. In short, it looked a lot like a Japanese company (cf. Shiba, Graham, and Walden, 1993, p. 282).[12] In this highly centralized environment, management was able to strongly push implementation of a fixed set of practices down through the hierarchy. FPL initially adopted the Japanese system intact. The weakness of the FPL approach was that it lacked a method for calibrating these innovative practices to their new U.S. business environment, and it was also vulnerable to a change in top management.

In 1990, not long after FPL won the Deming Prize, just such a management change took place. The new management team, headed by James Broadhead, was initially quite hostile to the quality initiative. He was able to tap a great deal of employee dissatisfaction. It became apparent that many employees had gagged on the large bureaucratic apparatus that had been created. There was a widespread feeling among employees that the quality program had become very mechanical and inflexible and had created a paper-oriented bureaucracy that in some cases was actually creating barriers to continuous improvement. Broadhead's view was that electric power was a commodity, that the real challenge for the company was how to adapt to the increasing threat posed by the pending deregulation of the industry. In this context, it didn't pay to worry so much about quality. He set in motion policies that dismantled much of the quality apparatus and instituted a major downsizing initiative to reduce costs. It was a traumatic time for those associated with the quality initiative, and many employees left the company (cf. Main, 1994).

Despite this, the quality initiative survived at FPL in streamlined fashion, and Broadhead's views mellowed over time. In the 1990s, a number of changes were made in the quality initiative, including the introduction of extensive benchmarking, an emphasis on self-managing teams, a greater stress on accountability, business process reengineering, and increased stress on giving employees more opportunities to be creative and flexible (Broadhead, 1996, p. 13). A variety of key measures showed continued quality improvement over the performance achieved when the company received the Deming Prize (e.g., further reduction in number of unplanned outages and dramatic improvement in quality performance of the Turkey Point nuclear plant). In summary, we see at FPL a very discontinuous process of implementation and adaptation that flowed in part from the lack of adaptability of a centralized management system.

In HP's case, the decentralized structure ensured a much more continuous process of adaptation as managers and lower level employees tried out various practices, used what seemed to work, adapted them as necessary, and discarded the rest. Those driving the HP corporate quality initiative instinctively modified and simplified the often complicated and resource-intensive Japanese procedures in order to gain acceptance by division managers and their subordinates. The closest HP came to a discontinuous process was with the changes introduced by the new corporate quality director, Richard LeVitt, after he took office at the end of 1992, but these changes were mild compared to the disruption that took place at FPL. All in all, the decentralized model at HP led to a robust and flexible approach to quality improvement, but one that was not necessarily sharply focused to respond quickly to specific problems.

While the use of one company to model desired behavior on the part of another is often presented as a simple matter of learning and imitation, our analysis suggests that YHP's effectiveness in having an impact on HP was closely related to the help it provided in turning learning into doing. It was most effective when it had practical iterative exchanges with HP personnel about solving real business problems. This mode maximizes transparency. YHP and HP personnel in effect become joint parties in a "community of practice" that was introducing new ideas into HP. In these cases, there was a very effective bridging of the gap between learning and practice. However, in many other areas, the YHP impact was more diffuse and only partially successful in bridging the learning-practice gap. Here its impact was felt more at the corporate level, with the inevitable dilution of impact at the divisions that comes from having a highly decentralized company.

Imitation of the desired model was often not successful and not even desirable as HP personnel modified YHP ideas to fit their perceived organizational culture. Thus, it can be said that *hoshin* management became institutionalized at HP in a way that furthered alignment around common breakthrough objectives and the development of common planning practices throughout the corporation. This was quite consistent with the spirit of *hoshin* management as implemented by Japanese companies like YHP. Nevertheless, we have seen that the specific mechanisms by which it came to operate at HP deviated sharply from many Japanese practices. Some purists will insist the half-empty glass means that even highly capable American companies like HP have failed to derive the full benefits of *hoshin* management. Yet, the case can be made that this half-empty glass is actually full, that HP did exactly what was required to have its employees successfully embrace and draw major benefits from *hoshin* management in a rapidly changing business and technological environment. No doubt, the truth lies somewhere between these polar positions.

Notes

1. At this time, the Japanese were particularly effective in capitalizing on their superior reliability performance across a broad range of industries. Other competitive dimensions of quality that came into play at varying times and places were performance, features, conformance, durability, serviceability, and aesthetics (cf. Garvin, 1988). The 1980s were a period in which an aura of Japanese superiority led to a high perceived quality of their products.

2. See Cole 1999.

3. Yokogawa Hewlett-Packard became Hewlett-Packard Japan in 1996. Since it was called Yokogawa Hewlett-Packard during the time covered by this analysis, we use that name in this chapter.

4. I am particularly indebted to the following individuals who gave generously of their time and provided many relevant corporate documents to make this analysis possible: Craig Walter, former corporate quality director at Hewlett-Packard; Richard LeVitt, current corporate quality director; Kenzo Sasaoka, former CEO, Yokogawa Hewlett-Packard; Katsu Yoshimoto, country quality manager for YHP in the 1980s; T. Michael Ward, TQM manager HP Quality; Bill Mohr, quality consultant, Finance and Remarketing Division, Hewlett-Packard and Prof. Noriaki Kano, quality counselor for HP from 1985 to 1992. All subsegment quotations from HP and YHP personnel, unless otherwise noted, are from interviews conducted in 1996 and 1997.

5. In fact, once the joint venture was formed, YHP's subsequent efforts to recruit management employees faced the same problems as experienced by other American subsidiaries and joint ventures; that is, they were forced to recruit at "B" rather than "A" schools.

6. While Hamel (1991, pp. 83–103) discusses the importance of transparency in interpartner learning within international strategic alliances, he doesn't explicitly link it to trustworthy information.

7. Text from notes provided by Kenzo Sasaoka, July 1996.

8. Presentation at 1997 NSF Design and Manufacturing Grantees Conference Seattle, January 8, 1997.

9. These conclusions are drawn in part from conversations with Bob King, executive director, GOAL/QPC, October 6, 1996.

10. YHP as a company is actually composed of a manufacturing division, and a sales division and the financial results of the company are a combination of both. The influence of YHP's financial performance on HP has been based primarily on the results of its manufacturing division.

11. After responding to the challenges of the 1980s with a move toward greater centralization, HP modified some of those changes and moved back toward a more decentralized model in the early 1990s (Packard, 1995). Thus, the corporate quality department was once again in a position of trying to sell its ideas to the divisions, rather than operating from the position of strength it had in the late 1980s.

12. Professor Kano worked as one of the Japanese counselors at FPL at roughly the same time as he served in that capacity at HP. Befitting their different management structures, he was able to work with the most senior management at FPL, while at HP he worked primarily at the division level.

References

Beckman, Sara. 1996. "Evolution of Management Roles in a Networked Organization." In Paul Osterman, ed., *Broken Ladders: Managerial Careers in the New Economy*. New York: Oxford University Press.

Bemowski, Karen. 1996. "Something Old, Something New." *Quality Progress* 29 (Oct.): 27–34.

Broadhead, James. 1996. *The Evolution of Quality at FPL*, pp. 11–17. International Conference on Quality, Oct. 15–18. Yokohama: Japanese Union of Scientists and Engineers.

Camp, Robert. 1989 *Benchmarking*. Milwaukee: ASQC Quality Press.

Cole, Robert E. 1999. *Managing Quality Fads: How American Business Learned to Play the Quality Game*. New York: Oxford University Press.

Garvin, David. 1988. *Managing Quality*. New York: Free Press.

Hamel, Gary. 1991. "Competition for Competence and Inter-partner Learning within International Strategic Alliances." *Strategic Management Journal* 12: 83–103.

Kanter, Rosabeth Moss. 1983. *The Changemasters*. New York: Simon and Shuster.

Keller, Maryann. 1989. *Rude Awakening*. New York: Harper Perennial.

King, Bob. 1989. *Hoshin Planning: The Developmental Approach*. Metheun, Mass.: GOAL/QPC.

Main, Jeremy. 1994. *Quality Wars*. New York: Free Press.

Mohr, William, and Harriet Mohr. 1983. *Quality Circles*. Reading, Mass.: Addison-Wesley.

Moore, Geoffrey. 1995. *Inside the Tornado*. New York: Harper Business.

Mozer, Clark. 1984. "Total Quality Control: A route to the Deming Prize." *Quality Progress* 17 (Sept.): 30–33.

Nelson, Richard, and Sidney Winter. 1982. *An Evolutionary Theory of Economic Change*. Cambridge: Belknap Press.

Packard, David. 1995. *The HP Way*. New York: Harper Business.

Sasaoka, Kenzo. 1996. "Sangyōkai kara mita hinshitsu kanri shikō" (Personal thoughts about how industry sees quality control). Paper presented at the meeting of the Japanese Society for Quality Control. Tokyo: Nihon Hinshitsu Kanri Gakkai.

Shiba, Shoji, Alan Graham, and David Walden. 1993. *A New American TQM*. Portland: Productivity Press.

Stacey, Ralph. 1996. *Complexity and Creativity in Organizations*. San Francisco: Berrett-Koehler.

Stinchcombe, Arthur. 1990. *Information and Organizations*. Berkeley: University of California Press.

Watson, Greg. 1991. "Understanding Hoshin Kanri." In Yoji Akao, ed., *Hoshin Kanri: Policy Deployment for Successful TQM*. Portland: Productivity Press.

Young, John. 1983. "One Company's Quest for Improved Quality." *Wall Street Journal*, July 25, 10.

7

Site-Specific Organization Learning in International Technology Transfer

Example from Toshiba

W. Mark Fruin

Japanese management systems (JMS) are diffusing rapidly around the world; witness the success of the Toyota Production System (TPS) and the worldwide renown of "lean production." JMS, we argue, are systems that incorporate more than just leanness or operational efficiency as seen in a number of techniques and tools, such as flexible automation, zero defects, and small batch manufacturing. (See Porter, 1996, for another view.) These additional factors are related to larger issues of organizational design and strategy and to their close links, embeddedness, really, in management systems.

A considerable amount of research has indicated that JMS factories in Japan are organized, staffed, and managed rather differently from prototypical North American and Western European factories (Abegglen, 1958; Cole, 1971, 1979; Dore, 1973; Fruin, 1992, 1997; Lincoln and Kalleberg, 1990; Whittaker, 1990; Womack et al, 1991) and that such differences add up to something more than a checklist of manufacturing tools and techniques, like those mentioned.[1]

Site-specific organizational learning (SSOL) is part of that something more. SSOL is the integration, motivation, and evolution of sensible, effective management and manufacturing practices at local factory sites. SSOL embodies active learning, in sharp contrast with notions of technology transfer where receiving sites merely copy or replicate technology. In short, critical features of JMS are *local* or *site-specific* in origin and evolution, and this is true whether the site is at home or abroad.

Learning and Technology Transfer

Technology transfer always requires some degree of active learning, but key questions are how much and in what ways. To the extent that change and transformation dominate the transfer process, that process is much more than error-free transmission and copying from one site to another. Instead of one-to-one transfer, SSOL underscores the likelihood of adaptation, mutation, and innovation during the copying process. Moreover, local selection and retention processes help to create an evolving set of receiver-specific practices that are notably different from site to site.

Differences between what is sent and what is locally realized are basic to Japanese management systems. They spring from the critical importance of factories in manufacturing strategies and from a concomitant concentration of all manner of resources at the factory level of organization. Once localized and situated, *kaizen, hoshin kanri*, and other learning practices, like total quality management (TQM) and total productivity (TP) campaigning, refine local learning (Fruin and Nakamura, 1997; Fruin, 1998). Compared with other production systems, Japan's firms rely heavily on adapting and accumulating know-how and capabilities at the factory level of organization.[2]

To the extent that SSOL is important at home, overseas factories are also likely to be SSOL-dependent. And whether at home or abroad, SSOL is something creative and idiosyncratic to particular sites. From simple practices and routines, more complex practices and routines build up and evolve through trial-and-error learning. Change is cumulative, incremental, and differentiated in that the more change happens, the greater the impact of SSOL.

For self-sustaining SSOL to evolve, however, overseas sites have to break free of parent company control. This means that they must possess enough autonomy and ability to act on their own, they must embrace the practice and not just the form of a parent factory's JMS, and on-site learning must be incorporated into local management and policy making. In short, JMS must be anchored by host factory adjustments to environmental conditions.[3] Although parent factory practices may serve as models of good manufacturing practice during early stages of technology transfer, SSOL assumes evolution to a stage when parent-offspring teaching relationships are supplanted.

Local experience in this model is akin to the role of environmental landscapes in models of complex adaptive systems.[4] As factories respond, adapt, and adjust to the rigors of the environment, they develop certain levels of environmental fitness and conditional sustainability. Random mutations, copying errors, adaptations, and successful imitations of home factory practices generate a wide range of routines and procedures that are further selected and refined according to local notions of fitness and suitability. Local experience is all-important in setting rules, measuring performance, modifying expectations, and assigning credit. Most important, idiosyncratic learning becomes shared learning through such practices as TQM, just-in-time delivery schedules (JIT), and TP campaigning at transfer sites (Fruin, 1997). In time SSOL defines the form and content of technology transfer and, thus, what is desirable and sustainable in internationalizing JMS.

Subsystem Complementarity and Local Learning

Two different sets of suborganizational processes are especially important for advancing SSOL. First, in some important ways JMS features and practices are complementary; they reinforce and resonate with each other. (See Chapter 2 on bundled subsystems and complementarity, and chapter 5 on supplier relations, both in this volume, for further expositions of this theme.) Hiring, training, and promotion practices, for example, have to dovetail with technical skill requirements, standard operating procedures, and locally salient routines. The more complex such requirements are, the more critical the fit between human resource practices and technical and organizational subsystems. Given the importance of fit, subsystem complementarity will likely emerge on-site, because it is difficult to specify in advance how system components will fit and evolve together.

Second, organizational learning is always rooted in local experience and knowledge creation. Although sources of learning may be vicarious and originate off-site, effective learning requires local implementation and assessment. On-site problem solving, in particular, is a key source of experiential learning, driven by a recurring demand for home-brewed interpretations and implementations of Japan-inspired production systems. What works well in Japan will not necessarily work well overseas. First, engineers and managers are not likely to understand completely why things are the way they are, at home and overseas. Second, extracting a subset of routines and practices from a full set necessarily changes the nature of what is extracted and what is left behind. Let me offer a garden variety example. Suppose you have evergreen shrubs in the midst of some annuals, like gladioli. Their requirements for watering, fertilizing, and sunlight differ. You decide to move the evergreens elsewhere. Not only are the evergreens affected by the transfer, but so are the gladioli. By analogy, technology transfer is always partial (entire gardens can't be moved intact), and it always requires a rebuilding of routines and practices at new sites.

SSOL is required at JMS sites in order to reach a certain level of fitness-based adaptation to environmental demands. Fitness-based means that organizations develop fitness based on the challenges they face. Both so-called single-and double-loop learning are part of fitness: single-loop when organizational learning remains localized in organizational subunits, as in particular factory teams and sections, and as a result they get better at doing particular tasks; double-loop when learning is generalized, repeated, and reused across a number of factory units, with the result that general task performance is enhanced (Fiol and Lyles, 1985; Levitt and March, 1988; Miner and Haunschild, 1995). In double-loop learning, in other words, routines that are useful in one unit or level are generalized across higher levels of aggregation, such as an entire factory. In both single-and double-loop learning, accumulating, diffusing, and refining on-site learning triggers a cascade of knowledge building that is site-and context-specific.

Given the pivotal role of the local environmental in developing fitness, a key issue with respect to internationalizing JMS is the degree to which manufacturing practices are both transferable and site-specific. Can something site-specific be transferred? Perhaps not. But the transformation of JMS features in new contexts can be anticipated and planned for; managers and workers can be encouraged to modify imported practice; local adaptation and learning can be stimulated. SSOL can be advanced, even accelerated, depending on management policies at the sending and receiving ends of technology transfer.

The Toshiba Corporation's efforts to develop and sustain JMS at home and abroad will be the means for testing the importance of SSOL in international technology transfer. Toshiba's Yanagicho Works in Kawasaki City is the JMS sending site; three overseas plants, one in France and two in the United States, are the receiving sites. Yanagicho is Toshiba's principal plant for the design, development, manufacture, and assembly of plain paper copiers (PPCs) and peripherals, like toner, along with other products like ATMs, optical disk drives, and laser printers (Fruin, 1997).

Generic JMS

At Toshiba's more advanced manufacturing sites, like Yanagicho, a number of preconditions underlie JMS. The first is a carefully selected, well motivated, and educated workforce that is rewarded on the basis of teamwork, productivity, and multiskilled capabilities. Second is a multitiered hierarchy of managers, from shop floor to factory head who provide on-site technical coordination in factories and at key affiliates and suppliers. Typically managers have had considerable shop floor experience.

A third is factory-based, multifunctional capabilities, including, at a minimum, design, development, product/process engineering and, of course, production. A fourth is a multifocal strategy that simultaneously targets low cost, high quality, high operations reliability, short time-to-market, volume and variety in manufacturing operations.[5] Fifth is a managerial system that effectively coordinates manufacturing processes and integrates factories with larger organizational (divisional and corporate) structures (Fruin, 1992). Finally, a sixth is a range of energetic small group activities that serve to refine, integrate, and diffuse knowledge and know-how. The comprehensiveness, thoroughness, and systematic character of small-group activities transform fairly low-level activities into strategic knowledge-management practices (Fruin, 1996, 1998).

Note well that JMS features, practices, and capabilities, like these, should not be construed as a checklist. Unless they make good sense locally and are fully incorporated into management in a coherent fashion, a sustainable, advanced manufacturing system will not emerge. Thus, a key feature of JMS is the effective linking of shop floor tools and routines with manufacturing organization and corporate strategy making. Production systems with these six characteristics are found most often in the larger factories of Japan's larger equipment and machinery manufacturing firms (Fruin, 1997). Elsewhere I have argued that such factories are found in circumstances of high product, process, and manufacturing systems complexity (Fruin, 1992, 1997).

Accordingly, there may be size, industry, and performance conditions with respect to the emergence, expression, and form of specific types of JMS. Toshiba, for example, claims to make and assemble 11,500 different kinds of final products in twenty-seven factories in Japan; that averages to 450 models and products per factory! Obviously, given the tremendous product variety, the conditions, including learning, that make for low-cost, low-time-to-market, high-quality products are situated in particular factory sites (Tyre and von Hippel, 1997). Just as obviously, such factories are not likely candidates for duplication overseas. What makes for SSOL at home in a particular industry or factory may not be sent abroad.

Universalism and Particularistism in JMS

There is little agreement in Japan concerning which JMS aspects and features are universal or particularistic. While some of these aspects may be found in any large and well-endowed factory, fieldwork in more than a dozen Toshiba factories and scores of discussions with Toshiba managers suggests that JMS features are not readily transferable from one factory to another. Nontransferability or the lack of direct imitability may arise from the way in which such features are expressed at specific sites.

That is, local learning and knowledge generation are based on a factory's efforts to create, design, and manufacture goods and to improve local design, development, and production processes. Site-specificity is path dependent; that is, management systems evolve as a result of local experience, experimentation, and effort. While issues of manufacturing systems integration and organizational learning are more or less universal, the particular ways in which practices and routines appear are not. Complex products like PPCs, with about 1,000 parts, components, manufacturing, and assembly steps, embody hundreds of thousands of choices with respect to which parts and components to use, whether they should be bought or locally made, who should do design, development and subassembly work, at what prices goods should be sold, and so on.

At the shop floor and factory levels of analysis, therefore, JMS features are particularistic. At the same time, however, JMS-like features are found in many, if not most, of Toshiba's larger factories, as well as in the factories of many other large firms. Thus, they are more or less universal in certain firms, industries, and circumstances. The same methods of, say, total quality management (TQM) might be found in any factory, but the way in which they are expressed in making particular products differs from one factory to the next. Accordingly, a distinction should be made between the degree to which such features are generally found (the degree of diffusion, universalism, or phenotypic detail) and the ways in which they are expressed and take on particular meaning (the mode of genesis, evolution, and sense-making).[6]

Perhaps this distinction can be captured in the difference between language syntax and use. Most of us know English syntax and grammar, but we use the rules and speak and write with varying degrees of skill and panache. In other words, what we do with largely similar language resources is singular and individualistic. This example assumes complete or nearly complete knowledge of language structure and usage. How much more (or less) variation would occur if language knowledge were partial and imperfect (Hutchins and Hazlehurst, 1995)? Since learning a language proceeds by using a language with imperfect knowledge, context is critical to what is expressed and how it is expressed.

The more localized JMS features and practices, the less likely that they will travel well, because, like language, the more localized a dialect, the greater the difficulty in communicating with outsiders. Language use is not standardized, vocabularly is idiosyncratic, and sources of authority are unclear. By studying three cases of the international transfer of PPC and toner technology, suggestions as to the limits and costs of transferring JMS and its underlying dialects or SSOL processes may be found. We believe that transferring JMS is possible but that transfer is highly contingent on context and that errors in copying, adaptation, and selection processes result in JMS-recipient sites that look different and behave quite differently from JMS-donor sites.

Toshiba's Plants in Mitchell, South Dakota, and Irvine, California

The Yanagicho Works is Toshiba's source of know-how and knowledge for photocopier (PPC) design and manufacture—a product in which Yanagicho has specialized since 1966. The crucial role of parent factories, like Yanagicho, in the overseas transfer of technical and organizational knowledge, like PPC technology, has been supported empirically in several studies (Brannen, 1992; Brannen, Liker & Fruin, chapter 4 in this book; Fruin, 1992, 1997; Kenney & Florida, 1992).

Under the authority of the Office Equipment Division of Toshiba's Information and Telecommunications Product Group, Yanagicho first went abroad with PPC technology with the opening of Toshiba Systems France near Dieppe, in Normandy, France, in 1986, and in the same year with the acquisition of a 3M toner plant in Mitchell, South Dakota. At about the same time, Yanagicho was instrumental in implementing three technology transfer agreements for PPC manufacture in India, South Korea, and China. Finally, early in 1989, a new line for PPC assembly opened in Irvine, California, where Toshiba was already making and assembling laptop computers, fax machines, X-ray equipment, PBXs, and telephones.

Yanagicho has only one small domestic branch factory that supplies parts and components in northeastern Japan but has six overseas branches or alliances for PPC and toner manufacture: two in the United States, one in France, one in China (the most recent), and technology licensing agreements in South Korea and India. Although it might seem that Yanagicho and Toshiba are already fairly international in these respects, in 1992, for example, Toshiba's export ratio, that is, how much of its domestic production was sold overseas, was 25 percent. Hitachi and Mitsubishi Electric's export ratios were lower, 16 percent for Hitachi and 18 percent for Mitsubishi Electric, suggesting how far Toshiba still has to go in locating its manufacturing facilities overseas.[7]

Mitchell, South Dakota

Toshiba America's Toner Product Division's (TPD) plant in Mitchell, South Dakota, was established in 1961 as a baby formula manufacturing factory run by Ross Laboratories. In May 1973, 3M purchased the plant from Ross and converted it to a toner manufacturing plant. Toner is the powdered, fine, black material that makes the actual photocopied image on either plain or speciality (thermal) paper. Toshiba bought the plant from 3M in October 1986 as part of a production localization strategy in North America. Toshiba had already been working with 3M for a number of years as a supplier of mid-size plain paper copiers on an OEM (original equipment maker) basis.[8]

There were about forty employees when Toshiba took over the facility in 1986; as of 1996, there were 160. The fourfold expansion of employees was matched by a doubling of plant size, from 81,000 to 185,000 square feet, on a twenty-five-acre site. Toshiba's cumulative investment in the Mitchell, South Dakota, facility is $30.55 million. The plant is nonunion, with three fixed shifts; it operates twenty-four hours a day and supplies not only the North American market but also Europe, Australia, and Japan.

The toner manufacturing process used at Mitchell was developed at the Yanagicho Works in Japan, Toshiba's mother factory for all photocopiers and supplies. Mitchell's toner is supplied to Toshiba's overseas sales subsidiaries and to other PPC makers on an OEM contract basis. Because the use of photocopier consummables, like toner and paper, is fairly predictable, Mitchell's production and Toshiba's sales of toner have been relatively stable, expanding 3–5 percent per annum. However, there is a certain amount of product choice when consummables are replenished, so high quality and low cost are the points of competition in the industry.

In the three years between 1990 and 1993, the Mitchell plant reduced material costs for manufacturing toner by 25 percent and energy costs by 50 percent. By the mid-1990s, Toshiba's Mitchell plant was well on its way to being an exemplary JMS site. But it took a good ten years from the time of initial purchase in 1986 for this to happen. What transpired during that ten-year period?

1986–1990

Initially, Toshiba merely bottled toner at Mitchell because there were time and technology transfer lags between purchase of the 3M facility and the transfer of production technology from Japan. Toshiba discontinued 3M's manufacturing process, intent on establishing and developing its own toner manufacturing process at Mitchell. But doing so was not so straightforward.

Although the sourcing of toner chemicals and developer (toner and carrier) was 100 percent localized, the manufacturing process was imported. Not surprisingly, quality assurance problems appeared within the first six months of Toshiba's buyout. Yanagicho's manufacturing process was not fine-tuned to the nature and quality of the available manufacturing materials. Temperature and humidity differences between South Dakota and Tokyo, for example, frustrated a simple transfer of Toshiba's domestic manufacturing process to Mitchell.

Moreover, Toshiba sought to increase production at Mitchell not only to supply 3M but also to supply Toshiba's PPC production sites inside and outside Japan. As a result, production jumped fourfold in the first year, but product quality did not hold up under the stress of increased manufacturing volumes. Beginning in 1987, therefore, Mitchell undertook a crash course in production quality assurance, total productive maintenance, and quality distribution practices, with the result that acceptable quality levels were realized within six months in spite of increased manufacturing output.

Mr. Tomonobu Shibamiya, the first general manager at Mitchell, was well equipped for the task of negotiating Mitchell's progress through the maze of problems associated with startup and full-scale production. He had been manager of the Manufacturing Engineering Department at Yanagicho before being sent to Mitchell, so he was easily able to tap into a wellspring of PPC manufacturing and engineering experience that had been accumulating at Yanagicho since 1966. Under his leadership, full and steady production with high quality and low cost were the first major problems to be solved at Mitchell. But in 1988, Shibamiya left for Toshiba's PPC production site in Irvine, California, of which more later.

1990–1991

Following Shibamiya's departure, there was a period of several months when the post of general manager, generally held by a Japanese expatriate manager, went unfilled at Mitchell. Then, in 1989, Mr. Ishizawa was sent to Mitchell from Yanagicho with a mandate to oversee an ambitious plan of expanding production, applied research, and logistical support functions. In May 1988 the original 3M production line was extended and a second added. In September 1990 lines 3 and 4 were established, along with a toner research unit and an expanded warehouse operation. At the same time, the production management system was overhauled with Yanagicho's assistance, and, in July 1991, a fifth and final line was added. By the end of summer 1991, the recently remodeled and expanded factory was running five lines, three shifts per day, seven days a week.

Unfortunately, Ishizawa's tenure at Mitchell was only a year and a quarter long, and, following his departure, there was another six-month hiatus before the new general manager, Mr. Mitsuo Komai, arrived. The breaks in leadership and the relatively short tenures of Shibamiya and Ishizawa meant that Mitchell was not able to cosolidate and assimilate the gains that were realized under the first two expatriate general managers. A vacuum at the top hindered Mitchell's efforts to realize JMS practices.

The choice of Komai to run the Mitchell facility was well considered. During the 1991 fiscal year, quality control, total productivity, and total productive maintenance programs had been introduced under Ishizawa. Given their newness and unfamiliarity at Mitchell, however, it was not clear how quickly or well they would take. But Komai was a quality assurance specialist, having been the head of the quality assurance department at Yanagicho and in charge of Yanagicho's overseas operations before being dispatched to South Dakota. He was the general manager under whom Mitchell would blossom.

1992–1996

Komai created and built the organizational substrates that supported the emergence of Mitchell as a world-class toner production site. During his tenure, profits trebled, while fixed and material costs were halved. These achievements were related to the considerable investment in plant and equipment that had accumulated during the four years prior to Komai's arrival. But investment in tools, techniques, and transfer lines might have come to little without the ambition and know-how of Mitchell's employees, who sought to use them well. That, Komai gave them.

Mitsuo Komai initiated or updated Mitchell's activities in the areas of cost reduction, preventive maintenance, quality assurance, QC circles, ISO accreditation, design for manufacture, production control and planning, and manufacturing information systems. In addition to these more or less well-known methods, Komai also introduced Total Productivity (TP) management, *hoshin kanri* (sequenced, organization-wide Total Quality Management methods), and visual performance management methods. As these were less well-known techniques, at least within the context of Toshiba's Mitchell facility, they may be termed soft or human-dependent technologies (see chapter 4 in this volume, by Brannen, Liker, and Fruin).

In the case of either hard or soft technologies, the give-and-take that occurs in the midst of implementing, experimenting, and adapting should be underscored and emphasized. Giving-and-taking both creates and uses a context for learning. Interactions, in other words, create conditions for learning, and they promote a goodness of fit among and between relationships and routines.

For example, in the area of visual performance reporting, there were fifty-three different kinds of visual reports extant in the Mitchell facility in October 1993, shortly after Komai's arrival. Komai felt that the number was too large to be effective. With the cooperation of employees, Komai was able to halve the number of factory management visualization items without reducing the overall effectiveness of the visual management program. Likewise, the number of totes (units) for holding work-in-process (WIP) inventories was reduced from 400 to 250. And, beginning with the 1991 introduction of QCC activities, by 1993 Mitchell's top performing QCC team was sent to Japan, where it walked away with a President's Award for Excellence in the All-Toshiba QCC Conference.

Under the watchful eye of Komai, by 1994–1995, each manager and each functional area had developed an elaborate statement of goals and objectives. Such goals and objectives were not imposed from above but, instead, emerged in the course of dialogues and negotiations among Komai, top and middle-level managers, and ordinary line-and-staff employees. While Komai had an idea of where he wanted the Mitchell plant to be, he did not really have a roadmap of how to get there. The roadmap emerged and evolved through discussion, negotiation, and dialogue. One measure of how far the work progressed is the ISO 9002 certificate Toshiba America's Toner Products Division (Mitchell) was awarded in February 1994.

As Komai describes these many victories, he characterizes the emergent process by which they were realized as one of "I decide but you recommend" (interview, Mitsuo Komai, Yanagicho Works, Kawasaki City, Japan, July 16, 1996.) This is consistent with *hoshin kanri* practices in Japan. According to Komai, a manager makes lots of decisions, but the ones that are made are not necessarily the ones that can be implemented and realized. Especially in a cross-cultural, transnational setting, it is difficult to know what can be done because that depends on local knowledge, practices, and routines. So, in Komai's view, workers recommend what they believe will work, and managers choose from among the recommendations.

Komai stressed that his main job at Mitchell was teaching local employees how to see and solve problems. He was famous for preaching and promulgating the story of the elephant and six blind men. In this story, six blind men are feeling different parts of an elephant and are asked to describe it. One, feeling the tail, thinks that it's a horse; another, feeling a leg, thinks it's a tree; another, touching the tusk, thinks it's a cylindrical rock, and so on. In other words, seeing what there is is critical to knowing what to do, but seeing depends on local knowledge. The real problem, therefore, is not really seeing the problem. Once we know what we're seeing, knowing what to do seems obvious.

Komai could not identify problems on his own, in other words, because finding problems depends on a kind of local knowledge that he did not possess. This is a generic problem for most managers, who are necessarily removed from day-to-day operations, but it is a special problem for overseas managers, who are removed culturally and organizationally from day-to-day operations.

Komai was not a Mitchell shop floor worker; he did not spend his days handling totes, mixing chemicals, and managing inventories. Local knowledge means embedded norms and practices. If locals could be encouraged to find and identify shop floor problems and make recommendations about what might be changed and how, Komai could decide which of the recommendations made sense in light of his extensive knowledge of management, quality assurance practices, and production operations. Komai's knowledge was grounded in Yanagicho's SSOL; Mitchell's was evolving and based in the historic and ongoing interactions, relations, negotiations, and improvisations that were taking place in South Dakota.

It would be difficult to describe the first ten years of Toshiba's operations at Mitchell according to standard models of management and organization. The structures and processes of work at Mitchell neither replicated what made sense in Japan nor were based on clearly defined notions of which practices and skills were needed in what amounts and where. But, as the course and content of the dialogue between managers and workers advanced, meanings emerged, scripts became clearer, and actions were more focused. That is, meanings were emergent and contingent on the understandings and interpretations that appeared and were shared and shaped by local actors. A jazzy-like, improvisational point and counterpoint among shop floor, supervisory, and managerial employees best characterizes the organizational evolution of Toshiba's Mitchell factory.

Irvine, California

Toshiba Systems America, a large and diversified staging, assembly, production, and distribution facility located amid the rapidly disappearing orange groves of Southern California, is located in Irvine. Irvine ships half a dozen different products, on the assembly and manufacturing side of its operations, including telephones, PBXs (private branch exchanges), faxes, laptop computers, computer boards, X-ray equipment, and PPC, as of 1989.

The original investment in plant and equipment for the PPC line in Irvine was $1.29 million ($1 = 100 yen), and most of this money went for the purchase of specialized equipment, such as conveyors, testing equipment, and simulation software (interview with Mr. Osada at Yanagicho, April 1988). Tomonobu Shibamiya, the manager responsible for photocopier production at Irvine (who had moved there from Mitchell, South Dakota), said:

> Originally, we had a three-year plan to produce two PPC models here. But we added two additional models on an OEM [supplying original equipment made by Toshiba to another firm] contract basis, and this threw off our original schedule. By adding models, the volumes predicted for the initial models dropped, and not surprisingly prices went up. Also, assembly cycle times shot up because workers had to learn

twice as many different assembly and testing routines. All our calculations about quality, time-to-market, and cost were thrown out the window.

At Irvine, PPC molds and dies still come from Japan, and this is likely to continue as long as overseas production runs are not long enough to make it economical to source molds and dies locally. In Japan, molds and dies for a particular PPC model might be used for twelve to eighteen months with a typical PPC model selling around 4,000 to 5,000 units per month. Irvine was running at 1,000 units a month for all models combined in the early 1990s.

Molds and dies come from Japan for a very simple reason: there are no PPC design engineers in Irvine. Their absence is not an act of prejudice but one of strategy. There are not nearly enough young, talented design engineers in Japan, and, of these, relatively few want to go overseas. In fact, few of them do. So, it makes good sense to concentrate engineering talent in Japan, where they can be more effectively trained, mobilized, and employed. But, as a result, it is nearly impossible to achieve cost reductions overseas through better engineering, better design, and better manufacturing practice, because there is not a critical mass of engineers to carry out those functions. Indeed, it is difficult enough to stabilize production and to achieve consistency and reliability in manufacturing operations.

Irvine had only fifteen PPC assemblers in 1990, a year after opening the line. (A short PPC line at Yanagicho in Japan would have about forty assemblers.) The small number reflects difficulties in recruiting local workers, as well as in assigning them at Irvine; there is a shortage of qualified workers on most of Irvine's lines. (The parent factory is also a multiproduct plant, but one where all the products share some historical and technical commonality.) At Irvine, PPC assembly competes with the assembly of digital phone exchanges, telephones, facsimiles, and laptop computers for the available labor supply.

It is unlikely that fifteen local employees will learn well four different assembly routines, according to expatriate Japanese managers. In fact, this is asking more of Irvine employees than of workers back home. Given the complexity of the multiple tasks involved in producing all four models with just fifteen assemblers, Irvine is operating at 60–70 percent over the standard operating times in Japan, and struggling.

Without enough volume and reliability in assembly operations, workers are not able to make independent, experience-based judgments about problems that arise during work. For example, they are not able to judge when a problem stems from the quality of a locally supplied part, the assembly process, or the manufacturability of the product itself. In effect, production volumes are too low to generate the learning that would allow assemblers to identify and diagnose problems easily. Such problem-solving skills are a major feature of JMS in Japan, and such skills are exactly the sort of thing that cannot be exported from Japan. They need to be developed locally.

Given these problems, the Yanagicho Works in Japan designed a PPC for ease of manufacturability at Irvine. The height of the line was raised because

Americans are on average taller than Japanese. Because Irvine's PPC was designed with fewer parts, it was easier to assemble; because it has fewer parts, it was less functional; that is, it did not do everything that a new PPC in Japan might do, such as enlarging and compressing images or printing on both sides of the page. Such adjustments in height of the transfer line, parts count, and functionality reduce flexibility, raise the cost of going overseas, and weaken the competitive position of Toshiba's PPCs in the international marketplace.

Since PPC manufacture is characterized by mid-size lots of extremely high quality—1,000 units per month of a certain size and performance, for example—it is extremely difficult to recruit local vendors who can supply such high-quality parts and components in relatively limited numbers. The investment needed to meet quality, performance, and cost requirements is considerable, and there is not enough experience binding suppliers and assemblers together to overcome the understandable reluctance of vendors to make such commitments. In Japan, supplier-asembler relations emerged in a context where credible commitments were sensible and mutually agreeable.[9] At Irvine, things were not so sensible and agreeable.

Performance measures at Irvine and Yanagicho were so different that the overseas yardstick was the number of hours required to assemble one unit (hours/unit), whereas in Japan, it was the number of minutes (minutes/unit). Part of the difference in assembly times springs from the six different nationalities represented among the fifteen different PPC assemblers at Irvine. (They did not have a common language of communication, training, work, or social experience.) Turnover on the PPC line had been running at 3 percent a month in the early 1990s; workers were young, twenty-seven or twenty-eight years of age on average, culturally and nationally heterogeneous, with lots of alternative work opportunities. The average age of assemblers at Yanagicho, by contrast, is forty-two or forty-three. Besides being culturally homogeneous (in the national sense), they are correspondingly more experienced, more settled in their lives, and more eager to be successful in their work.

Toshiba's PPC line at its Irvine plant was closed down in 1993, after five years of painstaking effort to transfer and implant PPC assembly and manufacture. The problems of making PPC, even in limited numbers, were overwhelming. The most important problems were macro-and micro-organizational. At the macro-organizational level, the differences between Yanagicho, a multifunction, multiproduct, well-integrated, virtuoso plant at home, and Irvine, an overseas plant that was not well integrated and that assembled many different products but with only limited functional capabilities, were stark. At the micro-organizational level, a site-specific, robust culture of discovery, initiative, and ambition at home contrasted sharply with Irvine's culture of organizational uncertainty, low operations integration, high employee turnover and *ukemi* (passivity).

Toshiba's Irvine plant included four different factory-based systems in one facility: the Fuchu, Ome, Hino, and Yanagicho Works had all transferred personnel, products, and processes from Japan. The four systems never co-alesced. They ran side by side with little or no cross-product learning and little leveraging of managerial experience or small-group activities from one business unit (BU) to another. Agreed-upon engineering practices and standard operating procedures (SOPs) to integrate routines across many product lines were missing. A single management, set of routines, and unifying culture did not imbue and integrate the facility. What characterized JMS at each of the donor sites in Japan was not present at Irvine in the early 1990s.

Evidence from Toshiba Systems France

Toshiba Systems France (TSF) began in 1986 as a 49–51 percent minority-shareholding joint venture with Regma, a subsidiary of Rhone Poulanc, to assemble PPC at Arques La Bataille. Within three years, or by 1989, the ownership position was reversed, giving Toshiba 80 percent and Rhone Poulanc 20 percent of the shares, respectively. At this time the Arques La Bataille factory had 270 employees, of whom seven came from Japan. The expatriate positions were vice president, chief of technology, technical department head, production manager, product coordinator, accounting head, and purchasing head. Early in 1990, the joint venture moved from Arques La Bataille, a medieval town inland of the Normandy coast, to Dieppe, a large industrial suburb some thirty kilometers from La Havre.[10]

There were three different work areas at the first French site: a parts delivery and kit marshaling warehouse in a detached, dilapidated brick building; a subassembly operation; and a final assembly and inspection line. Within three years and three months of the start of operations, seven different models of PPC were being assembled in France, although some of the models were acquired almost fully assembled from OEM suppliers. The total volume for all seven models was 5,000 units per month.

The parts storage area for PPC assembly was divided into two areas: one for parts from Japan and one for parts sourced within the EU. According to French and European Union (EU) rules of origin with respect to parts in inventory, a 5–10 percent random check of stored parts could occur at any time. Because of quality problems associated with locally sourced parts, however, Japanese managers stockpiled separately local and Japanese parts, and they had to set height limits for the highly piled, EU-sourced parts of questionable quality.

Problems in the quality of the sheet metal used in fabricating PPC panels and casings were typical of the range of problems encountered. Fabricated metal parts in the electronics industry in Japan use a high-quality sheet metal that is several grades higher than that used in construction and transportation applications, for example. Not only is it difficult to obtain the higher quality sheet metal in France, but also somewhat different metal bending and fabricating techniques are needed in working the material. As a result, EU-sourced parts and components using locally sourced sheet metal have to be carefully sorted and checked for quality before they are sent over for subassembly in the main building.

Since 1989, local efforts to improve the identification of parts and subassembly operations through color coding and better marking of work flow had notably enhanced the orderliness of these workplaces. Some of this effort was consistent with the Total Productivity (TP) activities that Toshiba had adopted companywide since 1985 (Fruin, 1997). But in terms of the direct transfer of explicit TP techniques from Japan, by late 1989 only the 5Ss from TP campaigning had been formally introduced into the French operation. Japanese expatriate managers felt that it would be rushing things to import more.

Informally, some of the biggest improvements in plant layout, flow, and production scheduling came as a result of importing the *me de miru kanri* or "eyeball management" campaign from Japan. The concept of "eyeball" or "visual" management is quite simple. If one can't look at a production layout and process and understand instantly how everything is linked, then the production process needs to be simplified. Much of visual management in France involved taking techniques that were considered implicit or nearly so in Japan and making them much more explicit.

In order to get this point in France, however, a prior understanding had to be reached concerning remuneration and rewards. The active consent of workers was much more easily gained when there was an understanding as to how gains in productivity would be redistributed as rewards. However, the agreement that was reached did not encompass larger issues of equity in the system of remuneration and reward. It covered only how incremental gains from the introduction of new production methods and techniques would be redistributed to workers who had actively joined in the design of new work activities.

The redefinition or recontextualization (see chapter 4 of this volume for a discussion of recontextualization) of the *me de miru kanri* campaign in France highlights the major problem of the Arques La Bataille plant in 1989–1990. The problem was how to adapt or modify Japanese work practices for French workers (actually, "operators" are what line workers are called at this plant and elsewhere in France). According to the French production manager on site, this redefinition was composed of five parts:

1. Gaining the active consent of workers to engage in job design and redesign (traditionally, French workers are not encouraged to do so)
2. Simplifying Japanese production and technology management ideas (trying to make explicit what is implicit)
3. Developing and reinforcing team organization (notions of teamwork and team participation were different)
4. Creating a subleader within teams who is responsible for team spirit, QC, and so on but who is not superior to other members of the team in a hierarchical sense (TSF workers had a hard time with

this concept because the line demarcating "superiors" is sharp in France)
5. Localizing sourcing arrangement and supplier relations so that aspects of visual management having to do with parts handling, inspection, and flow would have more of a French flavor

TSF moved to a new, physically imposing and integrated facility in Dieppe in 1991, took up the production of toner in 1991, and by 1992 had expanded to assembling six different PPC lines, with all of the lines clearing the EEC's 40 percent local sourcing hurdle. TSF did not yet boast the robustness of Yanagicho's multifunctional PPC Department, particularly its upstream design and development capabilities. Nor did TSF incorporate the depth and breadth of Yangicho's multiproduct capabilities.

But, by the mid-1990s, TSF was beginning to approach the cost, quality, delivery, and time-to-market characteristics of PPC and toner produced at its parent factory in Japan. This was no mean feat for a plant with less than ten years of operational history. Perhaps the EU's local content requirements should be partially credited for TSF's successful launch. Yet, TSF's lack of Yanagicho's full functionality meant that there were fewer cross-product and process learning opportunities and that the sources and numbers of organizational and technical adaptations were corresponding fewer.

Internationalizing PPC Production: A Discussion

In all three cases of internationalizing PPC and toner manufacture, there was a lengthy time lag between the initial acquisition of overseas facilities and the time they began to perform well. Several years were needed before technical and organizational features of JMS began to emerge and when plants reached targeted employment and output figures. This lag is related to the internationalization strategies of Japan's industrial firms.

Japanese industrial firms compete largely on the basis of adaptive or x-efficiency, as opposed to allocative efficiency. Allocative or financial efficiencies aim to allocate resources where they will realize the largest possible gains in the least possible time; quite often, this involves buying and selling assets and attracting investments through well capitalized financial markets, like Wall Street.

Adaptive efficiencies, in contrast, aim to gain more from what is already available, and in Japan they are evidenced by the highest rates of industrial productivity growth in the world, a concerted emphasis on factory-based product/process innovation, firm market share expansion and narrow diversification (clustering products within the same two-digit Standard Industrial Classification code), and long-term partnering with affiliates and suppliers (Aoki, 1988; Cole, 1989; Dore, 1987; Fransman, 1995, Fruin, 1992, 1997; Gerlach, 1992; Odagiri, 1992).

In short, whether at home or abroad, Japan's industrial firms aim to succeed primarily by getting more from less. Getting more from less typically revolves around strategies of cost cutting, productivity enhancement, and full-line production of related product lines and families of products to take advantage of economies of scope. These strategies are people-and routine-dependent in that they require employees to learn, refine, and constantly revise organizational practices. In effect, SSOL is the basis of such strategies.

People-and routine-dependent strategies are critical to the evolution of adaptative efficiency. When Japan's industrial firms go abroad, therefore, their intent is to do abroad what they have done at home. Yet, overseas employees and organizations are not at all like their home-grown cousins. They have not been reared in a domestic market where adaptive efficiencies have been and are emphasized above all others.

In this respect, the role of parent factories in guiding, monitoring, grading, and promoting offspring or overseas plants is crucial. Inevitably, a lag of several years separates the finalization of the international investment and the time the overseas facilities begin to perform well. This lag represents the time necessary for experimenting and learning in the plant, to develop generic and firm-specific practices, and to encourage plant-specific approaches.

During this same time, an offspring factory's repetoire of adaptive learning necessarily begins to diverge from a parent factory's. Divergence is necessary for two reason. First, the parent's whole system of routines and practices cannot be transferred and, hence, local adjustments to fill in the "holes" of what is being transferred are required; second, the "landscapes" in which overseas factories are located will encourage different patterns of environmentally conditioned adaptation. Selection forces are necessarily different, given different patterns of competition, organization, and management matched to different environments (Tyre and von Hippel, 1997).

Factory-to-factory transfer, therefore, is a model of both how things should and how they should not be. In the beginning, there is no other model the best that a local factory can do is to model itself on what the parent factory does. Before too long, however, offspring factories necessarily develop their own routines and practices, and these evolve into local models of best practice.

Even the initial periods of international technology transfer do not simply duplicate or replicate what was previously done in Japan. Something that makes sense for a new environment has to emerge. At Mitchell, the volume and quality of toner production and the design and development of new, sensor-based instrumentation products were advances on Yanagicho's state of the art. Yanagicho's toner production was limited to what is needed for engineering sample and prototype production, and Yanagicho did not manufacture the type of sensor-based instrumentation that Mitchell readied for the market.

Similarly, at Toshiba Systems France, combining large-scale production of photocopiers and toner, something that neither Yanagicho nor any other Toshiba factory has yet to do, provides evidence of TSF's novel efforts and successes. A comparison of some of the major differences at these sites is presented in Table 7.1. The biggest differences are seen in product complexity, numbers of products and parent factories, and labor turnover.

Both at home and abroad, Toshiba's operations pivot around SSOL. Site-specific learning is the crux of what is new and original at Yanagicho, Mitchell, and Toshiba Systems France. Successes at Mitchell and Dieppe and failure at Irvine offer evidence in support of this hypothesis. Irvine's five different product lines and four different parent plants made it difficult to focus its efforts on the transfer, application, and adaptation of PPC technology. The failure was critical because adaptive on-site discovery and learning are the heart of SSOL.

SSOL: More Than Co-location

In deciding which products to manufacture overseas, it is easy to forget the factory-based, site-specific characteristics that are responsible for the competitive advantages enjoyed by firms like Toshiba. Designing PPCs, even more than making them, requires complex organizational, technical, and managerial capabilities—precisely the sort of things that are hard to transfer overseas, if only because of a critical shortage of design, development, and systems engineers in overseas operations. Only now, ten years after its founding, is

Table 7.1 A Comparison of Key Factors Affecting Organizational Learning at Yanagicho and Three Overseas Plants[a]

	Yanagicho	Mitchell	Irvine	Dieppe
No. of employees	2,758+	150	150	100
Year established	1936	1986	1988[b]	1986
Greenfield/ brownfield	green	brown	green	brown
No. of shifts	1	3	1	1
No. of products	13	1+	5	2
Product complexity[c]	high	low	mixed	mixed
Employee turnover	low	low	high	low
No. of parent plants	0	1	4	1

a. Data collected at time of field interviews.

b. Year when photocopier production commenced.

c. Photocopier design, development, and manufacture represent high product complexity; photocopier knockdown kit assembly represents mixed complexity; toner manufacture represents low product complexity.

Toshiba's TPD plant beginning to nurture its own applied research and development capabilities.

The costs of hiring, training, and advancing local recruits in Toshiba's overseas manufacturing facilities obviously impede or promote SSOL processes. (At Irvine, a large number of non-American nationals, notably Mexican, Filipino, and Southeast Asian workers, complicated the training and socializing of PPC production employees.) Nevertheless, given a fairly positive public idea of what it is like to work for the Japanese, recruiting overseas has not been that much of a problem. In nearly ten years of operations at TSF and the former 3M toner plant in Mitchell, turnover rates have been quite low, generally 2–3 percent annually. Because TSF initially involved more assembly than manufacturing, the quality of work was quite acceptable, given low turnover, a basic education in quality control methods, and an accumulation of local know-how and adaptive routines.

But real problems may emerge in several years and in a number of ways. First, Toshiba's management and manufacturing systems depend heavily on internal promotion and in-company training, and in this Toshiba is representative of major Japanese firms as a whole. Given higher rates of voluntary and involuntary turnover in Western labor markets, can Japanese firms afford to maintain classical in-company training and "lifetime employment" policies? Further, if Japanese firms begin to bid competitively for the services of non-Japanese middle-and upper-level personnel to fill out and upgrade the quality of employees in their international operations, how will this affect the attitudes and ambitions of Japanese managers who are following more traditional paths of internal advancement?

With a product as complex as a multifunction PPC (digital, double-sided, color photocopying, for example), the challenge of taking production overseas is complex and daunting. At home, PPC manufacture depends on high levels of interunit and interfunctional integration and on site-specific experience and knowledge accumulated through processes of organizational learning and social and interpersonal relations. Such experiences and the resulting practices are highly particularistic to the manufacturing sites in question. The accumulation of SSOL and its strategic role in factory performance make it somewhat analogous to the notion of core competence. [11]

SSOL and Jumping Genes

SSOL never really took root and blossomed on the PPC line at Irvine. That plant's sources of organizational and technical knowledge were many, its production volumes low, and its workforce turnover high. Given these obstacles, it was practically impossible to create a single set of norms and standards for how things should be done, pulled together, and pushed ahead. Unlike Toshiba's two other international PPC factories, Irvine's operations were a welter of disparate policies, routines, and practices.

Given that the norm in Japan is not to cooperate too closely with other factories, it is doubly difficult for overseas plants—the receiving sites of technology transfer—to initiate international collaboration. As a result, organizational and technical transfer were stymied at Irvine; PPC production volumes remained too low, and turnover rates too high. On-site learning effects never took hold.

In sum, what happened at each of Toshiba's three overseas PPC and toner production sites was not like what had happened at home. Yanagicho's site-specific advantages emerged in the context of a historically situated, organizationally and technically integrated, advanced manufacturing system that embodied something more than the sum of its parts. Since the plant's founding in 1936, the people, products, and technologies of Yanagicho coalesced and combined in ways that were distinctive. Toshiba's core competence in photocopier design, development and manufacture are embodied in Yanagicho.

Nevertheless, Toshiba succeeded in transferring PPC technology to and internationalizing PPC production at Mitchell and Dieppe. In both cases, the process was more like reproducing than transplanting knowledge. In other words, a parent factory's generic knowledge was grafted onto a local host, but only after lots of experimentation, rejection, and recombination of the donor material were new, site-specific, JMS features expressed and evolved. JMS evolved more by site-specific genesis than by transmission, but something of the latter necessarily preceded the former.

At Mitchell and Dieppe, successful transfer of PPC technology was almost an act of creation, something in between the "jumping genes" of Barbara McCormick's Nobel prize–winning research on corn-kernel mutation and full-fledged reshuffling of genes or procreation. McCormick's research sought to explain Indian corn's changing patterns of colors; from one generation to the next, patterns do not breed true. Copying errors and random mutations were shown to be the major causes of variation.

By analogy, in technology transfer, a "contest" ensues between error-free transfer of knowledge and a host of copying, transferring, and implementing errors. Some errors happen naturally and some "on purpose," in that local selection and adaptation processes occur. Local actors always interpret what is being sent, what it means, and how it should be used. The more they do so, the more SSOL moves ahead. Even when they misinterpret what is being sent, SSOL advances.

"Jumping-gene" transfer contrasts with full-scale rethinking of production processes and product designs, which is analogous to genetic reshuffling or reproduction. To elaborate a bit on the biological metaphor, when a grape, say, cabernet sauvignon, is spread by cuttings taken from a single field, individual plantings may mutate, but they are genetically identical, as a population, with the parent plants. However, when varieties are interbred or crossbred, even a little, genes are recombined in numerous important ways.[12]

In this chapter, Toshiba's Irvine plant was more like propagation by cuttings, with an emphasis on straight transfer into a mixed-cropping environment. But the cuttings never took root and flourished. At Mitchell and Dieppe, in contrast, creating something locally distinctive was the aim, since both plants were brownfield sites, and nothing in the parent plant's product mix matched local offerings. Straight transfer or propagation by cuttings was never the goal. Propagation by grafting, by mixing and recombination of cultures, was the mode of transfer.

In sum, the existence of advanced manufacturing features, practices, and capabilities, on their own, is a necessary but not sufficient condition for the appearance of JMS. Something more than good models or tried-and-true templates is needed. Site-specific organizational learning is part of that something more. SSOL is what integrates and motivates JMS at home and abroad, and it best informs us as to the reasons for an unsuccessful transfer of PPC technology to Irvine and its successful birth and evolution at Mitchell and Dieppe.

Notes

1. Advanced means performing well in a business sense. There is a lively debate as to whether or not Japanese production systems are advanced in terms of their human relations outcomes.

2. The interdependency of factory, firm, and interfirm network is a basic feature of the Japanese enterprise system as outlined in *The Japanese Enterprise System—Competitive Strategies and Cooperative Structures* (New York: Oxford University Press, 1992).

3. It is fascinating to reflect on the makeup of the human chromosome. Only 5 percent of chromosomes carry traits to be transmitted; 95 percent are instructions on when and how traits should be expressed. By analogy, the traits and features to be transmitted in international technology transfer—JMS's genetic code, for example—are only a small part of what actually happens in the technology transfer process.

4. There is a rapidly growing literature on evolution, self-organization, and complex adaptive systems. Some of the most outstanding and accessible books are John H. Holland, *Hidden Order* (Menlo Park, Calif.: Addison-Wesley, 1995); Stuart Kauffman, *At Home in the Universe* (New York: Oxford University Press, 1995); Ralph D. Stacey, *Complexity and Creativity in Organizations* (San Francisco: Berrett-Koehler, 1996); and Manfred Eigen, *Steps Toward Life* (New York: Oxford University Press, 1992).

5. In Japan, such goals are sought and realized in a more or less synchronous fashion. Overseas, they are implemented more often in a stepwise fashion. Presumably, reliability in high-volume, high-quality production comes first (without these, market penetration is unlikely), with low cost, time-to-market, and model/product variety goals appearing subsequently. The order may differ from country to country and from product to product.

6. A phenotype is the totality of characteristics of an organism, in contrast with the genotype, which is the genetic constitution—or legacy—of an organism. Advanced manufacturing practices in this chapter are JMS phenotype features and attributes.

7. Martin Fransman, *Japan's Computer and Communications Industry* (Oxford: Oxford University Press, 1995), p. 335. The proportion of Japan's total manufacturing capacity located outside Japan is only 9–10 percent, two or three times less than the proportion for American industry. "Asian Promise—Japanese manufacturing," *Economist*, June 12–19, 1993, pp. 98–99.

8. Information about Toshiba's toner production plant in Mitchell, South Dakota, was obtained from data collection and interviews in Mitchell, South Dakota; Irvine, California; and Kawasaki City, Japan. Masao Nakamura and I conducted interviews in Mitchell in December 1995.

9. W. Mark Fruin and Toshihiro Nishiguchi, "Supplying the Toyota Production System," in Bruce Kogut, ed., *Country Competitiveness* (New York: Oxford University Press, 1993).

10. November 29, 1989, interview in Arques La Bataille with Philippe Delahaye, CEO, and other local TSF executives.

11. Along with the notion of core competence, SSOL argues that it is hard to know exactly why JMS sites work as well as they do; subsystem complementarity and situated learning effects are part of the reason why. Like core competence, SSOL acknowledges the causal ambiguity of knowing how, when, and why local capabilities are expressed.

The importance of local experience in triggering JMS needs to be distinguished from other notions of knowledge creation. Knowledge suggests a higher level of generalizability than learning does, in my opinion. Admittedly, an indeterminate amount of what diffuses from Japan and accumulates overseas is tacit knowledge. Tacit knowledge can be made more explicit, but doing so does not substitute for the necessity of accumulating local knowledge. SSOL emphasizes the importance of local knowledge creation, but, at the same time, a need for general knowledge transfer is noted.

12. David L. Wheeler, "Marrying the Science and the Art of Winemaking," *Chronicle of Higher Education*, May 30, 1997, pp. A24–25.

References

Abegglen, James. 1958. *The Japanese Factory*. Homewood, Ill.: Free Press.

Aoki, Masahiko. 1988. *Information, Incentives and Bargaining in the Japanese Economy*. Cambridge: Cambridge University Press.

Brannen, Mary Yoko. 1992, "Your Next Boss Is Japanese: Negotiating Culture at Japanese Paper Plant in Western Massachusetts." Ph.D. diss., University of Massachusetts, Amherst, Ph.D. School of Business Administration.

Chandler, Alfred D. 1990. *Scale and Scope*. Cambridge, Mass.: Belknap Press.

Cole, Robert. 1971. *Japanese Blue Collar*. Berkeley: University of California Press.

Cole, Robert. 1979. *Work, Mobility and Participation*. Berkeley: University of California Press.

Cole, Robert E. 1989. *Strategies for Learning*. Berkeley: University of California Press.

DiMaggio, P. J., and Powell, W. W. 1983. "The Iron Cage Revisited." *American Sociological Review* 48: 47–160.

Dore, Ronald. 1973. *British Factory–Japanese Factory*, Berkeley: University of California Press.

Dore, Ronald. 1987. *Flexible Ridgities*. Standford: Standford University Press.

Doz, Y. L., and Prahalad, C. K. 1984. "Patterns of Strategic Control within Multinational Corporations." *Journal of International Business Studies* Fall; 55–72.

Eigen, Manfred. 1992. *Steps Towards Life*. New York: Oxford University Press.

Fiol, C. Marlene, and Marjorie A. Lyles. 1985. "Organizational Learning." *Academy of Management Review* 10(4): 803–813.

Franco, Lawrence G. 1989. "Global Corporate Competition." *Strategic Management Journal* 10: 449–474.

Fransman, Martin. 1995. *Japan's Communications and Computer Industry*, Oxford: Oxford University Press.

Fruin, W. Mark. 1992. *The Japanese Enterprise System*. Oxford: Clarendon Press.

Fruin, W. Mark. 1995. "Localizing and Integrating Knowledge in Fast-to-Market Competition." in J. Liker et al., eds., *Engineered in Japan*. New York: Oxford University Press.

Fruin, W. Mark. 1996. "Manufacturing Knowledge in Japan: Organizational Campaigning and Time-based Competition." Paper prepared for PRISM, Seattle, Washington, Aug. 17.

Fruin, W. Mark. 1997. *Knowledge Works: Managing Intellectual Capital at Toshiba*. New York: Oxford University Press.

Fruin, W. Mark. 1998. "Manufacturing Knowledge in Japan: Organizational Campaigning and the Time Value of Knowledge." In Raghu Garud and Joseph Porac, eds., *Cognition, Knowledge, and Organization*. New York: Greenwood Press.

Fruin, W. Mark, and Masao Nakamura. 1997. "Top-Down Production Management: A Recent Trend in the Japanese Productivity-enhancement Movement." *Journal of Management and Decision Sciences* 18: 131–139.

Fruin, W. Mark, and Toshihiro Nishiguchi. 1993. "Supplying the Toyota Production System." In Bruce Kogut, ed., *Country Competitiveness*. New York: Oxford University Press.

Gerlach, Michael. 1992. *Alliance Capitalism*. Berkeley: University of California Press.

Ghoshal, S., and Westney, D. E., eds. 1993. *Organization Theory and the Multinational Corporation*. New York: St. Martin's Press.

Holland, John H. 1995. *Hidden Order*. Menlo Park, Calif.: Addison-Wesley.

Hutchins, Edwin, and Brian Hazlehurst. 1995. "How to Invent a Lexicon: The Development of Shared Symbols of Interaction." In E. Goody, ed., *Social Intelligence and Interaction*, pp. 157–189. Cambridge: Cambridge University Press.

Kauffman, Stuart. 1994. *At Home in the University*. New York: Oxford University Press.

Kenney, Martin, and Richard Florida. 1992. *Beyond Mass Production*. New York: Oxford University Press.

Kimura, Y. 1989. "Firm-Specific Strategic Advantages and Foreign Direct Investment Behavior of Firms." *Journal of International Business Studies* 10(2): 296–314.

Kogut, Bruce. 1989. "A Note on Global Strategies." *Strategic Management Journal* 10: 383–389.

Kogut, Bruce. 1993. *Country Competitiveness*. New York: Oxford University Press.

Leibenstein, Harvey. 1975. "Aspects of the X-efficiency of the Firm." *Bell Journal of Economics* 6(2): 580–606.

Levitt, Barbara, and James G. March. 1988. "Organizational Learning." *Annual Review of Sociology* 14: 319–340.

Lincoln, James, and Arne Kalleberg. 1990. *Culture, Control, and Commitment*. Cambridge: Cambridge University Press.

Miner, Anne S., and Pamela R. Haunschild. 1995. "Population Level Learning." *Research in Organization Behavior* 17: 115–166.

Odagiri, Hiroyuki. 1992. *Growth through Competition, Competition through Growth*. Oxford: Oxford University Press.

Porter, Michael. 1996. "What Is Strategy?" *Harvard Business Review* (Nov.–Dec.): 61–78.

Scott, Richard. 1995. *Institutions and Organizations*. Thousand Oaks, Calif.: Sage.

Stacey, Ralph D. 1996. *Complexity and Creativity in Organizations*. San Francisco: Berrett-Koehl.

Tyre, Marcie J., and Eric von Hippel. 1997. "The Situated Nature of Adaptive Learning in Organizations." *Organization Science*. 8(1): 71–83.

Wheeler, David L. 1997. "Marrying the Science and the Art of Winemaking." *Chronicle of Higher Education*, May 30, A24–24.

Whittaker, Hugh. 1990. *Managing Innovation*. Cambridge: Cambridge University Press.

Womack, James et al. 1991. *The Machine That Changed the World*. New York: Ralston Associates.

8

Transplantation?

A Comparison of Japanese Television Assembly Plants in Japan and the United States

Martin Kenney

The transfer and/or adoption of the Japanese management system in the United States has drawn much attention during the last fifteen years (Abo et al., 1994; Kenney and Florida, 1993 Womack et al., 1990). Global competition and Japanese success in several industries have captured the attention of politicians, businessmen, and scholars alike. The Japanese story has successfully motivated a dramatic rethinking of the nature of production management (see, for example, Adler 1993; Dertouzos et al. 1989).

Research has overwhelmingly concentrated on the Japanese automobile industry and its transplants. This is not surprising, since automobile production is a core industry in most large industrialized countries. Automobile firms have been either the largest or among the largest companies in their respective nations and employ large numbers of blue-collar and white-collar workers at relatively high wages. That an entire industrial period has been described by the term "Fordism" is explanation enough of the centrality of the automobile. The auto assembly line remains the dominant paradigm for thinking about production and industrial relations studies in the late twentieth century.

Western understanding of the factors behind Japanese success thus focuses on autos—witness the reception of Womack et al.'s *The Machine That Changed the World*. Japanese firms have also been remarkably successful in other industries, most notably, electronics. There is good evidence that the technical characteristics of product and process lead to rather different management systems in these other industries.

This chapter examines the transfer of Japanese television assembly operations to the United States. Despite its importance, the Japanese production system in the consumer electronics industry has received limited attention in Japan and the United States. This lack of interest is curious, because it has been a great Japanese industrial success story. In fact, the first great wave of Japanese transplants in the United States consisted of the television assembly factories established during the 1970s. In 1998 Japanese companies owned all the remaining television assembly factories operating in the United States.

There were important differences between the electronics and the automobile industries. For example, there was a significant difference in the relative importance of assembly factory performance and R&D performance. While automakers such as GM and Toyota invested less than 5 percent of sales in R&D, the typical electronics firm allocated between 7 and 10 percent of sales to R&D, though the percentage allocated to televisions per se may be much lower. R&D played a critical role in the competitive success of an electronics company and was a central contributor to a firm's total value added. Thus, for the electronics firm, manufacturing, though important, was not quite as dominant as for automakers. Having said this, it is also quite clear that Japanese electronics firms have been among the most efficient and highest quality manufacturers in the world. These companies used their factories as competitive assets (Fruin, 1997).

The first section of the chapter describes previous research and the research conducted for this chapter. The second section examines the television assembly production system in Japan. In the third section I describe the broader system of factory organization and management in these plants. The fourth section summarizes the differences between television assembly and automobile assembly in Japan. The fifth section examines the available evidence on the transfer of television assembly to the United States. The sixth section discusses the difficulties of the two factories acquired by Sanyo and Matsushita in the 1970s. In the seventh section I present the evidence on transfer to the greenfield factories, here called Factory Y, Factory Z, Factory M, and a Sony plant in San Diego. The concluding discussion reflects upon the reasons for the relative lack of transfer of the Japanese system to the television assembly transplants and the reasons for the differences between television and automobile assembly.

Previous Research and Methodology

There are remarkably few studies of the production systems and factory organization of consumer electronics factories in Japan. Moreover, comparing transplant television assembly facilities with those of Japan is difficult because the operations in the Japanese factories are changing. Since 1985 Japanese television assembly plants (that is, those located in Japan) have been the victims of rising costs and corporate decisions to relocate production to developing and developed countries. As a result, television assembly plants have reduced head count by not replacing retiring regular workers, not rehiring some contract workers, and shifting employees to other factories. The remaining production has been shifted to high value-added models, new models, or products exclusively for the Japanese market. With these products the companies can afford high wages, because they are tapping the deep reservoirs of skills among their Japanese workers.

For this chapter, two types of information were gathered on Japanese television assembly plants. First, day-long interviews were conducted at three Japanese television plants (two owned by the same company). These Factories are identified as Factory U, Factory S, and Factory I. One plant was visited in 1995, 1996, and 1997; the second was visited in 1996 and 1997; the third in 1997. I also interviewed a public relations official for a fourth company regarding its television assembly plant. Second, I conducted an extensive literature review in both English and Japanese. There have been few studies on television assembly in Japan, with the exceptions of Hiramoto (1994) and Nomura (1992a, 1992b), who have done comprehensive studies of the development of the Japanese television industry. Other important studies by Nakamura et al. (1994) and Nagano et al. (1996) focus on the organization of two Japanese VCR factories. Dore (1973) studied the heavy electrical industry, whose products were not consumer electronics. Fruin (1997) examined the multifaceted Toshiba Yanagicho factory, whose products and processes differ considerably from those in television assembly factories.

There have been a number of studies of the consumer electronics transplants; however, most studies have been done in the developing countries, particularly Malaysia or Mexico (Beechler and Taylor, 1995; Kenney and Florida, 1994; Kenney et al., 1997; Nomura 1992a) or the United Kingdom (Delbridge, 1995; Oliver and Wilkinson, 1988, Taylor et al., 1994 Trevor, 1988). The only comprehensive cross-national treatment of consumer electronics transplants was done by Abo and colleagues (1994). The difficulty with this particular study is that it uses a rating system to compare plant practices and provides little detail on the actual functioning of the plants; thus, it is difficult to use the study for further comparative work. Abo (1992; 1994) also provides cross-national comparisons of the television assembly facilities of Sanyo and Toshiba; however, these studies also provide little detail beyond ratings.

The U.S. portion of this paper draws upon interviews, done in 1991, at one U.S. television assembly transplant; interviews, done in 1992, at a television assembly transplant; interviews in Japan in 1995 with two managers who had been in the United States; a one-day battery of interviews at four different Japanese television assembly transplants and one Japanese television assembly transplant supplier; and various secondary sources, including newspaper and magazine articles. Research included a complete bibliographical search of the *Business Periodicals Index*, the *Wall Street Journal*, the *New York Times*, and the *Chicago Tribune* indices for 1972 through 1990—with few results. Notwithstanding the reliance on ratings, Abo (1992, 1994) and Abo et al. (1994) are important sources of information on the U.S. television transplants. An important secondary source is a series of case studies of Sanyo's Forrest City, Arkansas, television assembly factory (Harvard Business

School, 1981; Kotha and Dunbar, 1995; Yonekura 1985;). The other study of importance is Sato's (1991) study of the Toshiba factory in Tennessee.

The Production System in Television Plants

Television production has a complicated value chain that contains a number of production steps, each of which uses quite different mixes of labor, capital, knowledge, and skill. A television consists of the following major components: picture tube (CRT) with its flyback transformer and deflection yoke, printed circuit board (PCB), transformer, wire harness, tuner, plastic and metal parts, and various small parts. Table 8.1 shows cost breakdowns for a 20-inch and a 32-inch television built in Japan. As can be seen, the CRT is a preponderant (and growing) portion of the total value of a television. The printed circuit board is the next most valuable component. Television final assembly is only a small proportion of the total cost of a television set.

The amount of labor necessary to assemble a television set has dropped dramatically during the past twenty years. Assembly has been not so much automated as modularized, and the number of discrete parts has dropped precipitously. In the late 1970s, Japanese firms took nearly two hours to assemble a 21-inch color television set (Office of Technology Assessment, 1983, p. 238). U.S. and German firms took four hours, and the British firm nearly six hours. By 1997 labor time for a 20-inch television had decreased to twenty-seven minutes, and a 32-inch model took eighty-six minutes. In contrast, an automobile required ten to twenty hours.

The capabilities needed in one segment of the television value chain are often not relevant in other segments. Thus, it is possible to have a spatial

Table 8.1 Breakdown of Material Costs for Different Size Televisions, 1997 (in percentages)

Part	20-inch Television	32-inch Television
Cathode ray tube	50	57
Printed circuit board	20	24
Tuner	4	2
Flyback transformer	4	1
Deflection yoke	5	2
Cabinet	11	6
Other items	6	8
Total	100%	100%
Total assembly time (in minutes)	27	86

Source: Ohgai, 1997.

division of labor among the various value chain segments, based on different locational advantages. So, for example, the manufacture of larger CRTs was capital-intensive and required an engineering and technician-rich environment (for smaller CRTs, the technology was quite standardized, and they were produced for the world market in Malaysia and Thailand). In fact, CRT production is so different that it is organizationally located in the devices division, which is completely separate from the assembly division. Often, CRT production was not even housed at the same site as television assembly operation, and some television assemblers such as Sharp and Sanyo did not even produce CRTs (Khurana, 1994). Television assembly was relatively labor intensive, and required less capital investment and fewer engineers and other highly skilled technical personnel. Twenty years ago assembly of the PCB (formerly known from its electron tube days as the chassis) was highly labor intensive; in 1997 it was largely automated but located in low-wage environments to reduce the cost of the residual manual labor (Nomura, 1992a). Because of the ability to disaggregate the value chain, television manufacturers had significant flexibility regarding the location of these three major components of the value chain.

The television assembly factories I studied were organized around a conveyor belt assembly line that was approximately 100 meters long. Few of the jobs required significant interoperator coordination. The operators sat on chairs or stood. When the televisions arrived at the stations, they performed a set of routines in a prescribed time (usually around one minute), and then the sets continued down the line. In this assembly portion there was little robotization. The group leader (hancho) or an automated delivery vehicle delivered the parts to the operators, except the CRT (a heavy, bulky and expensive item), which arrived on an overhead conveyor. One factory had only recently automated the entire CRT delivery section to minimize breakage, though automation of CRT delivery seemed to be a general trend in the factories studied.

The rapid pace of market change has meant shorter product lives and production runs, and more frequent model changes. For example, in the 1970s, Factory U, located in Northern Japan, produced 500,000 of a single model. In 1997 an entire model run might be only 10,000. The preparation to introduce a new model usually was only two to three days. Production batch sizes had fallen to an average of 1,500 units. To accommodate such short runs, Factory U reduced the average time required to change a model from two to three hours in the late 1970s to thirty to forty minutes in the 1980s.

The shortening of production runs and model lives altered the economics of production from simply optimizing production time to optimizing production and model change periods. Accordingly, the factory manager at Factory U believed that further robotization and automation were no longer desirable, as they reduced flexibility while raising capital investment. Factory S in Japan produced a wide variety of televisions, such as wide-screen, LCD, and Internet televisions. In contrast, its sister U.S. factory manufactured large batches in a routinized production process. All managers said that the far larger variety of televisions produced in Japanese factories made comparison with their U.S. counterpart facilities difficult. By implication, though this was never articulated, Japanese workers were considered more flexible and capable of adjusting to change; model changeover is a more complicated and less patterned activity than routine production.

The Japanese television factories operated on a modified JIT system. Larger parts, such as CRTs, plastic cases, wire harnesses, and PCBs (in Japan PCB insertion was often outsourced) were delivered more than once per day. Smaller parts, such as resistors and capacitors, were delivered less frequently. However, little space was devoted to warehousing parts. Instead of a physical *kanban*, electronic ordering systems were used.

Product engineering was critical in television assembly. Reducing component counts and designing for simplified production were critical for market success. One significant advantage Japanese firms had over their U.S. competitors in the 1960s and 1970s was their quick substitution of the more reliable transistors for the bulky and less reliable tubes (Baranson, 1980). In the process, the "chassis," which was originally a heavy metal stand with numerous wires attached to it, shrank and became a PCB. This permitted the automation of chassis assembly and dramatically reduced shipment costs. The use of transistors and their successors, integrated circuits, decreased the number of parts, even while the television's functions were increased. As an example, by increasing its use of large-scale integrated circuits, Sanyo's Gifu factory decreased the parts count for its 20-inch televisions from 2,334 in 1970 to 1,006 in 1976 (Baranson, 1980, p. 103).

Part counts also dropped through the use of sophisticated plastic molds that combined several plastic parts into a single part (Hiramoto, 1994, p. 143). For example, one plastic injection molding company developed a new process capable of integrating the television cabinet and the speaker covers in one mold. This reduced the part count from five to one. Because of these improvements, there were fewer tasks to coordinate, and assembly lines could be shortened and head count reduced. Production quality improved because there were fewer opportunities for mistakes. Such simplification through product and component engineering appears to be easily as important as operator-driven continuous improvement.

In the factories there were many diagrams and documents that provided information on quality control (QC) results, yield, and other variables. There were also group pictures of various successful QC circles, and it was clear that both male and female workers were actively involved. On each line there was a large display indicating the number of televisions scheduled and produced. However, there were no *andon* lights like as those in a Toyota factory, except in the printed circuit board mounting section, where each machine has a light pole with green, yellow, and red lights to indicate its operational status.

Factory Organization and Management in Japanese Electronics

Divisions of the major Japanese electronics companies, such as Hitachi, JVC, Matsushita, Sanyo, Sharp, Sony, and Toshiba, operated Japanese television assembly factories. These plants' production systems were embedded in the broader factory management, corporate structure, and institutional environment. The management system was the same as that in other large Japanese firms and includes the long-term employment system, enterprise unions, and a complicated salary-setting system with an important seniority component, though there were many small differences because of the path-dependent development of each company. The following subsections address some of the important features of factory organization and management in consumer electronics assembly, though many of these features were actually company-wide.

Hiring and Initial Training

Because of the long-term employment system, hiring was a critical function. Manufacturing employees were recruited from among regular and industrial high school graduates (there are few terminal junior high school graduates in Japan). All recruits received written, oral, and medical examinations. The written examination was a corporation-wide exam that included surprisingly difficult algebra, contemporary economics, and English-language questions. The industrial high school graduates also received a technical examination in their major. The oral examination was meant to establish the worker's personality and motivation and was between thirty and sixty minutes in duration. Good oral answers were those that expressed a motivation to be successful, though one personnel manager said that the applicants were well coached on what to say.

The initial training for factory workers varied dramatically by company. At the VCR factory Nagano et al. (1996) studied, all the new workers received three months of initial training. The first month included an orientation to the firm and instruction in how to fasten screws and perform other basic procedures at the factory's training center. In the final two months the trainees rotated at two-week intervals through various workplaces. At the other television factories I visited, the off-the-job-training and orientation periods were much shorter, roughly three to five days in duration. After this, the newly hired employees spent three months rotating through various jobs throughout the plant, after which they were settled in one work group.

Worker Stratification

Production workers in the typical Japanese consumer electronics assembly facility were stratified on the basis of the type of contract held with the firm.

The bottom of the shop floor hierarchy consisted of fixed-term contract (i.e., temporary) workers. This first group of workers were predominantly, but not exclusively, female. Contract workers performed simple, routinized assembly tasks requiring a minimum level of skill and were paid relatively low wages (Nakamura et al., 1994). For example, in VCRs, Nakamura et al. (1994) found that nearly all the highly routinized tasks of physical assembly were done by contract workers. Though officially defined as contract workers, these employees (at least in Nakamura et al., 1994) had been relatively permanent workers in practice because historically their contracts were almost invariably renewed. The company union represented these contract workers.

Due to the strength of the yen in the 1991–1995 period, many of these long-term contract workers did not have their contracts renewed or were transferred out of the television assembly plants. Therefore, in contrast to the VCR factory Nakamura et al. (1994) studied, in 1997 the television factories had few contract workers. As an example, in Factory U there were few contract workers, except for the remote controller assembly section, where there was a room in which approximately twenty women contract workers manually assembled small lots of remote controllers. Because of the continuing transfer of television assembly offshore and the increasing automation at Factory I, only twenty-five of the 450 female workers were contract workers. Regular employees sometimes performed assembly tasks previously undertaken by contract workers or subcontractors.

The second group consisted of women doing relatively simple tasks working in final assembly. At the television assembly factories I studied, nearly all women were permanent employees, although in earlier times many contract assembly workers had been employed. Promotional opportunities for female regular employees were circumscribed. For example, Ohgai (1996) reported that women at Matsushita usually were promoted no higher than first-level supervisor or group leader. As described later, this limited mobility influenced the opportunities open to female shop floor workers for training and participation in higher-level work activities.

The third group was regular male workers. These men were the most highly trained group and were the source of most first-line supervisors. In these supervisorial positions they were responsible not only for managing employees but also for setting standard processing times, spearheading operational improvements, and conducting performance evaluations (Abo et al. 1994, p. 158). In a typical U.S. firm, these tasks were normally reserved for engineers and managers. In a 1996 visit to Factory I, only a few men were observed working on the highly automated assembly line (most workers were female regular employees).

While there were no legal or formal distinctions between male and female employees, in practice there was a stratification of regular shop floor workers on the basis of gender, particularly in the areas of opportunities for promotion, training, and engaging in "technician-like" work activities. Male regular employees were more often industrial high school graduates and typically had substantially greater opportunities for training. This meant that over their careers they were able to develop greater skills, and their "duties [became] mainly maintenance-related" (Abo et al., 1994, p. 157).

Nakamura et al. (1994, p. 64) found that, at the VCR factory, employees hired as regular workers typically did not perform any assembly work; the "regular employees (blue-collar) are mainly engaged in control and supervisory duties, while the persons actually engaged in assembly operations are the contract employees in each team." Moreover, for activities requiring greater skill and/or a broader range of knowledge, such as in the Adjustment and Inspection and Engineering subsections, there were no contract employees, while in the Materials Supply and Parts subsections there were only a few contract employees doing data entry and other "secretarial-type" functions. Because of the centrality of the regular workers, the remainder of the discussion focuses on them.

Training and Rotation

The commitment to training was universal in the Japanese consumer electronics assembly factories. Production workers within Japanese consumer electronics factories were stratified in terms of training. Regular workers received training on a range of subjects, including quality control, inspection, new machinery, machine maintenance, and special skills such as welding and soldering. At Factories U and I, in preparation for promotion to higher grades, an entire curriculum of classes was required. After promotion, another curriculum of classes was required. For regular employees, training was a constant feature of work.

An aspect of OJT training prominently featured in the literature was job rotation, whereby each member in a team was trained in all or most of the jobs undertaken by the team (Cole, 1989; Gronning, 1992). Three types of rotation were normally used. The first type of rotation was short-term rotation, which moves workers to different work positions to relieve boredom and ergonomic stress. In these factories this was not practiced except in certain inspection and visual balance adjustment activities that required alertness and visual concentration (most notably, projection television adjustment). In Japan, in Factory U, the assemblers worked all day at the same job, though they usually experienced some variation when models were changed, which was on average every two or three days. The lack of daily or short-term task rotation among assembly-line workers in Japan consumer electronics factories was not the result of workers' resistance or Western-style job control. Rather, managers believed it was better that the operators learn a single job well before being rotated.

The second type of rotation occurred when team members were missing; another worker was then transferred to the job temporarily. In the process, the second worker experienced and learned another job. Rotations of this kind were not even reported or logged in the personnel office.

The third type of rotation was designed to increase skills and create career paths. All workers received such a form of rotation. Male workers, more than female workers, received active job rotation that allowed them to perform a broad variety of tasks, from final assembly to PCB parts insertion. This cross-training was clearly oriented toward promoting workers into specialty sections such as equipment maintenance or production engineering. Compared to auto assembly, the routinized nature of tasks in both PCB insertion and television assembly made cross-training less important to ensure quality and continuous improvement.

Some workers, especially the graduates of industrial high schools, received intense training that transformed them into the equivalent of a technician or even a junior engineer in the United States. This was an interesting finding, because, in a recent article, Barley (1996), on the basis of his research in the United States., treats the technician as an objective category, while our findings suggest that the "technician" category was not present in Japanese television assembly factories.

Practices and findings concerning transfer through a broad variety of jobs by gender were inconsistent in their details. For example, Nakamura et al. (1994) found that all regular employees received this type of transfer, while Abo et al. (1994) found that it was restricted to male regular employees. Both studies agreed that cross-training within teams and job transfers within the factory were restricted to regular employees. The proper conclusion seems to be that female employees receive rotation, but because their careers were generally shorter (because of marriage and/or pregnancy) than those of their male counterparts, they received less training investment.

An example of training at one Japanese factory was a highly skilled industrial high school graduate. Table 8.2 illustrates his career pattern. With each change he received both on- and off-the-job training. Once during his career he was dispatched to the divisional product development section in another part of Japan, where he worked for six months with university-educated engineers developing a new video projection system. He then accompanied the product back to the factory and assisted in preparing it for manufacturing.

Labor Turnover

Although women were treated differently from men, labor turnover for both sexes was low in Japanese electronics factories. Hiramoto (1995, p. 246) found that annual turnover at a Hitachi television assembly facility in Japan was 1 percent for male workers and 4.2 percent for female workers. At the Matsushita Ibaraki television assembly facility, male turnover was "almost zero except for retirement," and women's turnover was 1 percent a year. Turnover was highest among the male employees because they had been hired during the massive growth in Matsushita's consumer electronics business in the early 1960s and were now retiring after thirty years of service

Table 8.2 Career Pattern for a Television Assembly Employee
Graduated from Industrial High School—18 Years

Job Classification	Time Phase
None	
PCB inspection	1 yr.
Material supply	1 yr.
G2	
Video projection system (VPS) assembly	1 yr.
Alignment of VPS	1 yr.
G3	
White balance in VPS	2 yrs.
G4	
Dispatched to product development	
Laboratory in other part of Japan	6 mos.
Returned to white balance in VPS	6 mos.
Production technology section	3 yrs.
During this period becomes G5	
G5	
Production maintenance section	3 yrs.
Production facility maintenance	4 yrs.

Usually, female turnover was the result of marriage and pregnancy (and the figure included women taking leave but planning on returning). The inclusion of women office workers raised turnover to approximately 5 percent per year (Nakamura et al., 1994). We can deduce that women assembly line workers had low turnover. In contrast, in the mid-1980s, when the Ibaraki television factory was operating at full capacity, female turnover was 10 percent per year (Ohgai, 1996). Turnover among contract workers and operators was not entirely negative from the company's viewpoint, because these workers could be replaced by less expensive younger workers. There would have been more damage had there been high turnover among the more skilled personnel, such as technicians and supervisors (Abo et al., 1994, p. 158).

Wages and Promotions

As in all major Japanese firms, wages were set according to a formula consisting of seniority (base), performance (merit), and ability components. The percentage weighting of these components differed by companies. There was also a bonus component that was approximately five months of salary paid in two installments. Salary increases were calculated once per year, and each individual received a unique raise; thus, every employee's salary was different (Ogasawara, 1992).

Japanese consumer electronics firms fill all higher level shop floor positions through internal promotion (Nakamura et al., 1994). At Factory U, even the factory manager was an industrial high school graduate. Many factory managers at this firm were industrial high school graduates. However, at the television assembly factories of the heavy electrical industry firms, such promotions for high school graduates were not as prevalent, so this pattern may not be generalizable.

The three different companies I studied had five grades of operators, and within these there were numerous smaller steps. Senior-level operators, what I call the "quasi-supervisor" category, carried no direct supervisory responsibility but wrote job descriptions and conducted various other supervisory tasks. Nakamura et al. (1994, p. 57) reported both male and female quasi-supervisors in the VCR factory, although the majority were males.

Table 8.3 provides the general job description for each category of worker in one firm's factories. The G1–G5 positions were nonsupervisory, and the H1–H3 were supervisory. After about two or three years with no classification, the newly hired factory operators were classified as G2 or G3. Most were classified as G2, though technical high school graduates usually became G3. At the G3 level, worker judgment was more important. The G4 and G5 levels corresponded to what in the United States would be considered technicians or a skilled-trades persons. They were expected to address complex problems and to work to solve them with a wide variety of personnel, including customers and suppliers. They also had an explicit training function—a supervisory function that has been delegated to them. The next step in their career would be to move to the H1 supervisory level, where the job description was more abstract.

Ogasawara (1992) presented a simplified diagram of how the criteria for promotion changed as a worker moved up the hierarchy (see Figure 8.1). The interesting aspect of this figure was that for mid-level operators, "managerial ability" was already being considered in worker evaluations. Then, for the senior-level operator, the "human aspect" emerged as an important criterion for promotion. The human aspect referred to modes of handling and motivating subordinates.

Workers for the supervisorial H1 to H3 categories were recruited entirely from among the production workers. This group was largely male (but not exclusively) and, often, industrial high school graduates. By the time workers reached this rank, they had a wide base of experience and had received significant training. The number of subordinates under an H1 supervisor varied, but on average it was about ten.

Teams and Small-Group Activities

Japanese factories operated on the principle that all workers should be organized into groups (Cole, 1989). Much analysis of the Japanese manufacturing system has emphasized the role of the group. In television assembly, all workers were members of groups with a group leader. Nevertheless, this "group" does not appear to have quite the same attributes as the "team" concept popularized by Toyota (Cole, 1989; Gronning, 1992). The plant

Table 8.3 Definition of Work Categories in Production

Group Classification	Job Duties
G1	Job duties according to fixed operational procedures; extremely limited range of simple, repetitive tasks.
G2	Based on elementary knowledge. Job duties according to fixed operational procedures, standards, etc. Relatively simple tasks.
	Although limited in scope, tasks in this work group will require a certain amount of worker judgment.
G3	Job duties require general knowledge and technical skills but are performed according to fixed operational procedures, standards, etc. Some fairly complex job duties requiring individual judgment in a relatively wide scope.
	In cases where product quality or production line problems arise, the worker is expected to handle simple problems independently; more complicated problems are to be solved according to the instructions from the responsible supervisor.
G4	Job duties require considerable specialized knowledge, technical skills, and on-the-job experience. They include the ability to carry out complex job duties independently and/or guide junior employees.
	In cases where complex product quality or production problems arise, the ability to resolve them in cooperation with concerned persons and departments both inside and outside the company is necessary.
G5	Job duties require considerable specialized knowledge and technical skills relating directly and indirectly to the workplace and extensive on-the-job experience. The ability to carry out complex and difficult job duties independently and to instruct junior employees in his/her charge are required.
	In cases where critical product quality or production line problems arise, job duties include devising remedies and working toward a resolution of the problem in cooperation with concerned persons and departments both inside and outside the company.
H1	A person possessing the ability to manage a work group, [han] or equivalent work unit. The H1 directly supervises junior employees and has the ability to effectively perform his or her assigned job duties.
	He or she has specialized technical skills, experience, and job know-how and has the ability to independently per-

Table 8.3 *(continued)*

Group Classification	Job Duties
	form job duties which are vital to the management strata at the subsection assistant manager and [work group] leader levels.
H2	A person possessing the ability to act as assistant manager of a section or equivalent work unit. He directly supervises junior employees and is capable of performing a wide array of practical and administrative job duties. He or she has a relatively high level of specialized knowledge, experience, and job know-how and has the ability to independently perform job duties which are vital to the management strata at the section or subsection level.
H3	A person possessing the ability to manage and monitor a section or equivalent work unit. The H3 possesses a high level of specialized knowledge, experience, and job know-how and has the ability to independently perform job duties which are vital to the management strata at the department and/or section level.

Source: Nakamura et al., 1994, pp. 50, 56.

manager at Factory U said that "we do not really work on the team concept." At his factory, groups were administrative units and did not engage in collective problem solving.

Though the actual work was not organized into teams, in every factory all regular workers, male and female, were involved in off-line small-group activities (SGAs). Some employees were members of a number of small groups, for example, a quality control circle and a safety group. (Small groups were a fundamental feature of Japanese production in the consumer electronics sector.) The most important and ubiquitous of these were quality control circles, which have had a long history in the Japanese consumer electronics industry. For example, Juran (1967) reported on a QC circle presentation by three Japanese women each under twenty-five years of age, who worked at the Matsushita car radio plant. In this case, the workers used information from assembly rejections and consumer complaints to prepare a Pareto analysis of these defects and to develop solutions for the problems.

Factory I provided me with a QC circle final report describing a circle in the quality management section. The report had two components. The first presented the technical aspects, including diagrams, timelines, and evaluations. The second was, in a sense, more interesting, since it described the social activities, such as outings, the QC circle members took part in as a group. The manager of quality control for the plant said these "social" events were a nec-

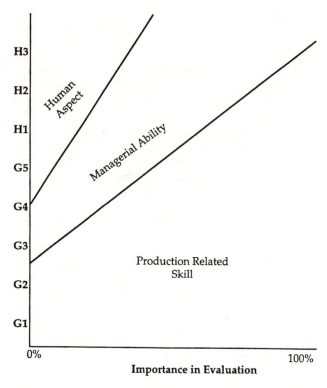

Figure 8.1 Importance of characteristics by hierarchical work categories (from Ogasawara 1992).

essary part of the QC circles activity. Here, the social role of SGAs was explicit. These activities were not merely to provide technical solutions but to also create camaraderie and to encourage information sharing and trust.

Job Characteristics

In Japanese television assembly facilities, line operators did not have the prerogative of stopping the line, even if they experienced problems. As Figure 8.2 shows, workers had to contact the group leader or the subsection leader, who then made the decision to stop the line. At Factory U the quality control manager said that if there were five successive cases of defects, then he would stop the line to analyze the problem. This differed dramatically from the practice at Toyota, where individual workers were empowered to push a button, and in sixty seconds the line would stop, unless the team or group leader overrode the worker's signal. Thus, responsibility and control were shared at the auto factory, whereas at the television assembly factory the supervisors controlled decisions.

In all three factories, at each work station there was a standardized worksheet posted in front of each operator. Figure 8.2 was a typical job description for a relatively junior G2 worker. The quasi-supervisor, with the approval of the group leader, the subsection leader, and the section leader (*kacho*), drew up the worksheet. From the worksheet, it can be seen that the content and specifications of the job order were quite highly standardized. The worksheet also contained information on the job, cautioning the operator about particular features. Supplementary tasks, such as checking operations and parts four times a day, were noted. The operator was instructed to notify the group leader or quasi-supervisor if anything irregular occurred. Notice that this low-level operator had no explicit checking functions. Checking was a more important aspect for operators above the G3 level.

At one factory I visited in 1996, the managers were reconsidering the intense decomposition of jobs. A description of the results of their systems' success is reproduced in Figure 8.3. The tasks of four operators were combined, so each operator did all of the tasks at each particular work station. As Figure 8.3 indicates, the operators were significantly more productive under the new system. Moreover, according to the plant manager, because the scope of the work was greater, operators were now able to offer better suggestions for improving operations. This rethinking of the production process resembles what Takashi and Fujimoto (1996) found at Toyota, where some plants were recombining short-cycle tasks and increasing the cycle time. Hikari Nohara, in personal communications, made a similar point, arguing that Toyota was losing out on worker suggestions because of the extreme fragmentation and lack of connectedness of tasks, which emptied their work of

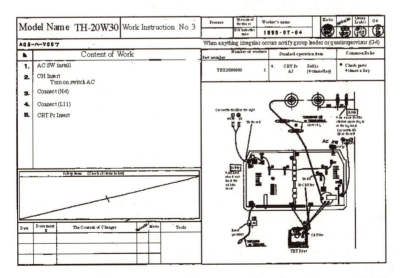

Figure 8.2 Standardized worksheet for a G2 worker (from Company X Television Division).

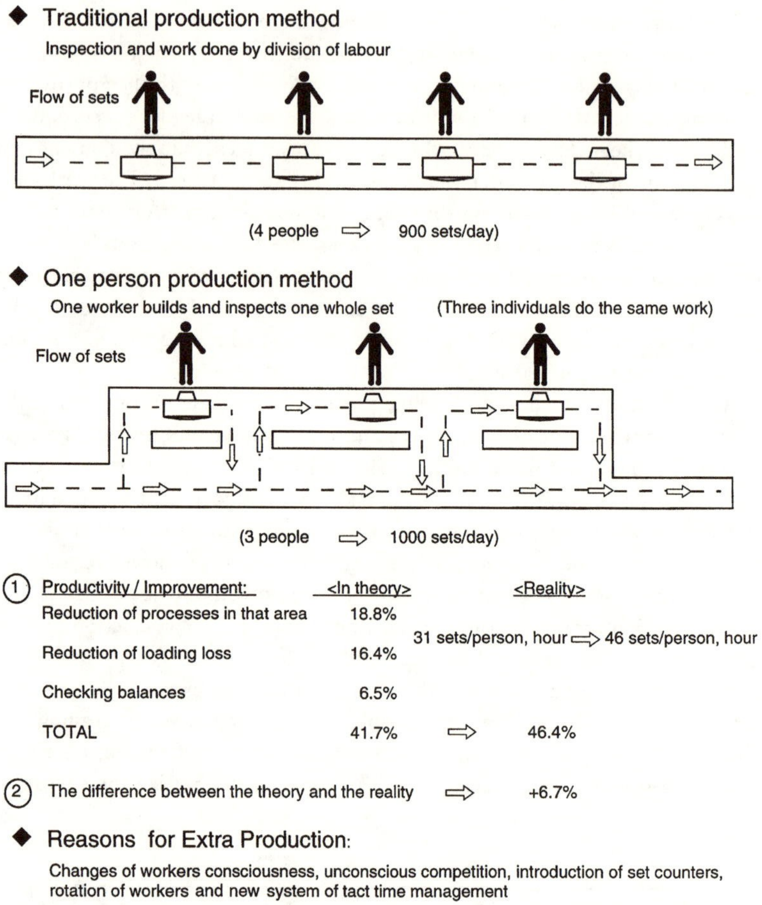

◆ Traditional production method

Inspection and work done by division of labour

(4 people ⇨ 900 sets/day)

◆ One person production method

One worker builds and inspects one whole set   (Three individuals do the same work)

(3 people ⇨ 1000 sets/day)

① Productivity / Improvement: <In theory>   <Reality>

Reduction of processes in that area   18.8%

                                                31 sets/person, hour ⇨ 46 sets/person, hour
Reduction of loading loss   16.4%

Checking balances   6.5%

TOTAL   41.7%   ⇨   46.4%

② The difference between the theory and the reality   ⇨   +6.7%

◆ Reasons for Extra Production:

Changes of workers consciousness, unconscious competition, introduction of set counters, rotation of workers and new system of tact time management

Figure 8.3 Reorganizing television assembly.

meaning. This concept underlies the restructuring of tasks at some Toyota plants.

Comparison of Television and Automobile Assembly

Fundamentally, television assembly is similar to auto assembly, in that it consists of discrete parts assembly. However, there are also significant differences. Table 8.4 outlines these differences. The institutional context is important to understand. Generally speaking, auto production is the primary activity of the auto industry. On the other hand, televisions are only one among many products made by consumer electronics firms. In the consumer electronics firms, the ratio of R&D to sales is greater than it is in the auto

Table 8.4 Comparison of Japanese Automobile and Television Assembly Factories

	Automobile	Television
DIFFERENCES		
Firm characteristics		
Firm product mix	Single most important	One of many
R&D /sales	Less than 5 percent	More than 7 percent
Engineer-to-operator ratio	Low	High
Physical aspects		
Automation[a]	Lower	Higher
Assembly line	1 kilometer	100 meters
No. of parts	30 to 40,000	Less than 2,000
Assembly time	10 to 20 hours	27 minutes[b]
Minimum efficient factory size	3,000 employees	600 employees
Factory cost	$500 million	$30–50 million
Nature of team	Interactive	Hierarchical
Role of operators in successful operation	Significant	Less significant
Ability of operator to stop line	Yes	No
Complexity of operator tasks	Relatively high	Relatively low
On-the-job training	Critical	Important, but less critical
Off-the-Job training	Less emphasis	More emphasis
Kaizen	Critical	Important, but less critical
SIMILARITIES		
Quality control circles	All workers involved	All workers involved
Suggestions	Mandatory	Mandatory
Role of supervisors	Extremely important	Extremely important
Wage system	Similar	Similar
Promotion system	Similar	Similar
Blue/white collar	No differences	No differences
Engineer-worker interaction	Close	Close

a. For televisions this includes printed circuit board insertion.

b. This for the standard 20-inch model.

industry, though it is important to note that the R&D-to-sales ratio related to televisions is likely quite low. Finally, Japanese consumer electronics firms have high engineer-to-operator ratios; those for autos are not as high.

The two assembly processes were different in their level of technical complexity. Television assembly was much simpler than automobile assembly. An auto assembly line was nearly one kilometer long; an auto contained approximately 30,000 parts, in contrast to between 1,000 and 2,000 for televisions. Put differently, in 1985 Abegglen and Stalk (p. 61) reported that television assembly had approximately 100 steps, whereas auto assembly had approximately 1,500 steps. In contrast, men's dress shirts had slightly more than twenty steps. There was a difference in the sheer scale of the three undertakings of at least an order of magnitude.

The physical nature of the work process was also different. Generally speaking, autoworkers moved around the vehicle. Their activity was more complex than sitting in a chair and inserting parts, connecting wires, or tightening screws. The generally more complex work task provided greater opportunity for operator contributions to the improvement effort. This was not to say that operator improvement in television assembly was without value—simply that the potential value added by operators was circumscribed by the technical nature of the product and the process.

The gender characteristics of the workforces were also different. In the television factories a large number of women were employed, whereas at the automobile factories there were only a few women. One important reason for this is that Japanese law forbade women working night shifts. Because in Japan autoworkers changed shifts on a regular schedule, women would have had to work at night when their shift changed. In contrast, most consumer electronics factories operated only two shifts.

Not only was the television assembly line shorter, it was also divided into fewer discrete segments. In a Toyota facility, there were many *andon* lights that signaled the status of the various segments of the line and a number of electric scoreboards that compared the number of vehicles or parts produced in a line segment with the target. In the typical television factory there were few *andon* lights in the line and only one large scoreboard for comparing the target and actual production. Responsibility for line operation was vested far more firmly in the supervisors. With fewer and simpler steps there was less risk of failure or error, and failures and errors were not as costly.

In television assembly, production was not done in teams, as described in the literature on Toyota. Neither was there a Toyota-style team leader present in the television assembly factories studied. Cross-training of workers within the group was not as systematically pursued as in the Toyota system. OJT, though important in television assembly, was not as important as in autos. In contrast, I was struck by the relatively heavy emphasis on off-the-job training.

This brief overview has delineated some of the major differences between television and auto assembly in Japan. Even in the same institutional environment, significant differences in production and management systems existed. One final difference I have not yet discussed—Japanese television assemblers began overseas production in the United States in the early 1970s, fifteen years before Honda built its first factory in Ohio. It is to this issue of Japanese investment in the United States that I now turn.

Transfer to the United States

With the possible exception of Sony, the consumer electronics firms—like Japanese firms in other industries—were "reluctant multinationals" (Trevor, 1988). However, their tremendous success in exporting televisions to the United States in the 1960s and 1970s resulted in significant trade friction (Porter, 1986). This increasing trade friction and fear of U.S. protectionism convinced Japanese television producers to establish assembly plants in the United States. As Table 8.5 indicates, from the early 1970s Japanese television producers opened or acquired factories in the United States. Initially, these plants were proverbial "screwdriver" factories, receiving both production equipment and critical components from Asia. Indeed, by the mid-1970s, U.S. makers themselves were largely dependent on parts imported from Asia, though the most vital component, the CRT, was still made in the United States by U.S. makers. Some of the CRTs used in the transplants and many of the assembled PCBs were imported from Japan. Later in the decade, the Japanese transplants purchased CRTs from U.S. manufacturers, and the PCBs were imported from other parts of Asia. Only in the mid- and late 1980s did Japanese manufacturers build CRT factories in the United States (one exception is Sony, which established its CRT factory in the mid-1970s because its Trinitron tube was unique and could not be purchased in the open market.) More recently, the number of assembly plants has dropped dramatically as assembly operations have been relocated to Mexico, with its lower labor costs.

The U.S. consumer electronics industry was quintessentially Fordist. Every ill that plagued the U.S. automobile industry existed in television production (MIT Commission on Industrial Productivity, 1988). Labor relations and quality were abysmal. For example, between 1970 and 1979 Japanese television makers had between nine and twenty-six field calls per 100 sets, whereas U.S. firms had between 100 and 200 field calls per 100 sets (Porter 1983). Similarly, the faults per 100 sets on a U.S.-operated assembly line was between 140 and 200, but for Japanese assemblers it was only between one and three. Baranson (1980) found that in 1979 the defect rate for U.S. sets was 5 percent, whereas for Japanese televisions sets it was 0.4 percent.

The consumer electronics transplants were pioneers in the relocation of production from Japan to the United States. At the time, there were few examples of successful Japanese production in the United States. (Yoshino, 1976). Most people judged the Japanese system to be so culturally different as to be unadaptable to Western countries (Nakane, 1970). Similarly, Japa-

Table 8.5 The Status of Japanese Television Assembly Plants in the United States as of 1997

	Sony	Matsushita	Sanyo	Mitsubishi	Toshiba	Hitachi	Sharp
Location	San Diego, California	Franklin Park, Illinois	Forrest City, Arkansas	Santa Ana, California	Lebanon, Tennessee	Anaheim, California	Memphis, Tennessee
Start of operation	1972	1974	1976	1977	1978	1979	1979
Type of operation	Startup	Acquisition	Acquisition	Startup	Startup	Startup	Startup
No. of employees, 1997[a]	4,000	0	400	0	600	0	600
No. of employees, 1988[b]	1,500	800	400	550	600	900	770
Products	TVs, CRTs, and monitors	TVs and PTVs	TVs	PTVs	TVs and microwave ovens	TVs and VCRs	TVs and microwave ovens
Maquila	Yes	Yes	Yes	Yes	Yes	Yes	No
Operations	TV assembly moved to maquila	Closed—moved to maquila	Most production in maquila	Merged with Georgia factory	Expanding maquila	Closed—moved to maquila	Considering maquila

a. No longer assembling televisions; now producing CRTs and computer monitors and other items.

b. Assembling televisions and producing CRTs.

Source: Electronics Industry Association 1989, Ohgai 1997, and various sources.

nese companies did not understand the pitfalls of acquiring U.S. operations, with their old facilities and entrenched work practices.

Evaluation of transfer is difficult because each company has taken a somewhat different path. Moreover, the available information on these factories is irregular and not comparable between firms. The following presentation uses case studies of the Sanyo Arkansas and the Matsushita Illinois factories because they have been the most studied. A discussion of some of the greenfield factories follows. The final section examines the magnitude of the transfer from Japan.

Two Acquisitions—Sanyo and Matsushita

The Sanyo Plant in Forrest City, Arkansas

In 1977 Sanyo purchased the failing Forrest City, Arkansas, facility from Warwick, the main supplier of Sears brand televisions. The Warwick factory

JVC	NEC	Matsushita	Mitsubishi	Orion	Pioneer	Sony
Elmwood Park, New Jersey	McDonough, Georgia	Vancouver, Washington	Braselton, Georgia	Princeton, Indiana	Chino, California	West Morland, Pennsylvania
1982	1985	1986	1986	1987	1988	1992
Startup	Startup	Startup	Startup	Startup	Startup	Startup
0	0	250	400	250	100	800
100	400	200	300	250	0	0
TVs	TVs	VCR-TV Combo	TVs and mobile telephones	TVs	PTVs	TVs and CRTs
Yes	No	Yes	Yes	No	No	Yes
Closed— moved to maquila	Closed	Stable	Expanding maquila	No	No	Large screens only

was, by all accounts, an example of the worst in U.S. manufacturing. It was organized by the International Union of Electronic, Electrical, Salaried, Machine and Furniture Workers (IUE) and operated in a traditional conflictual U.S. style (Beazley, 1988). The Sanyo quality assurance director described the plant when he came to the U.S.:

> Compared with Japan, my first impression was that there was too much specialization. Sectionalism, I felt, was wrong among the departments, lines, and workers. It seemed to me that line workers thought quality control was the responsibility of the inspection or quality departments. I also felt that the concept of cooperation was totally lacking. . . . Japanese workers would think of quality as the concern of the entire company. In addition, I noticed the working environment was very dirty. (Yonekura, 1985, p. 1)

Traditional U.S. Fordism was in full swing at the Forrest City plant, and workers could not be moved from one job to another without union agreement, so there was no possibility of job rotation.

After purchasing the Arkansas plant, Sanyo immediately revamped production by installing new machinery, using higher quality Japanese parts, and cleaning and upgrading the facility. The Warwick plant quality control manager was made the plant manager to signal the importance of quality (Kotha and Dunbar, 1995, p. 7). Sanyo also tried to create the feeling of a "big happy family atmosphere to enhance morale at the plant" (Reid, 1977). The company worked to eliminate the traditional layoff after the Christmas season and attempted to smooth out production in the hope of developing a rough equivalent to the long-term employment system (Kotha and Dunbar, 1995 p. 8).

Productivity and quality immediately rose, and there was a "halo" effect because the plant was saved from closure. Still, productivity was at least 25 percent below that of Sanyo's Japanese plants. The Japanese managers came from a continuous improvement environment and constantly pushed for better quality and greater productivity. This bothered U.S. workers, who wanted to know when the improvement process would end. One of the Japanese managers said:

> On the subject of productivity, the key element is teamwork, with the responsibility resting squarely on management to motivate workers. The reason there are workmanship problems in the U.S., I believe, is the different concept of teamwork. In a Japanese plant there is much more dialogue between blue-collar and white-collar workers; in fact, rapport is so natural, we take it for granted. Such however, is not the case in the U.S. In this respect we may even be more advanced in the concept of democracy than Americans. (Harvard Business School, 1981)

The Japanese tried to break the barriers created by the ingrained functional specialization in the Sanyo plant. In effect, they tried to transplant Japanese factory organization and management to the United States.

Factory employees had different conceptions of who was responsible for quality control. One Japanese manager, who found it difficult to get U.S. workers to inspect the work done by other workers, described them in these terms: "They feel that it is wrong to say that a fellow worker has made an error, or even to correct the errors they see. But surely this is essential if the company is to turn out good products. If we make defective products, who will buy them? And where will these people work if nobody buys them?" (Harvard Business School, 1981, p. 10).

Sanyo did not limit its efforts to personnel-related action. It also installed intermediate inspection stations along the line to intercept problems. In addition, Sanyo installed a tumbler that flipped the completed televisions into the air to find out "if a screw falls out"; the screw was then traced back to the responsible worker (Reid, 1977, p. A12). It was difficult to know whether these additions were in excess of those used in Japan. But my research in the Japanese television assembly plants in Mexico indicated that those factories had more inspectors than in the Japanese plants. The same was probably true in the U.S. transplants.

In contrast to U.S. managers, who in most cases remained in their offices, Japanese managers spent much time on the shop floor studying operations. U.S. workers interpreted this as a form of managerial surveillance. In Japan, this was considered only normal, and workers would have considered a manager's absence from the shop floor as negative.

Despite an apparently improved atmosphere, in 1979 the union struck for eight weeks over wages and other issues. Japanese managers, who expected a reciprocal relationship as part of their "family" ideology, were shocked. In 1985 the union struck again because of management's demands for medical insurance cuts, seniority system changes, and the right to shift workers from job to job. In other words, U.S. workers fought management's demands for control and flexibility comparable to what they enjoyed in Japan. The second strike was far more bitter and violent than the first. The union leadership felt that the "happy family" theme and emphasis on quality control was just a way to get improvement ideas from employees without providing greater compensation. Union leadership adopted the dominant position of U.S. unions in regard to worker involvement and quality control activities. The strike was settled, and management achieved most of its goals, but there was significant lingering animosity.

In contract talks in 1989, the union agreed to reduce the number of job classifications from eleven to five, in order to facilitate the movement of workers to different jobs (Abo et al., 1994, p. 207). The union had little choice but to acquiesce, because Sanyo made it clear that it was quite prepared to close the plant and move to Mexico. Moreover, in a return to traditional labor-management relations, Sanyo began using layoffs to adjust its staffing levels. In a sense, the plant's earlier conflictual relations with Warwick management were reproduced with the new Japanese management.

Sanyo attempted to transfer key elements of its Japanese management system to Arkansas but failed. The failure seems to have had two causes. The first was the cyclical nature of the U.S. market, both on an annual basis (because of the extraordinarily high Christmas demand), and in the long-term because of the sharp recessions that characterize the U.S. economy.

The second cause of Sanyo's failure was a breakdown in reciprocity. The counterpart of long-term employment was workers' commitment to job flexibility, to product and process improvement, and to involvement in off-line activities. Without these compensations, there was little economic rationale for the long-term employment commitment. However, in the conflictual atmosphere it was not surprising that at the Sanyo plant OJT was not emphasized, and promotion came through the traditional U.S. system of job posting (Abo, 1994). Sanyo did recruit some supervisors from the ranks of the unionized operators, but this was not a general policy. Moreover, the responsibility of the supervisors was largely confined to labor and personnel issues, and they had little involvement in technical activities, in contrast with the setup in Japan where supervisors had deep technical knowledge of the various jobs in their sections. Investment in worker training was limited, with little training in maintenance procedures. In 1982 the Sanyo plant successfully introduced "Quality Improvement Groups" aimed at lowering defects (Yonekura, 1985), but within a few years there were no QC circles or other small-group activities (Abo et al., 1994). There also were few other "Japanese-style" features, such as uniforms, morning exercises, or open-plan offices.

The Sanyo plant was a case study of the difficulties in transforming a badly managed operating brownfield facility into a high-performance factory. The different perspectives of Japanese and American quality control managers on the issue of improving quality best capture the difficulties. The Japanese QC manager stated, "Quality improvement can be achieved through cooperation among workers, lines, departments, and managers." His American assistant said, "The most important means [to achieve quality] is to introduce more advanced automation, digitalization, and consumer-oriented simple product design" (Yonekura, 1985, p. 4). In the Forrest City environment, it was difficult to evaluate which perspective was correct, but Sanyo gave up trying to transplant Japanese management to Arkansas. By 1997 total employment at the Sanyo factory had dropped to 400, which was quite close to the lower limit for an economically viable mass-production television assembly facility. Since the late 1980s Sanyo's additional consumer electronics investments in North America have gone to its plants in Tijuana, Mexico.

Matsushita's Motorola Factory

In 1974 Matsushita purchased Motorola's Quasar television division and quickly closed most of its factories. However, the firm continued to operate the Franklin Park, Illinois, assembly factory. Matsushita purchased the facility in 1974 and closed it in 1995. As with the other Motorola operations, Quasar was not unionized, but the factory management, organization, and operation were clearly Fordist. After acquiring the Quasar plant, the newly dispatched Japanese president said the plant's quality was unacceptable, but he maintained that before bringing in sophisticated equipment, "We're expecting employees to improve the quality, rather than sit and wait for the parent company to bring in the new machines. Eventually they'll come, but first Americans must show what they can do by their own efforts" (Kraar, 1975).

Matsushita revamped production and dramatically increased quality. Evidence from discussions with Matsushita television managers indicates that the introduction of superior equipment and the importation of higher quality parts from Japan were the most important factors in this improvement. For example, automatic insertion equipment was brought from Japan that allowed the factory to automatically insert 80 percent of the components on the PCB, and this equipment replaced the equivalent of 388 persons while improving quality significantly (Jameson 1978, p. 18). Initial press accounts described dramatic quality and productivity improvements as being attributed to superior management techniques. There was a report that, after Matsushita assumed management of Franklin Park plant, workers were allowed to stop the belt by pressing a button and to take the chassis off the line to complete their tasks (Hayes, 1981; Jameson, 1981), a practice not used in Japan.

However, as in the case of Sanyo, it was difficult to reorganize the plant—even though the Quasar plant was nonunionized. Abo (1994) found that:

> On-the-floor hourly jobs including maintenance have been differentiated into 100 different job categories, which are ranked across fourteen levels. Wages basically correspond to each respective job rank on a one-to-one basis. For operations, a fixed job-type system was adopted, in which a specific worker repeatedly performs a specific job. . . . In this plant, it is a fixed rule that an assembly worker only assembles, and an adjustment worker only adjusts. The promotion from one job rank to another in the production area is done through a system whereby those who have applied for a job posting are selected according to how well qualified they are by virtue of experience and outside professional training or education. For those with similar qualifications, seniority makes the difference. (Abo et al., 1994, p. 204)

Workers jealously guarded their jobs and were unwilling to transfer to new jobs. Matsushita also had little success in involving workers in quality control or kaizen programs (Abo et al., 1994). In contrast with Japan, where the quasi-supervisor and the group leader were actively involved in determining standard times for tasks and assigning jobs, in Chicago the industrial engineers undertook these tasks. Matsushita also did not transfer activities such as morning group meetings to the Motorola plant (Jameson, 1978, p. 18). In 1981 a newspaper report found that a form of QC circles was being used, but a later study found few SGAs (Abo et al., 1994).

Originally, the Motorola television production complex had 6,700 employees, but by 1990 this number had dropped to approximately 600, their work confined to assembly as other operations were closed. With the passage of the North American Free Trade Agreement (NAFTA) in 1995, Matsushita announced the closure of the Franklin Park factory and moved all television assembly operations to Tijuana, Mexico. Given the lack of flexibility and worker involvement, there was little economic justification for continuing the high-cost, relatively low-productivity operation.

The Greenfield Factories

The other Japanese television assembly factories were all established as greenfield factories. With the exception of those of Sony and, recently, Mitsubishi, all the factories were operated along American lines (Abo et al., 1994). There are, however, differences between the prototypical U.S. factory and these transplants. In all the Japanese transplants, former operators filled managerial and supervisorial positions—a typical promotion pattern in Japan. In all the factories, workers were charged with ensuring quality production and informing supervisors about quality problems. Suggestions were encouraged, though in most cases these programs did not generate a significant number of suggestions. There was one final difference between Japanese firms and the U.S.-based operations of non-Japanese television firms—some Japanese firms continued to assemble televisions in the United States. In contrast, after April 1998 there were no more non-Japanese television assembly plants in the United States.

Factories Y and Z

Factories Y and Z are in the Middle South and are examples of the adoption of the American pattern. They both opened in approximately 1980 (dates disguised) as "greenfield" factories. A large U.S. electrical workers union unionized both. Each has experienced only minor labor disturbances since its establishment. The union contracts each company signed were similar, but there were some differences.

At both factories, wages corresponded strictly to job ranks, maintenance worker positions were filled by hiring experienced workers, and production workers were not involved in maintenance (Abo et al., 1994, pp. 208–210). At Company Z there were seven separate labor grades, and within these grades there were various job classifications. In the entire factory there were eighteen separate job classifications. Factory Y has a job classification system typical of a U.S. unionized factory, with eight grades of workers and eight grades of skilled trades. Within these grades there are a number of job classifications, though the respondents would not specify them.

For both factories, there were tightly written contract rules regarding movement between job classifications, but temporary movement for clearly delineated emergencies was a possibility. Normal movement between these classifications came out of seniority-based job bidding and certification that the applicant met the minimum standard for the new job. Short of gross failure, only seniority bumping could move a person from his or her particular job. In other words, organized rotation for any purpose was impossible without the consent of every operator involved.

In both unionized factories, contract clauses prevented nonunion members from operating machines except in emergencies, to instruct workers, or to test repaired machines. Management did have the ability to move workers temporarily from one job to another in case of emergency. In other words, the union had agreed that, to keep the plant operating, union rules could be bent. These restrictions indicate that both factories had a fairly traditional type of job-control unionism, with only very delimited flexibility.

There was the usual clear separation between white- and blue-collar workers. However, there was another group, the technicians. At both factories a separate class of technicians did not belong to the union, in contrast with factories in Japan, where technicians were simply a higher grade of workers. In Factory Z, as in the other factories visited, the technicians were not in the operator pay category. To become a technician, it was necessary to have received a formal degree from an accredited institution such as a junior college or technical institute, although, in practice, some operators could learn a sufficient number of skills in the factory to be promoted to the technician category.

In all four U.S. factories studied in 1997, there was a separation between technical duties and supervisory duties in the factory hierarchy. Whereas in Japan work descriptions were drafted by the quasi-supervisor and supervisor, in the United States all of these activities were handled by the industrial engineering sections. U.S. supervisors were not expected to know each job in the group they supervised; in contrast, in Japan such knowledge was considered mandatory. A way of understanding this is that one important difference between Japan and the United States is not simply the separation between mental and manual labor but also a separation between job skills and knowledge and hierarchical control. In the Japanese transplants, this separation existed in the case of many supervisors.

When Factory Z was established, management accepted unionization and did not try to implement the Japanese management system. A manager at this factory was quoted as saying, "We try to keep things the way our American employees want. We have no uniform, no QC circle, and no flexible work arrangements. Like other American companies, we have a labor union and layoffs. We are profitable and have a good reputation for quality" (Sato, 1991, p. 9).

At Factory Z the Japanese managers told Sato (1991, p. 16), "High efficiency can be achieved without introducing flexible work arrangements and other shop floor practices common in Japan." Despite the inflexibilities introduced by unions, in 1997 Factory Z dramatically shortened production lines by eliminating excess length on the conveyor line, the "burn-in" for the CRTs, and automating adjustment for the CRT. I was unable to ascertain whether layoffs were used to eliminate excess workers. This reorganization and automation was part of an ongoing process of making television assembly less reliant on direct workers and more reliant on technicians.

In the 1990s one innovation to the traditional union-based system, the group leader, was introduced. Group leaders were bargaining-unit employees (all the factories were in right-to-work states, so not all bargaining unit members belonged to the union) who were appointed solely at the discretion of management to the group leader post. They were usually workers who knew the jobs and the equipment in the group. Their responsibilities encompassed what in Japan were the technical responsibilities of the group leader, such as assisting in model turnover, having responsibility for parts, reassigning workers, and regulating production flow. Importantly, the group leaders could also work on the line. But because they were bargaining-unit members they had no disciplinary authority over the group members.

The use of SGAs and QC circles was spotty. In 1990 Abo et al. (1990) found that Factory Y had QC circles for the purpose of "raising a sense of participation in plant management through communication between supervisors and workers." The Japanese manager they interviewed stated that the aim of the circles was to improve the work in terms of both product quality and productivity. The circles were voluntary, though the participation rate was 70 percent. However, from my interviews, I found that there was only limited voluntary participation in QC circles among the operators. The actual activity was limited to one hour a month after normal work hours. At one factory, management was also in the process of introducing a new channel of communication aimed at encouraging not only suggestions but more general feedback from operators.

Sato (1991) reported that she found a failing suggestion program. When I visited the factory in 1997, there was a relatively unused suggestion program. Similarly, the QC circle program barely operated, and a Japanese manager said that the union discouraged worker involvement. I was not able to verify this with any other managers.

These two companies had the largest workforces of the remaining television assembly transplants (the Sony San Diego workforce was larger, but it no longer assembles televisions). One factory recently integrated production even further by doing printed circuit board insertion at its factory—a surprising development, considering that all the other transplants imported completed boards from Southeast Asia or Mexico. These factories operated along the lines of the traditional U.S. unionized factories and were changing only gradually. However, both companies remain committed to producing in the United States and continue to invest in more automation.

Factory M

Factory M was established in approximately 1980 on the West Coast and was closed in the mid-1990s, when its production was moved to Mexico and to another factory in the United States. It was nonunionized, and the labor force was extremely diverse ethnically and linguistically—an attribute Japanese managers perceived as a cost and as an impediment to management.

The Japanese executive interviewed said that the factory was not organized in a Japanese style and the management had simply adopted U.S. customs. At Factory M the production hierarchy at the television assembly plant was operator, lead operator, supervisor, production supervisor, and production manager. Though the lead operators were promoted entirely from the operator group, only 70 percent of the supervisors had been operators. The production supervisors had been promoted from among the supervisors, and one assistant production manager had been promoted from among the supervisors. There was also a technician classification; some of the technicians were promoted from among the operators, and others were recruited externally. The company did not insist on hiring internally and often hired from the outside. Factory M did not guarantee employment security, but in 1991 it had not yet had a layoff. As buffer to prevent layoffs, about 20 percent of the work force was temporary.

Factory M also had a training program, but, according to the Japanese president, there was less training than in Japan. The firm would consider in-house training, but "as of today, very few people can be instructors." In Japan more training was conducted internally, with senior workers, super-visors, engineers, and managers serving as instructors. In the United States the training depended on outside resources, such as the local junior colleges. Rotation was used only in the picture adjustment area, because of the intense concentration required.

Factory M continued to produce large-screen televisions in California until it closed and moved its operations to the United States and to Mexico. For this company, the high costs of operations in California and the low quality of the labor force convinced the firm to leave.

The Sony Plant

The Sony San Diego plant was the oldest Japanese consumer electronics op-eration in the United States. In 1997 the plant was highly diversified and no longer assembled televisions, having transferred all television assembly to Mexico. The San Diego factory continued to produce television and computer CRTs, monitors, and various other products. In 1997 there were nearly 4,000 employees in the San Diego facility. The factory was not unionized; a union-ization campaign was defeated in 1985.

From its inception, the factory used an American management and labor relations style. This was sufficient for the first fifteen years, but due to com-petitive pressures, in 1988–1989 Sony management decided that the U.S. sys-tem it had adopted was not generating the efficiencies necessary to remain competitive. A major effort was launched to transform the factory to a more "Japanese-like" management system. Both managers and workers were told that, if productivity did not improve, the factory would be closed and relo-cated to Mexico (Sony Corporation, 1993). For U.S. workers and managers, this was a credible threat, because Sony had a successful Mexican factory only forty miles away. In the ensuing transformation of the factory, tech-niques such as flexible work teams, QC activities, "mutual checking of work," and open presentation of relevant information on productivity and defects were adopted. The factory's performance improved sufficiently to save it, though only a few years later all television assembly was switched to Mex-ico.

At Sony there were four ranks of workers and supervisors, including a lead person. Pay raises for operators were determined according to length of service, with a seven-year cap in the same ranking. This flexible system has some resemblance to a simplified Japanese pay system. Supervisors were pro-moted internally (Abo et al., 1994, p. 210). In a sense, Sony is the outlier among these companies, because it warned its employees and gave them a chance to transform the factory. As a result, though television assembly was moved to Mexico, the plant became sufficiently capable and dynamic to be able to receive new products such as the Sony Playstation and computer monitors from Japan and quickly ramp up production. The Sony plant had two important advantages that most of the other factories did not. The first was that capital-intensive CRT production was on the same site. The second was that Sony built a strong R&D and production engineering group on site, providing higher level capabilities. In effect, the San Diego plant moved from competency in production to competency in learning, thus allowing operations to add value.

General Comments

Though the television transplants differed in many ways, they all operated in a style far closer to that of U.S. factories than of Japanese factories. Even the companies, such as Sanyo, that consciously tried to introduce a Japanese-like system soon retreated and accepted the U.S. system. Given their superior quality control, automation, and engineering, the Japanese transplants were able to operate relatively successfully in the U.S. environment. A few, especially Sony, made significant profits from their U.S. operations. It is ironic that the three unionized transplants survived longer than almost all the nonunionized transplants, and no unionized transplant has been closed (there are now two nonunionized transplants still operating, Sony in Westmoreland, Pennsylvania, and Mitsubishi in Braselton, Georgia.).

Discussion

Key findings

The preceding section has examined several television assembly transplants. Although there are important lacunae in our understanding of the production and factory management systems in these plants, several patterns nevertheless emerge.

First, in general, the Japanese firms transferred their production equipment to the United States and, at least initially, imported many parts. The standardized worksheets in both the United States and Japan were quite similar. In general, the U.S. factories produced simpler televisions, but the factories in both countries worked to decrease changeover times. In Japan, responsibility for drawing up the standardized worksheets was given to the quasi-supervisor and to the group leader. In the United States the responsibility was placed in the industrial engineering section. Quality procedures in the U.S. and Japanese factories were similar, though in the Japanese factories there was mandatory worker involvement in more sophisticated off-line quality control and small-group activities. There was far greater worker and supervisor involvement in machine maintenance in Japan than in the United States, where these responsibilities were handled largely by skilled-trades persons and technicians.

Second, the factory organization and management systems differed markedly between the two countries. There were certain similarities; for example, the factory organization charts were quite similar with regard to how the different functions were classified, and a number of the transplants were unionized, though the U.S. industrial unions and the Japanese enterprise unions bargained for very different contracts. First and foremost, among the differences, the unionized transplants defended the clear distinction between labor and management. Japanese and U.S. supervisors differed markedly in terms of their technical capabilities, U.S. supervisors often were not highly capable technically, whereas Japanese supervisors had firm technical capabilities built through hands-on experience and off-the-job training. In the unionized transplants, supervisors were not allowed to actually work on the line, so they were often not fully capable of undertaking the jobs of those they managed.

In the unionized transplants there was little or no rotation. Moreover, the U.S. seniority system severely limited management's ability to redeploy workers. In all of the plants, the sheer number of job classifications had been lowered through time, but a comparatively large number of classifications still existed in the unionized transplants. Positions in the U.S. factories were filled on the basis of a qualifications test and then of seniority. In Japan there were active OJT and classroom training programs for workers at every level. In the U.S. technicians were a separate category that required formal qualifications received from nonfirm educational institutions, whereas in Japan workers who had technician-like functions were not treated differently from operators. In summary, little of the Japanese organization and management system was transplanted to the United States; rather these factories adopted prevailing U.S. patterns, whether unionized or nonunionized. Only in the past decade, under the pressure of competition from Mexican factories, did these factories, move to adopt a more Japanese-like production system.

Overall, the U.S. transplants (with certain exceptions) achieved relatively high efficiency, producing large numbers of standardized products, but there were limited improvements and only a slow growth in factory capabilities. The result was that a number of these factories were closed, and production was moved to Mexico.

The contrast with the auto industry is striking. In the auto transplants, as chapter 2 by Pil and MacDuffie shows, there has been extensive transfer of the practices that support dynamic learning capabilities, and the results have been correspondingly impressive. However, the U.S. television assembly transplants have diverged from the auto assembly transplants far more than their respective sister plants in Japan. Not only have they diverged in terms of management and production systems, but they have differed in the apparent eagerness or ability on the part of management to facilitate operator-and factory-based knowledge creation.

Causes of Limited Transfer

The technology of products and processes helps explain the difference between the relatively thorough transfer of Japanese management techniques to the auto assembly transplants and the relatively limited transfer to the television transplants. Simply put, television assembly is highly standardized and simplified. The transfer of Japanese management techniques may not have been considered necessary—quality has been built into the product and the equipment (Abo et al., 1990). The Japanese companies had little reason to transfer the Japanese system, because the skills of production workers would have limited impact on product quality and because cost-effective substitutes for Japanese approaches for ensuring high quality were available, such as increased inspection (Abo et al., 1994).

Indeed, comparing television to auto assembly, there were not nearly as many opportunities for worker input to create significant innovations, especially in cases where the production process consisted of long runs of highly standardized products. The auto production process was far more complicated, and the worker's tasks more physically complex; therefore, there was greater opportunity for worker improvement and greater importance to team coordination. The auto assembly plants had good reason to pursue a more active strategy of transfer—at least for those components of the Japanese management system focused on blue-collar commitment and involvement.

This technical explanation misses something important, however. Not only did the television transplants bypass the Japanese approaches that would have energized worker involvement, they did not implement the approaches that enabled their home-country plants to excel in engineering-driven innovation. Even if improvements in performance were relatively more engineering-driven than worker-driven in television assembly compared to auto assembly, this fact would not explain why the television transplants did not implement the approaches that enabled their home-country plants to perform so well.

Put in historical context, the relatively limited transfer of Japanese management style systems to the television assembly subsidiaries becomes easier to understand. These plants were built before Japanese managers were confident that their export successes could be attributed to the Japanese production and management system—as distinct from the weak yen or from less tangible factors like the Japanese work ethic—and before they had reason to believe that the critical parts of this Japanese system could indeed be transferred to a culture as foreign as that of the U.S. (Cutcher-Gershenfeld et al., 1994, found that a similar factor explained the limited use of Japanese approaches in the earliest auto parts transplants). On the U.S. side, U.S. unions were much stronger in the 1970s, and there was little sense of crisis in the unions to bring about the willingness to experiment with new approaches.

Moreover, the early television factories were "screwdriver" plants, simply assembling imported parts and subassemblies, so there was little need or opportunity for worker involvement. Once such a low-involvement system was established, it became a self-reinforcing structure that was difficult to change. Though the screwdriver role of the factories evolved over time, there was no urgency about overhauling the established systems (Sony represents an interesting exception.)

These technical and historical factors help us to understand the early patterns but do not fully explain why the newer plants did not attempt a more comprehensive implementation of the management systems found in their home-country plants. Two further hypotheses seem worth exploring. First, the transfer of a system that puts relatively greater weight on engineering-driven innovation and learning is perhaps, and paradoxically, more difficult than the transfer of a system that gives greater weight to worker-driven improvements. Even though the shift from Fordist shop floor relations to "self-managed teams" has not been easy for many U.S. workers, it was far easier than the transition to the more top-down management-led teams common in Japan (see Applebaum, 1992, on "lean" versus "team" work organizations. Other chapters in this volume—those by Adler; Brunner, Fruin, and Liker; Pil and MacDuffie; and Jerkins and Florida—have commented on the way in which auto transplants have implemented the "team concept" in a way rather different from its Japanese meaning). High-performing Japanese electronics plants needed extensive worker involvement, but the nature of that involvement was different from the self-management model. It was expressed in an ability to implement engineers' ideas effectively and flexibly and to give the engineers thoughtful feedback. It was an involvement that gave workers far less immediate autonomy than the self-managed model, an involvement that functions within a hierarchy of expertise. Transferring the shared understanding that underlay this organizational form was, understandably enough, a huge challenge.

The second hypothesis puts the focus on management strategy. If, indeed, innovation and improvements in television assembly were more engineering-driven than in auto assembly, perhaps it made strategic sense for the Japanese parent to centralize that innovation in Japanese mother plants. Mark Fruin (chapter 7) describes the distinctive capabilities of such mother plants and the difficulty of transferring the idiosyncratic, site-specific skills that are required. Strategically speaking, the U.S. television transplants were essentially "branch" plants. Even when they progressed beyond the screwdriver stage, they were not chartered to serve as autonomous businesses pursuing their own strategies. And the economics of television assembly meant that such branch plants could indeed be moved quickly and cheaply to areas of lower labor costs—rather than investing the management time and attention in building site-specific innovation capabilities.

Consequences of Limited Transfer

Our review of this combination of technical, historical, and strategic factors helps explain why the world-class dynamic learning capabilities of the Japanese electronics plants were not transferred to their U.S. transplants. In other words, producing large numbers of standardized products in television assembly environment was economically feasible, even though there were limited improvements and only a slow growth in factory capabilities. Given the relatively simple technologies in television assembly, the television transplants could compete on "static efficiency" terms (Klein, 1977), and thus these factories were slow-moving targets for similar factories in low-wage environments, which when first established were relatively unsophisticated but were rapidly learning.

Moreover, compared to auto assembly plants, electronics plants were smaller and less expensive to equip, and they relied on a much smaller supplier network, whose in-house design capabilities and geographic proximity were less critical. Television plants could be moved at relatively short notice. Management decisions had a short time horizon, and there was significantly less capital at risk. An investment in the United States—or Mexico—did not imply the same long-term commitment as did an investment in auto assembly.

On such terms, transplants in the United States could not compete for long against plants located in Mexico. Rather than attempt an overhaul of their U.S. plants in the 1990s, many, but not all, Japanese firms chose to close their U.S. assembly facilities and move to Mexico (five—Mitsubishi, Toshiba, Sharp, Sanyo, and Sony in Westmoreland, Pennsylvania—continued to have significant television assembly facilities in the United States).

It is true that even if the transplants managed to transplant the dynamic learning capabilities of their Japanese sister plants, the economics of television production might still have pushed production to Mexico. Indeed, production in Japan itself has been shifting off-shore to Southeast Asia. But failure to transplant dynamic learning capabilities meant that (a) the transfer to Mexico was urgent and the social dislocations thus much greater and (b) the plants and workforces left in the United States lacked the capabilities that would warrant assigning them new products whose economics could make U.S. production a viable proposition.

References

Abegglen, James, and George Stalk Jr. 1985. *Kaisha: The Japanese Corporation*. New York: Basic Books.

Abo, Tetsuo. 1992. "Toshiba's Overseas Production Activities: Seven Large Plants in the USA, Mexico, the UK, Germany, and France." Paper prepared for the Symposium of the Euro-Asia Management Studies Association, University of Bradford, Management Centre, Nov. 27–29.

Abo, Tetsuo. 1994. "Sanyo's Overseas Production Activities: Seven Large Plants in U.S., Mexico, U.K., Germany, Spain, and China." In Helmut Schutte, ed., *The Global Competitiveness of the Asian Firm*, pp. 179–202. New York: St. Martin's Press.

Abo, Tetsuo, ed. 1990. *Local Production of Japanese Automobile and Electronics Firms in the United States*. (Institute of Social Science, University of Tokyo Research Report No. 23, March).

Abo, Tetsuo, ed. 1994. *Hybrid Factories*. New York: Oxford University Press.

Adler, Paul. 1993. "Time-and-Motion Regained." *Harvard Business Review* Jan.–Feb.: 71(1): 97–109.

Adler, Paul. 1996. "Beyond Autonomy: The Socialization of Production? A Case of Teams at NUMMI." Draft chapter in J. Durand, J. Castillo, and P. Stewart, eds., *Teamwork in the Automotive Industry*. Oxford: Oxford University Press.

Applebaum, H. 1992. "Work and Its Future." *Futures* 4: 336–350.

Baranson, Jack. 1980. *Sources of Japan's International Competitiveness in the Consumer Electronics Industry*. Washington, DC: Developing World Industry & Technology.

Barley, Stephen. 1996. "Technicians in the Workplace—Ethnographic Evidence for Bringing Work into Organization Studies." *Administrative Science Quarterly* 41(3): 404–441.

Beazley, J. Ernest. 1988. "In Spite of Mystique, Japanese Plants in U.S. Find Problems Abound." *Wall Street Journal*, June 22: A1.

Beechler, Schon, and Sully Taylor. 1995. "The Transfer of Human Resource Management Systems Overseas." In Nigel Campbell and Fred Burton, eds., *Japanese Multinationals: Strategies and Management in the Global Kaisha*, pp. 157–185. London: Routledge.

Cole, Robert. 1989. *Strategies for Learning*. Berkeley: University of California Press.

Cutcher-Gershenfeld, Joel, et al. 1994. "Japanese Team-based Work Systems in North America: Explaining the Diversity." *California Management Review* 37(1): 42–64.

Delbridge, Rick. 1995. "Surviving JIT: Control and Resistance in a Japanese Transplant." *Journal of Management Studies* 32(6): 803–817.

Dertouzos, Michael, et al. 1989. *Made in America: Regaining the Productive Edge*. Cambridge, Mass.: MIT Press.

Dore, Ronald. 1973. *British Factory—Japanese Factory*. Berkeley: University of California Press.

Florida, Richard, and Martin Kenney. 1991. "Organizational Transplants: The Transfer of Japanese Industrial Organization to the U.S." *American Sociological Review* 56(3): 381–398.

Fruin, Mark. 1997. *Knowledge Works*. New York: Oxford University Press.

Grønning, Terje. 1992. "Human Value and 'Competitiveness': On the Social Organization of Production at Toyota Motor Corporation and New United Motor Manufacturing, Inc." Ph.D. diss., Ritsumeikan University, Kyoto, Japan.

Harvard Business School. 1981. "Sanyo Manufacturing Corporation—Forrest City, Arkansas." HBS Case No. 0-682-045.

Hayes, Thomas. 1981. "The Japanese Way at Quasar." *New York Times*, Oct. 16, D1, D9.

Hiramoto, Atsushi. 1995. "Overseas Japanese Plants under Global Strategies: TV Transplants in Asia." In S. Frenkel and J. Harrod, eds., *Industrialization and Labor Relations: Contemporary Research in Seven Countries*. Ithaca, N.Y.: ILR Press.

Hiramoto, Atsushi. 1994. *Nihon no terebi sangyo*. Tokyo: Minerva Shoten.

Jameson, Sam. 1978. "Japan Firm Puts Quasar into Focus." *Los Angeles Times*, Jan. 19, 1, 18.

Juran, J. M. 1967. "The QC Circle Phenomenon." *Industrial Quality Control* Jan.: 11(12): 329–336.

Kenney, Martin. 1997. "Strange Times: Knowledge Creation and Obsolescence in the Information Society." Unpublished paper.

Kenney, Martin, and Richard Florida. 1988. "Beyond Mass Production: Production and the Labor Process in Japan." *Politics and Society* 16(1): 121–158.

Kenney, Martin, and Richard Florida. 1993. *Beyond Mass Production: The Japanese System and Its Transfer to the U.S.* Oxford University Press, 1993.

Kenney, Martin, and Richard Florida. 1994. "Japanese Maquiladoras: Production Organization and Global Commodity Chains." *World Development* 22(1): 27–44.

Kenney, Martin, W. Richard Goe, Oscar Contreras, Jairo Romero, and Mauricio Bustos. 1997. "Learning Factories?: An Examination of Shopfloor Workers in the Japanese Electronics Maquiladoras." *Work and Occupations*

Khurana, Anil. 1994. "Quality in the Global Color Picture Tube Industry: Managing Complex Production Processes." Ph.D. diss., University of Michigan, Ann Arbor.

Klein, Burton H. 1977. *Dynamic Economics*. Cambridge, Mass.: Harvard University Press.

Koike, Kazuo. 1988. *Understanding Industrial Relations in Modern Japan*. New York: St. Martin's Press.

Kotha, Suresh, and Roger Dunbar. 1995. *Sanyo Manufacturing Corporation—1977–1990*. Leonard N. Stern School of Business, New York University case study.

Kraar, Louis. 1975. "The Japanese Are Coming—With Their Own Style of Management." *Fortune* March: 116–121, 160–164.

MIT Commission on Industrial Productivity. 1988. *The Decline of U.S. Consumer Electronics Manufacturing: History, Hypotheses, and Remedies*. Cambridge, Mass.: MIT Press.

Nagano et al. 1996. *Work Organization in Japan and Germany: A Research Report on VCR Production (2)*. Miscellanea, no. 13. Tokyo: Philipp-Franz-von-Siebold-Stiftung, Deutsches Institut für Japanstudien.

Nakamura, Keisuke, Helmut Demes, and Hitoshi Nagano. 1994. "Work Organization in Japan and Germany: A Research Report on VCR Production (1)." *Miscellanea*, no. 6. Tokyo: Philipp Franz von Siebold Stiftung, Deutsches Institut für Japanstudien.

Nakane, Chie. 1970. *Japanese Society*. Berkeley: University of California Press. Noble, David. 1977. *America by Design*. New York: Oxford University Press.

Nomura, Masami. 1992a. "Japanese Personnel Management Transferred." In S. Tokunaga, N. Altmann, and H. Demes, ed., *Internationalization and Changing Corporate Strategies*, pp. 117–132 Munich: Iudicum Verlag.

Nomura, Masami. 1992b. "Assembly Automation and Division of Labor in Japan." In P. Brodner and W. Karwowski, eds. *Ergonomics of Hybrid Automated Systems III*, pp. 21–28. New York: Elsevier.

Nonaka, Ikujiro, and Hirotaka Takeuchi. 1995. *The Knowledge-Creating Company*. New York: Oxford University Press.

Office of Technology Assessment. 1983. *International Competitiveness in Electronics* Washington, DC: Author.

Ogasawara, Koichi. 1992. "Japanese Personnel Appraisal: Individualized Race for Power and Imposed Involvement." Paper presented at the conference on "Japanese Management Styles: An International Comparative Perspective," Cardiff Business School, Wales, Sept. 28–29.

Ohgai, Takeyoshi. 1996. Personal communications. Various dates.

Ohgai, Takeyoshi. 1997. "Hollowing out and the Division of Labor with

Asia: The Japanese Television and VCR Industry." *Ryukoku Daigaku Keieigaku-ronshu* 36(4): 1–11.

Oliver, Nick, and Barry Wilkinson. 1988. *The Japanization of British Industry*. Oxford: Basil Blackwell.

Porter, Michael. 1983. *Cases in Competitive Strategy*. New York: Free Press.

Porter, Michael, ed. 1986. *Competition in Global Industries*. Cambridge, Mass.: Harvard Business School Press.

Reid, T. R. 1977. "Osaka-Arkansas Success." *Washington Post*, Sept. 2, A1, A12.

Sato, Akemi. 1991. "Business as Usual: Management Practices of Japanese Consumer Electronics Companies in the United States." Program on U.S.-Japan Relations, Harvard University Occasional Paper 91–10.

Sony Corporation. 1993. Personal interview, Sony manager, Tokyo, Japan, Dec. 12.

Takashi, Matsuo, and Takahiro Fujimoto. 1996. "Dynamic Capability of Integrating Divergence: Reorganizing the Process of Final Assembly at Toyota." Paper presented at the International conference "New Imperatives for Managing in Revolutionary Change," IBM Amagi Homestead, Aug. 25–27.

Taylor, Bill, Tony Elger, and Peter Fairbrother. 1994. "Transplants and Emulators: The Fate of the Japanese Model in British Electronics." In Tony Elger and Chris Smith, eds., pp. 196–228. *Global Japanization*. London: Routledge.

Trevor, Malcolm. 1988. *Toshiba's New British Company*. London: Policy Studies Institute.

Womack, John, Daniel Jones, and Daniel Roos. 1990. *The Machine That Changed the World*. New York: Rawson Associates Macmillan.

Yoffie, David. 1984. *Strategic Management in Information Technology*. Englewood Cliffs, N.J.: Prentice Hall.

Yonekura, Seiichiro. 1985. "Sanyo Manufacturing Corp. (B)." Harvard Business School Case Study. Unpublished paper.

Yoshino, M. 1976. *Japan's Multinational Enterprises*. Cambridge, Mass.: Harvard University Press.

9

Using Expatriate Supervisors to Promote Cross-Border Management Practice Transfer

The Experience of a Japanese Electronics Company

Mark F. Peterson

T. K. Peng

Peter B. Smith

The Japanese electronics companies that opened production facilities in the United States during the 1980s faced the same kinds of intercultural challenges in managing a foreign workforce that are common to all multinational corporations (MNCs). As several chapters in the present volume indicate, many MNCs have found these intercultural challenges to be an integral part of transferring advanced manufacturing practices. For example, Nakamura, Sakakibara, and Schroeder (chapter 11, this volume) effectively argue that the fluidity of the U.S. labor market may jeopardize the returns on investment in human capital in the United States that Japanese companies have come to expect at home. We describe here the complementary risks of investing in expatriate supervisors. In the present chapter, we illustrate these risks by analyzing the role that expatriate supervisors played in one such Japanese company.

American managers are accustomed to giving strategic priority to financial matters and operational priority to engineering problems of physical technology. The importance of managing the social side of the foreign direct investment (FDI) equation is easy to underestimate. Of course, we recognize that production technology is partially embodied in "tools"—physical equipment and facilities—developed by engineers. For example, in process production organizations like oil refineries, success of transfer depends mainly on the quality of the physical plant. When tools largely determine production technology effectiveness, transfer can be managed by carefully engineering tools and equipment in the home country.

However, to the extent that production technology is affected by human capabilities and social relationships that cannot be embodied in tools, the transfer process will have social uncertainties of complexity and interdependence (Boyacigiller, 1990). For example, as Kenney (chapter 8, this volume) describes in his discussion of television assembly, a great deal of an FDI's success can depend on how operators use the physical equipment. Throughout the electronics industry, if operators evade procedures intended to reduce dust or static electricity, for example, defect rates can become high. In the electronics industry plant described here, employees could step around a shallow water-filled tray designed to remove dust from their shoes rather than walk through it. To the extent that a production process depends on effectively using tools rather than on the tools themselves, transferring and controlling technology is fragile. That is the case in the FDI to be described here.

Expatriate Supervisors as Part of Startup and Ongoing Technology Transfer

Multinational corporations that are transferring fragile technologies sometimes choose to assign expatriates to extended overseas duty. They do so to facilitate initial technology transfer and to promote communication from the home office when production innovations and adjustments subsequently become necessary (Baliga and Jaeger, 1984). How extensively expatriates should be used is a point of controversy both between MNCs and host governments and within multinationals themselves (Kobrin, 1978). This controversy juxtaposes a host government's typical priority for local employment against a multinational's typical priority for promoting effective FDI performance. These matters of international policy are outside the scope of the present discussion. However, the controversy also includes matters of what actually happens when expatriates are used at lower supervisory levels. Both host governments and multinationals share an interest in knowing if transferring lower level expatriates is really necessary and effective and what issues arise when they are used. It is this question to which we speak here.

Implicit in a multinational's choice to incur the expense of using expatriates at low supervisory levels is that (1) technical information about equipment use is better transferred through supervisors than through such alternative mechanisms as formal procedures and training, (2) something about the home country's or home organization's informal norms and culture for managing production is critical, and (3) expatriates will be better able than will host country supervisors to implement the desired corporate culture or management approach. In the Japanese case, this desired culture may include scrupulous attention to quality and the many other distinctive characteristics supporting the advanced manufacturing practices described in various chapters of this volume. An MNC's judgment that it should use expatriate supervisors ordinarily recognizes a tradeoff. Relying on expatriates for ease in communicating and identifying with corporate management comes at the potential cost of difficulty in communicating and identifying with subordinate employees.

Figure 9.1 identifies three "practical challenges" to expatriate supervisors that affect whether they will genuinely prove helpful in transferring a production system. These are challenges of communication, influence, and circumvention. A supervisor's communication challenge is to act so that subordinates will accurately interpret the supervisor's intentions. Supervisors need to be concerned about whether subordinates will interpret as intended the objective actions they take as reflecting such elements of leadership style as support, concern for effective performance, and assistance in learning to do good work. The influence limitation is the constraint of cultural norms (e.g., power distance; Hofstede, 1980) that affect the legitimacy of a supervisor's influence attempts. Supervisors may be expected to play a larger role relative to, say, written procedures, group decisions, or personal discretion in some countries than in others. The circumvention challenge is a supervisor's need to effectively complement (or compete with) other sources—colleagues, norms, formal rules—on which subordinates can draw to govern and legitimate their actions and attitudes (Peterson, Smith, Bond, and Misumi, 1990). As we develop later, aspects of leadership style such as pressure to perform well can have different consequences depending on various aspects of the work situation, such as the extent to which work requirements are new or changing. In addition to these practical challenges, Figure 9.1 identifies a symbolic challenge. This is the challenge expatriate supervisors face in coming to grips with aspects of their subordinates' interpretation and re-

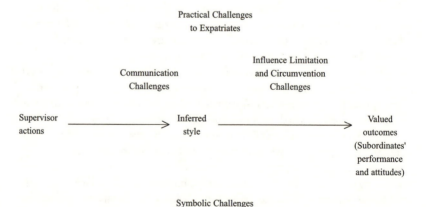

Figure 9.1 Categories of relationships and contingencies in intercultural leadership research.

sponse to their actions that are solely due to the subordinates's stereotypes about the supervisor's nationality.

The Site and Our Role

At the time we became involved in 1985, the organization we studied was struggling to face these challenges in its first U.S. production site. The company is an established, highly regarded Japanese organization with a significant global position in its product domain. In contrast to broader-scope companies like Matsushita or Sony, the company's product strategy was relatively focused. It had operated sales divisions in the United States for more than a decade, and its first production site, the one with which we became involved, had been open about three years. This greenfield U.S. operation included final assembly, packaging, inspection, and shipping. Components were manufactured at a facility in Japan and shipped to the United States. The Japanese production facility also did the final assembly and shipping for domestic sales. The U.S. facility was designed to replicate many of the procedures of its Japanese parent plant, with the exception that some of the more advanced technology of the Japanese facility—such as warehousing using robotics—was not transferred. At the time we became involved, the production system had been set up and the process had begun to replace at least some and possibly all of the Japanese supervisors with Americans. The supervisors' role in communicating the technical aspects of the production equipment had been largely completed by this time, so, in our view, the value of their continued presence rested increasingly on grounds of the role they might play in transferring the softer, social aspects of operations.

Structurally, the U.S. facility was headed by an experienced, expatriate Japanese manager. Reporting to him was a team of Japanese managers responsible for each of the technical functions of the plant (e.g., various engineering specialties, maintenance, production) and an American head of human resources. The human resources manager was then only beginning to learn Japanese. The meetings attended by the first author of this chapter were conducted in Japanese, with specific questions directed to him in English when his input was required. Both the Japanese expatriate and U.S. supervisors reported to one or another of the Japanese managers. The supervisors, in turn, directly supervised the workforce, including several production and maintenance groups.

The company had a long relationship with a Japanese leadership researcher and facilitator, Jyuji Misumi, then of Osaka University. Misumi had been frequently retained as a consultant and trainer and generally had a very close relationship with the company. He had developed a variety of training programs at the company's facilities in Japan (Misumi, 1985; Peterson, 1988). The plant manager of the U.S. site had been one of Misumi's students. Our invitation to work with the company came through the relationship between Misumi and this plant manager. As MacDuffie and Helper (chapter

5, this volume) note, a typical aspect of Japanese FDI is for an MNC not only to move the facilities it owns from home but also to recreate its home relationships with suppliers and customers. We were, in effect, acting as part of the process by which the company recreated the support for its management training. Our relationship with Misumi paralleled the American workforce's relationship with the company.

Our role was to administer and compile employee surveys to help the company adjust its supervisory practices and train its supervisors, as well as to provide feedback about other work attitudes (e.g., pay attitudes, trust in the organization). We designed and administered the surveys, drawing on both Japanese and U.S. sources of questions, then provided statistical information in two forms. One was plant-wide averages provided to the human resources manager and plant management group. The other was averages for each supervisor of the responses by subordinates in the supervisor's unit. We provided the unit-level averages directly and confidentially to each supervisor. The unit-level information was not provided to the plant management. Our involvement ended at the point of providing the statistical information. We understand that the human resources manager then distributed a letter-length summary of findings to the workforce, engaged in training, and otherwise facilitated use of the information in a manner consistent with the plant manager's preferences.

Performance-Maintenance Leadership Theory and Training

The basic thrust of the supervisory training that the company had been doing with Misumi resembles training often done throughout the world, but with some unique emphases. The training is based on the observation that leaders need to help maintain constructive work group processes and member attitudes and that they also need to see that the group contributes to other groups and to organization performance as a whole. One somewhat unique emphasis on this general theme for training that distinguishes it from some of the popular U.S. leadership training programs is that it is not the leader's attitudes or personality that are central or the leader's behavior in itself that is critical. The goal of training is only indirectly to change supervisor attitudes or to teach supervisors to carry out a specified set of actions. Instead, supervisors are trained to become aware of the way their attitudes and actions are being interpreted by subordinates. The emphasis in training, then, is on providing survey feedback, coaching supervisors to consider why their actions are being interpreted as they are, and encouraging supervisors to consider how to better communicate their interest in maintaining effective group process and promoting effective group performance. Within the larger scheme of social science, the training is rooted in the gestalt psychology/Lewinian field theory tradition (Misumi, 1985; Misumi & Peterson, 1985; Peterson, 1988).

In his own terms, Misumi's leadership research and training has centered on various specific aspects of leadership that fall broadly within the "Performance" (P) and "Maintenance" (M) group functions (Misumi, 1985; Misumi and Peterson, 1985). The P function includes various forms of leadership that followers experience as being directed toward reaching group goals. Aspects of leadership experienced as preserving group social stability constitute M function leadership.

For laboratory research purposes, researchers have represented the P and M functions by instructing leaders to carry out specified activities that followers are very likely to experience as contributing to the Performance and Maintenance functions (Misumi, 1985). For purposes of working with organizations, the Performance and Maintenance functions are included as part of questionnaire surveys. There is no single "PM survey" as such. Instead, different surveys are constructed to accommodate the specific kinds of leadership situations found not only at various hierarchical levels in various kinds of work organizations (e.g., manufacturing, coal mining, government) but also in other sorts of social situations like student clubs, elementary school classes, and political parties (Misumi, 1985; Misumi and Peterson, 1985). Depending on the specific setting (e.g., industrial, governmental, educational, political), anywhere from two to six or occasionally more separate factors have been found in Japan that represent different aspects of these two basic functions.

Some themes appear in this research and training that are also found throughout the present volume's discussion of Japanese human resources practice. One is that a supervisor's contribution to subordinate performance typically includes two main elements. First, it requires demonstrating technical competence and guiding subordinates in the way to do their work effectively. This contribution is reflected in the "planning-P" measure that is noted later. Second, it requires managing a complex dynamic between communicating external pressure and urgency, on the one hand, and adapting to the personal needs of the individual, on the other. This dynamic is illustrated in Figure 9.2. This dynamic is reflected in the "pressure" measure and its relationship to the "maintenance" measure.

Our experience when explaining the PM leadership approach in the United States and Europe suggests that leaders can combine pressure to work hard with personal support is foreign and contradictory even to most scholars. These same audiences find it immediately plausible that providing subordinates with instructions about how to do their work or technical assistance to do it better can be combined with support. Combining pressure and support seems somehow more difficult.

Figure 9.2 suggests that, when subordinates experience pressure from a leader to work very hard and very carefully, their interpretation and response to that pressure depends on their beliefs about the reason and the ultimate source of the pressure. If they believe that pressure originates in the self-interest of an elite group of power holders—the corporation, the supervisor,

Attributed Source of Pressure	Pressure from Leader	Response by Followers
PRINCIPAL'S SELF-INTEREST:		
Shareholder/senior management greed	High pressure implies low maintenance	Resentment, cohesive resistance, social loafing
Boss's personality		
Boss's personal situation		
COLLECTIVE (PRINCIPAL/AGENT) INTEREST:		
Long-term competition	High pressure implies high maintenance	Cooperation, cohesive performance, social facilitation
Short-term crisis		

Cultural Contingencies Affecting Interpretations:

Power distance

Collectivism

Recent historical situation

Figure 9.2 The sources, meaning, and implications of pressure.

shareholders—they will interpret pressure communicated by the leader as lack of concern for the well-being of the followers. The response is likely to have all the trappings of alienation—resentment, cohesive resistance, taking advantage of any individual foolish enough to cooperate by working hard for the authorities, shirking (Hill, 1995), and social loafing (Earley, 1989).

Alternatively, if pressure is viewed as originating in the shared interest of an in-group of which the subordinates, supervisor, and company are a part, then the pressure communicated by a superior may be viewed quite differently. Under such circumstances, followers will interpret the communication of pressure as reflecting the leader's concern for the well-being of the entire collectivity. Then, pressure can promote cooperation, high cohesion combined with high performance norms, and a propensity toward encouraging one another to work hard (social facilitation). Nowhere does Misumi spell out this line of argument about the varying effects of pressure, but some such dynamic implicit in his line of reasoning and results and in much of his laboratory research (Misumi, 1985).

Misumi's (1985) Japanese research indicates that supervisors do in fact vary in whether or not the pressure they communicate is viewed as reflecting a concern for collective well-being. This contrasts with U.S. leadership style research, which has long stumbled over the problem that pressure tends to have a high negative correlation with considerateness (Schriesheim and Stogdill, 1975). In other words, subordinates in Japan appear to readily identify circumstances where a supervisor's pressure is appropriate given the group's and the organization's situation and to respond cooperatively when that occurs. American subordinates tend not to make this distinction. In the typical U.S. view, taking care of external pressures is the job of management. If pressure is placed on the nonmanagerial workforce, then management is either inept or inconsiderate. Either way, our sense is that pressure communicated by supervisors in the United States typically tends to be viewed as inappropriate, illegitimate, and inherently at odds with personal or collective maintenance.

The idea that pressure from a leader is more likely to be viewed as supportive and legitimate in Japan than in the United States finds support in several sources. There is a conceptual basis for expecting that people coming from different cultural backgrounds may be predisposed to make different attributions about the reasons for their supervisor's actions (Maznevski and Peterson, 1997; Shaw, 1990). From a cultural view of psychology, Americans, as relatively individualistic (Hofstede, 1980), find it quite normal to radically separate what is good for themselves as individuals from what is good for any in-group of which they are part (Markus and Kitayama, 1991). Japanese, being more collective, do not separate their self-image from their group image quite so radically. From the perspective of agency and transaction cost theory, for various reasons rooted in the history of technological development of the two countries (Dore, 1973), there is a greater propensity in Japan than in the United States to ground transactions within a hierarchy in trust rather than in separate exchanges subject to risks of acting with guile (Hill, 1990). Hence, the openness to believe that pressure from a supervisor comes from collective rather than individual motives may be greater in Japan than in the United States. From an institutional perspective on group dynamics, groups in individualistic societies are more prone to engage in social loafing by taking advantage of a highly motivated individual than are groups in collective societies (Earley, 1989).

Adapting the Japanese Questionnaires

Items asking about a supervisor's leadership were translated from a Japanese industrial version of the PM questionnaire (Misumi and Peterson, 1985) and piloted in other organizations (Peterson, Maiya, and Herreid, 1994). As did Misumi, we viewed translating an originally Japanese questionnaire into English as less than optimal, even though this same questionnaire had been used extensively with the company's facility in Japan. It would have been preferable and more consistent with the usual practice in PM field research to first collect brief anecdotes and accounts of leadership in the U.S. facility, construct items from those accounts, and then derive a new survey, perhaps including both these new items and the existing, translated items. However, resource constraints made such a new survey development process infeasible at the time of our project. Instead, our role in transferring the supervisor training approach used by the company in Japan was restricted to working with a translation of the Japanese form.

For an approach to training like this one, the question of how survey measures administered to subordinates are linked to subordinates' attitudes and performance is quite critical. These relationships were well established and quite stable in research done in Japan, both within this company and with many others. The question of whether American employees would react similarly to supervisors within a Japanese-owned plant was not at all certain. Our assessment was being done during the era of the movie "Gung Ho" and of great public concern in the United States about what was feared to be excessive control by Japanese corporations.

What we have done is to assess the relationship between the supervisors' leadership, as viewed by their subordinates, and various sorts of performance-related attitudes and behaviors. This assessment was done for the set of supervisors as a whole, and also with an eye to differences between employee reactions to Japanese expatriates as compared to America supervisors. One supervisory function is to promote effective performance, so measures of employee performance were included as criteria. In particular, the plant was struggling to get employees to attend work on time and to conform to quality requirements such as those to minimize dust. Adler (chapter 3, this volume) notes that attendance was the most serious discipline problem for Toyota's and NUMMI's U.S. operations, and the situation was basically the same in the present site. As is more typical for a U.S. than for a Japanese workforce, many employees were in dual-career situations and raising children. Both the formal performance evaluation system and the leadership by supervisors were needed to motivate attendance in competition with other pressing employee needs and nonwork roles.

Another key supervisory role in many FDIs, and certainly in this one, is to promote confidence and trust in management's intentions. Consequently, the attitude criteria considered here include whether the organization can be trusted and whether it treats employees fairly. Of particular concern in this site was the potential for layoffs. There were, in fact, some workforce reductions between the two points of our assessment, and some uncertainty about both future reductions and future expansions (the latter actually occurred). As a result, satisfaction with job security is included as a particularly salient aspect of trust in the employer. Our assessment also considered whether subordinates working under an expatriate supervisor report relying more or less on their supervisor than do those working under a domestic supervisor. In particular, do U.S. workers find ways to work around Japanese supervisors?

Supervisor Nationality and the Implications of Leadership Style

Given the long history of domestic leadership research, one would hope to find good precedent to anticipate what effects the company could expect from supervisory leadership. However, studies of intercultural relations between people at different hierarchical levels are exceedingly rare. Brannen (1991, 1994) has analyzed some such dynamics over a five-year period in a Japanese takeover of a U.S. production facility. Her analysis supports the basic premise of the present study by concluding that there is a great deal more to transferring a production technology than transferring physical equipment (see also Brannen, Liker, and Fruin, chapter 4, this volume). She found that employees, particularly middle managers, in the facility experiencing the takeover she studied had the potential to become alienated. Various practices, such as sending U.S. employees to Japan and showing support for established traditions of the takeover target (e.g., holiday events), seemed to reduce intercultural tensions and misunderstandings. However, her study was actually done several years after our project. Her very careful literature search and our own indicates little other precedent for our sort of analysis in intercultural leadership studies.

Social Limitations on Hierarchical Influence

The lack of literature that provides a close counterpart to the situation faced in the company we studied drives us to draw preliminary inferences from more basic research about leadership in Japan and the United States and to speculate about how this literature applies to an intercultural supervisory situation. Among the relevant basic literatures are comparative analyses of U.S. and Japanese leadership, studies of communication, and leadership style contingency research.

Comparative leadership studies give reason to doubt whether *any* supervisors are able to exert as much influence on American subordinates as Japanese supervisors are accustomed to exercising in Japan. One line of research shows strong, continuing effects of subordinates' relationship with a first supervisor on subsequent promotion rates in a large Japanese retail chain (Wakabayashi & Graen, 1984). Misumi's extensive series of laboratory and field studies shows that the effects of supervisory leadership in Japan are consistently strong, although the specific kinds of effects are moderated by contingencies such as follower anxiety and task characteristics (Misumi & Peterson, 1985; Misumi & Seki, 1971; Peterson, 1988). In both research programs, the correlates and effects of supervisory leadership in Japan appear to be stronger and more consistent than they are found to be in Western countries (Smith & Peterson, 1988). Although his level of analysis is really country (or subsidiary) rather than individual, Hofstede's (1980) comparative study of work cultures in fifty countries indicates greater individualism in the United States than in Japan. This difference in individualism might encourage Americans to look more toward their personal experience and less toward their supervisor than Japanese expatriates would expect.

Communication Limitations

Not only may Japanese expatriates find that they have less influence over U.S. subordinates than they did over their subordinates at home, as Figure 9.1 notes; they may even have less influence than do their American counterparts. Language provides a guide to social reality and a means of communication. As one might expect, numerous studies indicate that communication is an essential element in leader-subordinate relationships. Mintzberg (1973) contended that senior managers spend as much as 50 percent of their work time interacting with subordinates. Easy and ready communication contributes to the ability of leaders and subordinates to interact effectively (Bass, 1981). The theoretical underpinnings of most supervisory leadership theories rest on verbal communication processes. For example, path-goal leadership theory argues that a leader influences subordinates' perceptions of work goals and personal goals by articulating the linkages or "paths" that connect these two sets of goals (House & Dessler, 1974). Cognitive and role theory perspectives (e.g., Pfeffer, 1981; Pondy, 1978; Smith & Peterson, 1988) treat organizations as systems of shared meanings within which formal leaders must communicate to intervene in ongoing processes. Both transactional and transformational leadership processes rest upon communication (Bass, 1985).

Since culturally sensitive use of language is critical to leadership, expatriate managers to whom U.S. English with its many American idioms is a second language may be at a disadvantage. Cultural similarities and differences are key factors in the communication process (Ronen, 1986). Language can be an important source of noise in intercultural communication (Samovar et al., 1981). Consequently, faced with difficulties in understanding their boss, American employees working under Japanese supervisors may use alternative sources to figure out what to do.

Supervisor Nationality and Alternative Sources of Meaning

A domestic leadership literature indicates that there are circumstances under which shop floor employees get their main work direction from other sources than from their supervisor (e.g., Howell, Dorfman, & Kerr, 1986). Peterson, Smith, Bond, and Misumi (1990) identify five sources of meaning that organization members can use to make sense of and to respond appropriately to work demands: the company's manuals on procedures and policies, unwritten but accepted policy, advice from a superior, advice from other experienced coworkers, and one's own previous experience and training. The U.S. data for the Peterson et al. (1990) study came from the same site being analyzed in the present chapter. The results indicated that people at this site report relying more on supervisors compared to the other sources of meaning studied than is reported by respondents at a similar level in electronics manufacturing plants in Japan. The differences between the Japanese data and the U.S. data from this site raised the question of whether there would be differences even within this site in sources relied upon between people working for Japanese supervisors and those working for U.S. supervisors.

Implications of the Three Basic Literatures

The literatures about social limitations and communication limitations so far described suggest that Japanese supervisors will face various struggles as they strive to effectively promote management practice transfer, while the event management study suggests that it will be important for them to work to successfully handle this struggle. This struggle is likely to increase at a stage like that in the site we studied, when the supervisors' role is increasingly to transfer the softer aspects of company culture rather than technical production information. Expatriates may find that the impact of their leadership differs markedly from what they were accustomed to in Japan. Kenney (chapter 7, this volume) describes the sense of power a Japanese manager can feel in the United States because he can try to initiate direct punitive action on a subordinate, and he contrasts this to the feeling of powerlessness experienced in Japan. However, very rarely does any supervisor in the United States have the power to make his or her subordinates voluntarily go out together for drinks most evenings instead of going home to the family. And, although the management system can terminate employment in the United States, the constraints on an individual supervisor who tries to do so are quite substantial. It is also uncertain whether Japanese corporate control will be able to provide Japanese supervisors with sufficient leadership influence to overcome their communication limitations.

Hence, the decision by an MNC to extend the use of expatriate supervisors beyond the immediate period needed for technical information transfer is ill-advised, unless unusual effort is put into anticipating and preparing supervisors for the situation in the United States and into monitoring their progress. Our involvement in the company we are describing here, then, is part of that sort of "unusual effort" that the company recognized would be necessary. Its process of increasing the proportion of U.S. supervisors to Japanese supervisors during this period also reflects its apparent sense that a new phase in managing the U.S. facility was approaching.

The Meaning of Leadership Style Measures

We were invited into the site to do a questionnaire survey project about leadership. The first author was invited to spend a day at the U.S. plant and a day at the sister plant in Japan. We also had opportunities to ask for limited follow-up information, Part of that information that a small number of employees provided in follow-up interviews is provided in the discussion section.

We have done several survey projects in Japan with Japanese organizations, including other electronics companies (Smith et al., 1989) and local governments (Peterson, Elliott, Bliese & Radford, 1996), we have closely observed other colleagues doing similar projects, and we have presented to and watched others present survey results to large audiences of Japanese managers. Our own experience and that of others (Lincoln & Kalleberg, 1990, pp. 43–44) in doing attitude surveys with Japanese organizations is different from what we find in the United States. In the United States, we ordinarily find surveys to be a technology used in selected human resources departments and begrudgingly accepted by other parties (e.g., production managers). We have found American managers' patience with means, correlations, and standard deviations applied to social indicators to be limited at best. Although we have experienced variability in reception to surveys in Japan, presentations of survey results to managers seem better attended to by a broader manager audience than we find in the United States. This appears to be particularly the case for the set of several dozen major organizations with which Misumi has worked since the 1950s, especially in the Osaka and the Fukuoka areas. For example, one striking experience occurred in a project being conducted at about the same time as this one when the TV crew for a local news channel in Fukuoka videotaped a colleague's presentation of means comparing work attitudes in Japan with those other countries. In interviews the media conducted with other presenters, it was clear that social science was a media event. In general, our sense is that the willingness of Japanese organizations to use quantitative social science statistics *can*, in some organizations, parallel the willingness to use other quantitative devices for problem solving. That was certainly the case for the MNC with which we were working.

The history of leadership style survey research is long and checkered (Smith & Peterson, 1988). It goes back to the development of the familiar "Likert scale" items, with five or seven response alternatives anchored by adjectives like "agree" and "disagree." In fact, Misumi had developed a close personal and professional relationship with the Likert who invented this sort of survey item and had also translated Likert's leadership and management books into Japanese during the 1960s. Rather than rely heavily on translations of Likert's questionnaire items, however, Misumi worked inductively from interviews with organization members in Japan to develop his own surveys.

Research Questions and Hypotheses

The problems the company faced were to assess the value of continuing to use expatriate supervisors and to evaluate the possible responses to the issues that had arisen in using them. Our involvement provided quite an unusual opportunity to look into this problem by comparing Japanese supervisors of U.S. employees with American supervisors of U.S. employees from the same community doing similar work in the same Japanese-owned plant. Our interest in expatriate supervisors, then, directs our attention to ways in which employees respond differently to Japanese supervisors' leadership than to American supervisors' leadership. Other studies using similar leadership measures deal with overall relationships between these measures and criteria, and with whether and how these measures interact in predicting various criteria (Peterson, Maiya, & Herreid, 1993; Peterson, Smith, & Tayeb, 1993; Smith, Misumi, Peterson, & Bond, 1992; Smith, Misumi, Tayeb, Peterson, & Bond, 1989).

Hypotheses can be tested on the basis of cross-sectional analyses at two times and on longitudinal analyses. Supervisor nationality is a contingency that can affect (1) the relationship of inferred leadership style to performance and attitudinal criteria and (2) employees' reports of their reliance on their supervisor. A basic hypothesis that precedes any comparisons of leadership by Japanese and U.S. supervisors is that supervisory leadership matters. This is not a trivial hypothesis, given a long history of mixed results about whether supervisory leadership style affects performance (Smith & Peterson, 1988).

The longitudinal quality of this project is an advantage and also provides a mixed blessing from the standpoint of making sense of the results. The advantage is that this research design helps avoid making attributions about Japanese management in general that really should take into account the particular historical situation of the facility studied. Single-time assessments make it easy to confuse "that which is Japanese" with "that which is Japanese at this particular stage of a plant's development." A mixed blessing derives from the fact that the two points in time are not simple replications. The T1 data were collected at a point where the production technology had been transferred and the first set of U.S. supervisors trained and installed in place of their Japanese predecessors. The history to this point had been one of continuing growth. The T2 data were collected about eighteen months later, at a point where additional U.S. supervisors had been trained and when there were rumors about possible retrenchment, possible expansion, and adjustments to the compensation of supervisors. These changes in situation may well have affected the way plant workers related to supervisors in general or to the Japanese compared to the U.S. supervisors, but specific predictions are difficult. Rather than try to make separate prediction for T1, T2, and longitudinal results, we base our hypotheses on more basic theory and leave interpretation about historical changes in context for the discussion section.

The hypotheses stated here rest on a basic proposition: supervisors generally intend to provide maintenance-oriented, planning, or pressuring leadership in order to have a positive effect on their subordinates' work and well-being. Maintenance-oriented (supportive, considerate) leadership is intended to establish good personal relationships with subordinates and to promote a generally constructive social situation in the group. Planning is intended to provide information about next steps and about what needs to be done in order to accomplish work. Pressure, when done constructively, communicates the realities of external competition and the need to work effectively in order to reach performance goals of mutual benefit.

Finding positive relationships between these leadership style dimensions and various criteria is consistent with a supervisor's usual intent but can also occur for other reasons (e.g., reverse causal effects, confounds between the criteria and the way respondents experience the supervisor's leadership). Finding negative relationships is also quite plausible—supervisors could, for example, put extra pressure on subordinates who are not performing well. We would expect over time that, if such pressure were effectual, the subordinates would "mend their ways" and perform better or, alternatively, that the supervisor would give up. In either case, a negative relationship would move toward either a zero or a positive relationship as part of a mutual social learning process. The present study allows this sort of learning process to become apparent, since two waves of cross-sectional analysis and a longitudinal analysis are all possible. Accepting such built-in limitations, the analysis is structured around tests of five hypotheses.

Hypothesis 1: Mean differences in leadership based on supervisor nationality. There are two defensible alternative hypotheses about the relative amount of each leadership function that U.S. and Japanese supervisors are viewed as providing. One alternative hypothesis is that the closer connection of Japanese supervisors with senior plant and corporate management and their knowledge of the production system in the home facilities will make it possible for them to provide even greater amounts of leadership than will the U.S. supervisors. This especially applies to planning-P and pressure-P and might be expected to decline in significance over time as U.S. workers and supervisors learn the production system. A second alternative hypothesis is that, because of the constraints on Japanese leaders' ability to communicate, Japanese supervisors will be seen as providing less of each aspect of leadership than will U.S. supervisors. This might be especially expected for M leadership, to the extent that showing support requires a more thorough mastery of cultural subtleties than does the more technically based planning-P or organizationally based pressure-P.

(1a) Maintenance, planning-P, and pressure-P will be *higher under U.S.* than under Japanese supervisors;

(1b) Maintenance, planning-P, and pressure-P will be *higher under Japanese* than under U.S. supervisors.

Hypothesis 2: Main effects of leadership on criteria. Hypothesis 2 is based on the typical purpose of leadership, as noted earlier—to promote subordinate performance and to maintain positive subordinate attitudes.

(2) The leadership style measures will be associated with high subordinate performance, high attendance, low turnover, and high satisfaction.

Hypothesis 3: Interactions of leadership with supervisor nationality. The constraints, discussed earlier, that affect Japanese supervisors suggest that the effects of leadership for employees working under them will be weaker than for employees under U.S. supervisors. Constraints affecting leadership by Japanese supervisors could be shown in one of two ways:

(3a) Average levels of performance, attendance, turnover, and satis-
      faction will be more positive under U.S. than under Japanese su-
      pervisors;
(3b) The positive cross-sectional and longitudinal relationship between
      leadership and subordinate performance, attendance, low turn-
      over, and satisfaction will be stronger under U.S. than under Jap-
      anese supervisors.

A logically competing set of hypotheses underlies the decision by this
MNC to use expatriate supervisors. This decision is based on the belief that
Japanese supervisors will promote the transfer of an effective Japanese man-
agement pattern. Hence, two alternative hypotheses to 3a and 3b are:

(3c) Average levels of performance, attendance, low turnover, and sat-
      isfaction will be greater under Japanese than under U.S. supervi-
      sors;
(3d) The cross-sectional and longitudinal relationship between lead-
      ership and subordinate performance, attendance, low turnover,
      and satisfaction will be stronger under Japanese than under U.S.
      supervisors.

Hypothesis 4: Sources of meaning. The final hypothesis, following on the
discussion of limitations that potentially affect Japanese supervisors' leadership, is about respondents' conscious tendency to overtly express reliance on
a supervisor.

(4) Production employees working under Japanese supervisors will
     report making more use of sources of meaning other than super-
     visory leadership and less use of supervisory leadership than will
     respondents working under American supervisors.

Method

Shop floor employees completed a questionnaire in groups during work hours
in a room within the plant at two points in time, eighteen months apart. The
project was described by the university-based researcher as a combined management research and survey feedback project. Questionnaires had a code
number identifying individuals that allowed the researchers to compare answers in different years and to link answers with performance data. Respondents were assured that their answers would be treated confidentially and
that no individual's responses would be communicated to management. The
Time 1 survey obtained 229 responses from 232 eligible respondents. Respondents were of average age 34.3 years and 76.3 percent were female. At
Time 2, 193 out of 199 eligible resondents completed the survey. Of these
respondents, the average age was 32.7 years, and 66.1 percent were female.
All of the more skilled employees were supervised by Japanese managers. In
order to avoid confounding supervisor nationality with job classification, the

analyses reported here are based exclusively on semiskilled production employees. There were 118 such employees at T1 and ninety-nine at T2. Of these T2 respondents, seventy had also been employed and responded to the survey at T1. The proportion of respondents working under U.S. supervisors at T1, T2, and for data combining the two waves is 44.1 percent, 69.7 percent, and 54.3 percent, respectively.

Attendance and performance data were obtained from company records. Supervisors were identified as either Japanese or American on the basis of company records. In most instances, the Japanese supervisors rotated between day and night shifts on a monthly basis, while the American supervisors maintained fixed shift assignments. Turnover was determined by comparing company employment lists at T1 and T2. People on the list at T1 but not T2 had left the plant.

Employee Questionnaires

The questionnaire completed by shop floor workers consisted of a series of closed-ended questions. Among these were questions about specific leadership behaviors, leadership style, sources of meaning, and attitude criteria. Descriptive statistics and reliability coefficients (alpha) for indices derived from these questions are shown in Table 9.1., and scale intercorrelations are shown in Table 9.2.

Experienced Leadership Style

The leadership style measure consisted predominately of a twenty-item questionnaire based on the Performance-Maintenance leadership work described earlier. Three subscales were constructed after factor analysis and scaling checks were conducted to evaluate the original scales. (Details are available from the authors.) The average of eight items was used to represent the maintenance-oriented (M) leadership that respondents experienced as being provided by their supervisor. For the performance (P) leadership function, separate measures were constructed for the two sorts of performance (P)-oriented leadership described earlier: planning-oriented P leadership (Planning-P) and pressure-oriented P leadership (Pressure-P). Five items were used to measure Planning-P, and three were used to measure Pressure-P. For each item, possible responses were "always," "usually," "sometimes," "rarely," and "never." Additional information about the items, translation checks, and pretests are presented elsewhere (Peterson, Smith, and Tayeb, 1993; Peterson, Maiya, and Herreid, 1994).

Sources of Meaning

The sources of meaning measures consisted of ten questions that asked respondents how much use they make of: (1) manuals, (2) unwritten but ac-

Table 9.1 Descriptive Statistics for Indices

	Time 1			Time 2		
	Mean	S.D.	Alpha	Mean	S.D.	Alpha
Leadership						
Maintenance	3.26	.75	.85	3.31	.90	.92
Planning	3.98	.57	.66	3.93	.57	.74
Pressure	4.21	.60	.54	4.15	.60	.59
Criteria						
On-time atten-dance	4.15	1.12	.94	4.29	.85	.95
Performance	3.84	.41	.80	3.59	.57	.86
Satisfaction—security	2.96	.69	.55	3.36	.77	.74
Satisfaction—trust	3.11	.48	.71	3.38	.73	.84
Satisfaction—fairness	3.05	.78	.67	3.00	.82	.71
Sources of Guidance						
Rules and manuals	2.88	1.16	.71	3.10	1.21	.79
Informal policy	3.37	.98	.74	3.30	1.01	.78
Superiors	4.01	.81	.72	3.84	.87	.75
Coworkers	3.24	.92	.80	3.18	1.03	.79
Personal experience	4.09	.71	.87	4.05	.66	.75

All measures are scored such that a higher value indicates a larger amount of the construct measured.

cepted policies, (3) the supervisor, (4) experienced coworkers, and (5) their own experience and training. One set of questions asked employees how much they used these sources in "day-to-day situations," and another set of questions asked how much they used them when facing "unusual problems" (Peterson et al., 1990). Parallel questions from each set were used to form five scales. A representative item is: "In your usual day-to-day work, to what extent do you use the company's manuals on procedures and policies?" For all items, the response alternatives were: "very great extent," "great extent," "moderate extent," "small extent," and "very small extent."

Attitude Criteria

Three attitude criteria were taken from the Michigan Organization Assessment Questionnaire (Cammann et al., 1983). Satisfaction—security (three items) is satisfaction with job security at the plant. Satisfaction—trust (four items) is satisfaction with the company's trustworthiness and confidence that what the plant hierarchy says is trustworthy. Satisfaction—fairness contains three items that ask whether the company is fair.

Table 9.2 Correlations Between Leadership and Criteria Measures

	1	2	3	4	5	6	7	8
1. Maintenance								
2. Planning	.29							
3. Pressure	.16	.28						
4. On-time attendance	.18	.07	.02					
5. Performance	−.03	−.12	−.14	.29				
6. Satisfaction—security	.32	.07	.13	.01	−.09			
7. Satisfaction—trust	.45	.16	.12	.14	−.06	.47		
8. Satisfaction—fairness	.43	.23	.06	.09	−.19	.40	.40	
Time 2								
1. Maintenance								
2. Planning	.47							
3. Pressure	.04	.21						
4. On-time attendance	−.01	−.00	.06					
5. Performance	.08	−.05	−.23	.13				
6. Satisfaction—security	.53	.10	.11	.11	.13			
7. Satisfaction—trust	.68	.44	.07	.12	−.09	.40		
8. Satisfaction—fairness	.55	.16	−.02	.19	−.00	.51	.74	

Correlations are based on pairwise deletion of missing data. Minimum N: 99 at T1, 87 at T2.

Performance and Turnover Criteria

Two performance measures were obtained from company records: on-time attendance and general performance. The records were based on subordinate performance evaluations made jointly by immediate superiors and section leaders at the next level. The eleven performance evaluation items were each headed by a brief descriptive label and were evaluated using five behaviorally anchored rating points. The on-time attendance scale is based on two items. The categories for the first item, headed "Times absent," were: 0, 1–2, 3–4, 5–7, and 8 or more. The categories for the second item, "Hours absent," were: 0–4, 5–16, 17–32, 33–56, and 57 or more. The general performance measure is based on nine items with the following headings: knowledge of job, quality of performance, quantity of performance, efficiency or perform-ing job functions, cooperation, safety habits, initiative, responsibility, and communication. The behavioral anchors for the evaluation categories were different for each item (details available from the authors). As an example, the responses (from positive to negative) for the "knowledge of job" item were: "has thorough knowledge of all phases of his/her job," "has good knowledge of most phases of his/her work," "knows the job well enough to do daily assignments," "more knowledge of practically all phases of the job is required," "needs considerably more knowledge of many phases of his/her job." For the present research, all items were coded on a 1–5 scale, with the positively phrased evaluation receiving a 5. As noted in Table 8.1, both performance measures had good reliability and variance.

Analysis Methods

Hypothesis 1 was tested using t tests. Hypotheses 2–3 were tested using a series of regressions. The cross-sectional regressions at T1 and T2 were conducted in three steps. The first step predicts each criterion from Supervisor Nationality (coded 0 for U.S. supervisors and 1 for Japanese supervisors). The second step adds the three leadership measures. The third step adds a block of interaction terms formed by multiplying Supervisor Nationality with each of the three leadership measures (see "Interactions of style and nationality," discussed later). A significant result at any of the three steps is inferred if there is a significant increase in variance explained (R^2 change) between one step and the next. The longitudinal regressions add one step to this procedure. This step, included before any other, controls for the Time 1 value of each criterion. Consequently, the regressions reflect the additional variance in Time 2 criterion values that the predictors explain beyond what would be expected based on Time 1 scores for the criterion (Macy & Peterson, 1983). (For one longitudinal criterion, Turnover, the added step is not relevant.) Due to the modest sample size, especially for subgroup comparisons, marginal significance levels ($p < .10$) are noted for incremental R^2. Where an interaction between leadership style and supervisor nationality is at least marginally significant, separate regressions are reported for each supervisor nationality. Beta coefficients in these regressions are then tested to evaluate whether a significant relationship between leadership and a criterion applies to only one nationality. A summary table in the discussion section of this chapter indicates the extent to which other regressions done separately for the two nationalities of supervisor are reasonably consistent with those that show statistically significant differences between the two groups.

The fourth hypothesis was tested using t tests to compare reliance on different sources of meaning depending on supervisor nationality.

Results

Mean Differences in Leadership Measures

Differences in the use of the three leadership styles are shown in Table 9.3. The results support Hypothesis 1a at T2, which suggests that higher levels of leadership will be experienced for respondents under U.S. than under Japanese leaders for Maintenance leadership. Hypothesis 1b, which suggests higher levels of leadership under the Japanese supervisors, is supported for Planning-P at T1.

Table 9.3 Mean Difference in Leadership by Supervisor Nationality

	T1			T2		
	U.S.	Japan	t	U.S.	Japan	t
Maintenance	3.25	3.27	− .11	3.61	2.77	4.02**
Pressure-P	4.12	4.27	−1.21	4.05	4.24	−1.36
Planning-P	3.80	4.12	−2.79**	3.89	3.86	.26

N for U.S. supervisors ranges from 41 to 45 at T1 and from 74 to 77 at T2, depending on missing data. N for Japanese supervisors ranges from 55 to 58 at T1 and from 31 to 34 at T2, depending on missing data.

**$p<.01$.

Main Effects Regressions of Attitudes and Performance

Cross-sectional results for T1 and T2 are shown in Table 9.4, and longitudinal results are shown in Table 9.5. Instances where the interaction of supervisor nationality and leadership style showed a significant increase in variance explained are noted here. In these cases, separate regressions (discussed later) were conducted for U.S. and for Japanese supervisors.

Significant main effects for supervisor nationality indicate that performance evaluations are higher under U.S. than under Japanese supervisors at Time 1 (but not Time 2), and that Satisfaction—Trust is marginally higher ($p < .10$) under U.S. than under Japanese supervisors at Time 2 (but not Time 1). The longitudinal results (Table 9.5) show no relationship between nationality and either the attitude or performance measures after controlling for T1 scores. Turnover is higher under Japanese than under U.S. supervisors. Thus, hypothesis (3a), suggesting that U.S. supervisors will be generally more successful than Japanese supervisors, finds some support.

The change in variance explained generally supports Hypothesis 2 for the cross-sectional main effects results. These results indicate that the leadership predictors are significantly related to Performance evaluations and to all three attitude criteria at both times, but not to On-time Attendance. The longitudinal results show more mixed results for Hypothesis 2. They indicate that Time 1 leadership contributes additional explained variance beyond Time 1 scores for Satisfaction—Security, and (marginally) Satisfaction—Trust. Turning to the specific style measures, Maintenance has significant positive relationships to all three attitude criteria at both times and in the longitudinal analysis. Planning has a significant negative relationship to Performance at both times. It also has a negative relationship to Satisfaction—Security at Time 2 and in the longitudinal analysis, and a positive relationship to Satisfaction—Trust at Time 2. Pressure has a marginal negative relationship to Performance at Time 2 and a significant negative relationship to Performance

Table 9.4 Main Effects Regression Predicting Attendance, Performance, and Attitudes from Supervisor Nationality and Leadership Style: T1 and T2

Criteria	Supervisor Nationality	Predictors (Beta coefficients)			
		M	PL	PR	R^2 change
Time 1					
On-time attendance	−.13				.02
	−.07	.29*	−.13	−.04	.06
Performance	−.24*				.06*
	−.12	.23	−.38**	−.04	.11*
Satisfaction—securty	.02				.00
	.01	.30*	.12	−.02	.14**
Satisfaction—trust	−.08				.01
	−.10	.37**	.17	−.07	.22**
Satisfaction—fairness	.01				.00
	.04	.48**	−.03	.03	.22**
Time 2					
On-time attendance	.02				.00
	−.00	−.03	.00	.05	.00
Performance	−.07				.00
	.03	.22	−.26*	−.20†	.10*
Satisfaction—security	−.11				.01
	.21*	.81**	−.40**	.14	.40**
Satisfaction—trust	−.21†				.04†
	.09	.62**	.19*	.05	.47**
Satisfaction—fairness	−.01				.01
	.32**	.74**	−.06	.02	.40**

†$p < .10$; *$p < .05$, two-tailed; **$p < .01$, two-tailed.

N at T1: 91 for On-time attendance and Performance, 90 for the Satisfaction criteria. N at T2: 84 for On-time attendance and Performance, 83 for the Satisfaction criteria, 164 for Turnover.

Nationality codes: 1 = Japanese supervisor, 0 = U.S. supervisor.

in the longitudinal analysis (although the overall contribution of the leadership predictors to increased variance explained is not significant in the longitudinal analysis).

Interactions of Style and Nationality

The interactions between leadership style and nationality in predicting the criteria show several significant nationality-based differences. Five regressions that incorporate leadership-by-nationality interaction terms showed increases in variance explained beyond the main effects. These were regressions pre-

Table 9.5 Main Effects Regression Predicting Attendance, Performance, Retention, and Attitudes at T2 from Supervisor Nationality and Leadership Style in the First Year

Criteria	T1	Sup. Nat.	M	PL	PR	R^2 change
On-time attendance	.35					.12**
	.35	.02				.00
	.36**	.10	.06	−.18	−.15	.06
Performance	.55**					.31**
	.55**	−.11				.01
	.50**	−.09	−.04	.06	−.27*	.06
Turnover						
	—	.25*				.06*
	—	.28*	.10	−.01	−.14	.02
Satisfaction—security	.45**					.20**
	.44**	.07				.00
	.39**	.05	.38*	−.43**	.05	.13†
Satisfaction—trust	.32*					.10*
	.31*	−.10				.01
	.20	−.07	.35*	−.14	.18	.11†
Satisfaction—fairness	.47**					.22**
	.47**	.05				.00
	.34**	.30	.34*	−.26	.15	.08

†$p < .10$; *$p < .05$, two-tailed; **$p < .01$, two-tailed.

$N = 54$ for on-time attendance and performance; $N = 78$ for turnover; $N = 53$ for the satisfaction criteria.

Nationality codes: 1 = Japanese supervisor, 0 = U.S. supervisor.

dicting Satisfaction-Trust at Time 1 (R^2 change = .07, $p < .05$), Performance at Time 2 (R^2 change = .07, $p < .10$), and On-time Attendance (R^2 change = .22, $p < .01$), Performance (R^2 change = .08, $p < .10$), and Satisfaction—Fairness (R^2 change = .09, $p < .10$) in the longitudinal analysis. Separate regressions for U.S. and Japanese supervisors showing the nature of these five interactions are presented in Table 9.6. Even in the three instances where the increase in variance explained by the leadership-by-nationality interaction is only marginally significant, the separate regressions clearly indicate different relationships between leadership and criteria depending on supervisor nationality. Maintenance-oriented leadership has generally positive implications for the attitudes, performance, and attendance of subordinates working under Japanese supervisors. However, it is associated negatively with some of these same variables for U.S. supervisors. Planning-oriented leadership is associated with Satisfaction—Trust for subordinates under U.S. supervisors but not for those under Japanese supervisors. However, it is associated with increases in Satisfaction—Fairness in the longitudinal analysis for respondents under Jap-

Table 9.6 Separate Regressions by Supervisor Nationality where Interactions Showed Contingent Relationships

	U.S. Supervisors					Japanese Supervisors				
	T1	M	PL	PR	R^2 change	T1	M	PL	PR	R^2 change
Variables showing significant T1 interactions										
Satisfaction—trust	—	.18	.44*	.01	.33**	—	.48**	.02	−.20	.24**
Variables showing significant T2 intractions										
Performance	—	−.24†	.20	.25*	.13*	—	.56*	−.42	.04	.19
Variables showing significant longitudinal intractions										
On-time attendance	.63**				.40**	.02				.00
	.55**	−.46**	.06	−.10	.18*	.12	.54*	−.13	−.38†	.27†
Performance	.66**				.43**	.43*				.19*
	.58**	−.16	.01	−.51**	.27	.46	−.07	.17	−.00	.02
Satisfaction—fairness	.51**				.26**	.42*				.17*
	.65**	−.17	−.21	.05	.09	.12	.68	−.17	.14	.34

†p < .10; * p < .05; ** p < .01.

a. For regrssions based on T1 data only or T2 data only, R^2 figures are main effects terms. For longitudinal analyses they are incremental variance explained after T1 scores are controlled, and the beta coefficients are similarly adjusted for T1 scores.

anese supervisors, but not for those under U.S. supervisors. For U.S. supervisors, Pressure is positively associated with Performance cross-sectionally at Time 2 but negatively associated with performance in the longitudinal analysis. Pressure also has a marginally significant negative longitudinal relationship with On-time Attendance for the Japanese supervisors. Hypotheses 3b and 3d predict interactions between leadership style and nationality. However, the interactions found show a more complex picture than the simple hypothesis that effects will be stronger for supervisors of one nationality than for those of the other.

T tests comparing reports about use of different sources of meaning under U.S. and Japanese supervisors are provided in Table 9.7. The results do not support Hypothesis 4, which predicts that subordinates will report relying more on their supervisor if the supervisor is American rather than Japanese. (Similarly, multiple criterion analysis of variance [MANOVA] show no significant effects; results not shown.)

Discussion

The focus of our analysis has been on the problem of whether, how, and for how long expatriates should be used at supervisory levels to help transfer management practices. The results indicate that the relative roles of Japanese and American supervisors clearly changed over time at the site studied. Comparing how much of each leadership aspect the two nationalities provided indicates that the Japanese supervisors' contribution to "planning" in the sense of transferring the production process was still clearly recognized at

Table 9.7 Student *t*-tests Comparing Reliance on Alternative Sources of Guidance for Respondents under U.S. and Japanese Supervisors

Use of Guidance from	1985 means			1986 means		
	U.S.	Japanese	*t*	U.S.	Japanese	*t*
Rules and manuals	2.85	2.90	−1.36	3.10	3.12	−.09
	(43)	(55)		(63)	(29)	
Informal policy	3.45	3.30	.75	3.28	3.35	−.29
	(43)	(53)		(60)	(27)	
Superiors	3.84	4.13	−1.82†	3.82	3.88	−.27
	(43)	(57)		(63)	(29)	
Coworkers	3.17	3.29	−.63	3.10	3.38	−1.24
	(41)	(57)		(63)	(29)	
Personal experience	4.20	4.01	1.31	3.99	4.18	−1.25
	(43)	(56)		(63)	(28)	

†*p* < .10.

Numbers in parentheses are the sample sizes.

T1. By T2, the unique contribution of the Japanese supervisors appears to have been less acknowledged. The means shown in Table 9.3 indicate that neither group is viewed as providing as much planning-P leadership at T2 as the Japanese were viewed as providing at T1. This change could well signal the maturation of the knowledge, skills, and habitual practices in operating the production system and a reduced need for supervisors to guide workers.

The higher turnover of people who were under Japanese supervisors at T1 would be consistent with a progressive increase in tension with these supervisors between T1 and T2. Although not statistically significant, the somewhat higher levels of pressure-P leadership by the Japanese supervisors viewed through the sort of American lens described in Figure 9.2 may have contributed to the sense of low M leadership. Results shown in Table 9.7 indicate that this change did not extend to the Americans supervisors being circumvented at T1 or the Japanese supervisors at T2. The Japanese supervisors had begun to be viewed as distinctly less supportive than were the Americans. The higher performance evaluations under U.S. than under Japanese supervisors at T1 might seem to indicate that there were some limitations in the ability of the Japanese to exert influence even at that time. However, an alternative explanation is that the evaluations are partly an artifact either of higher expectations for the performance of the Japanese supervisors and the people under them by the evaluators or of a perhaps unconscious intent to encourage the relatively new U.S. supervisors by supporting the work of their subordinates. Generally speaking, the company's decision to use Japanese supervisors during startup and to progressively replace them with Americans appears to have been a reasonable one.

Leadership-Style Training for U.S. and Japanese Supervisors

Apart from the question of whether and when a Japanese company may want to use Japanese expatriate supervisors, the results have implications for how to train and use them. It suggests learnings about leadership within Japanese FDIs in the United States (Peterson, Maiya, & Herreid, 1993; Peterson, Smith, & Tayeb, 1993). Some of these learnings are evident in the main effects relationships between leadership and the criteria, regardless of the nationality of the leader.

One learning is that some kinds of leadership typically found useful in Japan may be helpful in Japanese FDIs located in other countries, while others may not. Several leadership-style relationships to criteria were found here to be stable over time and consistent between supervisor nationalities. The finding that maintenance-oriented leadership was positively related to satisfaction at both times and in the longitudinal results should be comforting. This is what the company had experienced in Japan and what its supervisors had been trained to expect. However, planning-oriented leadership was negatively related to performance at both T1 and T2, while pressure-oriented leadership was negatively related to performance at T2 and in the longitudinal results. The Japanese PM theory of leadership, which formed the core of the leadership training provided to these managers in Japan, suggests that combining an above-average emphasis on both performance (planning and pressure) and maintenance will yield optimal performance. Other analyses (not shown) indicated that there is no interaction between planning or pressure and maintenance such that subordinates who experience high-maintenance leadership react more positively to pressure or planning than do others. In the present context, pressure and planning simply appear to generate negative reactions, at least when subordinates view them as being provided by their supervisor. Did the American workers want these functions to come from some other source, such as a formal training program, or from a formal reward system, or did they simply not want the supervisors to talk about work? These are the kinds of problems the Japanese management needed to face, problems that were not typical of its experience with a Japanese workforce.

The kinds of main-effect leadership-style results found here have been notoriously site-specific and difficult to replicate in the United States or to interpret in a generalized way (Smith & Peterson, 1988). In contrast, leadership is more consistently important in Japan (Misumi & Peterson, 1985) than in the United States. What might a Japanese management group learn from such results? One risk is that what it learns from its first U.S. experience will be generalized to all future U.S. sites. Alternatively, perhaps leadership may come over time to be equally important if a quasi-Japanese culture can be established in a U.S. site. Setting up that culture might require specific interventions targeted at increasing the reliance on supervisory leadership.

As noted at the beginning of this chapter, a broad range of "leadership substitutes" has been identified that makes leadership style results problematic. These make it unlikely that results from the present site will fully generalize to sites with different technologies, management philosophies, and workforce composition. At the site studied, however, there was no evidence (Table 9.7) that subordinates who work under Japanese supervisors are conscious of making greater use of one set of substitutes—nonsupervisory sources for understanding their situation and handling work problems—than do those who work under U.S. supervisors. This nonsignificant finding is meaningful, since such differences have been found in several studies that compared U.S. and Japanese sites (Peterson et al., 1990; Smith & Peterson, 1995).

Other evidence besides the present survey results suggests that substitutes for leadership operated that are not reflected in the sources of meaning measured. For example, briefings by the plant managers indicated that on-time attendance was given disproportionate weight over other aspects of performance in decisions about pay raises and assignments to desirable shifts. In effect, these particular rules, enforced through the personnel system, may have reduced the effect of supervisory leadership on attendance. The results, which indicate that leadership style has cross-sectional and longitudinal relationships to several important criteria, should be used in the organization studied. However, the history of U.S. leadership research indicates that the endurance of these relationships and their generalizability need to be periodically reassessed even at this site if training is to be based on them.

Implications of Nationality-linked Differences in Relationships between Leadership and Criteria

Results of the regressions comparing the two nationalities of supervisor are summarized in Table 9.8. Compared to the maintenance leadership results, the results for planning and pressuring show more idiosyncracies, depending on supervisor nationality, the criterion, and short-term (cross-sectional) versus long-term (longitudinal) relationships. Although some of these results (e.g., that pressure by U.S. supervisors may have negative long-term implications for performance) should be monitored by the organization, the pattern of results is too varied to attempt more general interpretations.

In the instances where significant interactions appear between leadership style and nationality, the separate beta coefficients for each supervisor nationality show a sufficiently consistent picture to pose future hypotheses. In

Table 9.8 Summary of Regression Results

Hypothesis	Performance	Attendance	Turnover	Satisfaction
1: Leadership style main effects	Supported at T1 and T2, partly over time	Partly supported at T1, not at T2 or over time	Not supported over time	Supported at T1, T2, and over time
2a: Criteria higher under U.S. supervisors	Supported at T1, consistent at T2 and over time	Not supported	Supported over time	Not supported
2b: Leadership effects stronger under U.S. supervisors	Not supported	Not supported	Not supported	Mixed support for Planning-P
3a: Criteria higher under Japanese supervisors	Not supported	Not supported	Not supported	Not supported
3b: Leadership effects stronger under Japanese supervisors	Supported for M at T2, consistent at T1	Supported for M over time, consistent at T1 and T2	Not supported	Mixed support for M

general, subordinates who view Japanese supervisors as showing considerate, "maintenance"-oriented leadership also show positive values on many criteria, including some aspects of performance. This tendency is reversed for U.S. supervisors, particularly for performance and attendance. In effect, subordinates at this site appeared to take advantage of any considerateness (perhaps interpreted as lenience) by U.S. supervisors, but to reciprocate with good performance the considerateness of Japanese supervisors. Such a dramatic difference has obvious implications for training at this site. If this pattern persists or generalizes to other sites, it suggests that simply being Japanese may give a performance-oriented meaning to considerate behavior that is subtle enough to remain tacit to subordinates when answering leadership-style questions. A supervisor's nationality may be part of the "ground" against which the "figure" of his or her action is interpreted. The process by which tacit and conscious organization learnings interrelate (Nonaka, 1994) requires consideration in intercultural management training. These results suggest that Japanese expatriates in the United States, and perhaps expatriates in general, would benefit from thinking through the implicit leadership theories and other social interpretation processes (e.g., Lord & Kernan, 1987; Peterson et al., 1990) that affect intercultural relationships between hierarchical levels.

Supplemental Interview Information about Behavior Meanings

The second year of data collection included an interview component that was designed to flesh out some of the statistical results and to guide subsequent research. Eighteen employees were interviewed about various aspects of their work situation, including the supervision they received. One pair of questions asked about typical differences between what the Japanese and American supervisors do (1) to encourage people to work hard or work carefully, and (2) to be friendly. Some of the comments were evaluative, indicating that one or another nationality placed particular emphasis on either hard work or being friendly. Some interview respondents were convinced that American supervisors "watch you more" than the Japanese, while others appear equally sure that the Japanese supervisors are more strict about getting the job done than are the Americans.

Perhaps more important for subsequent study, interviewees identified several nationality-specific ways of emphasizing hard work or being friendly. In the category of encouraging hard work, some respondents mentioned that Japanese supervisors used informal rewards (a free Coke, recognition in a shift meeting, thanks for good work), pressuring behavior ("tell" versus "ask" for extra work time, look upset and rush around, beg and plead versus ask to do extra work), punitive actions (scream or yell, refuse to speak to someone who has made a mistake), directing attention to work (explain importance of good quality, speak about safety, explain what to do). Also mentioned in the "working hard" domain were some impressions and images used to contrast Japanese and American supervisors. Among these are "inscrutability" comments about the Japanese, such as "you sometimes can't figure out their expression or tone of voice," reflecting differences in nonverbal cues.

The cues of friendliness that were mentioned included joking around, smiling, saying "hi," talking about sports or TV, arranging impromptu "parties," asking (or not asking) about family, and sharing candy. General images of degree of mutual understanding or misunderstanding also were mentioned in the "friendly behavior" context.

A separate section of the questionnaire asked respondents how often their supervisors showed a number of specific behaviors like sending notes or dressing similarly to workers. For example, a number of what on the surface would seem performance-oriented behavior patterns came over time to be interpreted as indicating group maintenance. Among these are expecting suggestions and discussing career plans. A complete report of the meanings that these specific behaviors were given is provided elsewhere (Peterson, Smith, & Peng, 1995).

Implications for FDI beyond Japanese MNCs

Technology transfer is a basic reason for engaging in FDI. The simplest way for a corporation to transfer a technology is to simply sell products abroad that are made at home. Selling finished goods has the advantage that an MNC needs to engage in intercultural relations only at the point of sale. For a Japanese company to produce VCRs in Japan and sell them in the United States is quite a bit simpler than to produce VCRs in the United States. However, multinationals continue to encounter constraints that mitigate against using this "simplest solution" (Davidson and McFetridge, 1985). Logistics uncertainties (e.g., costs of shipping finished goods) and host government interference with imports (e.g., tariffs) encourage multinationals to use FDI. Where an organization's competitive advantage lies in production process innovations as much as in product innovations, technology transfer problems are accentuated. For much of the electronics industry, certainly for the organization studied here, the competitive requirements of extremely high production quality and low manufacturing tolerances make production process transfer exceedingly important to an FDI's viability. Intercultural issues make replicating a home country's production processes abroad even more difficult than the already complex problem of taking the production process used at one plant and replicating it in another plant within the same country.

The kind of study presented here is extremely rare in the organization literature but is critical to addressing the intercultural problems faced in transfering technology. The present results can help evaluate a multinational's choice to use expatriates at low organization levels, the training provided for and the ongoing management of expatriate supervisors, and the kind of changes over time that an MNC might expect as a foreign direct investment matures. The research approach also has implications for future intercultural field studies, including domestic studies of workforce diversity as well as international intercultural studies.

Mainstream management research has historically paid little attention to cross-cultural issues and even less to international intercultural relations (Adler, 1983; Boyacigiller & Adler, 1991; Peng et al., 1991). In the recent past, special attention has been paid to Japan (Peng et al., 1991), initially because of its economic success, then because of its increased investment in manufacturing and real estate abroad (Kujawa, 1983, 1986). Intercultural relations on the shop floor, between Japanese and other parties though, have rarely been studied. Daily shop floor intercultural relations, however, are a significant element in technology transfer and ongoing control that affect any multinational corporation. These relations have been rarely studied (e.g., Brannen, 1994; Lincoln & Kalleberg, 1990), but assumptions about how they operate substantially affect MNC decisions.

An MNC's decision to use supervisory-level expatriates to help transfer its production technology to an FDI and to maintain subsequent control rests on a complex set of assumptions about intercultural relationships. The most generalizable theme in the present results is that a supervisor's ability to contribute to transferring a management system is influenced by the supervisor's nationality. The organization learning literature (e.g., Nonaka, 1994) recognizes that transferring a culture includes a system of tacit understandings. Transferring these understandings is a very different process from transferring even the most complex, sophisticated set of tools. At minimum, the model that expatriates will make "them" think like "us" is simplistic.

The long experience of site-specific results in U.S. leadership style research (Smith & Peterson, 1988) indicates that generalizing from the specific regression coefficients found here would be risky. For example, we expect that the small office staff and maintenance groups at the site studied may well react differently to their Japanese supervisors than do the larger production group studied here. The present research has several limitations beyond the typical limitations of leadership-style research. In particular, those drawing inferences from the results must recognize that they represent a single site, not a sample of FDIs. The "pressure" leadership measure, although strong enough to yield some interesting results, also shows reliability below the level ordinarily considered desirable. Sample sizes are also modest, especially for the longitudinal analyses. Nevertheless, the results are useful, given the lack of intercultural research (Boyacigiller and Adler, 1991, p. 268), especially in FDIs, and the large number of multinationals that seek to use expatriates to transfer home-country organization practices. There are learnings possible simply in the examples provided of the possible ways in which subordinates from one nation may react differently from what one might expect to supervisors from another nation.

References

Adler, N. J. 1983. "Cross-Cultural Management Research: The Ostrich and the Trend." *Academy of Management Review* 8: 226–232.

Baliga, B. R. and A. M. Jaeger. 1984. "Multinational Corporations: Control Systems and Delegation Issues." *Journal of International Business Studies* 15: 25–40.

Bass, B. M. 1981. *Stogdill's Handbook of Leadership*. New York: Free Press.

Bass, B. M. 1985. *Leadership and Performance beyond Expectations*. New York: Free Press.

Boyacigiller, N. A. 1990. "The Role of Expatriates in the Management of Interdependence, Complexity and Risk in Multinational Corporations." *Journal of International Business Studies* 21: 357–381.

Boyacigiller, N. A., and N. J. Adler. 1991. "The Parochial Dinosaur: Organizational Science in a Global Context." *Academy of Management Review* 16: 262–290.

Brannen, M. Y. 1991. "Culture, the Critical Factor in the Successful Implementation of Statistical Quality Control." *Business Horizons*, 35: 59–67.

Brannen, M. Y. 1994. " 'Your Next Boss Is Japanese': Negotiating Cultural Change at a Western Massachusetts Paper Plant." Ph.D., University of Massachusetts, Amherst.

Cammann, C., M. Fichman, G. D. Jenkins, and J. Klesh. 1983. "Michigan Organization Assessment Questionnaire." In S. E. Seashore, E. E. Lawler, P. H. Mirvis, and C. Cammann, eds., *Observing and Measuring Organizational Change: A Guide to Field Practice*, pp. 71–138. New York: Wiley-Interscience.

Davidson, W. H., and D. G. McFetridge. 1985. "Key Characteristics in the Choice of International Technology Transfer Mode." *Journal of International Business Studies* 16: 5–21.

Dore, R. 1973. *British Factory—Japanese Factory*. London: George Allen and Unwin.

Earley, P. C. 1989. "Social Loafing and Collectivism: A Comparison of the United States and the People's Republic of China." *Administrative Science Quarterly* 34: 565–581.

Hill, C. W. L. 1995. "National Institutional Structures, Transaction Cost Economizing and Competitive Advantage: The Case of Japan." *Organization Science* 6: 119–131.

Hofstede, G. 1980. *Culture's Consequences: National Differences in Thinking and Organizing*. Beverly Hills, Calif.: Sage.

House, R. J., and G. Dessler. 1974. "The Path-goal Theory of Leadership: Some post hoc and a priori Tests." In J. G. Hunt and L. L. Larson, eds., *Contingency Approaches to Leadership*. Carbondale: Southern Illinois University.

Howell, J. P., P. W. Dorfman, and S. Kerr. 1986. "Moderator Variables in Leadership Research." *Academy of Management Review* 11: 88–102.

Kobrin, S. J. 1978. "Expatriate Reduction and Strategic Control in American Multinational Corporations." *Human Resource Management* 27: 63–75.

Kujawa, D. 1983. "Technology Strategy and Industrial Relations: Case Studies of Japanese Multinationals in the United States." *Journal of International Business Studies* 14: 9–22.

Kujawa, D. 1986. *Japanese Multinationals in the United States: Case Studies*. New York: Praeger.

Lincoln, J. R., and A. L. Kalleberg. 1990. *Culture, Control, and Commitment: A Study of Work Organization and Work Attitudes in the United States and Japan*. Cambridge: Cambridge University Press.

Lord, R. G., and M. C. Kernan. 1987. "Script as Determinants of Purposive Behavior in Organizations." *Academy of Management Review* 12: 265–277.

Macy, B. A., and M. F. Peterson. 1983. "Evaluating Change in a Longitudinal Quality of Work Life Intervention." In S. Seashore, E. E. Lawler, P. A. Mirvis, and C. Cammann, eds., *Assessing Organizational Change: A Guide to Field Practice*, pp. 453–476. New York: Wiley-Interscience.

Markus, H., and S. Kitayama. 1991. "Culture and the Self: Implications for Cognition, Emotion, and Motivation." *Psychological Review* 98: 224–253.

Maznevski, M., and M. F. Peterson. 1997. "Societal Values, Social Interpretation and Multinational Executive Teams." In C. S. Granrose and S. Oskamp, eds., *Cross-Cultural Work Groups*, pp. 61–89. Thousand Oaks, Calif.: Sage.

Mintzberg, H. 1973. *The Nature of Managerial Work*. New York: Harper and Row.

Misumi, J. 1985. *The Behavioral Science of Leadership: An Interdisciplinary Japanese Research Program*. Ann Arbor: University of Michigan Press.

Misumi, J., and M. F. Peterson. 1985. "The Performance-maintenance (PM) Theory of Leadership: Review of a Japanese Research Program." *Administrative Science Quarterly* 30: 198–223.

Misumi, J., and F. Seki. 1971. "The Effects of Achievement Motivation on the Effectiveness of Leadership Patterns." *Administrative Science Quarterly* 16: 51–59.

Nonaka, I. 1994. "A Dynamic Theory of Organizational Knowledge Creation." *Organization Science* 5: 14–37.

Peng, T. K., M. F. Peterson, and Y. P. Shyi. 1991. "Quantitative Methods in Cross-national Organizational Research: Trends and Equivalence Issues." *Journal of Organizational Behavior* 12: 87–108.

Peterson, M. F. 1988. "Organization Development Programs in Japan and China based on the Performance-Maintenance (PM) Theory of Leadership." *Organizational Dynamics* 16: 22–38.

Peterson, M. F., J. R. Elliott, P. D. Bliese, and M. H. B. Radford. 1996. "Profile Analysis of the Sources of Meaning Reported by U.S. and Japanese Local Government Managers." In P. Bamberger, M. Erez, and S. B. Bacharach, eds., *Research in the Sociology of Organizations*, pp. 91–147. Greenwich, Conn.: JAI Press.

Peterson, M. F., K. Maiya, and C. Herreid. 1993. "Adapting Japanese PM Leadership Field Research for Use in Western Organizations." *Applied Psychology: An International Review* 43: 49–74.

Peterson, M. F., P. B. Smith, M. H. Bond, and J. Misumi. 1990. "Personal Reliance on Alternative Event-management Processes in Four Countries." *Group and Organization Studies* 15: 75–91.

Peterson, M. F., P. B. Smith, and T. K. Peng, 1995. "Japanese and American Supervisors of a U.S. Workforce: An Intercultural Analysis of Behavior Meanings." In S. El-Badry, H. Lopez-Cero, and T. Hoppe, eds., *Navigating the Japanese Market: Business and Socio-economic Perspectives*, pp. 229–249. Austin, Tex.: IC² Institute.

Peterson, M. F., P. B. Smith, and M. H. Tayeb. 1993. "Development and Use of English Versions of Japanese PM Leadership Style Measures in Electronics Plants." *Journal of Organizational Behavior* 14: 251–267.

Pfeffer, J. 1981. "Management as Symbolic Action: The Creation and Maintenance of Organizational Paradigms." In L. L. Cummings and B. M. Staw, eds., *Research in Organizational Behavior*. Greenwich, Conn.: JAI Press.

Pondy, L. R. 1978. "Leadership Is a Language Game." In M. W. McCall and M. M. Lombardo, eds., *Leadership: Where Else Can We Go?* Durham, N.C.: Duke University Press.

Ronen, S. 1986. *Comparative and Multinational Management*. New York: Wiley.

Samovar, L. A., R. E., Porter, and N. C. Jain. 1981. *Understanding Intercultural Communication*. Belmont, Calif.: Wadsworth.

Schriesheim, C. A., and R. M. Stogdill. 1975. "Differences in Factor Structure across Three Versions of the Ohio State Leadership Scales." *Personnel Psychology* 28: 186–209.

Shaw, J. B. 1990. "A Cognitive Categorization Model for the Study of Intercultural Management." *Academy of Management Review* 15: 626–645.

Smith, P. B., J., Misumi, M. F. Peterson, and M. H. Bond. 1992. "A Cross-cultural Test of the Japanese PM Leadership Theory." *Applied Psychology: An International Review* 41: 5–19.

Smith, P. B., J. Misumi, M. Tayeb, M. F., Peterson, and M. H. Bond. 1989. "On the Generality of Leadership Style Measures across Cultures." *Journal of Occupational Psychology* 62: 97–110.

Smith, P. B., and M. F. Peterson. 1988. *Leadership, Organizations and Culture*. Beverly Hills, Calif.: Sage.

Wakabayashi, M., and G. B. Graen. 1984. "The Japanese Career Progress Study: A Seven-year Follow-up. *Journal of Applied Psychology* 69: 603–614.

Part III

Surveys across Industries

10

Work System Innovation among Japanese Transplants in the United States

Davis Jenkins

Richard Florida

In 1972, Sony opened a television plant in San Diego, ushering in an era of expanding investment by Japanese companies in U.S. manufacturing operations, or what are often referred to as the "transplants." The amount of new investment by Japanese companies in U.S.-based manufacturing transplants reached flood proportions in the mid-1980s, peaking in 1989 at around $9 billion. During the early 1990s, Japanese direct investment in U.S. manufacturing declined precipitously in line with the overall decline in foreign direct investment in the United States that accompanied recessions in the United States, Europe and Japan. Since then, such investment has rebounded somewhat, especially as Japanese companies have expanded production in existing facilities. It is not likely to return to the heady levels of the 1980s any time soon, however, in part because Japanese firms are now directing an increasing share of their foreign investment to Asia (Ministry of Finance, 1995).

Nevertheless, the transfer to the United States of Japanese manufacturing might remains an important factor for U.S. industrial competitiveness, not just because of the magnitude of the investment to date, which has created jobs for American workers and new business opportunities for U.S.-based suppliers, but because of what Japanese manufacturers have to teach U.S. industry. Foremost among the knowledge that Japanese manufacturers bring to the U.S. is expertise in innovative methods for managing production work. These practices are regarded as a key source of the competitive advantage that Japanese companies in industries such as automobiles and electronics have enjoyed in recent decades (see, for example, Womack et al., 1990). Some see such practices as the foundation for a new and superior form of capitalist industrial organization (Abo, 1990, 1993; Kenney and Florida, 1993; Lazonick 1990).

Even as investment by Japanese companies in U.S. transplant operations has moderated, U.S. manufacturers have been rushing to implement new approaches to managing production work that are commonly associated with manufacturing in Japan. Some of the practices involved in these new work systems, which are referred to by various labels such as "flexible" and "transformed" and "high performance," are actually quite foreign to manufacturing practice in Japan. They are associated with Japan because, in their broad designs, they resemble the work organization characteristic of large Japanese automobile and electronics manufacturers in a number of respects. Among these are their tendency to organize front-line production workers in groups or teams, to involve production workers in decisions regarding job design and quality control, and to stress the skill upgrading of workers at all levels. Moreover, used in concert with one another as a system, these practices are designed to foster continuous improvement in the performance of the production system, a process of innovation that is often referred to by the Japanese term *kaizen*.

As a result, there has been intense interest in ways in which Japanese manufacturers manage production work in their U.S. transplant operations. Most of the research on this topic has revealed a varied pattern of transfer and adaptation. A series of comparative case studies by the University of Tokyo (Abo, 1990, 1993) found that the approach to work organization among the transplants differs by industry, with automotive-related transplants exhibiting a greatest propensity to transfer Japanese practices to the United States, while electronics transplants tend to emulate U.S. practices and thus adapt to the U.S. environment. In general, the study revealed a tendency to create a "hybrid factory" organization reflecting a mix of Japanese and American approaches. Similar conclusions were reached by a study of Japanese transplants in the United States and Europe by Fujimoto, Nishiguchi, and Sei (1994), who found evidence of transfer of Japanese-style production management practices but noted that practices associated with labor markets—recruitment, training, promotion, wage systems and labor relations—tend to conform to the local environment. Case studies by a team from Michigan State (Cutcher-Gershenfeld et al., 1995) showed that Japanese transplants differ markedly in their approach to implementing work teams. The Michigan State team attributed these differences to a number of factors, including the nature of the production process, whether the plant was wholly Japanese-owned or a joint venture, and whether it was a new plant or an older acquired facility.

The literature on the transplants has been heavily influenced by studies of the automobile sector and, to a lesser extent, electronics—both sectors known for their innovative approach to work organization in Japan. Most of the research on the transplants has relied on case studies, with several of these studies focusing on a single case: the NUMMI joint venture between Toyota and General Motors (Adler, 1993a, 1993b; Brown and Reich, 1989; Krafcik, 1986; Wilms et al., 1995). The handful of surveys to date have been confined to a single industry or sector (see, e.g., Florida and Kenny 1991; Kenney and Florida, 1992; MacDuffie 1994; MacDuffie and Pil 1994 Milkman 1991;). Hence, there have not been data from which to make generalizations about the pattern of innovation across the broad range of industries in which Japanese companies have transplants operations in the United States.

This chapter examines the management of production work among Japanese transplants across the full range of industries in which Japanese manufacturers have a significant presence in the United States. To do so, it reports the results of the first survey of the production work practices of the population of Japanese transplants in the United States. Also included in the survey was a sample of U.S.-owned plants that serve as suppliers to the Japanese automotive assembly transplants. These data allow us to compare the pattern of practice among the transplants with that among U.S. plants that are involved in similar activities and have relations in some cases with the same focal organizations (i.e., Japanese transplant customers).

We cannot make definitive claims about the *transfer* by the transplants of Japanese work organization to the U.S. because we lack data on the practices of a comparable set of manufacturing plants in Japan. Instead, our focus is on the extent to which U.S.-based Japanese transplants have adopted innovative approaches to managing production work that are commonly associated with manufacturing practice in Japan but that may in fact reflect a blending of Japanese and American practices. Recognizing that there is likely to be wide variation in practice, we also attempt to identify distinct approaches to organizing work among the transplants and to understand the factors that underlie the decision to adopt one approach versus another.

Following a summary description of the survey data, we present a model of work system innovation that enables us to test empirically which innovative practices the Japanese transplants and their U.S.-owned suppliers are using in conjunction with one another in managing production work on the factory floor. We then categorize the plants in our survey sample according to extent to which they are and are not using these innovative practices in conjunction with one another as a "work system" and examine how the pattern of work system innovation differs among the transplants across industries and industry sectors and between the transplants and their U.S.-owned suppliers.

The Data

The data were collected through a 1994 survey by the authors of the entire population of Japanese transplants in the United States. The survey obtained plant-level data on organizational practices, supplier relations, plant charac-teristics, and performance. Transplants are defined as establishments that are either wholly Japanese-owned or have a significant level of Japanese partic-ipation (at least 20 percent ownership) in cross-national joint ventures.

The survey was administered to the population of Japanese transplants in the United States and a smaller sample of U.S.-owned suppliers to the auto-motive transplants. The sampling frame for the survey was based on the 1993 Japan External Trade Organization (JETRO, 1993) database and supple-mented with information from other sources.[1] The sample of U.S. suppliers was drawn from the ELM database on U.S. automotive suppliers and sup-plemented by data from the U.S. Department of Commerce on U.S.-owned suppliers to the Japanese transplants. The survey was administered by the Center for Survey Research at the University of Massachusetts—Boston in two phases; the first involved a mail survey, and the second relied on tele-phone interviews. On the basis of an initial screening, 238 transplants were found to be ineligible for the sample, resulting in a sample size of 1,195 transplants and 338 U.S.-owned suppliers to the transplants.

The intended respondent was the plant manager, although in some cases the survey was filled out by a manufacturing manager or a human resource manager. There are indications that in more than one case the survey was completed by individuals from multiple departments. A total of 601 surveys were completed and returned, for a response rate of 40.1 percent.

Field research was conducted at a small sample of transplants and U.S.-owned manufacturing plants. Interviews were conducted with managers, en-gineers, and staff in production, purchasing, and human resources. The re-search team also observed the production process at each site, where possible talking with workers on the production floor. The field research played an important role in shaping the questions and hypotheses examined by analyz-ing the survey data.

Japanese Transplants and the New Work Systems

Much of the previous research on work organization and the transplants has focused on the adoption of particular practices considered to be "innovative." More recent thinking and research on innovative forms of work organization stress the value of examining the use of sets of work practices in conjunction with one another as a "work system." We begin our analysis by looking at individual practices, but then broaden the focus to systems of innovative work practices.

Table 10.1 compares the adoption of "innovative" work practices by the Japanese-affiliated manufacturing plants that responded to our 1994 survey with that by manufacturing plants in Osterman's 1992 survey of work or-ganization among a size-stratified sample of establishments in the U.S.[2] This comparison allows us to see the extent of use of particular innovative prac-

Table 10.1 Adoption of Innovative Work Practices: U.S.-based Japanese Transplants and U.S. Manufacturing Plants Generally

Practice[a]	Japanese Transplants[b]	Manufacturing Plants in the U.S.[c]
Quality Circles: % of plants	77.5	50.7
Quality circles: % participation	41.7	34.1
Self-directed teams: % of plants	43.7	50.0
Self-directed teams: % participation	31.5	34.9
Job rotation: % of plants	63.1	52.0
Job rotation: % participation	NA	33.9
Statistical process control: % of plants	70.1	52.3
Statistical process control: % participation	30.8	28.6
Off-the-job training for production workers: % of plants	79.2	70.9
Off-the-job training for production workers: % participation	39.7	27.8
No layoff pledge to production workers?	52.1	40.2
Group incentive compensation (e.g., gain sharing) for production workers: % of plants	13.4	12.4
Pay for skills for production workers: % of plants	45.6	36.9
Profit sharing for production workers: % of plants	50.3	42.1
TQM: % of plants	62.1	47.6
TQM: % participation	40.1	34.9

a. "% of plants" indicates the percentage of plants in each sample that use the given practice. "% participation" indicates the percentage of production workers in a plant who participate in the given practice.

b. Data for Japanese-affiliated manufacturing plants in the United States are from a 1994 survey by Richard Florida and Davis Jenkins of Carnegie Mellon University.

c. Data for U.S. manufacturing plants are from a 1992 survey by Paul Osterman published in Osterman (1994). Only data for plants in industries comparable to those in the Florida and Jenkins sample are reported here.

Observations have been weighted to produce estimates for the entire population of plants sampled in each case.

tices among Japanese-affiliated manufacturing plants in the United States compared to that among a representative sample of manufacturing plants in the United States. Overall, the transplants were more likely to use innovative methods for managing production work than were manufacturing plants in the United States generally.[3] The only exception is that U.S. manufacturing plants generally showed a greater propensity to use self-directed worker teams. It is important to note, however, that our survey used a more restrictive definition of "self-directed teams" than did Osterman's.[4] The transplants were also more likely to complement innovative approaches to managing production work on the shop floor with supportive human resource policies. For example, the transplants were more likely than their U.S. counterparts to make a no-layoff pledge to their production workers, to provide production workers with off-the-job training, and to remunerate workers for skills and knowledge developed on the job.

Some of the practices listed in Table 10.1 are found in plants of large Japanese manufacturers in Japan (particularly those in automobiles and electronics)—for example, "quality circles," in which production workers meet "off-line" to discuss problems with production processes. Others are more likely American adaptations of Japanese practices or ideas. For example, the "self-directed team," in which production workers carry out their work under the direction of a team leader who is a production worker rather than a supervisor, is more an American invention than an Japanese one, although it reflects the Japanese approach of involving front-line workers in designing work methods and contributing to the improvement of manufacturing processes. Similarly, pledging not to lay off production workers (except in dire circumstances) can be seen as an effort to recreate in the U.S. labor market environment the "permanent employment" for core manufacturing workers that has been a prominent feature of labor relations in large companies in Japan. This supports the findings of previous research that the approach of the Japanese transplants to managing production work reflects a transfer of some practices from Japan and a borrowing of other practices of American origin.

This hybridization of work organization by the Japanese transplants has led to varying conceptions of what is "innovative" about the transplants' approach to managing production. At least two points of consensus emerge from research on the work practices of Japanese manufacturers in Japan and abroad and the larger literature on new forms of work organization. First, "innovative" work practices are those that foster the improvement of organizational performance over time. Scholars of Japanese industrial organization have argued that the propensity to promote continuous improvement of organizational systems, or what is sometimes called "organizational learning," is the distinguishing characteristic of the innovative methods of managing work that were pioneered in Japan and are now diffusing to Western industry (Cole, 1989, 1992, 1994; Nonaka, 1991; Nonaka and Takeuchi, 1995, Rohlen 1992). Second, there seems to be agreement, and some solid supporting evidence, that innovative work practices are most effective when they are implemented as a "system" of mutually reinforcing practices (Bailey, 1993; Ichniowski and Shaw, 1995, Levine and Tyson, 1990; MacDuffie 1994).

A Model of Work System Innovation

To examine the use by the Japanese transplants and their U.S. suppliers of innovative approaches to managing production work, we constructed a framework or model in which such approaches are seen as a system of work practices. We included individual practices in the model only to the extent that they contribute to organizational learning or improvement. Because our focus is on the management of direct production work, we are interested in practices that contribute to the ongoing improvement of manufacturing processes. For a system of work practices to promote manufacturing process improvement, they must not only motivate workers to want to make improvements but also enable them to develop the necessary know-how and give them the authority to do so (Cole, 1994). Table 10.2 lists the practices that make up our innovative work system model and shows their link to the conditions for manufacturing process improvement. This list was drawn from research on production management in large Japanese manufacturing firms, studies of work organization among Japanese transplants in this United States, and the burgeoning literature on "organizational transformation."[5] The practices that constitute the model have been grouped into three dimensions according to how they are thought to interact in bringing about the improvement of manufacturing processes: teamwork, worker involvement, and skill development.[6] The variables used to operationalize the model are defined in Table 10.3 and described in more detail below under the appropriate work system dimension.

Teamwork

Organizing workers in teams to carry out the direct work of production motivates workers by encouraging mutual monitoring of performance and by engendering team spirit (Cole, 1989). Work teams promote skill development required for manufacturing process improvement by facilitating learning by example, coaching, and learning by teaching others. To the extent that such teams have the authority to decide how to carry out their work and to solve problems as they arise, work teams can benefit process improvement by providing multiple feedback channels to ensure speedy response to problems and by affording multiple perspectives for problem solving. Two variables are included in the model to indicate the use of production worker teams in a given plant: %TEAMS, which is the percentage of production workers who regularly work in teams, and TEAMSAY, which measures the scope of authority given to these teams.

   In addition to carrying out the direct work of production in teams, workers can also take part in problem-solving groups or "quality circles," where

Table 10.2 Hypothesized Practices of an Innovative Work System and Their Links to the Conditions for Manufacturing Process Improvement

Dimension and Element	Motivates Initiative/ Commitment	Develops Skill/ Knowledge	Enhances Authority/ Opportunity
Teamwork			
Worker teams	√	√	√
Problem-solving groups	√	√	?
Compensation tied to group performance	√		
Low status differentiation	√		
Worker Involvement			
Product/business information shared with workers	√	√	
Low functional specialization	√	√	√
Workers define work methods	√	√	√
Decentralization of quality-related tasks	√	√	√
Suggestion system	√	√	?
Skill Development			
Training of production workers	√	√	
Promotion from within	√	√	√
Job rotation	√	√	√
Training of supervisors and managers	√	√	

they meet off-line, apart from their regular production duties, to discuss particular problems with the production system and work environment. Participation by workers in such groups promotes manufacturing process improvement by teaching workers to identify problems and their root causes, to work together to devise solutions, and to present those solutions to others within the work group (Cole, 1994). To the extent that the ideas generated by these groups are implemented and that workers are involved in the implementation, problem-solving groups also offer workers a chance to contribute to manufacturing process improvement directly (Cole, 1989; Lincoln and Kalleberg 1990). The variable %QCS is included to measure the percentage of production workers actively involved in such off-line problem-solving groups. In

Table 10.3 Definitions of Work System Model Variables

Dimension and Variable	Definition
Teamwork	
% TEAMS	= percentage of production workers who regularly work in teams
TEAMSAY	0 = work teams have little authority, ...5 = work teams have extensive authority
%QCS	= percentage of production workers currently involved in off-line problem-solving groups or quality circles
GROUPPAY	0 = pay tied to job classification and/or seniority, ...4 = pay based on group performance and skills learned
STATUS	0 = extensive status differentiation, ...5 = little status differentiation?
Worker Involvement	
INFOSHARE	0 = management shares little information with production workers, ...5 = extensive information sharing
JOBCLASS	0 = 20 or more formal job titles for production workers, ...4 = 1 job title for production workers
CONTROLMETH	0 = production workers have little say in the design of work methods, ...3 = production workers have extensive say in design of work methods
%SPC	= percentage of workers who regularly use statistical process control (SPC) in their work
CONTROLQUAL	0 = production workers have little responsibility for quality control, ...3 = workers have extensive responsibility for quality control
IDEARATE	= number of suggestions per plant employee in 1993.
Skill Development	
%WKRTRAIND	= percentage of production workers who received off-the-job training in the past 12 months
TRAINSCOPE	0 = no or limited range of training for production workers, ...5 = extensive range of training provided to production workers
JOBROTA	0 = no job rotation of production workers, ...3 = extensive rotation

Table 10.3 *(continued)*

Dimension and Variable	Definition
PROMOTEIN	= percentage of supervisors and managers who were promoted from a production worker job
%MGRTRAIND	= percentage of supervisors and managers who received off-the-job training in the past 12 months
Manufacturing Process Improvements	
MPIRATE	= number of times in past 12 months that changes were made to the manufacturing process for the plant's largest selling product.
MPISCOPE	0 = limited range of reasons for quality-oriented manufacturing process improvements,. . . .3 = extensive range of reasons

addition to these two types of team structures, efforts to minimize status distinctions between workers and managers (measured in the model by the STATUS variable) and pay systems that provide incentives for group performance (measured by the GROUPPAY variable) motivate workers to contribute to organizational performance by giving the sense that they are part of the same "team" as managers and rewarding them for acting in the collective interest.

Worker Involvement

The second dimension consists of practices that involve front-line production workers in job design, quality control, and other functions that, in the U.S. at least, were traditionally the purview of managers and other professional employees. A key step toward involving production workers is for managers to provide them with information about the performance of the products they produce as well as of the company by which they are employed. The IN-FOSHARE variable is included in the model to measures the extent of such information sharing in a plant. Where production workers do not have broad discretion over how to do their jobs, and where the variety of tasks they do is limited, there is less opportunity for workers to develop the kinds of knowledge and insights about the production process that would enable them to devise suggestions for improving the production system. If workers are forced to carry out job protocols dictated by others removed from the production floor, they have little incentive to learn as part of their work. Relegated to performing highly specified job tasks, workers have cause to resist taking part in innovation, since they could well be displaced from their jobs by the productivity improvements that may result. In contrast, where workers have more control over their work and are able to develop deep knowledge about the production system in the process, they have more to contribute to process improvement and are more likely to want to do so. The variable CONTROLMETH is included as a measure of the extent to which production workers have a say in the design and updating of work methods. The JOBCLASS variable indicates the number of job classifications for production workers at a plant. It is reverse coded, so a higher value indicates lower functional specialization (or higher functional integration) of production jobs.

Another dimension of worker involvement that can enhance organizational innovation is the practice of giving workers responsibility for monitoring the quality of products they produce. This promotes process improvement because front-line workers are in many respects best positioned to see problems with the production system as they arise and to figure out how best to solve them. Centralizing responsibility for quality tasks can be detrimental, since it excludes those who are closest to the point of production where the information relevant to quality control is in many respects richest (Cole, 1989, 1992, 1994). Hence, shop floor quality improvement will be limited to the extent that such tasks are the purview of managers, engineers, and quality control specialists as opposed to production workers. Two measures are included in the model to gauge the extent of production worker involvement in quality control. %SPC is the percentage of a plant's production workers who regularly use statistical process control in their work. CONTROLQUAL measures the extent to which production workers have responsibility for quality control at different phases of the production process: supplied components, work in progress, and finished products. Suggestion systems, in which workers can recommend ways to improve operations or working conditions, are another way that production workers can take part in quality control and improvement. Cole (1989, 1994) argues that allowing workers to exercise initiative in solving problems enhances their self-esteem by giving them the sense that their ideas are valued. As a result, they are more likely to feel that they are part of the larger organization and to be committed to its purposes. The variable IDEARATE is included in the model to measure the number of suggestions for improvement per employee that were offered by plant employees in the year preceding the survey.

Skill Development

Skill development can take place both through formal training outside of regular job activities and through structured learning on the job. In the latter, learning is embedded in the everyday work of production and is aimed at developing knowledge specific to the organization. In the plants of large manufacturers in Japan, practices such as rotating workers among jobs and departments and promoting supervisors and managers from the ranks of production workers foster the development of a broad base of knowledge specific to the organization and its operations (Koike, 1994). With a prodigious supply of home-grown talent and strong commitment to the shared goals that these practices engender, the organization has both the means and the impetus not only for bringing about incremental improvements to production processes but also to make the transition to entirely new forms of technology. The proprietary nature of these structures for learning makes them difficult to duplicate. Hence, the competitive advantage they help to create is likely to endure. Three variables are included in the model to indicate the extent of formal training: %WRKTRAIND, which is the percentage of a plant's production workers who received off-the-job training in the past twelve months; %MGRTRAIND, the percentage of production supervisors and managers trained in the past year; and TRAINSCOPE, which measures the range of training topics offered to production workers and managers. Structures for informal skill development are measured by JOBROTA, which indicates the extent to which production workers are rotated within and across work groups and departments, and PROMOTEIN, which is the percentage of the plant's supervisors and managers who were promoted from a production worker job.

To test the hypothesized relation of the practices entailed by the three work system dimensions to manufacturing process improvement, we included in the model measures of the scale and scope of quality-related manufacturing process improvement activity in the plant. MPIRATE indicates the number of times in the past twelve months that changes were made to the manufacturing process for the plant's largest-selling product. The MPISCOPE variable measures the extent to which such changes were motivated by efforts to enhance product quality, eliminate waste, or improve product flow, rather than merely by changes in product specifications or product demand.

Validating the Model Using the Survey Data

We estimated our model of an innovative production work system using our survey data and a structural equations modeling technique that makes it possible to test hypotheses concerning not only which practices are used in conjunction with one another but how they are interrelated (Anderson and Gerbing, 1988; Kim and Miller, 1978). In this method, which is also known "confirmatory factor analysis," the model is specified as a series of equations in which the observed variables (which in this case measure the particular work practices) are assumed to be caused by the latent variables (which in this case represent the work system dimensions) (Anderson and Gerbing, 1988; Kim and Miller, 1978). The equations are estimated simultaneously, and the covariances among the variables are decomposed to describe the relationship between the unobserved and the observed variables as well as among the unobserved variables themselves. This method has several advantages over exploratory factor analysis and other techniques used in previous research to validate models of organizational innovation. For one, it allows statistical tests to be performed to determine if the sample data are consistent with the imposed constraints, or, in other words, whether the data *confirm* the conceptually generated model. As such, the method provides a rigorous test of the conceptual model (Long, 1983a, 1983b). A fuller exposition of the method is given elsewhere by the authors (Jenkins, 1995; Jenkins and Florida, 1995).

The model was estimated separately using four subsamples of our data: (1) all Japanese transplants; (2) Japanese transplants not involved in the supply of products for automobile production; (3) transplant automobile parts suppliers; and (4) U.S.-owned suppliers to the Japanese transplant automotive assemblers. The transplant automotive suppliers are split out not only to allow comparison with the U.S. automotive suppliers but to determine if they differ markedly in their approach to managing production work from transplants not involved in the production of automobiles, given that the literature on the transplants has been so heavily influenced by studies of the automobile sector.

Table 10.4 shows the means of the variables measuring the use of particular practices for each of the four subsamples of interest. Differences of means tests indicate varying patterns in the use of certain practices not only between Japanese-affiliated and U.S.-owned plants but between those plants in our sample that are involved in the production of automobile components compared to those that are not. For example, workers teams are given greater authority in U.S.-owned automotive supplier plants than in the Japanese-affiliated plants in our sample, whether or not they are involved in auto parts production. This is consistent with the finding, mentioned earlier in the comparison of our survey results with those of Osterman, that U.S. manufacturers are more likely to use "self-directed" worker teams, which are more of an American invention, although they reflect Japanese ideas. Plants that are involved in the supply of components for automobile production, whether they are affiliated with Japanese or U.S. firms, are more likely to adopt innovative practices such as teams and suggestion systems. Automotive supplier plants, whether transplant or U.S.-owned, are also more likely to give production workers greater responsibility for quality control and to offer extensive training to production workers and managers. Hence, it seems that some artifact of the automotive sector, rather than national affiliation of the firm, is responsible for a greater propensity to adopt these innovations.

The results of the confirmatory factor analysis show a statistically significant association between most of the variables that represent innovative work practices and the work system dimensions with which they were hypothesized to be associated. This indicates that, in general, plants in the four samples are using these innovative practices in conjunction with one another as expected. A few variables failed to exhibit the expected relationship with the latent work system dimensions. For example, the STATUS variable, which is reversed coded to measure the lack of status differentiation in a plant, is

Table 10.4 Innovative Work System Model: Means (Standard Deviations) of Indicator Variables

Dimension and Indicators	Japanese Transplants	Japanese Transplants, Not in Autos	Japanese Transplants Auto Suppliers	U.S.-owned Auto Suppliers
Teamwork				
%TEAMS	45.8	43.2*	50.3*	46.0
	(42.6)	(42.8)	(41.9)	(39.6)
TEAMSAY	2.0*	1.8	2.2	2.6*
	(1.7)	(1.7)	(1.6)	(1.7)
%QCS	41.8	41.8	41.8	38.0
	(39.1)	(40.5)	(36.5)	(35.4)
GROUPPAY	1.2	1.2	1.2	1.2
	(1.0)	(1.0)	(0.9)	(0.9)
STATUS	3.5*	3.3*	3.9*	2.8*
	(1.1)	(1.0)	(1.0)	(0.9)
Worker Involvement				
INFOSHARE	3.5	3.5	3.4	3.7
	(1.4)	(1.4)	(1.4)	(1.3)
JOBCLASS	2.0	2.0	2.0*	1.5*
	(1.2)	(1.2)	(1.2)	(1.2)
CONTROLMETH	−0.1	−0.03	−0.1	0.1
	(1.0)	(1.1)	(1.0)	(0.9)
%SPC	30.8*	26.7*	38.3*	45.7*
	(36.4)	(34.7)	(38.2)	(34.8)
CONTROLQUAL	0.0	−0.1*	0.2*	0.0
	(1.0)	(1.1)	(0.8)	(1.0)
IDEARATE	1.2	1.1*	1.4*	1.3
	(1.2)	(1.2)	(1.2)	(1.2)
Skill Development				
%WKRTRAIND	39.6	34.3*	49.3*	50.1
	(41.4)	(40.3)	(41.7)	(40.9)
TRAINSCOPE	2.9	2.5*	3.6*	3.8
	(1.7)	(1.7)	(1.4)	(1.3)
JOBROTA	1.8	1.8	1.8	1.8
	(1.0)	(1.1)	(1.0)	(1.0)
PROMOTEIN	44.5	44.3*	50.6*	54.6
	(35.0)	(34.6)	(35.0)	(30.5)
%MGRTRAIND	52.1	44.4*	66.6*	65.8
	(40.3)	(40.3)	(36.6)	(38.0)
Manufacturing Process Improvement				
MPIRATE	11.5*	10.6	13.1	20.0*
	(25.0)	(23.8)	(26.9)	(33.2)
MPISCOPE	1.5*	1.5	1.6	2.0*
	(1.3)	(1.3)	(1.3)	(1.2)
N	390	250	140	127

* Difference of means statistically significant at $p < 0.01$ based on t tests.

significantly associated with teamwork only for the U.S.-owned sample of plants. Similarly, contrary to the practice of large automotive and electronics manufacturers in Japan, the transplants do not seem to use consolidation of production worker job classifications (JOBCLASS) as a means of expanding worker involvement or authority, whereas among the U.S.-owned suppliers examined here, such functional integration of production jobs is associated with other efforts to promote worker involvement. In these respects, the U.S. automotive suppliers surveyed here seem in general to be more "Japanese" than the Japanese-affiliated plants. For neither the transplants nor the U.S. suppliers do job rotation (JOBROTA) or promotion of managers from within (PROMOTEIN) seem to play a role in skill enhancement, despite the fact that these practices have been recognized as means of skill development in the plants of large manufacturers in Japan (Koike, 1994).

Consistent with accepted practice in structural equations modeling (Long, 1983b), we deleted from the model those variables that showed no statistically significant loading on the latent work system dimensions to which they were assigned.[7] The elements of the revised model are illustrated in Figure 10.1. Note that, in addition to removing the variables for which no significant effect is evident, we renamed the "Skill Development" work system dimension "Training," since only training-related variables remain under that dimension of the model.

Figure 10.2 shows the covariances among the (latent) work system dimensions for the Japanese transplants. All such covariances are statistically significant. The relatively strong covariances among the "Worker Involve-

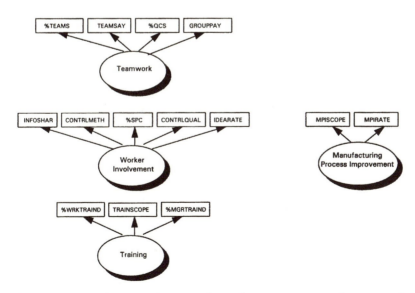

Figure 10.1 Confirmatory factor analysis of an innovative production work system (revised measurement model).

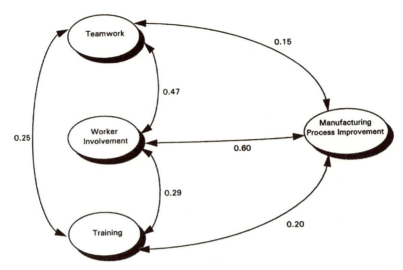

Figure 10.2 Covariance structure model of an innovative production work system: Covariances among latent work system dimensions for U.S.-based Japanese transplants. All covariances are statistically significant at $p < 0.01$.

ment" and the "Teamwork" and "Training" dimensions suggest that, where production workers are involved in job design and quality control, it is deemed appropriate to organize workers into teams and to provide them with a broad range of off-the-job training. A similar pattern of covariances among the work system dimensions is evident for the U.S.-owned supplier subsample.

The three dimensions of the work system model are also significantly associated with the intensity of manufacturing process improvement activity in the manufacturing plants in our survey sample. By far the strongest link to process improvement activity is through the "Worker Involvement" dimension. This suggests that giving front-line workers responsibility for deciding how to carry out their jobs is an effective way to foster continuous improvement and to achieve the gains in organizational learning that are likely to result from such activity.

In the revised model, we have identified a set of innovative work practices that are positively related to the level of manufacturing process improvement activity in our sample of plants and are used in conjunction with one another as a work system by both Japanese transplants across a wide range of industries and by U.S.-owned suppliers to the transplant automotive assemblers. The practices that make up the three dimensions of the model reflect a blend of Japanese and American influences. The fact that the same model of work system innovation is evident among the U.S.-owned supplier plants suggests that this approach is not unique to Japanese manufacturers.

The Pattern of Work System Innovation among the Transplants

To examine the pattern of work system innovation among the U.S.-based Japanese transplants and their U.S.-owned suppliers, we used cluster analysis to group the plants that responded to our survey according to their use of the production work practices that were found to be interrelated by the structural equations analysis of the preceding section. We then examined the factors associated with the adoption of the different work system types or "regimes" identified.

Clustering Plants by Work System Regimes

We hypothesize that the plants in our sample will fall along a continuum of approaches to managing production work ranging from what we term "Taylorist" to "Innovative." Table 10.5 summarizes the sorts of contrasts we expect to observe between plants that take a Taylorist approach to managing production worker and those where the work system can be classified as Innovative.[8] In general, we expect the Taylorist plants to be characterized by greater functional specialization, centralization of control over job design and quality control, and lack of emphasis on training for production workers in particular. Innovative plants will exhibit greater degrees of teamwork,

Table 10.5 Hypothesized Contrasts between Taylorist and Innovative Work Systems

Dimension and Element	Taylorist System	Innovative System
Teamwork		
Production management	Closely supervised, narrowly defined tasks	Worker-led teams
Quality circles	No	Yes
Pay	Tied to job classification and/or seniority	Based on group performance
Worker Involvement		
Information sharing with workers	Limited	Extensive
Control of job design	Industrial engineers and supervisors	Production workers
Responsibility for quality control	Quality specialists	Production workers
Suggestion systems	No	Yes
Training		
Training of production workers	Limited	Extensive
Training of managers	Moderate	Extensive

worker involvement, training, and other practices shown by the structural equations analysis of the preceding section to be associated with higher levels of manufacturing process improvement activity in the plants in our survey sample.

Five clustering techniques were used to group our sample of plants according to their use of the innovative work system practices validated in the preceding section. Four of the five methods produced similar two-and three-cluster solutions.[9] Comparing the results of these four methods, we chose Ward's method as producing the most useful cluster pattern for our purposes here.[10] The means of the work practice variable for the two-and three-cluster solutions produced by Ward's method are shown in Tables 10.6 and 10.7 respectively. Note that all variables have been standardized by transformation to z-scores to facilitate comparison among them.

In the two cluster solution (Table 10.6), one cluster consists of plants that score below the sample mean on all measures, while the other cluster consists of plants that score above the sample mean. Supporting our hypothesis, the plants in the first cluster exhibit an approach to managing production work that can be characterized as Taylorist, while those in the second cluster exhibit the functional integration, worker involvement, and emphasis on training that are characteristic of the Innovative work system model.

Table 10.6 Means of Work System Variables by Plant Cluster: Two-Cluster Solution by Ward's Method for Pooled Sample of Plants

Dimension and Variable	Cluster 1 (Taylorist)	Cluster 2 (Innovative)
Teamwork		
%TEAMS	−0.52	0.64
TEAMSAY	−0.57	0.71
%QCS	−0.30	0.38
GROUPPAY	−0.21	0.26
Worker Involvement		
INFOSHARE	−0.25	0.31
CONTROLMETH	−0.36	0.45
%SPC	−0.34	0.41
CONTROLQUAL	−0.31	0.39
IDEARATE	−0.18	0.22
Skill Development		
%WKRTRAIND	−0.25	0.31
TRAINSCOPE	−0.38	0.47
%MGRTRAIND	−0.25	0.31
N	286	231

All variables have been standardized using the z-score transformation.

Table 10.7 Means of Work System Variables by Plant Cluster: Three-Cluster Solution by Ward's Method for Pooled Sample of Plants

Dimension and Variable	Cluster 1 (Taylorist)	Cluster 2 (Mixed)	Cluster 3 (Innovative)
Teamwork			
%TEAMS	−0.37	−0.93	0.64
TEAMSAY	−0.47	−0.87	0.71
%QCS	−0.32	−0.27	0.38
GROUPPAY	−0.23	−0.15	0.26
Worker Involvement			
INFOSHARE	−0.27	−0.18	0.31
CONTROLMETH	−0.48	−0.05	0.45
%SPC	−0.42	−0.12	0.41
CONTROLQUAL	−0.60	−0.13	0.39
IDEARATE	−0.23	−0.01	0.22
Skill Development			
%WKRTRAIND	−0.64	0.84	0.31
TRAINSCOPE	−0.61	0.25	0.47
%MGRTRAIND	−0.62	0.78	0.31
N	210	76	231

All variables have been standardized using the z-score transformation.

In the three-cluster solution produced by Ward's method (Table 10.7), the plants in the Taylorist cluster have been split into two clusters, one in which the plants score below the mean on all practices and the other in which the plants score below the mean on most practices, except those related to training. Plants in this latter group tend to place a great emphasis on providing formal off-the-job training for workers and mangers but have not adopted teams, worker involvement, and other practices related to the organization of work on the shop floor. We refer to the approach to managing production work exhibited by this second cluster of plants as "Mixed," since it may reflect two or more strategies. On one hand, it could represent a strategy that sees deficiencies in the skills of individual workers, rather than the system by which production work is managed, as the chief impediment to problem solving and performance improvement and seeks to remedy these deficiencies by providing extensive off-the-job training to individual workers, while managing work on the shop floor using traditional Taylorist methods. One the other hand, it might be seen as a effort to use training to "transition" workers from a Taylorist to an innovative work system regime. Evidence that both strategies are present among the Mixed group of plants is given later in this chapter.

Plants in these three clusters can be seen as representing a continuum of "innovativeness" in the approach to managing production work that stretches from the low end with the Taylorist plants to the high end with the Innovative plants. Table 10.8 summarizes statistical analyses of the correlation between the three work system types and measures of innovative activity gleaned from the survey.[11] The structural equations modeling of the previous section showed a connection between practices entailed in an innovative work system and efforts to bring about ongoing improvement of manufacturing processes within the plant. As is indicated in Table 10.8, plants in the Innovative work system group exhibit higher levels of manufacturing process improvement activity than do plants whose approach to production management has been classified as Mixed or Tayorist. When compared to Taylorist plants especially, Innovative plants are also more likely to engage in other sorts of innovative activity, including concurrent engineering of products, environmentally conscious or "green" product design, and benchmarking the practices of other plants. There is also a strong association between the use of innovative production work practices and formal, plant-wide programs for systematically improving product quality, such as total quality management (TQM).[12] In addition, innovative work systems are also associated with "lean" management, as measured by the ratio of managers to workers, and, among plants in our sample that supply parts for use in automobile production in particular, with "leaner" levels of inventory for raw materials, work in process, and final goods.[13]

Table 10.9 summarizes the characteristics of the plants in the three clusters.[14] Plants that have adopted Innovative production work systems tend to use production technology of greater capital intensity and to hire more educated workers for production work than do plants that take a Taylorist approach to managing production work. In analyses not reported here in which we controlled for the effect of other factors such as plant size and age of plant, capital intensity was found still to have a strong association with the adoption of an Innovative work system. This makes sense, given that the high fixed costs of a capital intensive production system put a premium on ensuring high capacity utilization. Capital intensity therefore creates an incentive to manage production work in ways that facilitate troubleshooting and continuous improvement of the production system. In short, advanced plant and equipment is likely to require advanced organizational practices for their optimal utilization and performance. The use of Innovative work methods that give workers greater authority for job design and quality control seem to require in turn a more highly educated workforce. Perhaps related to this is the fact that Innovative plants are not only more likely than Taylorist plants to make a pledge of job security to workers but also tend to make good on such pledges with active efforts to avoid layoffs. This provides support for the view that efforts to transform the management of work so that workers are more involved in and responsible for the ongoing improvement of organizational processes need to be accompanied by assurances that workers' jobs will not be jeopardized as a result of their contribution to

Table 10.8 Measures of Innovative Activity by Work System Type

		Work System Type	
Measure of Innovative Activity	Taylorist (Cluster 1)	Mixed (Cluster 2)[a]	Innovative (Cluster 3)
Manufacturing process improvement activity	Low	Moderate	High
Quality-oriented product design activity	Limited	ns	Extensive
"Green" product design	No	ns	Yes
Concurrent engineering	Limited	ns	Extensive
Benchmarking of other plants	No	ns	Yes
TQM program	No	Yes	Yes
Ratio of managers to workers	High	ns	Low
Inventory levels	High (among auto suppliers especially)	Moderate (among auto suppliers)	Low (among auto suppliers especially)

a. "ns" indicates there is no statistically significant relation between the given characteristic and work system type at the $p < .01$ level.

Table 10.9 Typical Plant Characteristics by Work System Type

| | Work System Type[a] | | |
Plant Characteristic	Taylorist (Cluster 1)	Mixed (Cluster 2)	Innovative (Cluster 3)
Employment size	Small	Large	Midsize
Brownfield (vs. greenfield)	Yes (U.S. plants)	ns	No (U.S. plants)
Capital intensity	Low	ns	High
Wages	Low	High	Midrange
Union	No	Yes	ns
% workers who are H.S. grads	Lower	ns	Higher
Hiring criteria: Production workers	Experience in similar job	ns	Teamwork, problem-solving skills, technical training
No-layoff pledge to workers	No	ns	Yes
Active efforts to avoid layoffs	Limited	Extensive	Extensive
Recent downsizing?	ns	Yes	ns
Turnover rate	ns	High	ns
Obstacles to performance improvement	ns	"Inadequate skills of prod. workers" "Programs still new"	"Programs still new"
Relations w/customers and suppliers	Arm's length	ns	Cooperative
Place in supply chain	Finished goods producer	ns	Components supplier
EDI with customers and suppliers	No	ns	Yes

a. "ns" indicates that there is no statistically significant relation between the given characteristic and work system type at the $p < .01$ level.

productivity improvement and by active steps to ensure their job security. Innovative plants are also more likely to have cooperative relationships with their customers and suppliers than Taylorist plants, whose customer and supplier relations can be characterized generally as "arm's length."[15]

The "Mixed" plants tend to be larger and older plants that pay relatively high wages and are more likely to be unionized. These plants are more likely to have experienced recent restructuring or downsizing, as well as greater turnover of production workers. The instability of plants in this cluster may have provided an impetus for some of them to adopt a Mixed work system strategy, with its heavy emphasis on training. Thus, the large investment by some of these plants in off-the-job training for production workers seems to reflect an attempt to reassure workers (and their unions) that management has their interests and well-being in mind during a period of turbulence and uncertainty for the plant. By the same token, these efforts may also represent an effort by management to correct through training problems perceived to be contributing to the current instability at the plant. There is evidence from our survey to suggest that both strategies are evident among plants in the "Mixed" cluster.[16]

Pattern of Innovation among the Japanese Transplants

Table 10.10 shows the distribution of the three work system types or "regimes" among the U.S.-based Japanese transplants in 1994. More than 40 percent of the transplants had adopted approaches to managing production

Table 10.10 Adoption of Work System Regimes among Manufacturing Plants by Ownership and Industry Sector

	Percentage of Plants by Work System Regime		
	Taylorist	Mixed	Innovative
Japanese Transplants	44.7	14.6	40.7
Automotive suppliers	29.2*	18.4*	52.4*
Not automotive suppliers	53.2*	12.5	34.3*
Automotive Suppliers	32.8	13.4	53.8
Japanese transplants	29.2	18.4	52.4
Japanese-owned	28.8	20.7*	50.5
Japan-U.S. J.V.s	30.4	12.4	57.2
U.S.-owned	32.6	15.0	52.4

* Difference of means is statistically significant at the $p < .001$ level by the chi-square test. Observations have been weighted to create estimates for the entire population from which the sample was drawn.

work that can be classified as Innovative. However, nearly 45 percent of transplants were found to use Taylorist work practices. These transplants made little, if any, use of innovative practices. Approximately 15 percent of transplants followed a "mixed" approach, characterized by heavy investment in training but with a tendency to use Taylorist approaches to manage the work of production on the factory floor.

A key finding, then, of this first survey of the work practices of the population of Japanese transplants in the United States is that there is considerable variation in the pattern of adoption of work system innovations. While a sizable proportion of the transplants have adopted methods of managing production work that are conducive to manufacturing process improvement and that mirror in general respects practices associated with large automobile and electronics firms in Japan, others rely on Taylorist methods characteristic of traditional heavy industry in the United States.

In exploring further the variation in the pattern of adoption of work system innovations among the Japanese transplants, we find that there are key differences by industry sector. (See Table 10.10 again.) A strong finding that holds up under further analysis is that Japanese transplants involved in the supply of parts and other products for use in automobile production were significantly more likely than plants not involved in automobile production to take an innovative approach to managing production work and significantly less likely to follow the Taylorist model.

Japanese Transplants Compared with U.S. Suppliers

Earlier we compared data from our survey of the transplants and a survey by Osterman of a representative sample of U.S. manufacturing establishments to show that the transplants were on the whole more likely to use certain innovative methods for managing production work than were manufacturing plants in the United States generally.[17] The distribution of the three work system regimes among transplant and U.S.-owned automotive parts supplier plants is compared in Table 10.10.[18] These data show that, among plants in automotive parts supply, U.S.-owned plants are just as innovative in their approach to managing production work as are the transplants. This is perhaps not so surprising in light of evidence from studies of the efforts of Japanese transplant automotive assemblers to identify and cultivate suppliers that are innovative.[19] Of course, the U.S.-owned supplier plants in our sample were also found to supply U.S.-owned automotive assemblers in addition to the transplants. Only 16 percent of the U.S.-owned automotive supplier plants supplied a majority of their output to Japanese-affiliated customers. Therefore, the fact that these plants supply Japanese customers is probably not the only or even the main reason that they tend to be so innovative in their approach to managing production work. These findings, combined with evidence presented earlier, suggest that work system innovation is more prevalent among plants in the automotive sector generally, whether or not they are affiliated with or heavily dependent on Japanese companies.

Conclusion

Using data from the first survey of the production management methods of the population of Japanese transplants in the United States, we succeeded in identifying a set of work practices that are used in conjunction with one another by both Japanese transplants across a wide range of industries and U.S.-owned suppliers to the transplant automobile assemblers. These practices are used together as part of a production work system consisting of three dimensions—teamwork, worker involvement, and training—that are positively associated with the level of manufacturing process improvement activity in the manufacturing plants in our survey sample. The practices that make up the three dimensions of this work system model reflect of blend of Japanese and American influences. This supports the findings of previous research that the approach of the Japanese transplants to managing production work reflects a transfer of some practices from Japan and a borrowing of other practices of American origin as part of a process of adaptation to the American economic environment. The fact that the same general model of work system innovation is as evident among the U.S.-owned supplier plants as among Japanese-affiliated plants suggests that this approach is not unique to Japanese manufacturers and may well be prevalent among manufacturers in the United States not related in any way to the transplants.

There is considerable variation among the U.S.-based Japanese transplants in their approach to managing production work. While a sizable proportion of the transplants have adopted Innovative approaches to managing production work that are conducive to manufacturing process improvement and that mirror in general respects the stylized model of work organization associated with large automobile and electronics firms in Japan, others have adopted a Taylorist approach characteristic of heavy industry in the United States. Still others follow a "mixed" approach, characterized by heavy investment in off-the-job training but with a tendency to use Taylorist methods of managing production work on the factory floor. At least two strategies are evident among the plants in the Mixed work system group: some see the skill deficiencies of production workers, rather than the system by which production work is managed, as impediments to performance improvement and therefore use training to raise skill levels among employees, and some attempt to use training as a means of "transitioning" workers from a traditional Taylorist to an Innovative system of production management.

The adoption of innovative work systems is significantly more prevalent among transplants involved in the supply of parts and other products for use in automobile production than among those outside of the automotive sector. This finding is important because the literature on work organization among the transplants has been heavily influenced by studies of the automotive sector. The U.S.-owned automotive supplier plants we surveyed are found in general to be equally as innovative in their approach to managing production work as the Japanese transplant automotive suppliers. Hence, we find evidence of a greater propensity to adopt work system innovations among plants in the automotive sector that is independent of affiliation with or dependence upon Japanese companies.

Notes

1. These included the list of Japanese-affiliated plants in the United States as of 1990 compiled by the Japan Economic Institute (MacKnight, 1992), directories of Japanese-affiliated companies operating in the U.S., such as Toyo Keizai (1993), and various newsletters, news articles, and other publications.

2. Osterman's sample was limited to establishments with fifty or more employees. Osterman's survey was conducted by telephone, resulting in a response rate of 65.5 percent.

3. Note, however, that Osterman's survey was conducted two years prior to ours. It could be the case, therefore, that in the interim the plants in Osterman's survey "caught up" to those in our sample in the extent to which they use these practices.

4. In his survey, Osterman simply asked respondents whether their establishment had "self-directed teams" and what percentage of "core employees" (in manufacturing plants, this refers to blue-collar production workers) participated in such teams. Our survey asked a series of questions about the roles and responsibilities of work teams at a plant and then requested respondents to estimate the percentage of production workers who regularly worked in such teams. Only if a respondent indicated that "each team has a leader who is a production worker (not a supervisor)" did we consider teams to be "self-directed." Similarly, Osterman's survey does not distinguish between rotation of workers *within* work groups and *between* work groups. Our survey was designed to get at this distinction, since the literature indicates that it may be important. For example, Cole (1989) argues that rotation *within* a work group helps to relieve boredom and prevent repetitive stress disorders, but it does not promote multiskilling and "systems thinking" to the extent that rotation *between* work groups does.

5. For reviews of this literature, see Bailey (1993) and Jenkins (1995).

6. The model assumes that these practices interact with one another as a *system* in bringing about ongoing improvement of manufacturing processes. However, we depart from previous studies that have distinguished between practices that govern the way work tasks are carried out on the factory floor and those that reflect plant or firm-level human resource policies. MacDuffie (1995) groups his "bundles" of practices this way, following Osterman (1994), who distinguishes between practices by which the direct work of production or service is organized, on the one hand, and supporting human resource management policies, on the other hand. Many of the studies in the "organizational transformation" literature reviewed by Bailey (1993) use a similar taxonomy. In a test not reported here, we estimated MacDuffie's model of human resource bundles using data from our 1994 survey and the structural equations modeling method we employ here to validate our model. The results fail to support the discriminate validity of MacDuffie's grouping

of practices into two "bundles," where one bundle includes practices related to the organization of work on the factory floor and the other consists of a set of supporting human resource policies.

7. Statistical tests not reported here showed no "cross-loading" among of any of these nonsignificant variables on any other latent dimension in the model.

8. "Taylorist" is an appropriate antipode to "Innovative" in the context of this study from the perspective of those, ourselves among them, who see Taylorist approaches to managing work as inhibiting manufacturing process improvement and other forms of organizational learning, while Innovative work systems are seen to enhance it. A compelling statement of this view is given by Cole (1994) in a discussion of the implications for organization learning of two contrasting paradigms of work organization, one of which he labels "Taylorist" and the other of which he calls "the quality improvement paradigm that has emerged over the past few decades in Japan and is now diffusing to Western industry." The latter paradigm is the one we see as governing the design of the "Innovative" work systems observed here. Cole argues that the inspection-oriented approach of Taylorism to quality control discourages continuous improvement in a number of ways.

9. All clustering methods produce solutions (Aldenderfer and Blashfield 1984; Everitt 1980). Only the Single Linkage method produced widely divergent results. This method grouped most of the observations in a single cluster, with the remaining clusters consisting of only one or two observations. This "chaining" effect is characteristic of the Single Linkage method and provides an indication of how closely grouped the data are along the dimensions measured. For this reason, we decided that the Single Linkage method is not appropriate for use in this analysis.

10. Ward's method yielded cluster solutions with the highest sum of eigenvalues based on canonical discriminant variables. This means that, of the methods tried here, Ward's method produced the most statistically distinct clusters, although such a test should not be seen as formally validating the resulting cluster structure.

11. Details on these analyses are given by Jenkins (1995).

12. Interestingly, the connection between work system innovation and total quality management is just as strong for the Japanese-affiliated plants in our sample as for the U.S.-owned establishments.

13. The finding regarding inventories applies to both Japanese-affiliated and U.S.-owned automobile parts suppliers.

14. These findings are based on statistical analysis of the correlates of the three plant clusters with other data collected through the survey. The details of this analysis are given in Jenkins (1995).

15. The connection between an Innovative approach to managing production work within the factory and cooperative relations with external customers and suppliers is explored by the authors in greater depth elsewhere (Jenkins, 1995; Jenkins and Florida, 1995).

16. In our survey, respondents were asked to rate a list of factors by the extent to which each has been an obstacle to recent efforts to improve productivity, quality, and costs at the plant. Of all the factors rated, only two have statistically significant relationships with a particular work system regime. Plants in the Mixed cluster were significantly more likely to cite "inadequate skills of production workers" and "programs are still new" as obstacles, while the Innovative plants were significantly more likely to see the newness of programs as an impediment. The responses from plants in the Mixed cluster indicate that the Mixed work system group actually represents

a mix of strategies. Among plants that see the "inadequate skills of production workers" as an impediment to improvement efforts, a Mixed strategy
makes sense as an attempt to remedy the perceived problem—skill deficiencies—by providing off-the-job training for these workers. Plants that see the
individual worker as the source of the problem are unlikely to seek to change
the system by which workers are managed. Among Mixed plants that indicated that the "programs are still new," the approach of such plants can be
seen as an attempt to use the training of workers and other employees as a
means of "transitioning" the plant from a Taylorist to an Innovative system
of production management. Hence, it is likely that a mix of strategies is at
work among the plants in the Mixed cluster.

17. It is important to point out again that Osterman's survey (1992) preceded ours (1994) by two years and that Osterman's sample was limited to
establishments of fifty or more employees, whereas our sample had no size
limit.

18. The "Other Foreign" plants listed in the table are the fourteen plants
in our sample that were affiliated with foreign firms other than Japanese. The
majority of these were German firms.

19. See, for example, the chapter in this volume by MacDuffie and Helper.

References

Abo Tetsuo, ed. 1990. *Local Production of Japanese Automobile and Electronics Firms in the United States: The "Application" and "Adaption"
of Japanese Style Management.* University of Tokyo, Institute of Social
Science, Research Report No. 23.

Abo, Tetsuo. 1993. *Hybrid Factory: The Japanese Production System in the
U.S.* New York: Oxford University Press.

Adler, Paul. 1993a. "The 'Learning Bureaucracy': New United Motor Manufacturing, Inc." In Barry M. Staw and Larry L. Cummings, eds., *Research in Organizational Behavior.* Greenwich, Conn.: JAI Press.

Adler, Paul. 1993b. "Time-and-Motion Regained." *Harvard Business Review*
Jan.–Feb.: 71(1): 97–108.

Aldenderfer, Mark S., and Roger K. Blashfield. 1984. *Cluster Analysis.* Beverly Hills Calif.: Sage.

Anderson, J. C., and D. W. Gerbing. 1988. "Structural Equation Modeling
in Practice: A Review and Recommended Two-Step Approach." *Psychological Bulletin* 103: 411–423.

Bailey, Thomas. 1993. "Discretionary Effort and the Organization of Work:
Employee Participation and Work Reform since Hawthorne." Paper prepared for the Alfred P. Sloan Foundation. Teachers College and Con-
servation of Human Resources Project, Columbia University.

Brown, Clair, and Michael Reich. 1989. "When Does Union-Management
Cooperation Work: A Look at NUMMI and GM-Van Nuys." *California
Management Review* 31: 26–44.

Cole, Robert. 1989. *Strategies for Learning: Small-Group Activities in American, Japanese and Swedish Industry.* Berkeley: University of California
Press.

Cole, Robert. 1992. "Issues in Skill Formation in Japanese Approaches to
Automation." In Paul Adler, ed., *Technology and the Future of Work*,
pp. 187–209. New York: Oxford University Press.

Cole, Robert. 1994. "Different Quality Paradigms and their Implications for
Organizational Learning." In Masahiko Aoki and Ronald Dore, eds.,

The Japanese Firm: Sources of Competitive Strength, pp. 66–83. New York: Oxford University Press.

Cutcher-Gershenfeld, Joel, Michio Nitta, Betty Barrett, Nejib Belhed, and others. 1995. "Japanese Team-Based Work Systems in North America: Explaining the Diversity." California Management Review 37(1): 42–64.

DiMaggio, Paul, and Walter Powell. 1983. "The Iron Cage Revisited: Institutional Isomorphism and Collective Rationality in Organizational Fields." American Sociological Review 48: 147–160.

Everitt, B., 1980. Cluster Analysis. New York: Halstead.

Florida, Richard, and Martin Kenney. 1991. "Transplanted Organizations: The Transfer of Japanese Industrial Organization to the U.S." American Sociological Review 56 (June): 381–398.

Florida, Richard, Martin Kenney, and Davis Jenkins. 1994. Survey of Japanese-Affiliated Manufacturers and Their U.S. Suppliers. Pittsburgh: Center for Economic Development, Carnegie Mellon University.

Fujimoto, Takahiro, Toshihiro Nishiguchi, and Shoichiro Sei. 1994. "The Strategy and Structure of Japanese Automobile Manufacturing in Europe." In Dennis Encarnation and Mark Mason, eds., Does Ownership Matter? Japanese Multinational in Europe, pp. 367–406. Oxford: Oxford University Press.

Ichniowski, Casey, and Kathryn Shaw. 1995. Old Dogs and New Tricks: Determinants of the Adoption of Productivity-Enhancing Work Practices. Brookings Papers on Economic Activity: Microeconomics. Washington, D.C.: Brookings Institution.

Jenkins, Davis. 1995. "Japanese Transplants and the Work System Revolution in U.S. Manufacturing." Ph.D. diss. Carnegie Mellon University, Pittsburgh.

Jenkins, Davis, and Richard Florida. 1995. "Modeling Structures for Learning within Factories and between Them." Unpublished paper, University of Illinois-Chicago and Harvard University.

JETRO. 1993. Directory of Japanese-affiliated Companies in the USA and Canada: 1993–94. Tokyo: Japan External Trade Organization.

Kenney, Martin, and Richard Florida. 1992. "The Japanese Transplants, Production Organization and Regional Development." Journal of the American Planning Association 58 (1): 21–38.

Kenney, Martin, and Richard Florida. 1993. Beyond Mass Production: The Japanese System and Its Transfer to the U.S. New York: Oxford University Press.

Kim, Jae-On, and Charles W. Miller. 1978. Factor Analysis: Statistical Methods and Practical Issues. Beverly Hills, Calif.: Sage.

Klecka, W. R. 1980. Discriminant Analysis. Beverly Hills, Calif.: Sage.

Koike, Kazuo. 1994. "Learning and Incentive Systems in Japanese Industry." In Masahko Aoki and Ronald Dore, eds., The Japanese Firm: Sources of Competitive Strength, pp. 41–65. New York: Oxford University Press.

Krafcik, John. 1986. "Learning from NUMMI." Unpublished paper, Massachusetts Institute of Technology, International Motor Vehicle Program.

Lazonick, William. 1990. Competitive Advantage on the Shop Floor. Cambridge, Mass.: Harvard University Press.

Levine, David I., and Laura D'Andrea Tyson. 1990. "Participation, Productivity, and the Firm's Environment." In Alan S. Blinder, ed., Paying for Productivity. Washington, D.C.: Brookings Institution.

Lincoln, James, and Arne Kalleberg. 1990. Culture, Control and Commitment: A Study of Work Organization and Work Attitudes in the United States and Japan. New York: Cambridge University Press.

Long, J. Scott. 1983a. "Confirmatory Factor Analysis." Beverly Hills, Calif.: Sage.

Long, J. Scott. 1983b. "Covariance Structure Models." Beverly Hills, Calif.: Sage.

MacDuffie, John Paul. 1994. "Human Resource Bundles and Manufacturing Performance: Flexible Production Systems in the World Auto Industry." Unpublished paper, Wharton School, University of Pennsylvania.

MacDuffie, John Paul, and Frits Pil. 1994. "Transferring Japanese Human Resource Practices: Japanese Auto Plants in Japan and the U.S." Paper presented to the International Management Division, Academy of Management, Jan. Philadelphia, PA: Wharton School, Jan. 4.

MacKnight, Susan. 1992. *Japan's Expanding U.S. Manufacturing Presence: 1990 Update*. Washington, D.C.: Japan Economic Institute.

Milkman, Ruth. 1991. *Japan's California Factories: Labor Relations and Economic Globalization*. Los Angeles: Institute of Industrial Relations, University of California.

Ministry of Finance. 1995. *Base Notification Statistics*. Annual reports for the years 1987–1994.

Nonaka, Ikujiro. 1991. "The Knowledge-Creating Company." *Harvard Business Review* 69(6): 96–104.

Nonaka, Ikujiro, and Hirotaka Takeuchi. 1995. *The Knowledge-Creating Company*. New York: Oxford University Press.

Osterman, Paul. 1992. "How Common Is Workplace Transformation and Who Adopts It?" *Industrial and Labor Relations Review* 47(2): 173–188.

Rohlen, Thomas P. 1992. "Learning: The Mobilization of Knowledge in the Japanese Political Economy." In Shumpei Kumon and Henry Rosovsky, eds., *The Political Economy of Japan*. Vol. 3: *Cultural and Social Dynamics*, pp. 321–363. Stanford: Stanford University Press.

Toyo Keizai. 1993. *Japanese Overseas Investment: A Complete Listing by Firms and Countries*. Tokyo: Author.

Wilms, Welford W., Alan J. Hardcastle, and Deone M. Zell. 1994. "A Cultural Transformation: New United Motor Manufacturing, Inc." *Sloan Management Review* 36(1): 99–113.

Womack, James, Daniel Jones, and Daniel Roos. 1990. *The Machine That Changed the World*. New York: Rawson Associates Macmillan.

11

Just-in-Time and Other Manufacturing Practices

Implications for U.S. Manufacturing Performance

Masao Nakamura

Sadao Sakakibara

Roger G. Schroeder

Toyota was the first company to successfully implement what are now known as just-in-time (JIT) manufacturing practices. Toyota began disseminating these practices to other Japanese manufacturers, including its competitors, in the 1970s. The domestic dissemination process was largely complete by the late 1970s.

The JIT concept was first introduced to English-speaking engineering and management practitioners in an article by a group of Toyota employees, Sugimori, Kusunoki, Cho, and Uchikawa (1977). They characterize the Toyota production system as having two equally important features: (1) the JIT production system, which provides "only the necessary products, at the necessary time, in the necessary quantity," and (2) Toyota's "respect-for-human" system of encouraging active employee participation, eliminating wasteful movement by workers, protecting workers' safety, and empowering workers with greater responsibility and authority in the workplace. Kimura and Terada (1981), also Toyota employees, describe Toyota's JIT production system as a "pull system" with three goals: (1) preventing the transmission of the amplified fluctuations of demand or production volume from a succeeding process to the preceding process; (2) minimizing the fluctuation of in-process inventory so as to simplify inventory control; and (3) decentralizing management authority by allowing shop floor supervisors and foremen to make decisions on production and inventory control.

Monden (1981a, 1981b, 1981c), in addressing practicing U.S. industrial engineers, describes Toyota's views on the philosophy of JIT, the *kanban* system, production smoothing in JIT, and set-up time reduction. These articles place particular emphasis on the importance of small lot sizes, mixed model production, multifunction workers, preventive maintenance, and JIT delivery by suppliers.

Schonberger (1982) was one of the first to point out the applicability of JIT in the United States. Contemporary notions were that JIT could not be transplanted to U.S. manufacturing because of cultural obstacles. Shonberger, like Monden, stressed the importance of the shopfloor practices. Hall (1983) also recognized the importance of quality management, product design, supplier networks, and manufacturing strategy in successful implementation of JIT systems in the United States.

JIT manufacturing, which constitutes an integral part of Japanese management systems (JMS), is a complex production management system. Transfer of such a production management system across national boundaries is considerably more difficult than transfer of specific technical knowledge because of the difficulties associated with different languages, cultures, economic functioning, and business practices.

In particular, many of the practices that the "authentic Toyota style JIT system" seemed to require were unknown on the U.S. shop floor in the early 1980s. Nevertheless, the serious competition facing some key U.S. manufacturing industries generated significant U.S. interest in JIT practices by the mid-1980s.[1] The objective of this chapter is to provide an empirical perspective on the international transfer of multilayered production and technology management systems such as JIT.

Core and Infrastructure JIT Practices

JIT manufacturing practices in Japan consist of core and infrastructure practices. The description of JIT at Toyota given by Sugimori, Kusunoki, Cho, and Uchikawa (1977) and others clearly puts forward the notion that there are certain practices that define the core of JIT manufacturing, and some other practices (called infrastructure practices in this chapter) support the JIT practices. There is agreement in the manufacturing literature that the core JIT practices need to be implemented for JIT systems to operate mechanically. We follow Sakakibara, Flynn, Schroeder, and Morris (1993) in our definition of the core JIT and infrastructure practices. Note that the degree of implementation of core and infrastructure JIT practices is likely to be firm-specific as well as industry-specific. That is, some firms in the same industry will employ more JIT practices and some fewer, but there are likely to be well-defined industry norms with respect to the approaches to implementing JIT manufacturing.

Level 1. *Core JIT practices*

(J1) Set-up time reduction. Steps are taken to reduce set-up time.

(J2) Schedule flexibility. Each day's schedule, including time for catching up after stoppages for quality or machine breakdowns, is planned locally.

(J3) Maintenance. Maintenance: practices are part of workers' daily routines, with shift time allowed for maintenance work; maintenance is incorporated into manufacturing strategy.

(J4) Equipment layout. Production is modified to make use of manufacturing cells, improved machine and process layout, and flexible floor layout.[2]

(J5) *Kanban*. Plants and suppliers adopt kanban cards and containers.

(J6) Pull system support. Plants utilize features that support pull systems, such as stopping the line for quality problems, efficient floor layout, and worker-directed production.

(J7) JIT supplier relationships. Suppliers make frequent deliveries and achieve quality certification at the behest of plant managers.

Level 2. *Infrastructure JIT practices*
  Product design

(P1) New product quality. Quality considerations are built into designs and new product introductions.

(P2) Design characteristics. Product design encourage a minimum number of parts and ease of manufacturability and assembly.

(P3) Interfunctional design efforts. Manufacturing has input and cooperates in new product introductions across functional boundaries.

  Work force management

(W1) Supervisory leadership. Supervisors are involved in problem solving and encouraging workers to take steps to improve production and solve problems.

(W2) Incentives for group performance. Pay, promotion and other incentives encourage group/team behavior of workers and managers.

(W3) Labor flexibility. Plant management is commited to training workers for multiple tasks and to maintaining high worker skill levels relative to industry norms.

(W4) Small-group problem solving. Small groups of workers and managers are used for solving production problems and for encouraging workers to bring production-related problems to team problem-solving sessions.

(W5) Recruiting and selection. Plant management considers knowledge and skill levels, problem-solving ability, team performance, values, and ethics in selecting employees.

(W6) Supervisors as team leaders. Supervisors successfully encourage workers to work as a team, express their opinions, and cooperate with each other to improve production.

Organizational characteristics

(O1) Coordination of decision making. Employees are encouraged to discuss how they feel about different plant departments' abilities to coordinate and communicate decisions.

(O2) Decentralization of authority. Employees make some decisions without consulting their supervisors.

(O3) Plant-wide culture. Employees have a plant-wide culture and esprit de corps.

Quality management

(Q1) Process control. Statistical process control is used in production and in designing ways to "foolproof" the process and use of self-inspection.

(Q2) Feedback. Employees receive feedback on manufacturing performance measures such as quality, schedule compliance, and productivity.

(Q3) Rewards for quality. Plant workers and managers perceive that quality improvement is rewarded.

(Q4) Top management leadership for quality. Top management is committed to and has personal involvement in pursuing quality improvement.

(Q5) Supplier quality involvement. Suppliers are involved in efforts to resolve quality concerns.

Manufacturing strategy

(M1) Communication of strategy. Management communicates its goals, objectives, and strategies to employees.

(M2) Long-range orientation. Management takes into account long-term considerations such as quality and operations management in planning strategy goals.

(M3) Manufacturing strategy strength. Management understands and successfully enacts operations strategy.

(M4) New practices. Management adopts new industry practices to maintain a competitive edge.

(M5) Interfunctional competitive edge. Management actively seeks new processes, proprietary technology, and unique ways of using operations to increase a firm's competitive edge in interfunctional efforts.

The role of these infrastructure practices in the successful implementation of JIT is substantial. Good product design for JIT typically uses fewer parts, carefully tailored to meet consumers' demands. Such a design allows JIT manufacturing processes to operate with fewer quality problems and yet produce many differentiated products in time-varying quantities at low cost. Interfunctional cooperation in product design is essential for achieving this goal. The ideal batch size for JIT production is one, which would allow JIT to operate as a continuous production process. Good workforce management encourages workers to cooperate in operating JIT without major production downtimes. For example, any minor repair should be done by shop floor workers on site who have been delegated the authority to do so. Their multifunctional skill has to be developed for this purpose. Quality management of parts and production processes is essential for JIT, which assumes zero defects in general.

JIT is a system tied to and pulled by consumer demands. For this reason, whether or not a firm has a manufacturing strategy that matches JIT production systems to time-varying consumer demands affects the effectiveness with which JIT can function. Finally, implementation of many, if not all, JIT practices requires firm organizational characteristics that foster positive corporate culture. We should also point out that some infrastructure practices (for example, training multiskilled workers and worker incentives) may require changes in the current industry- or economy-wide practices involving unions.

Using respondents' answers at sample plants to scale questions for items J1–M5, it is possible to estimate the degree to which individual JIT practices have been successfully implemented.[3] Aggregate scales for subcategories can also be calculated. For example, aggregating J1–J7 provides a summary measure for the degree to which core JIT practices are implemented at a particular plant. Some empirical estimates obtained for these items are discussed in a later section.

Some practicing engineers in the United States thought that certain JIT practices, *in isolation from others*, could be adopted by U.S. manufacturing plants to reduce inventories, thus saving millions of dollars tied to the inventories. Others, however, were skeptical about the transfer of the JIT concept to the United States without the simultaneous transfer of the infrastructure practices that support the JIT system in Japan. The simple observation that, under certain circumstances, JIT can reduce inventory and hence the costs, with little additional investment, encouraged some U.S. manufacturing firms to experiment with it.[4]

An example of a successful JIT implementation of this type took place at Kawasaki U.S.A. in Lincoln, Nebraska. As early as 1980, Kawasaki U.S.A. started implementing JIT, where various models of motorcycles were made on a single line (Shonberger, 1986). Because the model mix approximately tracks the final demand this JIT-based, mixed-model production resulted in reduced inventory (Schroeder, 1993). In motorcycle production, JIT implementation has given inventory turns (defined by sales/inventory) of about twenty compared with three to five in traditional production settings (Pegels, 1982).

This Kawasaki example, other anecdotal evidence, and our empirical evidence suggest that selective transfer of JIT practices can effectively enhance U.S. manufacturing performance. In the next section, we argue that it seems unlikely that the whole JIT system, *as originally envisioned by Toyota*, will be transferred to the United States. Rather, a successful transfer of JIT requires firms to be selective about which practices to transfer to the United States and how to transfer them.

JIT, Japanese Business Practices, and the Functioning of Japanese Markets

JIT practices depend on certain business and market practices in Japan. These business and market practices are often prevalent across industries. In this section we summarize the role of these economy-wide business and market practices in the implementation of JIT in the United States (These practices are discussed in detail in Nakamura, 1993, and Nakamura and Vertinsky, 1994).

Industrial Relations and Labor Markets

JIT requires workers who are well trained in multifunctional skills. Such skills are necessary, for example, for scheduling flexibility, short setup times, and maintenance efforts on the shop floor. Japanese long-term employment practices allow workers and firms to invest in workers' human capital over long periods of time. Firms are able to reap returns from their investments in human capital, such as expensive on-the-job training (OJT) and job rotations. Moreover, workers can learn new skills, which are typically firm-specific and hence not necessarily highly valued in the labor market, without fear of being laid off. Enterprise labor unions also encourage workers to achieve multifunctional skills.

This internal labor market approach to worker training has worked well in Japan, where the labor market for skilled workers in midcareer is not well developed. However, such an approach is not necessarily in the interests of workers and employers in the United States, where labor market flexibility and worker mobility exist. In the United States, unionized plants have labor unions that are, unlike Japanese enterprise unions, organized across firms. Union rules may make it difficult for firms to establish, for example, fewer job classifications and multifunctional skill classes. Brannen, Liker, and Fruin, this volume, discuss the difficulty Nippon Seiko has experienced in training multifunctional workers in its transplants in the U.S.

Also, investing in workers' human capital over long periods of time may not be compatible with the incentives of U.S. firms and workers. Firms may be unwilling to invest in workers because of their concern that the workers may quit before the firms can reap the returns from human capital investment, and workers may be unwilling to invest time in learning firm-specific skills that may not be rewarded well in the labor market if they are laid off.

While the incentives of post–World War II large-firm industrial relations in Japan are well aligned with the objectives of JIT, new incentive mechanisms have to be created on U.S. shop floors to successfully implement JIT. Different incentive mechanisms are instituted, depending on the type of industry to which firms belong, whether or not plants are unionized, and other factors.[5]

The success of JIT implementation on the U.S. shop floor may also depend on the type of personnel management. For example, Peterson, Peng and

Smith, this volume, find some evidence that using Japanese expatriate managers may lead to less effective personnel management at transplants than using U.S. managers. Since transferring shop floor work practices is an important part of transferring JIT (or, more broadly, JMS) to the United States, firms may have considerable room to exercise ingenuity in how shop floor work and, perhaps, managerial work are organized.

Pil and MacDuffie, this volume, argue that Japanese auto assemblers have used extensive innovation and adaptation to successfully transfer their shop floor work practices to the United States. In particular, they show that Japanese auto assemblers' successful transfer of shop floor work practices to the United States has not been accompanied by the full transfer of the three pillars of the Japanese employment system: lifetime employment, enterprise unionism, and seniority wages. These three pillars are still prevalent in Japan.

Adler, this volume, presents examples of innovative efforts to design appropriate work organization methods for JIT plants in the United States. Adler finds that human resource management (HRM) methods at both NUMMI (New United Motor Manufacturing Inc., a fifty-fifty joint venture between Toyota and GM) and TMM (Toyota Motor Manufacturing, a fully owned subsidiary of Toyota) are neither purely Japanese nor American. Despite their hybrid HRM policies, Adler finds the manufacturing performance levels of NUMMI and TMM to be world class.

Similarly, in this study, we suggest that hybridization processes in HRM practices have taken place at our sample plants (which do not include auto assemblers such as NUMMI and TMM).

Suppliers and Corporate Groups (Capital Keiretsu)

JIT is particularly effective in industries where a large number of parts are assembled into final products (e.g., the auto and appliance industries). In such industries, it has been customary for Japanese assemblers to rely on many suppliers for parts. Therefore, successful JIT implementation requires the integration of the operations of both assemblers and suppliers, and, largely as a result, business relationships between large assemblers and their suppliers are long term in Japan. Moreover, firms' incentives are often carefully aligned, using small but effective equity participation in suppliers by assemblers or other means of risk sharing, joint product development, and technology transfer. Such interfirm arrangements require significant amounts of effort to maintain, since large assemblers often have overwhelming bargaining power against smaller suppliers.

In the United States, where the rights of control of distinct individual corporations are more valued than in Japan, the subtle, potentially unstable, and yet long-term business relationships that characterize Japanese capital *keiretsu* are unattractive. This may explain why Honda has experienced difficulty in developing a reliable network of suppliers in the United States.[6] (MacDuffie and Helper, this volume).

A consequence of long-term interfirm relationships in Japan is that price-based competition in open markets is often sidestepped in favor of relationship-based business transactions. Such behavior in the United States would potentially be subject to antitrust prosecution. (Such antitrust concerns are much more significant in the United States than in Japan.) Traditionally, U.S. corporations have chosen either to vertically integrate parts operations (like GM) or to outsource parts in the spot market. Vertically integrated operations in large firms can suffer from serious agency and bureaucratization problems caused by their size. On the other hand, complete outsourcing from independent suppliers causes problems of coordination because the buyer has no control over the suppliers. The Japanese capital *keiretsu* system, involving suppliers loosely connected and centered around their assembler firms, lies between these two extreme cases and is thus a solution to such interfirm problems.

Successful implementation of JIT for assembly-based operations requires a good coordination of both assemblers' and suppliers' operations concerning core and infrastructure JIT practices. For example, just-in-time arrival of needed parts from suppliers (J7) is a good first step for implementing JIT but may not be adequate for maintaining a long-run supply of quality parts. The assembler and suppliers will undoubtedly need to interact regarding quality management (Q5) and also product design. While there is no a priori reason to believe that implementing core JIT practice (J7) requires any particular form of industrial organization, U.S. firms' experiences so far seem to suggest that some new incentive mechanisms must be devised to incorporate suppliers successfully within a JIT system in the United States. Some U.S. firms have been able to accomplish this.

Functioning of Markets in Japan and the United States

Japanese industrial relations and capital *keiretsu* interfirm relationships, which are prevalent across industries, have serious implications for the functioning of markets and implementation of JIT in Japan. Yet there is no indication that the United States has transferred Japanese practices that would alter the functioning of U.S. labor markets or supplier-assembler relationships fundamentally. In the next section we show that many U.S. manufacturing plants, both U.S. and Japanese owned, have been able to implement core JIT and, to a lesser extent, infrastructure JIT practices in their own ways.

This finding is consistent with Shimada (1988), who advises Japanese manufacturers to (1) ascertain which aspects of their production technologies are essential to their competitiveness and yet independent of market and cultural conditions, and (2) study methods for transferring them to overseas production units in an organizationally effective manner (Nakamura, 1993, p. 247).

Interestingly, the implementation levels of JIT and other management practices at U.S. world-class plants and Japanese transplants in the United

States are quite similar; however, the implementation levels of these practices at Japanese transplants are quite different from the implementation levels at world-class manufacturing plants in Japan. (See Figures 11.1 and 11.2) We also note in Figures 11.3 and 11.4 that world-class Japanese manufacturers emphasize horizontal communication more than their U.S. counterparts. These figures also suggest that the communication practices of Japanese transplants are considerably closer to those of U.S. firms than to those of Japanese world-class plants.[7]

The Japanese transplants have implemented many of the infrastructure practices to a lesser degree than have Japanese manufacturing plants. While some may view this as a reflection of the shortcomings of implementing the Toyota system in the United States, our view is that U.S. world-class manufacturers and Japanese transplants alike have been following the aforementioned strategy put forward by Shimada.

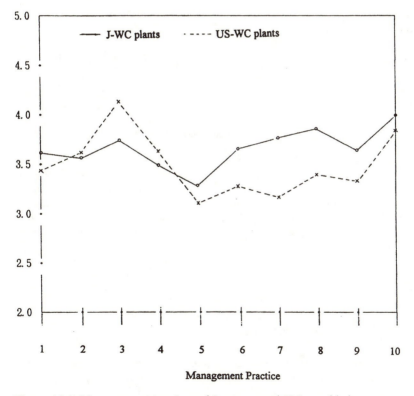

Figure 11.1 Management practices of Japanese and U.S. world-class manufacturers. 1 = shop floor communication and cooperation; 2 = management consistency; 3 = worker attitudes; 4 = human capital development; 5 = JIT practice; 6 = production system development; 7 = shop floor quality control; 8 = organizational quality control; 9 = response to new technology; and 10 = manufacturing strategy.

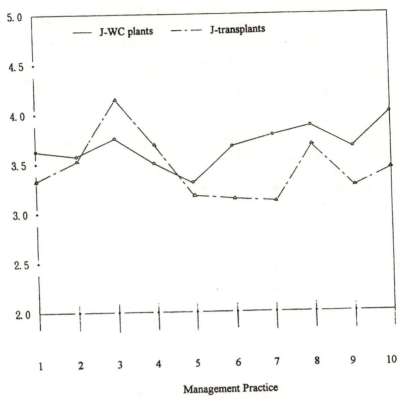

Figure 11.2 Management practices of Japanese and U.S. world-class manu-facturers and Japanese transplants in the United States. 1 = shop floor com-munication and cooperation; 2 = management consistency; 3 = worker at-titudes; 4 = human capital development; 5 = JIT practice; 6 = production system development; 7 = shop floor quality control; 8 = organizational qual-ity control; 9 = response to new technology; and 10 = manufacturing strat-egy.

Empirical Relationships between Core and Infrastructure JIT Practices

The original Toyota JIT system was presented with much emphasis on the infrastructure practices that support implementation of JIT. We have argued that the JIT infrastructure practices developed in Japan are closely tied to Japanese business practices and market functioning. The successful imple-mentation of core JIT practices is positively correlated with the successful implementation of infrastructure practices in Japan.[8] It is of interest to see if such positive correlation is found for implementation of JIT in North America as well, where the assumptions that govern such infrastructure practices are quite different from those that operate in Japan.[9] For this reason, we consider the empirical relationship between core and infrastructure JIT practices.

The core JIT practices are generic in that the successful implementation of these practices *alone* is likely to lead to a successful JIT system. Implementing the core JIT practices, however, can be aided by the presence of JIT infrastructure practices. As we discussed earlier, many of these infrastructure practices are easier to implement in Japan. Firms in the United States, including Japanese transplants, however, must devise methods to deal with U.S. production and industrial relations practices. Thus, it is also interesting to empirically investigate the relationships between plant performance and core and infrastructure practices.

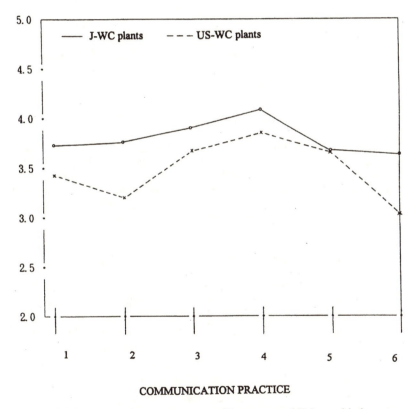

COMMUNICATION PRACTICE

Figure 11.3 Communication practices of Japanese and U.S. world-class manufacturers. 1 = shop floor; 2 = interfunctional; 3 = planned; 4 = between head offices; 5 = supplier relations, product development; 6 = supplier relations, logistics.

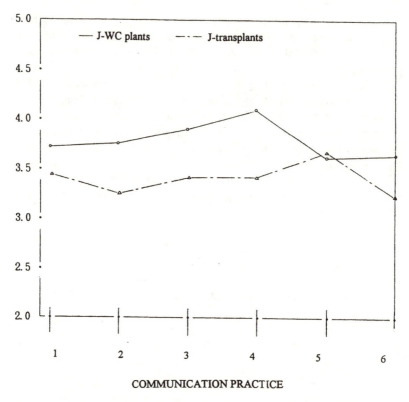

Figure 11.4 Communication practices of Japanese and U.S. world-class manufacturers and Japanese transplants in the United States. 1= shop floor; 2 =
interfunctional; 3 = planned; 4 = between head offices; 5 = supplier relations, product development; 6 = supplier relations, logistics.

Description of Our Sample Plants

First, we present empirical results based on our own sample of twenty-nine
United States owned and thirteen Japanese-owned manufacturing plants located in the United States. The U.S. subsample consists of seventeen world-
class plants and twelve traditional plants where we have used Schonberger's
(1986) definitions for world-class and traditional plants.[10] Our sample plants
belong to the machinery, auto parts, and electronics industries. No auto assemblers (for example, the Big Three) are included in our sample. Florida
and Jenkins, this volume, find that the degree of adoption of organizational
innovation among U.S.-and Japanese-owned plants in the United States varies
significantly by industry. Our sample includes multiple manufacturing industries and thus should reflect such industry effects. In 1990, we obtained detailed responses to scale questions from selected managers and workers at
each sample plant. The scale questions measure the degree of implementation

of each of the core and infrastructure JIT practices discussed earlier. Information on plant performance and specifications were also obtained.[11] Tables 11.1 and 11.2 describe our sample plants.

From Table 11.1 we see that Japanese transplants are considerably smaller than U.S.-owned plants in sales and value added. Small value added implies the transplants' small stock of capital equipment compared to their U.S.-owned counterparts. This is also consistent with the fact that the transplants and their equipment are both quite young (52 percent of their equipment is less than two years old, compared to 16 percent and 12 percent, respectively, for world-class and traditional plants.) Young age provides an advantage to

Table 11.1 Characteristics of Sample Plants[a]

Variable	WC	T	J
Industry			
Machinery	4	5	4
Auto parts	4	3	5
Electronics	9	4	4
Sales ($000)	213,657	127,220	78,397
Sales per employee ($000)	344	203	184
Value added per employee ($000)	226	119	42
Cost of goods sold/sales	94%	68%	95%
Manufacturing costs			
Direct labor	7%	10%	10%
Materials	61	61	74
Overhead	32	28	15
Net investment in plant and equipment ($000)	20,035	22,398	23,494
Original year when plant was built	1964	1939	1986
Equipment age			
LT 2 years	16%	12	52
3–5 years	25	8	35
6–10 years	25	28	10
11–20 years	21	29	3
GT 20 years	13	23	0
Production processes			
One of a kind	3%	15%	1%
Small batch	36	44	17
Large batch	7	37	8
Repetitive/semicontinuous	40	10	39
Continuous	11	3	39

a. Our sample firms were randomly selected from master lists of plants in each subgroup. The sources used were: Dun's Industrial Guide (1986) for traditional plants, Schonberger's (1986) Honor Roll for world-class plants, and JETRO's directory of Japanese FDI.

Table 11.2 Performance of Sample Plants[a]

	WC	T	J
JIT performance variables			
Lead time (days)	20	96	61
Cycle time (days)	46	80	68
Inventory turns	6.5	3.4	14.2
On-time delivery (%)	66.9	79.0	82.8
Competitive advantage variables[b]			
Unit cost of manufacturing	2.4	2.7	2.9
Quality of goods and services	1.6	1.9	1.3
Fast delivery	1.9	2.6	1.8
Flexibility to change production volume	2.4	2.5	2.6

a. Our sample firms were randomly selected from master lists of plants in each subgroup. The sources used were: Dun's Industrial Guide (1986) for traditional plants, Schonberger's (1986) Honor Roll for world-class plants, and JETRO's directory of Japanese FDI.

b. These are scale variables representing 1 to 5 (1 = highly competitive, 5 = not competitive).

the transplants in one respect; the new equipment they use typically incorporates JIT hardware requirements. Given this significant difference in the age of equipment, it is interesting to note that U.S.-owned world-class plants record better performance in lead time and cycle time than the transplants, while the transplants do better in inventory turns and on-time delivery (first panel in Table 11.2). There seems to be little difference in competitive advantage variables between world-class and transplants (second panel in Table 11.2). Because of the small sample size, it is not possible to test the ranking of performance by plant type. Yet the variation we observe in plant performance and plant characteristics by plant type is reassuring for our statistical analysis to follow.

Relationships between Core JIT and Infrastructure JIT Practices

An appropriate statistical method to test the relationship between two sets of variables (core and infrastructure JIT practices here) is canonical correlation analysis. Canonical correlation is a technique for analyzing the relationship between two sets of variables. Each set can contain several variables. To capture all possible sources of correlation between two sets of variables, it is customary to find several independent dimensions (axes) along which the correlation between the two sets is measured. The correlation coefficients measured along such dimensions are ordered by their magnitudes into first canonical correlation, second canonical correlation, and so on.

Simple and multiple correlation are by definition special cases of canonical correlation in which one or both sets contain a single variable. Therefore, in our empirical analysis to follow, canonical correlation is interpreted simply as a statistic representing correlation between two sets of variables. (A detailed statistical description of canonical correlation is given in the Appendix.)

The extent to which a canonical pair of combinations of variables can explain (span) the original variables is the Redundancy Index (RI). Thus, RI is a simple extension of the standard R^2 in regression analysis and reduces to R^2 when one or both sets of variables contain a single variable. RI can be interpreted as the goodness of fit associated with a particular canonical pair. The sum of the RIs associated with all statistically significant canonical pairs represent the goodness of fit for the model. By definition, each RI, as well as its sum over all canonical pairs, lies between 0 and 1.

Our canonical correlation analysis for measuring the strength of the relationships between core and infrastructure JIT practices, reported in Table 11.3, shows that the first two canonical correlations (.8258 and .6826) are both statistically significant (at the 0.02 percent and 5.7 percent levels, respectively) and infrastructure practices explain 52.36 percent (RI = .5236 = .4097 + .1139) of the core JIT practices variance.[12] We conclude, therefore, that the successful implementations of the core JIT and infrastructure practices are positively correlated. We also note that a significant portion (about 50 percent) of the variance of core JIT practices cannot be explained by infrastructure practices. That is, some of the JIT core practices can be implemented as generic practices for reducing inventory without regard to the infrastructure practices.

Relationship between JIT Performance and Core and Infrastructure JIT Practices

We measure JIT Performance by four quantitative variables for each plant: inventory turnover (cost of goods sold/total inventory), cycle time (average time between raw material procurement and customer delivery), lead time (average amount of time to fill an order), and on-time delivery (percentage of on-time delivery to customers).

Table 11.3 Relationships between Core JIT and Infrastructure Practices: Correlation Estimates[a]

	First Canonical Pair	Second Canonical Pair
Canonical correlation (*p* value)	.8258 (.0002)	.6826 (.0570)
Goodness of fit: Redundancy index (RI)	.4097	.1139

a. Only the first two canonical pairs are statistically significant at at least an 80 percent level and are reported here.

Table 11.4 shows that the canonical correlation between the core JIT practices and JIT performance is .7827, which is statistically significant at a 10 percent level ($p=.0847$). The fraction of the variance in the JIT performance practices that can be explained by the core JIT variables is 39.2 percent.

We have already seen that JIT core and infrastructure practices are highly correlated. It is, then, of interest to see the correlation between the combined core JIT and infrastructure practices and the JIT performance practices. From Table 11.4 we see that the correlation is .8041, which is statistically significant at 1 percent ($p=.0078$), and 44.7 percent of the variance in the JIT performance practices is explained by combined core JIT and infrastructure practices.

We conclude that implementing core JIT practices is associated with a significant improvement in the performance of U.S. manufacturing industries.[13] This is consistent with many successful implementations of JIT in the United States where plant management used its ingenuity in implementing generic core aspects of JIT practices over which the plant management had control.[14]

JIT as a Source of Competitive Advantage

JIT performance variables are generally thought to reflect various operational performance levels of manufacturing plants. They do not, however, measure the competitiveness of plants' products in the market place. We use the following factors to describe the competitiveness of a manufacturing plant: cost of manufacturing, quality of product and service, fast delivery, and flexibility to change volume. We then used the five perceptual five-point Likert scale variables corresponding to these factors to measure plant management's opinion of the plant's performance.

We find that competitive advantage is highly correlated with JIT performance, having a canonical correlation of .8302 ($p = .0024$) and the goodness of fit RI = 54.05 percent.

Table 11.4 Relationships between JIT Performance and Core JIT/Infrastructure Variables: Correlation Estimates[a]

	JIT Performance and Core JIT Practices	JIT Performance and Core JIT/ Infrastructure Practices
Canonical correlation (p value)	.7827 (0.847)	.8041 (.0078)
Goodness of fit: Redundancy index (RI)	.3920	.4472

a. Only the first canonical pair is significant at at least an 80 percent level and is reported here.

Canonical Correlations for U.S.-owned Plants

Our results so far are for the entire sample of both U.S.-owned and Japanese-owned manufacturing plants. It is of interest to see if similar results hold for U.S.-owned plants alone. The behavior of the canonical correlations for the U.S.-owned plants in our sample, shown in Table 11.5, is quite consistent with that of the canonical correlations for the entire sample. We conclude that the patterns of transfer of JIT to U.S.-owned plants are similar to those for the entire sample. (Because of the small sample size, it is not possible to conduct similar analysis for the Japanese-owned plants.)

Concluding Remarks

In this chapter we have discussed implementation of core and infrastructure JIT practices in the United States We have argued that while the original Toyota production system was consistent with the business practices and market functioning that prevail in Japan, transfer of such Japanese business practices and market functioning to North America has not taken place and is unlikely to take place in the future. This does not imply, however, that a successful transfer of JIT to North America is not possible.

Our empirical evidence suggests that both world-class U.S. manufacturers and Japanese transplants in various industries have been able to adapt the core JIT and infrastructure practices to the U.S. environment. In particular, we have shown that the implementation of Core JIT practices alone is associated with a significant improvement in U.S. manufacturing performance. This also means that U.S. manufacturers have successfully implemented certain Japanese practices without having to adopt Japanese country-specific business practices.

Table 11.5 U.S.-Owned Plants: Correlation Estimates[a]

	Core and Infrastructure JIT Practices	Core JIT Practice and JIT Performance	Core/ Infrastructure JIT and JIT Performance	Competitive Advantage and JIT Performance
Canonical correlation (p value)	.881 (.0061)	.822 (.2719)	.862 (.0618)	.828 (.0144)
Goodness of fit: Redundancy index (RI)	.494	.415	.526	.501

a. Only the first canonical pair is significant at at least an 80 percent level and reported here. The sample size is 22 for all columns except the second column (Core JIT practices and JIT performance) for which the sample size is 28.

In examining HRM practices at NUMMI and TMM, Adler, this volume, states that "foreign subsidiaries in the U.S. (or elsewhere) operate within a complete cultural, social, and institutional context that affords them—indeed, demands of them—interpretation, choice, and learning." Our findings on the implementation of JIT at Japanese- and U.S.-owned plants in the United States are consistent with Adler's interpretation. We believe that similar environments face U.S.-owned firms that try to implement JIT and JMS practices in their own domestic plants.

Appendix: Canonical Correlation

This method finds a linear combination from each set of variables, called a canonical variable, such that the correlation between the two canonical variables is maximized. This correlation between the two combinations is the first canonical correlation. The coefficients of the linear combinations are canonical coefficients (canonical weights). The method continues by finding a second set of canonical variables, uncorrelated with the first pair, that produces the second highest correlation coefficient. The process of constructing canonical variables continues until the number of pairs of canonical variables equals the number of variables in the smaller group. Each canonical variable is uncorrelated with all other canonical variables, of either set except for the one corresponding canonical variable in the opposite set. In most empirical analysis, only a first few canonical correlations are statistically significant, which means that the corresponding pairs of canonical variables are statistically sufficient to describe fully the relationships that exist between the two sets of variables under investigation. For statistical inference, canonical correlation analysis requires multivariate normality of the variables in the data sets. Normality of variables in our data set is accepted by the Shapiro and Wilk test (1965) at a 5 percent level. It is also shown that, for multivariate analysis with aggregate data of our type, our sample size (41) is acceptable (Hofstede et al., 1990).

Notes

1. More than 700 articles on JIT were written in the United States during the period 1985–1990. While some studies regard JIT practices as merely shop floor management practices, many others view them more broadly, as in the original descriptions of the Toyota system, as affected by various other aspects of management practices: manufacturing strategy, human resource management, and quality management and supplier management practices, among others.

2. The Toyota production system emphasizes cellular work arrangements where the machines that would ordinarily be dispersed in various process departments are arranged in small groups in work cells. In a work cell, batches of related but different products can be processed, often simultaneously. One of the implications of using a work cell is reduced work-in-process

inventory; hence, JIT manufacturing typically requires use of work cells. The idea of work cells was first presented in the United States by Flanders (1925).

3. To measure the scale for each of items J1–M5, respondents (representative workers and some management personnel of a sample plant) were asked several (three to five) questions for each item. The specific questions asked are given in Sakakibara, Flynn, Schroeder, and Morris (1997).

4. These firms include Ford, GE, GM, Eaton, Motorola, Black & Decker, Briggs and Stratten, Hewlett-Packard, IBM, John Deere, Bendix, Mercury Marine, Omark, Rockwell, Westinghouse, Tennant, 3M and Honeywell. (Schroeder (1993).)

5. Labor unions' objections to outsourcing has been traditionally stronger in the United States than in Japan. This may also explain U.S. firms' traditional tendency to vertically integrate. Unionization varies from one industry to another. For example, the auto industry (e.g., the Big Three) is generally unionized, but the electronics industry is less so. Neither IBM nor HP is unionized. Kenney, this volume, also argues that there are far greater inter-industry differences in the United States than in Japan in many prevailing business practices.

6. Toyota's Vice CEO states that "Toyota buys parts from about 400 U.S. suppliers. There is, however, considerable variance in performance among these suppliers. Japanese suppliers are still better in continuous *kaizen* movement and product quality" (Nihon Keizai shimbun, Tokyo, June 29, 1996). We believe that the variance in performance among U.S. suppliers comes from the difference in performance between world-class and traditional manufacturing plants. (See Tables 11.1 and 11.2). Such variance is very low for Japanese transplants or, more generally, Japanese suppliers. We do not have explanations for why high variance persists in U.S. plants.

7. Fruin and Nakamura (1997) report that top-down production management methods are being implemented in improving the productivity of many Japanese corporations.

8. These two types of practices are highly correlated in Japan. For example, analyzing a sample of thirty-two Japanese manufacturing plants with world-class reputations, Morita, Sakakibara, and Flynn (1995) find that good plants (above average plants) score better in all of the ten manufacturing performance measures including JIT and infrastructure practices measures than poor plants (below average plants).

9. Such positive correlation might be observed, for example, when: (1) firms copy both JIT core and infrastructure practices from Japan to their U.S. plants (institutional explanation), and (2) the implementation of JIT core practices naturally leads to the subsequent implementation of JIT infrastructure practices (causal explanation). We are indebted to Jeff Liker for this footnote.

10. Schonberger's (1960) Honor Roll identifies world-class plants chosen on the basis of manufacturing excellence, quality management, top management support, technology management, and other factors. We consulted with industry leaders before placing plants from Schonberger's Honor Roll on our master list of world-class plants.

11. See Flynn, Sakakibara, and Schroeder (1995) and Flynn, Schroeder, and Sakakibara (1994, 1995, 1996) for detailed descriptions of the sample and the questionnaire used and for additional empirical applications.

12. Note that, prior to our canonical correlation analysis, the individual scales within each of the infrastructure groups are combined into a superscale. A superscale is the mean of the scores on individual scales. For example, the Product Design superscale is the mean of the scores on three scales: New

Product Quality, Design Characteristics, and Interfunctional Design Efforts. We also standardize scales and superscale scores by industry. All four JIT performance criteria are also standardized to have a mean of 0 and a variance of 1 for each industry. Such standardization is necessary for the following reason. Suppose that transportation industry (T) has a better JIT performance than machinery industry (M). This may be because T uses fewer components than M or because T tends to use more continuous processes than M. Standardization removes these issues from our consideration.

13. We should note that, in obtaining our canonical correlation between JIT core practices and JIT performance, reported in Table 11.4, we do not control for the effects of JIT infrastructure practices. Obtaining canonical correlations after controlling for (partialing out) the effects of variables not included is beyond the scope of this paper.

14. This conclusion is also consistent with empirical results based on regressions in Nakamura, Sakakibara, and Schroeder (1998).

References

Dun & Bradstreet Corporation, Dun's Industrial Guide, Dun Bradstreet, NY, NY, 1986.

Flanders, R. E. 1925. "Design Manufacture and Production Control of a Standard Machine." *Transactions of the American Society of Mechanical Engineers* 46: 28–37.

Flynn, B. B., S., Sakakibara, and R. G. Schroeder. 1995. "The Interrelationship between JIT and TQM: Practices and Performance." *Academy of Management Journal* 38: 1325–1360.

Flynn, B. B., R. G., Schroeder, and S. Sakakibara, 1994. "A Framework for Quality Management Research and an Associated Measurement Instrument." *Journal of Operations Management* 11: 339–366.

Flynn, B. B., R. G., Schroeder, and S. Sakakibara. 1995. "The Impact of Quality Management Practices on Performance and Competitive Advantage." *Decision Sciences* 26: 659–691.

Flynn, B. B., R. G., Schroeder, and S. Sakakibara. 1996. "The Relationship between Quality Management Practices and Performance: Synthesis of Findings from the World-Class Manufacturing Project." *Advances in the Management of Organizational Quality*, Stanford, CT: JAI Press, 1: 141–185.

Fruin, M., and M. Nakamura. 1997. "Top-Down Production Management: A Recent Trend in the Japanese Productivity Enhancement Movement." *Managerial and Decision Economics* 18: 131–139.

Hall, R. W. 1983. *Zero Inventories*. Homewood, Ill: Dow Jones-Irwin.

Hofstede, G., B., Neuijen, D. D., Ohayv, and G., Sanders. 1990. "Measuring Organizational Cultures: A Qualitative and Quantitative Study across Twenty Cases." *Administrative Sciences Quarterly* 35: 286–316.

Kimura, O., and H. Terada. 1981. "Design and Analysis of Pull System: A Method of Multistate Production Control." *International Journal of Production Research* 19: 241–253.

Monden, Y. 1981a. "What Makes the Toyota System Really Tick?" *Industrial Engineering* 13 (Jan.): 36–46.

Monden, Y. 1981b. "Adaptable Kanban System Helps Toyota Maintain Just-in-Time Production." *Industrial Engineering* 13 (May): 29–46.

Monden, Y. 1981c. "Toyota's Production Smoothing Method: Part II." *Industrial Engineering* 13 (Sept.): 22–30.

Morita, M., S. Sakakibara, and E. J. Flynn, 1995. "Properties of Fit in World-Class Manufacturing Management: Analyses and Implications for Competitiveness." Paper presented at the annual meeting of the Academy of Management, Vancouver, Aug. 10.

Nakamura, M. 1993. "Japanese Industrial Relations in an International Business Environment." *North American Journal of Economics and Finance* 4: 225–251.

Nakamura, M., and I. Vertinsky. 1994. *Japanese Economic Policies and Growth: Implications for Businesses in Canada and North America.* Edmonton: University of Alberta Press.

Nakamura, M., S. Sakakibara, and R. G. Schroeder. 1998. "Adoption of Just-in-Time Manufacturing Methods at U.S.-and Japanese-owned Plants: Some Empirical Evidence." *1998 IEEE Transactions on Engineering Management,* 45: 230–240.

Pegels, C. C. 1982. "The Kanban Production Management Information System." In S. Lee and G. Schwendiman, eds., *Management by Japanese Systems,* pp. 152–164. New York: Praeger.

Sakakibara, S., B. B., Flynn. R. G., Schroeder, and W. T. Morris. 1997. "The Impact of Just-in-Time Manufacturing and Its Infrastructure on Manufacturing Performance." *Management Science* 43: 1246–1257.

Schonberger, R. J. 1982. *Japanese Manufacturing Techniques: Nine Hidden Lessons in Simplicity.* New York: Free Press.

Schonberger, R. J. 1986. *World-Class Manufacturing.* New York: Free Press.

Schroeder, R. G. 1993. *Operations Management: Decision Making in the Operations Function,* 4th ed. New York: McGraw-Hill.

Shapiro, S. S., and Wilk, M. B. 1965. "An Analysis of Variance Test for Normality." *Biometrika* 52: 591–611.

Shimada, H. 1988. *The Economics of Humanware* (in Japanese). Tokyo: Iwanami.

Sugimori, Y., K. Kusuniki, F. Cho, and S. Uchikawa. 1977. "Toyota Production System and Kanban System: Materialization of Just-in-Time and Respect-for-Human System." *International Journal of Production Research* 15: 553–563.

Vesey, J. T. 1992. "Time-to-Market: Put Speed in Product Development." *Industrial Marketing Management* 21: 151–158.

Part IV

Synthesis

12

Organization Theory Perspectives on the Cross-Border Transfer of Organizational Patterns

D. Eleanor Westney

The transfer of Japanese production systems to the United States in the 1980s and 1990s must rank as the most widely discussed and intensively studied case of cross-border organizational learning in modern history. But the nature of the discussion has shifted over time. In the early 1980s, when the establishment of Japanese auto plants like Honda's in Ohio and Toyota's joint venture with GM in California first drew extensive popular attention to the issue, much of the discussion was over whether Japanese systems were at all transferable to the U.S. social context, which differed in so many ways from the Japanese setting in which they had evolved. Time and many careful studies have demonstrated that many Japanese practices do in fact "work" in the U.S. industrial setting but that they—or the larger organizational system of which they are a part—require some adaptation or modification to do so. This is the central theme of many of the chapters in this volume, and although the various authors differ in the terms they use—hybridization, recontextualization, adaptation, transplantation, localization, learning—they are talking about the same phenomenon: when complex organizational systems developed in one social context (in this case Japan) are transferred to a different setting (the United States), they change, and the resulting system is neither a copy of the original model nor a replica of existing local patterns, but something different. In some cases, the outcome is an organizational form that has ongoing problems and is seen as less successful than either the original model or comparable local organizations. In other cases, however, such as the Japanese auto transplants that are the focus of many of the chapters of this book, hybridization becomes adaptive innovation, producing new organizational patterns that become part of the organizational landscape in the new setting.

In today's era of increasing internationalization of organizations and organizational networks, the processes involved in the cross-societal transfer of organizational patterns constitute a topic of broad interest to managers, workers, and scholars of organizations. The increasing cross-border integration of activities within multinational corporations (MNCs), learning from "global best practice," the emulation of the social organization of market economies in the formerly state socialist countries of the former Soviet bloc— all involve the transfer of organizational patterns developed in one context into another. The experience with Japanese production systems in the United States is of great interest in its own right, but it has a much broader relevance.

In exploring the wider implications of the experience with the Japanese transplants, one would expect that organization theory would provide well-developed perspectives on which to build. After all, for more than three decades organization theory has been dominated by "open systems" models of organizations, which begin with the premise that organizational structures and processes can best be understood in terms of their relationships with their environment. But although organization theory provides several useful perspectives on cross-societal organizational transfers, there have been remarkably few systematic studies, either empirical or conceptual, of the specific issues involved in such transfers and the subsequent change processes. As a result, established theory provides very little in the way of specific hypotheses. This chapter identifies three perspectives on organization-environment relations (the organization as "strategic design" as "social construct," and as "political system") and then builds on them and on the chapters in this volume to develop generalizations about what patterns organizations are most likely to want to transfer across borders, what changes are likely to take place in those transfers, and what processes of change are likely to be observed.

Three Organizational Perspectives

The proliferation of schools of organization theory has led to an array of taxonomies to cluster various schools of thought into more general categories, whose utility depends on the purpose for which it is used. In the organizational literature produced over the past four decades—which mark the introduction and ascendancy of the open systems perspective on organizations— we can identify three broad perspectives that are particularly useful for looking at organization-environment relations.[1] The perspective that is most common in management regards organizations as "strategic designs"—systems consciously constructed for the efficient accomplishment of certain tasks. Another perspective sees them instead primarily as ideational constructs defined by shared interpretations, meaning, and value (hereafter referred to as the "social construct perspective"). And the third perspective portrays them as both arenas for and tools of power and interests (the "political" perspective). All three perspectives can trace their lineage to Max Weber, widely regarded as the progenitor of organization theory. His seminal work on bureaucracy contains many of the key elements of the strategic design perspective, while his comparative studies of religious worldviews and the rise of capitalism contains the seeds of elements of the social construct perspective, and his discussion of power and authority provides a touchstone for much subsequent development in the political perspective. As the possibility of anchoring all three perspectives in Weber shows, these perspectives are not mutually exclusive theoretical domains; rather, they are potentially complementary ways of viewing the complex processes of organizational change and organization-environment interactions.

Organizational analysis in the strategic design perspective focuses on organizational structures and processes—how activities are clustered and linked so that they contribute to (or, in some cases, stand in the way of) the efficient achievement of organizational goals. The environment, in keeping with the "systems" model of the organization as an input-throughput-output system (which is fundamental to much of the work in this perspective), is portrayed as a source of necessary inputs and an absorber of outputs—the "task environment" (Dill, 1958), the "organization-set" (Evan, 1966), or the "organizational domain" (Thompson, 1967).

A number of paradigms and schools of thought come under the umbrella of this perspective: the Aston school, early work on technology and organization (including Woodward, 1965; Thompson, 1967, and the early work [1970] of Perrow), contingency theory (Lawrence & Lorsch, 1967), organization design (Galbraith, 1973), the strategy-structure approach of Alfred Chandler (1962, 1977), the strategic choice approach (Child, 1972), transaction cost analysis (Williamson, 1975, 1985), and much of the recent work in the strategy field on the resource-based view of the firm (e.g., Aaker, 1989; Conner, 1991). Obviously, these various paradigms differ considerably in the specific variables they use to analyze organizations and the ways they characterize environments. However, they share certain fundamentals: for example, the micro foundation in terms of the model of individual behavior is basically utilitarian, in that human behavior is assumed to be means-rational in the Weberian sense, within the limits of available information ("bounded rationality"), and responsive to material incentives. The key features of organization are its design and the relationships among design, task, and environment (for example, the division of labor, coordination, and the provision and generation of the resources necessary to perform required tasks). Change in organizations is fundamentally driven by problems of lack of *fit*, both internal fit among the various elements of structure and process and external fit with the resource configurations and exigencies of the environment. When organizations face problems because of lack of internal fit (a problem, for example, because a unit is given a certain task but is not assigned the skills or resources needed to accomplish it) or external fit (for example, the products or services a firm provides no longer match the needs of customers), their managers can and should change the organization design in order to improve the organization's efficiency and effectiveness. One of the key tools in redesigning organizations is the realignment of rewards and incentives to fit the goals of the organization and the requirements of the new design.

Organizational analysis in the social construct perspective centers on understanding how the participants themselves view and interpret their own organization and with how organizational patterns are viewed and interpreted in the larger social context; see, for example, the work of Karl Weick (1977, 1995), organizational ethnography (e.g., Kunda, 1992; Van Maanen, 1988), the structuration theory of Anthony Giddens, the vast literature on organizational culture, and institutional theory. The micro foundation of the perspective is built on individuals as "sense makers," drawing on shared, collective models of how the world works and how it ought to work. As Scott has pointed out in the context of institutional theory (one of the variants of this perspective), this has both a cognitive aspect—the "taken-for-granted" assumptions about how organizations work that are captured in concepts like cognitive schema, mental maps, and Meyer and Rowan's (1977, p. 345) colorful metaphor of "the building blocks for organizations [that] come to be littered around the societal landscape"—and a normative component— patterns that are invested with value and ideas about what is good, right, and appropriate. In most analyses that use the social construct model, organizational change is seen as a slow, emergent process, and managers face severe limitations on their ability to alter its direction or its speed, in part because internal cognitive and normative patterns are reinforced by the external environment. There are two related models of the environment in this perspective. One portrays it in terms of larger national or occupational cultures that shape and reinforce internal patterns (Hofstede, 1980), or even in terms of broader civilizational patterns (Hamilton, 1994). The other model is the "organizational field" of institutional theory, which portrays a set of interacting organizations within an arena of activity (comparable to an industry) that share certain expectations of other participants in that arena and that shape and reinforce cognitive and normative aspects of organizations within the entire field (DiMaggio and Powell, 1983).

The third perspective, the political, sees organizations as arenas for contending interests and the struggle for power. Organizational analysis centers here on conflict, coalition building, interests, negotiation, power, and influence. Resources are a focus of interest, not (as in the strategic design perspective) in terms of their efficient utilization but because of who controls them and the power such control confers. Within this perspective, one can identify several levels of analysis. Some authors, particularly those who concentrate on the factory and on the organization of work, focus on organizations as arenas for occupational and class conflict (Clegg and Dunkerley, 1980; Crozier, 1964; Edwards, 1979; Perrow, 1981); others focus on the struggle for power among managers (Mintzberg, 1983; Pfeffer, 1981, 1992); still others (such as the resource dependency school) focus on the power of the organization relative to the other organizations with which it interacts (Pfeffer & Salancik, 1978). For all three, however, the micro model of human behavior involves the drive for power and influence on the one hand and the drive for autonomy on the other (resource dependency extrapolates this micro model directly to the organization as a whole).

The organizational environment is therefore portrayed as a set of actors who are potential allies or foes in the internal struggles for ascendancy and/ or a set of strategic resources whose control affects the power balance within the organization or the power of the organization in its network. The most common political model of the environment in the study of business organizations today is the *stakeholders* model (see, for example, Donaldson & Preston, 1995; *Economist*, 1996; Freeman & Reed, 1983; Kochan & Rubenstein, 1997). Stakeholders are internal and external actors with a stake in the organization—meaning those whose well-being is affected by the actions of (and within) the organization (e.g., the local community, interest groups such as consumers' groups or environmental activists, shareholders, and unions). These external stakeholders also control or have access to resources that can affect the internal power balance. This perspective focuses on organizational change that occurs as a result of a change in the power balance of the organization, which is often linked to the mobilization of external stakeholders in alliance with a set of internal stakeholders.

Despite the very different premises on which these perspectives are based (or perhaps because of them), they rarely generate directly competing hypotheses about adaptation processes when organizational patterns move across borders. More often, they direct attention to different sets of variables and processes, or they predict similar outcomes but for different reasons (equifinality). All three perspectives, for example, would predict that over time, organizations of a similar scale in a given industry will come to exhibit very similar organizational patterns; however, they differ on their explanations for this commonality. The strategic design perspective would interpret this as a consequence of the shared patterns' fit with the demands of the industry environment. The social construct perspective would assert that the shared patterns come to be regarded as an appropriate and conveniently accessible recipe within an organizational field. And the political perspective would see the dissemination of a particular set of patterns as a playing out of the power configurations across stakeholders. Let us turn now to how each of these perspectives speaks to cross-border organizational transfers.

Cross-Border Transfers of Organizational Patterns

This section addresses three issues. The first is the question of what patterns are likely to be transferred across borders in two contexts: from MNC parent to local subsidiary (as in the case of the Japanese transplants), and from a foreign model to a local emulator (as in the case of U.S. firms "learning" from their Japanese competitors).[2] The second concerns the factors that drive changes in those patterns in their new environment. The third is the kind of processes by which adaptation takes place.

The Logic of Transfer

Each of the three perspectives would put forward a different logic of transfer. In other words, each has a different answer to the question of what organizational patterns are most likely to be transferred across borders—or, more accurately, which patterns organizations are likely to try to transfer. Within a multinational corporation (MNC), a strategic design perspective would argue that a parent company will transfer to its subsidiaries abroad those organizational patterns that optimize the company's efficiency and effectiveness and that give it a competitive advantage in its industry (see chapter 2, by Adler, in this volume, and also Kogut and Zander, 1993). Analogously, in the case of firms in one country emulating patterns from another country, local firms will try to learn from the competitively superior patterns of their key foreign competitors, especially in industries where those competitors are successfully invading local markets and in which their success is attributed to superior organizational capabilities, rather than to lower factor costs or better products. In this strategic design perspective, the Japanese production system is fundamentally a set of organizational structures, processes, practices, and routines that have enabled Japanese industrial firms to lower production costs, improve quality, and increase flexibility, thus conferring a competitive advantage in many industries over firms that have not adopted such systems (or their functional equivalents). Therefore, both Japanese MNCs moving production offshore and U.S. firms competing with Japanese companies will make a strategic choice to transfer or emulate the key elements of the organization design that produce this competitive advantage (chapter 11, by Nakamura, Sakakibara, & Schroeder, in this volume, provides an excellent example of this perspective for both sets of actors, Japanese MNCs and U.S. firms trying to compete with Japanese firms). Aspects of organization design that are not central to competitive advantage can be filled in with patterns that conform to local practice. Therefore, one would expect that, among MNCs from a given country, one would observe considerable variation in what parent companies try to transfer to their subsidiaries across industries, because organizational practices differ in their salience for competitive advantage across industries, (as Martin Kenney points out in chapter 8 of this volume, in which he contrasts the low level of transfer of the social organization of production from Japan to the transplants in television assembly with the much more extensive transfers in later-arriving auto assembly plants). One might also expect some variation across individual firms: Sony will differ from Matsushita, for example, because it has tried to differentiate its strategy and organization from its older, more established competitor, and Honda may well differ from Toyota in its approach to building and maintaining a local supplier network, given its latecomer status in the industry and its consequent challenges in building a supplier network in its home country (see chapter 5, by MacDuffie & Helper, in this volume). Similar industry-level and firm-level differences can be expected in the emulation of Japanese patterns by local firms; cross-border emulation of organizational patterns will be greatest in those industries where Japanese competitors are extremely strong, to the point of threatening the home market, and where organization-based capabilities constitute key competitive advantages. Therefore, according to this perspective, we would expect learning from Japan on the part of local firms to be greatest in such industries as autos, auto parts, semiconductors, and copiers and for particular firms in which the competitive challenge assails their core businesses.

The social construct perspective would argue that this view ignores the difficulty of identifying which particular aspects of a complex organizational system constitute the core of its efficiency and effectiveness (an argument that is substantiated in chapter 6, this volume, on Hewlett-Packard). While the social construct perspective would not deny the strategic design view of the Japanese production system as a set of organizational structures, processes, practices, and routines that have enabled Japanese industrial firms to improve their competitiveness, it would insist that it is more. It is an organizational model—a social construct—composed of certain patterns and the rationales for those patterns that have evolved gradually, in interaction with the Japanese cultural and institutional context, and that have become institutionalized in Japan—that is, both accepted as the taken-for-granted way to organize production efficiently and as having many patterns valued as good in themselves.

From a social construct perspective, the answer to the question of which organizational patterns an MNC is likely to transfer to new operations may seem obvious: it will try, often unsuccessfully, to transfer the patterns that are strongly institutionalized—that is, patterns that are highly valued and that are taken for granted—in its home environment. But, although this answer may be obvious in the context of a new plant in the home country, the move across borders complicates the issue. On the one hand, in some cases (for example, the European auto producers now establishing plants in the United States), one of the motives for moving outside the home country may be to escape patterns that are strongly institutionalized there. On the other hand—more relevant for Japanese firms—a parent firm may be unwilling even to try to export some of its most deeply institutionalized patterns, on the grounds that they are regarded as culturally specific and distinctive, rooted in national culture or even in a local community, and managers may have a shared belief that they are not transferable. Given the strong emphasis in much of the 1970s and early 1980s management literature (both in English and in Japanese) on the importance of cultural factors in shaping Japanese-style management, Japan's managers may have been particularly susceptible to such a belief during those years (Martin Kenney, in chapter 8 in this volume, suggests that this "period effect" may be a factor in the lower level of transfer of Japanese production organization in the early moves into manufacturing in the United States in consumer electronics). Moreover, highly valued patterns may be seen as transferable to some environments but not to others (to other Asian environments but not to Western countries, for example, or to other highly developed countries but not to developing countries). Taken-for-granted patterns are more likely than normatively valued patterns to be transferred regardless of environment, in large part because they are transferred almost automatically. But, as Paul Adler has suggested in chapter 3, the internationalization process itself may well be a "deinstitutionalizing" process, exposing a firm to different ways of managing and organizing and calling into question patterns that were previously taken for granted. By this argument, firms are likely to have fewer cognitively institutionalized patterns as their international experience expands. The social construct perspective, therefore, finds this question—what does a parent firm try to transfer—a particularly difficult one to answer a priori.

It has similar difficulty with specifying the patterns most likely to be emulated across borders by firms learning from their competitors. But this perspective highlights what might be called the social construction of competitiveness—the building of models of what makes for competitive firms (and also societies). What gets transferred is a *model* that is constructed by the emulating organization, with contributions of varying importance from the organization being emulated and from model builders in the organizational field (consultants, business journalists, and, of course, academics). This model is grounded in and legitimated by deeply held assumptions in the organizational field of the emulating organization about what makes firms competitive. The social construction of competitiveness is a topic that organization theorists working in this perspective have not pursued as vigorously as one might expect. This may be attributable to a long-standing but increasingly criticized assumption that institutional theory is less relevant in the "technical environments" of business organization (Scott, 1983)—environments where clear performance criteria reduce the conditions of uncertainty about effective organizational patterns under which social construction of elaborate models thrives.

Given the complexity of the processes of the social construction of competitiveness and the paucity of research and theory about it, advocates of this perspective probably feel on safer ground predicting what *won't* be transferred across borders in the "learning from foreign competitors" process. These are patterns that conflict with those that are deeply institutionalized in the environment of the emulating organizations—that is, those that run counter to deeply held assumptions about what makes for a competitive company or that violate highly valued patterns. For example, leading Japanese firms are characterized by comparatively small salary differences between managers and workers, and they customarily reduce managers' bonuses and even salaries before any major attempt is made to shed workers (Robinson & Yokokawa, 1997). After a decade of assiduous learning from the Japanese, however, the gap in rewards between top management and workers in U.S. firms and, even more strikingly, the practice of providing princely bonuses for managers who reduce their workforce are both at an unprecedented level, even in companies that have most assiduously attempted to "learn from" their Japanese competitors. The strong belief that the top managers deserve to have the profit performance of the firm reflected in their rewards has become deeply institutionalized in the United States, to the point where elements of Japanese practice that run counter to it are not included in the model. In this perspective, the perceptual filters involved in building models of "best practice" are a critical part of cross-border learning; they are discussed at greater length in terms of "imperfect information" in the following section.

The political perspective, like the strategic design perspective, has a fairly parsimonious answer to the question of what is most likely to get transferred: patterns that serve the interests of powerful stakeholders. In the MNC, according to this perspective, the parent-subsidiary relationship is a political arena, in which the parent tries to maintain or increase its control over its subsidiary and the subsidiary struggles to maintain or increase its autonomy. What the parent does and does not transfer to the subsidiary becomes a tool for ascendancy in this struggle. This perspective does not find it surprising that few if any of the Japanese transplants overseas come close to the integrated knowledge creation capabilities of the "knowledge factories" in Japan, especially in terms of their capacity to generate product and process innovations (Fruin, 1997). It would ascribe this not to a "life cycle effect"—that is, to the stage of the subsidiary's development and the time required to develop advanced capabilities in subsidiaries, factors that are likely to change over time, an explanation that is likely to be favored by the strategic design perspective.[3] Nor would it share the social construct interpretation that it might be ascribable to incompatible concepts of and organizational models of innovation in Japan and the United States. The real explanation, in this perspective, lies in the unwillingness of home-country managers to lose their control over the company's technology trajectory, and therefore the situation is likely to persist until the subsidiaries have the power to insist on building their own R&D organizations.

In cross-border learning across organizations, stakeholders are likely to seize on organizational models and on specific patterns that increase their power in the organization. The appeal of the Japanese production system to U.S. managers, in this perspective, is that it provides tools for reducing union control of the work process and ways of increasing productivity without increasing the rewards for workers. The criteria for transfer on which the political perspective focuses our attention are therefore, obviously, concerned with competing interests and the relative power of stakeholder coalitions, rather than the efficiency and competitiveness criteria of the strategic design perspective or the cognitive and normative criteria of the social construct approach.

Hybridization

All three perspectives would predict that transferring complex organizational systems across societies will change those systems. Each perspective, however, supplies a slightly different logic for this change (or hybridization, the term used throughout this chapter to refer to the phenomenon of the emergence of distinctive patterns in the cross-border transfer of organizational patterns). This section looks at how each perspective views three drivers of hybridization: the interaction of foreign and local patterns within the organization, imperfect information, and the interaction between internal patterns and key elements of the environment.

The Interaction of Foreign and Local Patterns

From the strategic design perspective, an organization that combines patterns from one organizational model with those from a very different model will, as an overall system, differ by definition from both and, indeed, may well constitute a new organizational form. Recent work on the organization of the multinational corporation has shown an increasing interest in how the two forces of local responsiveness and global integration (concepts that throughout the past decade have dominated the analysis of strategy in the MNC) have played out in terms of the analogous competing pulls on organizational structure: those from the parent organizational model and those from prevailing local patterns (see for example, Robinson, 1994; Westney, 1993; and the work cited in chapter 3, by Paul Adler, in this volume). Adler builds on this literature in his chapter, looking at whether specific HRM practices resemble those that prevail in the parent organization or in the local environment. But, as he finds, many patterns involve some combination of parent and local features ("hybridization"). And, although he finds overall that one of the two U.S. transplants he studies (NUMMI) tends to resemble more closely the patterns of the parent, Toyota, while the other is more similar to a local model (Toyota's Kentucky plant follows the U.S. union substitution model), the resemblance is not total; each is to some extent a hybrid of parent and local patterns.

A similar logic creates pressures for hybridization in companies that are adopting patterns from their foreign competitors. In this perspective, strong pressures for change in organizations in general and for hybridization in cross-border learning in particular come from a lack of fit between different aspects of structure or practice. This approach would predict that in the Japanese-owned factories in the United States, one would find "clusters" of tightly coupled patterns that would tend towards either the parent or the local model, with hybridization occurring where those "clusters" intersect. For example, in both Brannen, Fruin, and Liker's study of the ball-bearing plant in Ann Arbor (NSK) and Adler's analysis of the two Toyota transplants, the minimization of job categories and the use of production teams—patterns that are tightly coupled in the production system—followed Japanese practice fairly closely. On the other hand, labor relations, grievance procedures, and discipline policies followed local patterns (the union model in NSK and NUMMI, the union substitution model in the Kentucky plant). This affected the supervisor role—a role that links the two clusters of work organization and work discipline—in all three cases. At NSK, the supervisor spent more time dealing with worker complaints and allocation of work and less time on process improvement than in Japan (but more time on process improvement than in comparable U.S. plants, a topic not directly addressed in the NSK study but directly assessed in the case of Toyota plants).

A further aspect of emergent change as a result of the combining of parent and local patterns was observed in the Toyota plants. Both used a higher level of job rotation than was found in the Japanese Toyota plants (and a much higher level than in the Big Three's U.S. plants). Moreover, the rationale was the relief of boredom and physical stress, rather than the multitask training goal dominant in Japan. This is an emergent pattern that, one can argue, develops from the interaction of the parent-dominated work organization cluster and the locally dominated industrial relations system. It is a pattern that is designed to reduce stress and discontent in the work process system, because of the greater recourse open to the worker in the industrial relations cluster. In this perspective, not only does hybridization occur at points where parent and local patterns are inconsistent with each other, but innovative patterns that make for a new organizational form are most likely to emerge at the interface between clusters of patterns that are internally tightly coupled and moderately tightly coupled across clusters that follow different models.

From the social construct approach, the transfer of patterns across borders always produces something different in the new setting, if only because the foreign patterns are perceived and interpreted differently in their home setting and in their environments abroad (see chapter 4, by Brannen, Liker, and Fruin in this volume). Peterson, Peng, and Smith provide an interesting example in MNCs in their study of how expatriate managers' behavior is perceived by their American subordinates—which differs significantly from how very similar behavior by American managers is regarded. When an organizational practice or structure moves across borders, therefore, it will be interpreted very differently in the new setting—and that new interpretation may well lead to changes in how it actually operates. The evolution of teams in the Japanese transplants is an example. As several chapters in this volume attest, the combination of the team structure with American interpretations of teamwork in the workplace (which includes elements of empowerment and internal governance that are not present in Japan) have produced a structure that differs considerably from the original model. Robert Cole, in his book on small group activities in Japan, the United States, and Sweden in the early and mid-1980s, shows how the proclivity in the United States for seeing Japanese quality circles in terms of "quality of work life" models was an important factor in American companies' setting up QC organizations that differed substantially from the Japanese patterns these companies thought they were emulating (Cole, 1989).

From the political perspective, the combination of foreign and local patterns constitutes a potential arena for contending interests and for the enhancement of power within the firm. Association with the dominant organizational patterns can be an important power base in an MNC subsidiary. To the extent that parent patterns are being transferred, expatriate managers have an important source of power in their knowledge of home country organization. But expatriate managers are caught in a dilemma: their role depends on their mastery of home-country patterns, but success in their posting can come only if local employees accept their position and their agenda. Hybridization strategies provide an attractive way out of this dilemma: the expatriates preserve the value of their privileged knowledge of the parent organization but increase the psychological investment of local personnel. Local managers, on the other hand, especially those in companies with a significant expatriate manager presence, will never be able to match the expatriate mastery of home-country patterns; they derive their influence in their organization from their local knowledge. But, if they insist on applying only local patterns, they will be regarded as obstructive by powerful Japanese managers. For them, too, hybridization strategies are attractive: they provide a way of simultaneously building alliances with the Japanese expatriates and leveraging their local knowledge.

Imperfect Information

All three perspectives would acknowledge that when complex organizational patterns are transferred across societies, imperfect information causes departures from the original model in the new setting. But each has a different approach to this information problem.

From the strategic design perspective, imperfect information in cross-border transfers is a function of the complexity of organizational systems and the resulting problems of limited knowledge, especially positional limitations on knowledge. As many theorists have pointed out (e.g., Nelson and Winter, 1982; Nonaka and Takeuchi, 1995), much of what makes an organizational system work is tacit knowledge, and that knowledge is widely dispersed in the organization. It tends to be positional; that is, individuals know best the organizational patterns in which they themselves work, and the more distant the system is from their own positions, the thinner is the knowledge and the more confined to the formal structures. And most transfers of organizational patterns across borders have been carried out by upper-level managers, whose knowledge of the routines of the workplace can be limited.

The problems of imperfect information will therefore probably be more acute in independent organizations trying to learn from foreign rivals than within MNCs. In MNCs, the transfer of people across borders has long been recognized as a key mechanism of transferring organizational knowledge. It is impossible, however, to replicate home-country organizational patterns by staffing a foreign unit entirely with expatriates, except in extremely small offices (such as the early offshore units of Japanese trading companies). Hiring locals means that when information on the original model is inadequate, organizational participants will resort to models familiar from their past working experience or prevalent in the local environment, therefore causing unintended departures from the desired patterns.

In this perspective, the problem of imperfect information can be managed by providing better information, targeted to the parts of the organization where transfer is most desired. The Japanese auto transplants epitomize this approach, in the unprecedented scale of their transfers of employees across borders. This includes not only sending significant numbers of upper-and middle-level managers and technical people from Japan to the United States but also the dispatch of hundreds of blue-collar workers from the United States to gain direct experience and knowledge on the parent-plant assembly lines in Japan. The goal is to provide detailed, experiential knowledge of key organizational patterns to ensure their effective transfer to the new setting.

In the social construct perspective, "imperfect information" is less a question of how much information is available than of how it is interpreted, and it is a variable that is not directly controllable by managers. In the process of transferring information across societies, as chapter 4, by Brannen et al., and 6, Cole, by this volume, make clear, information is filtered both by senders and by recipients. Senders often present an idealized version of the original model, providing information more about how it is supposed to work than how it actually works. Receivers interpret information in the light of their own experience, values, and basic assumptions. Both types of "filters" affect the resulting perceptions of organizational patterns. Some illuminating examples can be found among management scholars trying to understand the roots of Japan's competitive success, who discovered that they lay in the particular individual's field of study, whatever that happened to be. Operations management experts wrote articles with titles such as "Japan—Where Operations Really Are Strategic" (Wheelwright, 1981); marketing experts found the secret of Japanese success in Japan's marketing practices (Kotler, Fahey, and Jatusripitak, 1985); human resource management experts found that Japanese HRM practices explained Japan's rise; even accounting experts located the key to Japanese success in their own field (see, for example, Hiromoto's *Harvard Business Review* article, "Another Hidden Edge—Japanese Management Accounting" Hiromoto, 1988). Japanese management provided for each group both a validation of its fundamental assumption that its own field provided the base for competitive success and a source of new ideas for specific practices that built on that base. The models that each group built were often extremely useful to U.S. companies, but they were far from providing perfect information on Japanese organizational systems.

In the political perspective, imperfect information stems from the assumption that knowledge is power. This perspective forces our attention to the issue of the deliberate concealing of information in cross-border transfers, driven by a desire to maintain or increase the power of individuals, groups, or functions, and of the parent in the multinational system. One of the key sources of power for individual managers in the MNC is a knowledge of how decisions are made and of the power networks of the organization, and this perspective would predict that information in these areas would be the most jealously guarded and the least likely to be transferred.

A critical question at the more organizational level in the MNC, given the recent debates over the "hollowing out" of home-country operations in U.S. and Japanese MNCs, is why home-country employees would be willing to provide information and knowledge that would enable a subsidiary to take jobs away from the home country. The extent of concealment and its effect on the transfer of capabilities has attracted some speculation but very little research (indeed, the very nature of the problem is such as to defy systematic research). But, in the case of the Japanese auto transplants, this perspective would argue that the voluntary export restraints (VERs) in autos provided a context where resistance to knowledge transfers from home-country operations was unusually low, since under the VERs the transplants were building vehicles that would increase the company's market share but were not expected to reduce exports significantly or to be imported back into Japan. This is a key factor, this perspective would argue, in the outstanding success of the transplants in transferring production systems from Japan to the United States. But it would also predict that the rise of the yen in the 1990s and the accompanying growth of reverse imports may well complicate organizational knowledge transfers in the future.

Key Elements of the Environment

Organizational systems that are moved into an environment that differs from that in which they evolved can be expected to change at those points where the environment and the organization interact. But, given that each perspective defines the environment differently, it is hardly surprising that each directs attention to a different aspect of environmentally induced hybridization.

If we take the organization-set as a prototypical model of the environment in the strategic design perspective, a key locus of hybridization in the organizational system when it is transferred across borders would be the interface between the organization and key elements of the organization-set that are missing or differently configured in the new environment (for examples of this in Japan's borrowing of Western organizational forms in the Meiji period, see Westney, 1987). The organization can be expected to change in its new environment depending on which of the following steps it takes to deal with the missing or anomalous element:

1. By doing without that particular input or activity (for example, by doing without the dense industry networking provided in Japan by industry associations or the external support for QC activities provided by professional organizations like the Japan Union of Scientists and Engineers)
2. By internalizing the activity performed in its home environment by external actors (for example, by internalizing training in basic mathematical skills)

3. By turning to the nearest local functional equivalent and adjusting its internal system accordingly (for example, by building a network of independent dealerships, rather than relying on a distribution *keiretsu* of wholly or partially owned distributors)

4. By acting as what Stinchcombe (1965) has called an "organization-creating organization"—that is, by providing information and other resources to help set up organizations of the kind on which the organization relied in its original setting (such as supplier networks)

The strategies chosen by the organization to deal with the organization-set problems in turn affect the organization design, not only in terms of the boundary-spanning unit that deals directly with that particular element of the set (the personnel department on recruitment, for example, or the purchasing department for suppliers) but also with any other aspects of organizational patterns that are tightly coupled to that boundary-spanning unit or to the external actor.

While this array of options holds for both MNCs and for firms that emulate foreign models, the chapters in this volume provide the most striking information on the MNCs—specifically, on the Japanese MNCs that have established production facilities in the United States. For these firms, the most problematic elements of the organization-set were those in the input-set. Most had already dealt with the challenges of building the output-set—that is, in autos by setting up their own distribution and sales networks, serviced by exports from Japan, and in consumer electronics by developing relationships with existing distributors and retailers. But, as several of the chapters in this volume make clear, the input-set posed major challenges for moving Japanese production systems to the United States, particularly in terms of suppliers of components and suppliers of labor (that is, the educational systems that produced potential employees).

As several researchers have demonstrated (e.g., Abo, 1994; Kenney and Florida, 1993; and MacDuffie and Helper, chapter 5, this volume), in dealing with the supplier issue, Japanese auto firms in particular have chosen the strategy of "organization creation"—recreating as closely as possible the kinds of organizations that supported their activities in their home environment. And, as MacDuffie and Helper show in their chapter, this was no simple task. Their study indicates some departures from the home-country model, such as the elimination of a charge for Honda's services in building supplier capabilities—2 percent of sales in Japan. We lack the data at this point on whether there are additional adaptations in how supplier relations are sustained and coordinated. For example, Jeff Dyer has found that Japanese auto firms meet with their closely affiliated suppliers in Japan seven times more frequently than the U.S. Big Three auto firms meet with their U.S.-based suppliers (Dyer, 1996a, 1996b). We do not yet know how often the Japanese interact with their U.S.-based suppliers, whether there is a difference in interaction levels according to whether the suppliers are Japanese-owned or U.S.-owned, or what mechanisms the Japanese firms might use to substitute for face-to-face contact in the United States, but the strategic design perspective would predict considerable hybridization of organizational patterns at the supplier-customer interface.

The social construct perspective, as we have seen, asserts that the processes of filtering and reinterpretation make departures from the original organizational model inevitable in a new setting. It would predict, however, that substantial innovation would be most likely to occur where the patterns being transferred are simultaneously strongly institutionalized in the original environment and encounter very different and incompatible patterns that are strongly institutionalized in the local environment. In some cases, particularly independent organizations learning from foreign models, the initial outcome is most likely to be the abandonment of the transfer of that particular pattern, but in MNCs the parent is likely to persist. In that case (and also where, in the context of cross-border emulation outside the MNC, the local firm continues its efforts to emulate the foreign patterns), innovation in the form of hybridization (the combining of elements of the patterns of the model and the local) is likely to result.

The example most cited in this volume is teamwork. Teamwork in production is a complex organizational pattern whose practices are undergirded, according to this perspective, by values and behaviors learned and reinforced in other key organizations (including schools) and institutional agents such as the mass media and reinforced by patterns adopted in organizations regarded as exemplars of good practice in the field. Chapter 3 (by Adler), 4 (by Brannen et al.), and 7 (by Fruin) in this volume, and other work on the Japanese transplants (e.g., Cutcher-Gershenfeld et al., 1995) have shown how the Japanese model of work teams has been modified and adapted to the U.S. values of autonomy and worker empowerment. Jenkins and Florida illustrate the same point with regard to U.S. firms' use of "self-directed teams," which has been strongly influenced by the ubiquity of teams in the Japanese production system. Indeed, Jenkins and Florida's very definition of the emerging innovative work practice of teams (they define a team as innovative only if it is "self-directed," which is operationalized by whether or not it has a leader who is a production worker, not a supervisor) can be seen as a hybrid that combines certain features of Japanese work organization with U.S. values and patterns. This interpretation of "innovative" work systems illustrates how hybrid organizational patterns can become widely accepted and disseminated within an organizational field, to such an extent that the original company patterns (themselves originally seen as highly innovative) can come to be regarded as less advanced.

This perspective would predict that such innovative hybrids would be most common in organizational fields where both the Japanese transplants and American firms are salient actors, a feature that would force continuing reinterpretation and experimentation in the combination of patterns from the two systems. That is, they would be most common in such fields as autos and its supplier industries—and Jenkins and Florida did in fact find that firms in the auto parts industry were likely to adopt innovative (i.e., "hybrid") work systems, regardless of the ownership of the firm or the level of dependence on Japanese firms as customers.

From the political perspective, the environment acts as a force for hybridization through the behavior of external stakeholders. These stakeholders sometimes have their own agendas that they wish to impose on organizations; they are also sometimes mobilized by competing groups of internal stakeholders seeking greater leverage in intraorganizational conflicts.

The external stakeholders with the most direct interests in how a production system is organized, whether it be in an MNC subsidiary or a home-country firm, are groups representing labor. The introduction of the Japanese production system in the transplants and its emulation by U.S. firms learning from Japan has been of particular concern to organized labor in the United States, and the unions' efforts to organize the laborforce in the transplants and their determination to validate their role in unionized transplants have played a considerable role in the hybridization of work organization. The portrayal of the NSK plant in Michigan in chapter 4, by Brannen et al., and Adler's analysis of NUMMI in chapter 2 show the effects of the union in both, particularly in enforcing certain practices around seniority and in shaping the grievance and discipline processes. And Adler demonstrates that the potential threat of unionization exerts pressures on nonunionized plants to consider the demands of workers as internal stakeholders more seriously, given the ever-present threat of mobilization of the external stakeholder (the union) if discontent reaches certain levels within the plant.

This perspective looks for hybridization in the production system to occur in those structures and practices that have been the arenas for conflict between management and labor in U.S. industry in the past, and where labor has won significant concessions from management, particularly concerning worker rights (for example, issues of seniority rights and due process for grievances). Both the union model and the union avoidance model presented in Adler's chapter exert strong pulls for hybridization and an accommodation of Japan-based practices to U.S. stakeholders, both in the transplants and on U.S. firms learning from Japan.

Second-Order Effects: Internal Adjustments to Adaptations to the Environment

Although the previous discussion has discussed each perspective separately, in reality, of course, changes are occurring on all three aspects of organizational adaptation simultaneously. And the changes to adapt to the external environment discussed in the preceding section affect the other aspects of the organization. Adaptations to a different stakeholder configuration, for example, result in internal changes that alter the alignment of the internal design and create pressures for further changes. Those political and design changes also challenge the mental models or norms of organizational participants, leading to further pressure for change on the social construct dimension. Each adjustment to the external environment, in other words, has a ripple effect on other dimensions, leading to a set of interdependent changes across the dimensions identified in the three perspectives.

These changes are complex and difficult to trace empirically. Some predictability to these changes—the "lid on the garbage can," in the words of Levitt and Nass (1989)—is generated by the strong inclination of managers to scan their immediate environment to see how other companies are handling these continuing pressures for adaptation. But one of the few reliable predictions that can be made about these adaptation processes is that the organizational forms that result from the cross-societal transfer of organizational patterns will be neither clones of the original forms nor clones of the prevailing local forms; they will be hybrids.

The Processes of Hybridization

The three perspectives differ considerably in their focus of analysis in addressing the question of how hybridization is actually carried out. The strategic design perspective sees hybridization as a consequence of deliberate organizational redesign (usually by managers), to accommodate conflicting pulls from local and imported patterns, to improve the internal fit within the organization and fit with the external environment, and to improve the organization's performance. The key processes in hybridization are the identification and analysis of problems in the organization and the development of design solutions. The social construct perspective, in contrast, sees hybridization as an ongoing process of gradual change in shared cognitive schema and normative orders. It is an emergent process, which can be accelerated by managerial actions but not determined by them. Managers can, for example, provide settings for making the tacit assumptions of organizational culture explicit and for articulating the cognitive maps of different groups within the organization (expatriate and local managers, for example, or advocates for following a foreign model and those opposed). Ikujiro Nonaka's model of the "knowledge spiral," in which tacit and explicit knowledge are enhanced and interact in various processes and settings, can also be seen as a social construct model for hybridization (Nonaka, 1994; Nonaka and Takeuchi, 1995).

From the political perspective, hybridization occurs through conflict and negotiation driven by competing interests; the outcome is determined largely by the relative power of the contending groups, both internal and external. Managers cannot shape the hybridization outcome solely by identifying the solution that contributes to performance most efficiently (strategic design) or by providing venues for surfacing basic assumptions and cognitive maps (social construct). In fact, in the political perspective, both those types of actions are regarded as tactics in the struggle to dominate the process. They shape the outcomes and processes of hybridization by mobilizing stakeholders and identifying accurately the interests of the various groups involved and by either negotiating or imposing hybrid organizational patterns.

Conclusion

The approaches to the issues of what gets transferred, what drives hybridization, and how hybridization occurs in each perspective are summarized in Table 12.1. This summary of the preceding discussion illustrates, probably more clearly than the text, the extent to which the three perspectives are complementary, each providing the analogue of a flashlight in a dark and overcrowded attic, directing the observer to different and potentially equally useful things.

An organization is, in fact, simultaneously a strategic design, a social construct, and an arena for political conflict. While honing the conceptual and theoretical base for understanding organization often benefits from mining one of these perspectives as deeply as possible, the empirical analysis of organizational processes like hybridization is most illuminating when it pays attention to all three (see the discussion in Cole, 1995, of the differences between Japanese and U.S. companies' approaches to organizational learning for an example). Even the most dedicated advocate of the social construct perspective would, at a minimum, admit that the strategic design perspective dominates most managers' thinking, and even the most single-minded wielder of the political perspective would admit that managers who can lay claim to the validation of the performance-based strategic design model thereby gain a powerful weapon in internal power struggles.

The study of hybridization processes in Japanese firms also raises the complex issue of the role of hybridization in the coevolution of organizations and environments. Several chapters in this book contribute to the large and growing literature on how powerfully America's production systems have been influenced by the Japanese model, especially in the auto industry (see also such works as Dertouzos, Lester, and Solow, 1989; Womack, Jones, and Roos, 1990). Clearly, major factors in the strength of this influence were the number of Japanese firms—six of Japan's ten firms in auto assembly and more than 300 auto parts suppliers (Kenney and Florida, 1993, p. 126)—the compression in time of entry (all within less than a decade), and their geographic concentration in the lower Midwest (Florida and Kenney, 1993, pp. 128–129).

Each of the three perspectives provides a different explanation of how the numbers and the concentration of Japanese entrants would magnify the impact of the Japanese production system on the U.S. environment. From the strategic design perspective, the numbers of transplants increases the amount and detail of information available about the Japanese production system and its strengths and weaknesses in the U.S. environment, making it easier for U.S. firms to learn from them and for the transplants to learn about successful hybridization strategies from each other. It also increases the likelihood that the transplants will deal with the problem of a missing or differently configured organization-set by organization creation—by setting up organizations that provide the quality of inputs in the manner to which the firm

Table 12.1 Three Perspectives on the Hybridization of Organizational Patterns in Cross-border Transfers

	Strategic Design	Social Construct	Political
What patterns are most likely to be transferred across borders?	Patterns that produce a competitive advantage	MNC: Patterns cognitively institutionalized in parent *Emulator:* Patterns that resonate with basic assumptions about competitiveness	MNC: Criterion of transfer is maintenance of parental control *Emulator:* Patterns that enhance the power of the dominant coalition
Why do patterns change in the new context?			
(a) Interaction of parent and local patterns within the transplant[a]	Lack of fit between foreign and local patterns; innovative hybridization where clusters of patterns intersect	Reinterpretation of patterns	Political advantages of hybridization strategies
(b) Imperfect information	Complexity	Sender and receiver filters	"Knowledge is power"—reluctance to share
(c) Environmental factors	Incomplete or differently configured organization-set	Different values, deliberate hybridization to maintain valued patterns	Stakeholder resistance
(d) Internal adjustments to changes in response to external environment	Changes to respond to lack of fit between new patterns introduced to respond to new environment and other tightly coupled patterns in the original model	Reinterpretation of organizational patterns introduced to respond to new environment; different configuration of subcultures	Power shifts and changes in conflict and negotiation patterns as a result of changes responding to new environment
How does hybridization occur?	Managerial redesign for efficiency and effectiveness in the new environment	Emergent process of developing new, shared cognitive and normative models	Conflict and negotiation

a. The entries in this row refer to MNCs only; other rows cover both MNCs and organizations that emulate organizational patterns from other countries.

has become accustomed. And this, in turn, changes the organizational environment.

From the social construct perspective, the scale of entry increases the likelihood that locals will regard it as an "invasion," prompting the transplants and their parents to develop a hybrid model of the organization that asserts the local dimensions of its identify and underplays the Japanese dimensions. One way to do this is to foster the view that the Japanese production system is not Japanese but next-generation—post-Fordist, lean production, high commitment. In this process, the model becomes both more susceptible to the introduction of patterns not present in the parent company original and more adoptable by local firms.

Finally, the political perspective would emphasize the impact of the transplants on the balance of power among stakeholders in the industry (which has long been one of the flagships of the union movement in the United States). The transplants are predominantly nonunion; those that are unionized have been able to exact major concessions from the unions as a price for coming under the umbrella of organized labor. This has further weakened unions in their bargaining with the U.S. Big Three and has made them more willing to allow experiments like Saturn, which accelerated the process of hybridization of Japanese and U.S. production systems.

Over time, the hybrid patterns themselves become part of the evolving organizational environment. The fact that the transferring of the Japanese production system to the United States is so recent and so compressed in time gives social scientists an important advantage in their efforts to understand the transfer process, the accompanying patterns of hybridization, and the effect of hybridization on the organizational environment, as the chapters in this volume demonstrate. This analysis, in turn, provides insights and models that are useful in understanding organizational transfers in other contexts and that may also help to advance concepts and paradigms across the various schools of organization theory.

Notes

1. The following typology is drawn from Ancona, Kochan, Scully, Van Maanen, and Westney (1996).

2. There is a third context, MNC parents learning from their foreign subsidiaries, as in Cole's chapter on Hewlett-Packard. Because the element of "coercive isomorphism"—the ability of the parent to impose patterns on its subsidiary—is missing in this context, it is virtually identical to the second case of emulation of a foreign model, with the single exception of the "imperfect information" factor discussed later in this chapter.

3. An alternative strategic design view might be that it is inefficient to duplicate innovation capabilities and technology trajectories and that concentrating these in and driving them from the home country makes strategic sense in the industries in which the Japanese have excelled, where the returns to global integration are greater than in industries where European firms have been more successful internrationally than the Japanese (from packaged foods to power systems).

References

Aaker, D. A. 1989. "Managing Assets and Skills: The Key to a Sustainable Competitive Advantage." *California Management Review* 31(2): 91–106.

Abo, T., ed.. 1994. *Hybrid Factory: The Japanese Production System in the United States.* New York: Oxford University Press.

Ancona, D., Kochan, T., Scully, M., Van Maanen, J., and Westney, E. 1996. *Managing for the Future: Organizational Behavior and Processes.* Cincinnati: Southwestern Press.

Chandler, A. D., Jr. 1962. *Strategy and Structure: Chapters in the History of the American Industrial Enterprise.* Cambridge, Mass: MIT Press.

Chandler, A. D., Jr. 1977. *The Visible Hand: The Managerial Revolution in American Business.* Cambridge, Mass.: Harvard University Press.

Child, J. 1972. "Organizational Structure, Environment and Performance: The Role of Strategic Choice." *Sociology* 6: 1–22.

Clegg, S. R., and Dunkerley, D. 1980. *Organization, Class, and Control.* London: Routledge and Kegan Paul.

Cole, R. E. 1989. *Strategies for Learning: Small-Group Activities in American, Japanese, and Swedish Industry.* Berkeley: University of California Press.

Cole, R. E. 1995. "Reflections on Organizational Learning in U.S. and Japanese Industry." In J. Liker, J. E. Ettlie, and J. C. Campbell, eds., *Engineered in Japan: Japanese Technology-Management Practices.* New York: Oxford University Press.

Conner, K. R. 1991. "A Historical Comparison of Resource-based Theory and Five Schools of Thought within Industrial Organisation Economics: Do We Have a New Theory of the Firm?" *Journal of Management,* 17(1): 121–154.

Crozier, M. 1964. *The Bureaucratic Phenomenon.* Chicago: University of Chicago Press.

Cutcher-Gershenfeld, J., et al. 1995. "Japanese Team-based Work Systems in North America: Explaining the Diversity." *California Management Review* 37(1): 42–64.

Dertouzos, M. L., R. K. Lester, and R. M. Solow. 1989. *Made in America: Regaining the Productivity Edge.* Cambridge, Mass: MIT Press.

Dill, W. R. 1958. "Environment as an Influence on Managerial Autonomy." *Administrative Science Quarterly* 2: 409–443.

DiMaggio, P. J., and W. W. Powell. 1983. "The Iron Cage Revisited: Institutional Isomorphism and Collective Rationality in Organizational Fields." *American Sociological Review* 48(2): 147–160.

Donaldson, T., and L. E. Preston. 1995. "The Stakeholders Theory of the Corporation: Concept, Evidence, and Implications." *Academy of Management Review* 20(1): 65–91.

Dyer, J. H. 1996a. "Does Governance Matter? *Keiretsu* Alliances and Asset Specificity as Sources of Competitive Advantage." *Organization Science* 7(6): 649–666.

Dyer, J. H. 1996b. "Specialized Supplier Networks as a Source of Competitive Advantage: Evidence from the Auto Industry." *Strategic Management Journal* 17(4): 271–292.

Edwards, R. 1979. *Contested Terrain: The Transformation of Work in the Twentieth Century.* New York: Basic Books.

Evan, W. 1966. "The Organization-Set." In J. D. Thompson, ed., *Approaches to Organization Design.* Pittsburgh: University of Pittsburgh Press.

Freeman, R. E., and D. Reed, 1983. "Stockholders and Stakeholders: A New Perspective on Corporate Governance." In C. Huizinga, ed., *Corporate Governance*, pp. 89–109. Los Angeles: University Press.

Fruin, W. M. 1997. *Knowledge Works: Managing Intellectual Capital at Toshiba*. New York: Oxford University Press.

Galbraith, J. 1973. *Designing Complex Organizations*. Reading, Mass.: Addison-Wesley.

Hamilton, G. G. 1994. "Civilizations and the Organization of Economies." In N. J. Smelser and R. Swedberg, eds., *The Handbook of Economic Sociology*. Princeton, N.J.: Princeton University Press.

Hiromoto, Toshihiro. 1988. "Another Hidden Edge—Japanese Management Accounting." *Harvard Business Review* 66(4): 22–26.

Hofstede, G. T. 1980. *Culture's Consequences: International Differences in Work-Related Values*. Beverly Hills, Calif.: Sage.

Kenney, M., and R. Florida. 1993. *Beyond Mass Production: The Japanese System and Its Transfer to the United States*. New York: Oxford University Press.

Kochan, T. A., and S. Rubenstein. 1997. *Toward a Stakeholder Theory of the Firm: The Case of the Saturn Partnership*. Working Paper. Cambridge: Massachusetts Institute of Technology.

Kogut, B., and U. Zander. 1993. "Knowledge of the Firm and the Evolutionary Theory of the Multinational Corporation." *Journal of International Business Studies* 24(4): 625–645.

Kotler, P., L., Fahey, and S. Jatusripitak. 1985. *The New Competition: What Theory Z Didn't Tell You about Marketing*. Englewood Cliffs, N.J.: Prentice Hall.

Kunda, G. 1992. *Engineering Culture: Control and Commitment in a High-Tech Corporation*. Philadelphia: Temple University Press.

Lawrence, P. R., and J. W. Lorsch. 1967. *Organization and Environment: Managing Differentiation and Integration*. Boston: Harvard University, Graduate School of Business Administration.

Levitt, B., and C. Nass. 1989. "The Lid on the Garbage Can: Institutional Constraints on Decision Making in the Technical Core of College-Text Publishers." *Administrative Science Quarterly* 34(2): 190–207.

Meyer, J. W., and B. Rowan. 1977. "Institutionalized Organizations as Myth and Ceremony." *American Journal of Sociology* 83(2): 340–363.

Mintzberg, H. 1983. *Power in and around Organizations*. Englewood Cliffs, N.J.: Prentice Hall.

Nelson, R., and S. Winter. 1982. *An Evolutionary Theory of Economic Change*. Cambridge, Mass.: Harvard University Press.

Nonaka, I. 1994. "A Dynamic Theory of Organization Knowledge Creation." *Organization Science* 5(1): 14–37.

Nonaka, I., and H. Takeuchi. 1995. *The Knowledge-Creating Company: How Japanese Companies Create the Dynamics of Innovation*. New York: Oxford University Press.

Perrow, C. 1970. *Organizational Analysis: A Sociological View*. Belmont, Calif.: Wadsworth.

Perrow, C. 1981. "Markets, Hierarchies, and Hegemony: A Critique of Chandler and Williamson." In A. Van de Ven and W. Joyce, eds., *Perspectives on Organizational Design and Behavior*. New York: Wiley.

Pfeffer, J. 1981. *Power in Organizations*. Marshfield, Mass.: Pitman.

Pfeffer, J. 1992. *Managing with Power: Politics and Influence in Organizations*. Boston: Harvard Business School Press.

Pfeffer, J., and G. Salancik. 1978. *The External Control of Organizations*. New York: Harper and Row.

Robinson, P. 1994. "Applying Institutional Theory to the Study of the Multinational Enterprise: Parental Control and Isomorphism among Personnel Practices in American Manufacturers in Japan." Ph.D. diss., Massachusetts Institute of Technology, Sloan School of Management.

Robinson, Patricia, and Jun Yokokawa. 1997. "Comparing Corporate Governance Structures in Japan and the United States." Paper presented at the annual meeting of the American Sociological Association, Toronto, Aug. 13.

Scott, W. R. 1983. "The Organization of Environments." In John W. Meyer and W. Richard Scott, eds., *Organizational Environments: Ritual and Rationality*. Beverly Hills: Sage Publications.

"Stakeholder Capitalism" 1996. *The Economist* Aug. 10, pp. 23–25.

Stinchcombe, A. L. 1965. "Social Structure and Organizations." In J. G. March, ed., *Handbook of Organizations*. Chicago: Rand-McNally.

Thompson, J. D. 1967. *Organizations in Action*. New York: McGraw-Hill.

Van Maanen, J. 1988. *Tales of the Field: On Writing Ethnography*. Chicago: University of Chicago Press.

Weick, K. 1977. "Enactment Processes in Organizations." In B. M. Staw and G. Salancik, eds., *New Directions in Organizational Behavior*, pp. 267–300. Chicago: St. Clair.

Weick, K. 1995. *Sensemaking in Organizations*. Thousand Oaks, Calif.: Sage.

Westney, D. E. 1987. *Imitation and Innovation: The Transfer of Western Organizational Patterns to Meiji Japan*. Cambridge, Mass.: Harvard University Press.

Westney, D. E. 1993. "Institutionalization Theory and the Multinational Corporation." In Sumantra Ghoshal and D. E. Westney, eds., *Organization Theory and the Multinational Corporation*, pp. 53–76. London: Macmillan.

Wheelwright, S. C. 1981. "Japan—Where Operations Really Are Strategic." *Harvard Business Review* 67–74.

Williamson, O. E. 1975. *Markets and Hierarchies: Analysis and Antitrust Implications*. New York: Free Press.

Williamson, O. E. 1985. *The Economic Institutions of Capitalism: Firms, Markets, Rational Contracting*. New York: Free Press.

Womack, J. P., D. T. Jones, and D. Roose. 1990. *The Machine That Changed the World*. New York: Rawson Associates/Macmillan.

Woodward, J. 1965. *Industrial Organization: Theory and Practice*. New York: Oxford University Press.

Index